The Raj

The Raj

A Journey through Ten Documents

Pramod K. Nayar

B L O O M S B U R Y
NEW DELHI • LONDON • OXFORD • NEW YORK • SYDNEY

BLOOMSBURY INDIA
Bloomsbury Publishing India Pvt. Ltd
Second Floor, LSC Building No. 4, DDA Complex, Pocket C – 6 & 7,
Vasant Kunj, New Delhi, 110070

BLOOMSBURY, BLOOMSBURY ACADEMIC INDIA and the Diana logo are trademarks of Bloomsbury Publishing Plc

First published in India 2023
This edition published 2023

Bloomsbury Academic India
An imprint of Bloomsbury Publishing Plc

ISBN: HB: 978-93-54355-47-9; eBook: 978-93-54355-63-9

2 4 6 8 10 9 7 5 3 1

Printed & bound in India by Replika Press Pvt. Ltd.

CONTENTS

PREFATORY NOTE

The archival texts have been retained in their original font, style and content in order to clearly show the environment of the time when these documents were produced. It is important to show in a book such as this the views held at that time and the profound effect they had on society. We acknowledge that several of the texts are derogatory about Indians, women and communities of different religious faiths like many hundreds of other colonial-era-based works. While these are clearly unacceptable to us today, we have not attempted to change any wording or redact the texts so that the contemporary reader may experience the rhetoric, attitude and ideologies that so clearly marked the Raj. In places, where the text had been smudged and rendered impossible to read, that specific segment has been deleted.

We would like to make clear that these are not the views held by the editor or Bloomsbury India and do not reflect our mission and values which are clearly stated on our website (https://www.bloomsbury.com/in/connect/about-us/missions-and-values/).

INTRODUCTION

This is neither a study of the East India Company (EIC) nor of the Raj. It is not a political or social history of the 400-plus years of the British in India. Rather, it plucks a handful of texts from one of the largest imperial archives in the world and brings them together for us to take a peek at how the British saw their Company—the antecedent of the multinational corporation, as Nick Robins has demonstrated (2006)—their potential subjects ('potential' until the Company becomes the Company-Raj after 1757), their own life in India and the land. It, however, excludes from its ambit the legislation and various India Acts.

Understandably, the texts examined here could be replaced by other texts—in fact, several others. This is beyond dispute given that there are plenty of options to choose from. What this book sets out to do is to read a group of texts that capture a set of ideological positions, attitudes and actions. The texts chosen here are not imaginative literature but an assortment of ethnographic studies, advice books, 'Minutes', and others broadly classified as 'non-literary'. They range from 'inquiries' into India to the taxonomic classification of the people, from a Charter document bestowing particular rights and privileges to a domestic advice manual.

This book reads the colonial texts not merely as reflective of practices and processes, whether this was a scientific questionnaire or advice on how to deal with native servants, but as *shaping* the material history of these practices and processes, informing them and influencing them. As cultural materialists and New Historicists have argued, the relations between imaginative productions (novels, poetry), artistic productions (paintings), and the economic and political domains are always mutually informative and influential. In other words, India was defined in and through these discourses, and administered through those definitions (primitive, a once-great-civilisation, superstition-ridden but with the potential for improvement, made of effeminate men and seductive/helpless/dangerous women, among others) and discourses. India became a field of study, a geopolitical entity, a burden, a mission, and multiple other 'meanings' as the discourse of the era determined.[1]

The discourse of adventure and discovery, of novelty and wonder, are to be found in the earliest writings of the 16th- and 17th-century explorers Ralph Fitch, William Hawkins, John Fryer, John Ovington, Thomas Herbert, but also in later-day travellers like Emily Eden (who, as the sister of the governor general, Lord Auckland, travelled in luxury across the country) and Fanny Parkes in her mid-19th-century travelogue, *Wanderings of a Pilgrim in Search of the Picturesque* (1850). The quest for the exotic in the Mughal empire, among the people of India, in the fauna and flora, undergirds the paintings of Thomas and William Daniell and William Hodges, and even later collectors and scientific observers such as Joseph Hooker in *Himalayan Journals* (1854), as much as it does the 'moral exotic' (in which the Indians' indolence and lack of work ethic are emphasised) in Robert Orme's *Historical Fragments of the Mogul Empire* (1782) and Jemima Kindersley's *Letters from the Island of Teneriffe, Brazil, the Cape of Good Hope, and the East Indies* (1777). Exploration and discovery are also written into memoirs such as Francis Younghusband's *Kashmir* (1909) but also in other genres related to hunting, sports and wildlife—Henry Shakespear's *Wild Sports of India* (1862), William Rice's *Tiger Shooting in India* (1857) and Thomas Williamson's *Oriental Field Sports* (1802).

The derisive discourse around Indian religions, specifically Hinduism, can be found in John Fryer's *A New Account of East-India and Persia* (1698) and in the writings of W.H. Sleeman (*Thugs, or, Phansigars of India,* 1839) in which he attributed the cult of thuggee to the pernicious evils of Hinduism. The ruin geography of the subcontinent is found in William Hodges' *Travels in India, During the Years 1780, 1781, 1782* and *1783* (1793), James Rennell's *Memoir of a Map of Hindoostan* (1788) which was a geographical-cartographic account of the subcontinent, as well as in histories such as Alexander Dow's *The History of Hindostan* (1768).

The wars of the subcontinent produced captivity narratives that sought to reinforce stereotypes of the heroic Englishman and the cruel native. In this genre, we can think of, among others, J.Z. Holwell's *A Genuine Narrative of the Deplorable Deaths of the English Gentlemen, and Others, Who Were Suffocated in the Black Hole, in Fort William, in Calcutta* (1758), Joseph Bristow's *A Narrative of the Sufferings of James Bristow* (1793) and Innes Munro's *A Narrative of the Military Operations, on the Coromandel Coast, Against the Combined Forces of the French, Dutch and Hyder Ally Cawn, from the Year 1780 to the Peace in 1784; In a Series of Letters* (1789) from the Anglo-Mysore wars, and the Anglo-Afghan wars (Lady Florentina Sale, 1843). Then, of course, there were the 'Mutiny' accounts of 1857 in Julia Inglis's *Siege of Lucknow* (1892), among others. These texts often depicted the collapse of Indian civilisation into ruin, attributed this to the despotic monarchies of the subcontinent, and implicitly or explicitly, proposed that British rule alone could restore peace and prosperity to the land and its people.

The civilisational discourse, which finds its rationale and justification in the ruin rhetoric of the 18th century, informed writings as diverse as Macaulay's 1835 'Minute' and Charles Grant's *Observations on the State of Society Among the Asiatic Subjects of Great Britain* (1792), all the way to R.S.S Baden-Powell's *Memories of India* (1920). These tracts proposed everything from English education to sports in schools as a way of civilising the native.

In the field of religion, missionary texts such as William Ward's *A View of the History, Literature, and Religion of the Hindoos* (1817), Claudius Buchanan's *An Apology for Promoting Christianity in India* (1813) were critical of Hinduism even as they presented Christianity as a necessary instrument of civilisation. Campaign and propaganda texts on various subjects such as women's education also share discursive frames of the civilisational mission in Mary Carpenter's *Six Months in India* (1868), Marcus Fuller's *The Wrongs of Indian Womanhood* (1900), Priscilla Chapman's *Hindoo Female Education* (1839), Margaret Cousins' *Indian Womanhood Today* (1941), and others. The discourse can also be found in the sati and female infanticide tracts ranging from Edward Moor's *Hindu Infanticide* (1811), John Cormack's *Account of Female Infanticide in Guzerat* (1815) to James Peggs' *India's Cries to British Humanity* (1830).

The classificatory and enumerative discourses that developed taxonomies of people, fauna and flora took recourse to surveys, which included writings on architecture, topography and other features of the subcontinent. Thus, James Tod's *Annals and Antiquities of Rajasthan* (1829), J.D. Hooker's *Flora Indica, Being a Systematic Account of the Plants of British India* (1855), Alexander Cunningham's *Archaeological Survey of India: Four Reports Made During the Years 1862–63–64–65* (1871) and Herbert Risley's *The People of India* (1908) are all texts that aim to survey, document and order the subcontinent into a manageable form, whether in the form of detailed tables of data or descriptive accounts. Tracts like Cunningham's and Tod's also initiated the discourse of conservation, arguing that ancient Indian culture, its architecture and texts have to be preserved for posterity. In the same vein, we see the efforts of the Asiatic Society and the Orientalists like H.H. Wilkins and William Jones at translation, compilation and codification of Sanskrit texts as a movement towards not only an imperial control over the knowledge production about the subcontinent but also towards their global circulation.

***

Within the dominant discourse of discovery and exploration in the 17th century, the texts speak of both, the thrill of navigating through new territories and the *difficulties* of mapping the vast variety of the subcontinent. This means that the early texts were full of expressions of awe and bewilderment at the sights of India, and we can discern a rhetoric of wonder in them. The rhetoric emphasised visual discovery and visual interpretations of what the traveller saw. The EIC chaplain, Edward Terry (1655), writes in his first topographical descriptions:

> This most spacious and fertile land (called by the inhabitants Indostan) so much abounds in all necessaries for the use and service of man, to

> feed, and cloathe and enrich him, as that it is able to subsist and flourish of itself, without any help from any neighbour prince or nation....
>
> When the ground there hath been destitute of rain nine months together, and looks all of it like the barren sands in the deserts of Arabia, where there is not one spire of green grass to be found, within a few days after those fat enriching showers begin to fall, the face of the earth there (as it were by a new Resurrection) is so revived, and throughout so renewed, as that it is presently covered all over with a pure green mantle ... amongst the many hundred acres of corn of diverse kinds I have there beheld, I never saw any but what was very rich and good, standing as thick on the ground as the land could well bear it. (Terry, 92, 100)

Later, when this same process of navigating and documenting the territory became institutionalised in the form of the Great Trigonometrical Survey and the mapping projects of the late 18th–early 19th centuries, the narratives took the form of tables and maps, almost as though the map organised the wonder that was the subcontinent into a set of mathematical and—again—visually legible data, as we can see in the James Rennell chapter in this volume. But even Rennell is anticipated in Thomas Roe's account of his visit to the court of Jahangir: Roe points to the 'errors' of the Mercator maps before offering a detailed geographical and navigational mapping (1990, 91).

Further, the tone of the discourse and the narrative embodiment of this depended on the audience the traveller was appealing to. The early Ralph Fitch, writing ostensibly for merchant-travellers of the future, focused on commodities: 'Here is great traffic for all sorts of spices and drugs, silk and cloth of silk, sandals, elephants' teeth and much China work, and much sugar' (cited in Locke 1997, 76). Comparably, William Hawkins, a merchant with the EIC, attempts to compute the annual income of the Mughal empire (cited in Purchas 1905, 3: 30–33, 34–35, 41–42). Hawkins describes the Mughal emperor thus:

> He is exceeding rich in diamonds, and all other precious stones, and usually wears every day a fair diamond of great price.... He also wears a chain of pearl, very faire and great, and another chain of emeralds, and ... rubies. (cited in Purchas 1905, 3: 42)

A century later, John Ovington, speculating on the possibility of a slow but steady English hold on the region, wrote of the incomplete nature of Mughal power:

> The introduction of a language concurs towards completing the conquest of a nation which yet the Mughals have not been able to effect in India, neither totally to reduce the old natives to a cheerful undisturbed compliance with the government. (1696, 247)

Alongside this rhetoric of wonder and awe was the discourse of difficulty when the traveller wished to describe what he saw as the excesses of the landscape. The same Edward Terry is now not a little unsettled by the sight of the Mughal army encampment:

> Now to make it appear that the number of people of all sorts is *so exceeding great*, which here get, and keep together in the Mogol's leskar [lashkar], or Camp Royal; first there are one hundred thousand soldiers, which always wait about that king (as before observed) and all his Grandees have a great train of followers and servants to attend them there, and so have all other men according to their several qualities, and all these carry their wives and children, and whole families with them, which must needs amount to a very exceeding great number. And further to demonstrate this, when that King removes from one place to another, for the space of twelve hours, a broad passage is continually fill'd with passengers, and elephants, and horses, and asses, and oxen, (on which the manner sort of men and women with their little children, ride), so full as they may well pass one by the other. Now in such a broad passage, and in such a long time, a very great number of people, the company continually moving on forward, may pass. (420)

Other kinds of difficulty are also mapped. There is the impenetrable Hindu (and occasionally Islam) religion, the nature of Indian houses and temples and the kind of literature and theology—all of which defeat decoding by the English traveller. Thus, Ovington refers to Sanskrit as the language where the 'mysteries of their theology' are written (248). Terry refers to the 'Mohammedan who lives in the dark' (239). Thomas Herbert refers to the Hindu religion as 'rare and wonderful, beyond apprehension', and the priests of Cambay as 'veiled and obscure in their best aspect' (1634, 38, 42). A letter in the newspaper, *The Englishman*, for instance, writes: 'gloomy terrors, abstracted solitudes, painful penances, and bodily mortifications, are the dreadful acts by which the Anti-Christian world is deluded' (29–31 October 1713, n.p.).

In the process of mapping the country, the English documented differences, often adapting the rhetorical strategies associated with exoticism (Rousseau and Porter 1990).

With mapping and increased documentation of all things on the subcontinent—from weather patterns to fauna and flora, cultural practices to ancient Indian texts—the writings produced provided the source for both, imaginative accounts of India and theories or histories of other cultures. This also meant theories of 'improving' the barbaric native and the discourse of a certain moral imperialism. Determined to paint the land and its people as effeminate, primitive (translated as unable to rule themselves), innocent (and yet dangerous), the discourses of difference from the latter half of the 17th century painted geographical, scientific and the moral exotic. Note, for instance, how Robert Orme constructs the Indians:

> Breathing in the softest of climates; having so few real wants; and receiving even the luxuries of other nations with little labour, from the fertility of their own soil; the Indian must become the most effeminate inhabitant of the globe; and this is the very point at which we now see him. (Orme 1974 [1782], 306)

The exotic was also a place distanced in time: the Indian ruin represented, for the British, a past glory, whose wonderful civilisations had been destroyed by invaders such as the Mughals. From the late 17th century, therefore, considerable attention was paid to the ruins of temples, buildings, agricultural lands and towns. George Forster's description of Raj Mahal goes like this:

> It would be difficult to discover, that this place had been, so lately, the principal city of a powerful and opulent chief ... the instability of monuments of human grandeur cannot, in any region of the globe, I apprehend, be more faithfully, or more grievously exemplified than at Raj Mahal. (1798, 1: 13–14)

Robert Orme refers to the 'miserable villages thinly interspersed, desolated towns, and the number of inhabitants as much diminished as their miseries multiplied' (1974 [1782]: 261).

The famous painter William Hodges would write in his travelogue:

> This hall was, by order of the Emperor Jehangire, the son of Acbar, highly decorated with painting and gilding; but in the lapse of time it was found to be gone greatly to decay; and the Emperor Aurangazebe, either from superstition or avarice, ordered it to be entirely defaced. (1793: 119–120)

The ruin was attributed to local rulers, their wars and the general dissipated culture of the natives. It was to be studied as evidence of both antiquarian history and cultural collapse, then. James Fergusson, one of British India's first architectural historians, wrote in *On the Study of Indian Architecture* (1866):

> When I was in India between twenty and thirty years ago, the subject of Indian architecture had hardly been touched. Views of Indian buildings had, it is true, been published by Daniell and others, but no attempt had been made to classify them, and the vaguest possible ideas prevailed as to their age or relative antiquity. (1977, 5)

Fergusson represents the British attempt to 'unravel the mystery' (as he called it) of India's past. Like the Orientalist project to translate, understand, and codify India's languages, people, laws, history and architecture, Fergusson set out to classify and analyse Indian buildings and monuments. This eventually led to the establishment of the Archaeological Society of India in the 1860s, all of which contributed to the discourse of Indian antiquity and primitivism, which, in turn, appealed as the exotic, for, as Natasha Eaton (2006) argues, the exotic represented an early or primal stage of civilisation for the spectator and this was precisely India for the English: an old, even ancient, place.

But in the midst of these ruins, the English traveller also encountered another kind of exotic and picturesque: the native woman. The Indian woman was dangerously seductive, but some of them were vulnerable. The former was embodied in the 'nautch girls', and the latter in sati. John Fryer wrote:

> Their dancing wenches ... with ephods of silk and gold upon their breasts; with these in a ring hand in hand, were the dancing boys, all naked but a clout about their privities, like the Bacchanalian youths that used to revel it with Flora's strumpets through the streets of Rome. (44)

Jemima Kindersley describes a nautch she witnesses: the girls first appear 'frightful', and their eroticism lies in 'their languishing glances, wanton smiles and attitudes not quite consistent with decency' (1777, 230–231). Godfrey Charles Mundy refers to their 'snake-like suppleness' (1995 [1832], 1: 88–92) and Katharine Elwood terms them 'coquettish' (1830, 1: 81-82). Another commentator writes:

> By the continuation of wanton attitudes, they acquire, as they grow warm in the dance, a frantic lasciviousness, and communicate, by a natural contagion, the most voluptuous desires to the beholders. (*Asiatic Annual Register* 1782, 36)

Forster, writing about the women of Kashmir in the *Asiatic Annual Register*, complains: 'The dress of the women is no less awkward than that of the men and is ill adapted to display the beauties they naturally possess' (*Asiatic Annual Register* 1799, 95). Robert Orme spends considerable time describing the Indian woman:

> Nature seems to have showered beauty on the fairer sex throughout Indostan, with a more lavish hand than in most other countries. They are all, without exception, fit to be married before thirteen, and wrinkled before thirty—flowers of too short a duration not to be delicate; and too delicate to last long. Segregated from the company of the other sex, and strangers to the ideas of attracting attention, they are only handsomer for this ignorance; as we see in them, beauty in the noble simplicity of nature. Hints have already been given of their

> physiognomy: their skins are of a polish and softness beyond that of all their rivals on the globe... (301)

Widows and satis constituted the helpless Indian woman for most English. William Hodges writes of Muslim women mourning at tombs:

> It is a custom with the women of the family to attend these tombs of their friends ... it is both affecting and curious to see them proceeding in groups, carrying lamps in their hands, which they place at the head of the tomb: the effect, considered in a picturesque light, is highly beautiful with that of sentiment, it is delightful. (1999 [1793]: 28)

There was also a moral exotic in the discourse, which accused the natives of not only being effeminate (Sinha 1995) but also lazy and unwilling to work. For instance, Orme writes: 'This general tendency to indolence being admitted, we shall find nature encouraging them in it' (303–305). In the same tone, Charles Hamilton writes in *Asiatic Researches* of 1788:

> The true character of the lower order of natives in their most supine indolence and sloth; owing chiefly, perhaps, to the ignorance and stupid rapacity of their Rajahs, zamindars and other landholders, and their total inattention to the welfare of those dejected wretches. (1 [1806 ed], 305).

It was the emphasis on the native inability to govern themselves, improve and be productive that enabled the making of the civilisational discourse of the latter Raj.

The civilisational and improvement discourse was, of course, embedded in racial and evolutionary discourses such as that enunciated by those like James Welsh:

> A race of beings seemingly intended by nature to complete the link between man, the image of his Maker, and the tribe of apes and monkeys. (1830, 1: 2)

James Mill's *The History of British India* (1817) mapped the human races, with the Europeans at the pinnacle of progress and civilisation. Mill pronounced the Indians an evolved race, but their civilisation had stagnated so their present state of civilisation was 'rude and ignorant' (I: 103, 131). Other 'scientific' and ethnographic accounts such as *The Hill Tribes of India* (1891) showcased the tribes of central and southern India, highlighting their primitiveness. It was believed, and strongly at that, the natives were craving for improvement. Here is George Campbell:

> The Bengalis seemed infinitely to prefer literature, law, and politics to anything that required some physical as well as mental exertion.... When I introduced gymnastics, riding, and physical training in the colleges, they heartily accepted these things, and seemed quite ready to emulate Europeans in that respect. (1893, 273–274)

Physical and moral improvement had to be instilled through discipline—from English textbooks to sport. C.E. Tyndale-Biscoe, the headmaster of the Srinagar Boys' School, argued that casteism was at the root of the effeminate body shape of the Brahmin:

> This probably was the root of the whole business, namely, that the act of pulling an oar might produce muscle on the arms and, as muscle was only worn by coolies, my worthies might be mistaken for such low-caste beings. No Brahman had so vulgar an appendage as muscle on the arm. (7)

He decides then that the natives need reform, and 'what better beginning could one desire than a school of young boys?' (12). English education was indispensable too. Charles Grant writes in his *Observations on the State of Society Among the Asiatic Subjects of Great Britain*:

> Hence the Hindus would see the great use we make of reason on all subjects, and in all affairs; they would also learn to reason, they would become acquainted with the history of their own species, the past and present state of the world; their affections would gradually become interested by various engaging works, composed to recommend virtue, and to deter from vice; the general mass of their opinions would be rectified; and above all, they would see a system of principles and morals. New views of duty as rational creatures would open upon them; and that mental bondage in which they have long holden would gradually dissolve. (2020, 22)

Like Macaulay before him, Charles Trevelyan writes:

> the languages of India will be assimilated to the languages of Europe as far as the arts and sciences and general literature are concerned.... When English shall everywhere be established as the language of education, when the vernacular literature shall everywhere be formed from materials drawn from this source.... We shall leave a united and enlightened nation where we found a people broken up into sections. (1838, 124)

In his *India, and India Missions*, Alexander Duff declared that peace in India could be achieved only through the Evangelical educational project. The purpose must be

> the intellectual, moral, and spiritual regeneration of the universal mind;—or, in the speediest and most effectual manner, the reaching and vitally imbuing the entire body of the people with the leaven of Gospel truth. (1839: 284)

Texts from the later 19th century described the advances made by English missionaries, doctors and statesmen in terms of improving the natives. *The*

Gospel in Santhalisthan describes the Santhal tribes as having 'resisted the false religions that have been thrust upon them' (Anon. 1875, vii). An essay on Assam speaks of tribals who had been induced to 'form an agricultural settlement' (*Classified Digest, 1701–1892* [1894], 606–608). Sarah Tucker emphasises that the 'lower' classes were more anxious for education (1842–1843, 1: 74).

William Clarkson declared: '[Indians] separated from each other for ages by human laws, they are brought together by the Divine law of love', thus underscoring the need for a Christianising of the land and its people (1850, 55). In all such cases, as Saurubh Dube has argued, the English treated the natives as innocent children (2004, 38–39).

Such a discourse of colonial management and control extended to the plant and animal life of the subcontinent. Arguing that tigers and wild animals were a threat to the *native*, the English set themselves up as protectors: hunters who would deal with the scourge. When the English arrive at a village, they are 'hailed as … friendly deliverers' (Inglis 1892, 106). Campbell (1853, 224) also uses the 'rescue theme' in his narrative. Savory (1900, 124) mentions how one Jemadar came up to the English and described a bear attack, and pleaded with them to visit the bear cave (1853, 224). Henry Shakespear even links hunting to evangelical activity:

> To him who has been blessed with the gifts of good nerve, energy, and strength, that he may save the bodies of these same ignorant heathen from the fell destroyer that lives in the forest and preys upon them. Who shall say that the poor idolater saved by the latter from destruction shall not become converted to Christianity by the former? (1862, 3)

Kate Martelli is unequivocal in her assessment about the shikar: 'Tigers are shot in India, not as game is in England for hunting, to give amusement to men, horses and dogs … but to save the lives of natives and their cattle' (quoted in Trollope 1983: 207–08). Proposing both adventure *and* an imperial mission (protecting the natives), numerous hunting manuals and memoirs appeared in the 19th century. The sporting memoir also implicitly and very often explicitly proposed the hunt as an index of the British sportsman's temperament, the English *man*'s masculinity and authority, and the triumphant colonial in an alien land. Major Dalbiac declared that pig-sticking ensured the development of 'those attributes so necessary for every soldier': 'a firm seat, a light hand, a good eye for the country, a bold heart, and a cool head' (*English Illustrated Magazine*, 22 [1899], 87–92). 'Hunters of the large game of India's magnificent forests', writes Henry Shakespear, 'keep[s] them [the young British boys serving in India] out of a thousand temptations and injurious pursuits' (1862, 2). Robert Baden-Powell, famous for the boy scouts movement declared in 1920:

> If polo and pig-sticking have not altered the history of British India, they have at any rate altered the lives and careers of many young officers.... They have complete driven out from the British subaltern the drinking and betting habits of the former generation, and have given him in place of these a healthy exercise which also has its moral attributes in playing the game unselfishly. (31)

The shikar thus encoded a discourse of discipline, imperial mission (to rescue the native) and the protector of *other* animals—and thus emerges a discourse of conservation—and control (Pandian 2001, Rangarajan 1996).

It was not only the *public* spectacle and program of improvement that appeared in the discourses. English writings on India were deeply concerned about domestic spaces—of both Indian homes and English homes—from the 1770s when smaller towns like Meerut or Jabalpur had cantonments with family lines and barracks for both Indian and British soldiers. 'Settling' a home in India was not an innocent act: they were 'strategies of rule' (Joseph 2004, 92). As early as 1795, H.T. Colebrooke had proposed that allowing Englishmen to own lands and settle homes in India would be a good step:

> European families residing longer in India, and enjoying the affluence there; will adorn the country, and increase its stock, with useful and ornamented buildings. Their taste for the elegant superfluities of life, will give encouragement to the industry of the laborious classes of the native inhabitants. Numbers of the natives sharing in the riches, which will again flow into India, will constitute a class of opulent individuals ... it is certain that they are sufficiently disposed for gratifications, which tend to encourage ornamental arts. (1795, 103–104)

A few decades later, Surgeon Johnson wrote:

> The elegant budgerows and pleasure boats, conveying whole families of Europeans to and from their country seats, contrasting finely with the rude and curiously constructed vessels of the natives, forming altogether a scene the most picturesque and engaging that can be imagined! (1806, 29)

It was in the process and practice of settling an Indian home that the discourse of femininity becomes organised around racial 'types'. It was the English *woman's* task and responsibility to retain English 'honor' and 'virtue'. This meant attention to the 'work' of wifedom and motherhood. The emphasis on the 'woman's role' enabled the discourse of domesticity to present the Englishwoman as the ideal woman, as opposed to the hypersexual and sensual Indian one as Inderpal Grewal has argued (1996, 45). This role demanded that the English memsahib assert control over her dominion—the home—and the native servants, as we shall see in the essay on the work by Flora Annie Steel and Helen Gardiner. For instance, while native ayahs, wet nurses and servants were an integral part of the English home, they were also sources of considerable anxiety. There was the anxiety over racial mixing and the fear that the English children would develop strong emotional ties to their native carers or pick up habits and personalities from them (Glover 2004, 75). We see an expression of this anxiety in Charles D'Oyly's *The European in India* (1813):

> No children are put out to nurse: the *Dhood-Dhye*, or wet nurse, is invariably accommodated in the house, where she assumes no small degree of consequence, especially if she thinks her services indispensable. In the course of time she becomes one of the family, and changes from wet to dry nurse. Many of these women, whose first entrance into the service of Europeans is quite accidental, retain their situations for a great many years, and amass very comfortable independencies.

Yet, even this discourse of the memsahib working towards settling her home in India was undercut by those who believed that the Englishwoman in India had very little to do. G.O. Trevelyan writes in his *The Competitionwallah* (1866):

> The ladies, poor things, come in for all the disagreeables of up-country life. Without plenty of work, India is unbearable. That alone can stave off languor and a depth of ennui of which a person who has never left Europe can form no conception. In a climate which keeps every one within doors from eight in the morning till five in the evening, it is, humanly speaking, impossible to make sufficient occupation for yourself, if it does not come to you in the way of business. After a prolonged absence from home, reviews and newspapers become uninteresting. Good novels are limited in number, and it is too much to expect that a lady should read history and poetry for six hours every day. What well-regulated female can dress an object in a society of a dozen people, who know her rank to a title, and her income to a pice; or music, when her audience consists of a Punkah-wallah and a Portuguese Ayah? Some ladies, as a matter of conscience go very closely into the details of household affairs; but after a time they come to the conclusion that it is better to allow the servants to cheat within a certain margin, for the sake of peace and quietness; for cheat they will, do what you may. Oh! The dreariness of that hour in the middle of the long day, when the children are asleep, and your husband has gone to tiffin with the judge, and the book-club has nothing but Latham's "Nationalities of Europe" … and the English post has come in yesterday, with nothing but a letter from your old governess, congratulating you for being settled among the associations of the Mahommedan conquerors of India, and asking you to take some

> notice of her nephew, who is in the office of the Accountant-General of Bombay. It is very up-hill work for a lady out here to keep up her spirits and pluck, and her interest in general subjects. The race-week, the visit to her sister in the Punjab, the hope of being ordered down to Calcutta, the reminiscences of the sick-leave, and the anticipations of the furlough, are the consolations of a life which none but a very brave or a very stupid woman can endure long without suffering in mind, health, and tournure. If a lady becomes dowdy, it is all up to her; and the temptations to dowdiness in the Moffusil cannot be well exaggerated. (120)

Indeed, Flora Annie Steel, co-author of one of the largest advice manuals in the heyday of the Empire, herself declared in her autobiography, *The Garden of Fidelity*: 'The majority of European women in India have nothing to do' (1929, 122).

Moving outward from the English home, the social sphere was equally significant in terms of the imperial discourse of control and management. As commentators have noted, the bungalow, the club, and the garden thus became sovereign English spaces within an 'alien' landscape. Here tennis and bridge parties, polo and dances ensured that a locus of English culture was firmly inserted into a foreign setting. 'The club is open' wrote a member of the Himalaya Club, 'to the members of the civil and military services, to the members of the bar, the clergy, and to such other private gentlemen who are on the government-house list, which signifies "in society"' (*Household Words* 15 [1857]: 365). The club was a public space where English men and women gathered and participated in public life and nation-building for the Empire (Morris 1982, Sinha 2001, Cohen 2009).

It can be seen, even from this brief survey of select discourses, that the very *context*—from discovery to civilisational mission—of imperial rule and colonial subjectivity (by which I mean both, the subjectivity of the colonial and the colonial subject, conjoined in an unequal dynamic relation) enabled these academic, personal, administrative and imaginative texts, which very often distilled the contexts into themes, theories and tenets. These distillations could occur in the form of W.H. Sleeman's emphasis on the religious foundations of banditry in India (the thuggee texts) or the Macaulay pronouncement of the need to produce Indian clerks for British offices in India. The material but also the affective and the social-administrative contexts inform the texts in the colonial archive.

The obverse is also true. The texts, especially those by influential figures like Macaulay or William Jones but also from observers and literary authors, shape the cultural imaginary of present and future statesmen, volunteer workers, philanthropists and teachers, even as they echo in resonant but fragmented ways in events such as the parliamentary debates around, say, sati, in England. Shaped by material histories of the Raj, and shaping the histories in turn, these texts have played an important role in how the British saw, behaved in and responded to the subcontinent.

Colonial discourse is multilayered, and overlaps in terms of emphasis, across the centuries of English writings on India. It also cuts across genres and forms—memoir, fiction, travelogue, administrative reports, diaries and compendia of advice.

***

This book is organised around 10 documents that it identifies as representing specific ideological discourses that operated in British India.

The Charter ('Charter Granted by Queen Elizabeth, to the Governor and Company of Merchants of London, Trading into the East Indies') that licensed the English East India Company (EIC) to trade with the countries of the 'East', signed by Queen Elizabeth I on the last day of the century, 31 December 1600, set in motion the processes and practices, discourses and attitudes that would eventually, over the next century-and-a-half, enable the making of, first a Company-Raj and then a full-fledged imperial dominion in the subcontinent. The Charter empowers the Company officials in many domains, constructs particular identities for these officials and conveys clearly the sense that trade with the 'East' is in the national interest, thereby linking mercantilism, capitalism and nationalism in one fell swoop.

Robert Boyle, the celebrity scientist, fascinated by the ships setting out to the East, saw the voyages as an opportunity to both, generate and codify knowledge of these distant nations and their peoples. His 'Inquiries for Suratte and other Parts of the East-Indies' (1666–1667) was a questionnaire that the travellers carried with them to the East and the answers they provided were to become the foundation for empirical (since this was the dominant epistemological position of Boyle and institutions such as the Royal Society) and imperial knowledge.

If Boyle sought information from the English travellers to the East, the surveyor general of British India, after the battle of Plassey (Palashi) of 1757 and the acquisition of both territory and diwani rights in Bengal, undertook both actual surveys and combined the information gleaned through these with extant sources. Rennell's *Memoir of a Map of Hindoostan* (1788) was a sustained cartographic memoir and study that integrated the diverse regions of the country into a manageable textual form, which laid the foundations for integrated revenue collection, administration and, of course, military control.

J.Z. Holwell's account of the 'Black Hole' events, *A Genuine Narrative of the Deplorable Deaths of the English Gentlemen, and Others, Who Were Suffocated in the Black-Hole in Fort William, in Calcutta, in the Kingdom of Bengal; in the Night Succeeding the 20th Day of June, 1756* (1758), was one of the first captivity narratives to emerge from the subcontinent. It became, as critics have argued, a foundational story and mythography for the Empire. Holwell's account rehearses specific stereotypes of the brave Englishman and the barbarian native. He speaks of Christian fortitude and endurance and uses the trauma narrative to foreground cultural differences but in the process also engages in a project of individual self-fashioning.

Joseph Wilson's eyewitness account of sati, published in *The Weekly Miscellany* under the heading, 'The Custom of Women Burning Themselves with their Husbands' (1788), embodies several of the discourses around the theme of widow burning. Wilson documents the rituals and focuses on the woman's volitional act and agency. He presents himself as the English observer, tasked with ensuring that the woman had the freedom to *not* ascend the pyre. Wilson looks forward to many of the elements of colonial discourse that would emerge in the campaign against sati from the early 19th century.

Contributing to the corpus of Orientalist learning and European romanticism, and unleashing a literary storm among the European connoisseurs, William Jones's translation of *Shakuntala, Sacontalá or The Fatal Ring* (1789) initiated the making of a literary canon of Indian texts. In the process, he established the similarity and difference between the 'Eastern' and 'Western', or European, literary aesthetics and traditions. The relationship between the textual tradition and the native scholars that framed Jones's work also constituted a major moment in the epistemological conquest and construction of India.

Perhaps one of the most criticised and scrutinised texts of the colonial archive, T.B. Macaulay's 'Minute on Indian Education' (1835) was an iteration in a debate on educating the Indians that had been underway for some decades. The Minute presents a case for funding and administering Western/English education founded on the premise that Indian/vernacular education has only myths and mysticism and offers no practical knowledge. Macaulay proffers utilitarian goals for education, as the tract foregrounds the economics of educating Indians but also the larger political advantages of doing so.

In what can be thought of as the textual embodiment of the major military and social campaign directed at controlling native subjects, W.H. Sleeman's account of the thugs in *Thugs or, Phansigars of India* (1839) identifies their origins and attributes their depredations to their religious affiliations. Sleeman thus inaugurates a surveillance discourse that eventually produced specific law-and-order administrative offices and propaganda, as well as an entire taxonomy of 'dangerous' natives.

If running a colonial administration was the 'man's work' in the gendered ethos of imperialism, the memsahib, argue Flora Annie Steel and Grace Gardiner in *The Complete Indian Housekeeper & Cook* (1888), needs to run the Englishman's home just as efficiently. In their advice and instruction book, a bestseller running into multiple editions in the decades following its first publication, Steel and Gardiner construct stereotypes of the Indian servant class. They encode in the process a discourse of imperial domesticity, with assigned roles for the men and women (both English and native).

Herbert Risley's *The People of India* (1908) was akin to the census in that it set out to construct a demographic catalogue of the subcontinent. Identifying castes, their origins and languages, Risley also employed anthropometry to classify and describe the peoples. Exploring their religions and customs, Risley constructed a particular ethnological account of the Indian peoples, and, in the process, laid the grounds for the amplification of the 'ethnographic state', and used his studies' results to ponder on the possibilities of Indian nationalism.

***

To even propose that these 10 are representative texts of the Raj is an absurdity—since they barely capture the expanse, intricacies and nuances of the imperial discourse. Rather, these can only be seen as a sampler of the archive. Taking any single discourse, whether of exoticism or the civilisational mission, entails discovering and engaging with not only the overt prejudices and racism but also very often the wonder, awe and puzzlement the British encountered as they set out to explore, examine and understand the subcontinent.

ACKNOWLEDGEMENTS

The Raj has been a perennial favourite when it comes to research and writing, and I cannot remember a year when I did *not* do some 'Raj work'.

Chandra Sekhar of Bloomsbury was very receptive to the project idea, and has been incisive and encouraging when it came to subjects like the volume's organisation, content and final form—to him, this project owes much.

I express my thanks to journals and anthologies, and their editors and reviewers whose comments have enabled me to sharpen my thoughts on the Raj-topic-of-the-moment. Among journals, I acknowledge: *South Asia, South Asian Review, Anglo-Saxonica* and *Asiatic*. Among the anthologies, I acknowledge *Ireland's Imperial Connections*; *The Edinburgh History of Reading*; *The English Renaissance, Orientalism, and the Idea of Asia*; *Cultural Histories of India*. To Debra Johanyak and Walter S. Lim, Rita Banerjee, Daniel Roberts and Jonathan Wright, Mary Hammond and Jonathan Rose, editors of these fabulous anthologies, many thanks for your invitation to contribute and the work you put into the volumes of which I am now a part.

To Kate Teltscher, whose work *India Inscribed* showed me where to go way back in the mid-1990s, I owe an intellectual debt of enormous proportions.

I am also grateful to publishers and editors at Penguin, Bloomsbury, Palgrave-Macmillan, Edinburgh University Press, Orient BlackSwan, Wiley-Blackwell and Routledge for their comments, suggestions and, above all, interest in this area and my contributions to it.

To Soma Ghosh, Librarian (English) at the Salar Jung Museum, Hyderabad, and her constant efforts, all undertaken with cheer and grace, to obtain materials when I have worked there, immeasurable gratitude.

Many books germinate in conversations with Anna Kurian, who is always enthusiastic about any Raj-work I do, especially if they are multivolume projects. For the constant-traveller role that you assay with such commitment, solidarity and affection, it is my privilege, Anna, to acknowledge you.

Thank you, Molly ('Chechu'), for enquiring lovingly about her 'little one'.

Nandana Dutta has been unceasing in her interest in my work, and her always gentle and loving urging to think in certain ways, even as she tries to catch up with her reading of what I publish. To your attention, insights and perspicacity, Nandana—much, much gratitude.

Professor K. Narayana Chandran established, for some of us willing ones, the standards in academic scholarship and publishing—that he sustains these standards even now, after four decades, is nothing short of the marvellous. To

KNC's indomitable spirit of inquiry and work ethic, and showing us the way to do things, I am very grateful.

Friends who drop in 'WhatsAppingly', regularly, to check on me—Neelu, Bhalla, Ajeet, Kulsoom, Om, Archana, Ashish, Krishna Ram, Sai Jawahar, Savita, Vaishali, Soma and Zahid—thank you.

To Nandini, Pranav, my parents and parents-in-law, I owe unquantifiable gratitude, for never complaining at the volume of work I take on, my frequently distracted state of being and, more importantly, for creating an extraordinarily supportive environment.

And thank you, Shubha, for obtaining, wizard-like, essays and journal articles in minutes, and for your enthusiasm for my work.

To the works of P.G. Wodehouse, Agatha Christie, Stephen King, the comics around Batman—my regular reading—many of which unwittingly capture the horror, the abyss and the comedy of academia, I can never express enough gratitude.

It is a pleasure to thank Atul Nair who compiled many of the materials meticulously.

I am grateful to the Institution of Eminence (IoE) project's Professional Development Fund.

1

IMPERIAL BUSINESS

The English East India Company (EIC)—a name that was coined much later—came into being through a Royal Charter signed and issued by Queen Elizabeth I, titled, *Charter Granted by Queen Elizabeth, to the Governor and Company of Merchants of London Trading Into the East Indies, Dated the 31st December, in the 43rd Year of Her Reign, Anno Domini, 1600.* This occurred after a series of sustained petitions and pressures from 218 members of the merchant community of England and the duke of Cumberland. This community, whose members had been a part of the Levant Company (formed in 1592), and which saw the Dutch prosper from the spice trade, and having taken cognisance of the successful maritime perambulations by James Lancaster (1591–1594), noted that England, too, could benefit from the trade with the 'East Indies'. (In 1599, the Dutch ships came back laden with pepper, the price of which tripled in England.) The English merchants raised upwards of £30,000 towards a trading voyage to the Indies. The queen relented after much delay and issued the Charter for the 'Governor and Company of Merchants of London' to acquire sole rights within England for the East Indies trade.

In order to finance the first set of four ships (*Hector, Dragon, Ascension* and *Susan*) under this Charter, the 200-plus investors raised a total of £68,373. The Company itself was initially created for a period of 15 years, from the date of the Charter. The ships sailed under the captaincy of James Lancaster in 1601. They returned in 1603.

The Charter and its later iterations appeared in a compilation, *The Lawes or Standing Orders of the East India Company*, published in 1621.

Structure and Content

The Royal Charter is a formal legal document. It opens with the granting of trading rights. In the process, it bestowed upon the group of merchants the status and privileges of a 'body corporate and politick' (its description), giving it a name, 'Governor and Company of Merchants of London'.

Later, the document would define the organisational structure of the Company.

There would be a governor—Thomas Smith/Smythe was appointed as the first—and 24 members would form a committee (later called directors). The committee members were to be appointed every year but they had the privilege of having their sons also automatically authorised to trade with the

East. By 'East', the Charter indicated Africa and Asia. It extended to Pegu, Malacca and Java, and all the 'Spice Islands' the Company ships hoped to reach. 'East' was not, in the Charter and the first imaginaries of trade, 'India', although, over the century, the two terms would indeed merge and become synonyms.

The rights of the Company are then spelt out: the right to draft laws, the right to re-export the products they brought from India, the freedom from customs duties and interference by any English authority (including the Lord Admiral), the right to grant trading licences of its own, the right to bring in gold, the right to own property such as offices and warehouses ('to enjoy and retain lands', as the Charter words it), and even to establish factories in the countries they would be trading with (unless this came into conflict with other European countries trading therein, or with the laws of England).

The Charter also outlines the procedures for decision-making, the election of members and the rights and privileges of the association, such as having its own seal.

Adventurers and Traders

The Charter defined the structure of the Company, which British historian John Keay summarises as follows:

> From the start the Company's stock had appealed to two very different types of investor. On the one hand there was the shareholder interested primarily in a quick and substantial return on his investment.... On the other hand there were those who perceived some collateral advantage in the trade itself. This group consisted of wealthy and influential City merchants with extensive commercial and financial interests outside the Company ... these two types of investor may be roughly identified with the Company's two institutional bodies, the General Court (later the Court of Proprietors) and the Court of Committees. The General Court comprised all those with voting rights, the qualification for which in the early seventeenth century was a minimum holding of, usually, £200. It therefore represented the generality of investors amongst whom those interested primarily in profits and dividends predominated. It was also, of course, the supreme authority within the Company. But, several hundred strong, it necessarily met infrequently and had little to do with the day-to-day running of the business.
>
> Under the terms of the original charter this was left to the Court of Committees consisting of the Governor, Deputy-Governor and twenty-four 'committees', or directors, all of whom were elected by the General Court. The Court of Committees was the Company's

> executive, making policy decisions which had to be ratified by the General Court as well as directing all operations. For specific and recurrent functions like purchasing bullion, timber, provisions, etc., handling correspondence with overseas factors, and managing the Company's sales it divided into a host of influential sub-committees. Both these and the Court of Committees met frequently. Naturally their work demanded managerial and commercial experience, and so naturally the 'committees' were predominantly City merchants. (1993, 25–26)

But beyond the organisation of the company of merchants, it is the rhetoric of the Charter that offers us insights into the aims and aspirations of the merchants, and of the English monarchy.

The second sentence of the Charter states that the petitioners had asked for royal 'assent and licence' so that they 'might adventure and set forth on one or more voyages', at their 'own adventures, costs and charges' (1918, 1). The word 'adventure' and its cognate occurs twice in the same sentence, and thus constructs the figure of the merchant-adventurer.

The Company then was a group of adventurers who sought the twin freedoms of *travel* and *trade*. Keay writes in his popular history of the EIC:

> The Company stands forth as a robust association of adventurers engaged in hazarding all in a series of preposterous gambles. Some paid off; many did not but are no less memorable for it. Bizarre locations, exotic produce, and recalcitrant personalities combine to induce a sense of romance which, however repugnant to the scholar, is in no way contrived. (1993, xx)

The Charter itself outlines the *possibility* of adventure, and the fulfilment of the twin ambitions of the freedoms sought and granted. But before the statement of these freedoms and expressions of ambition, the Charter speaks of 'commodities and merchandizes' that the Company merchants have 'not yet experienced'. Suggesting newness and novelty—features of the early modern travel discourse—the Charter implies unusual experiences lie in wait for those who 'adventure' beyond the known. Essentially, the Charter presents the lure of the exotic and the different—'not yet experienced'—as inspiring the merchant-adventurer.

The Company, it says, is free to trade

> In the countries and parts of Asia and Africa and to as many of the islands, ports and cities, towns and places, thereabouts, as where trade and traffic may by all likelihood be discovered, established or had; divers [sic] of which countries and many of the islands, cities and ports, thereof, have long been discovered by others of our subjects, albeit not frequented in trade of merchandize. (1–2)

The Charter, I suggest, combines trade and adventure into the theme of discovery. It calls upon the Company's merchants to not only pay attention to those routes, places and products that have *already* been on the trading maps of England and others but also those which 'may by all likelihood be discovered'. This rhetorical move enables, indeed persuades, the merchant to be an adventurer and a discoverer of opportunities in the form of possible places for trade. In the second part of the sentence, the Charter also calls upon the merchant-adventurer to observe those lands and places that have been discovered by their contemporaries but whose trading potential has not been fully utilised by the others. In other words, the Charter is gesturing at first, a *terra incognita* that warrants discovery and exploration, and second, a *terra potentia* that is not undiscovered but remains under-explored.[1] The merchant-adventurer is projected, therefore, as the vanguard not just of the English trading community but of the country and race itself. Further, by implying that there may be lands beyond what has already been discovered, the Charter opens up the world for imagining and therefore as a field of potentialities. Composed in the context of the Dutch, and before that, the Portuguese advances into transnational trade, the Charter assumes significance as an aspirational document and not simply a charter of rights.

The monopoly granted to the Company for all East Indies trade made this collective of adventurers a powerful group, even though the Company itself 'competed against other European organisations in Asia—and happily traded with them' (Erikson 2014, 2). The quantum of profits and trade generated was, as K.N. Chaudhuri has noted, more than sufficient for the Charter and the monopoly to be renewed by successive English monarchs (Chaudhuri 1978).[2]

National Needs

The group of merchants had pleaded with the queen for permission to trade. The Charter demonstrates another interesting move when granting them the rights.

After recording that the group would go forth at their 'own adventures, costs and charges', the Charter swerves onto an entirely different discursive route when it says, following the above phrase, 'for the honour of this our realm of England'. The trading enterprise of a group of merchants is re-designated as a national project, geared towards amplifying the honour of the realm. Thus, it is no longer just trade for profit but for the abstract quality of 'national' honour.

Then, when granting the licence, the Charter would reiterate this discourse:

> We, greatly tendering the honour of our nation, the wealth of our people, and the encouragement of them, and others of our loving

> subjects in their good enterprizes [sic], for the increase of our navigation and the advancement of our lawful traffick to the benefit of our Commonwealth… (2)

The shift in emphasis is clear: the aims of the Charter are, of course, to enable the trade and profits of the individual members (the Charter names the 200-plus members). Beyond that, however, there is also the larger, and presumably nobler, goal of serving the national interest.

It is possible to read the Charter as merging business with national interests, identifying one with the other. It tempers the question of fiduciary profiteering by implying profits of multiple kinds—the happiness of the people of the realm who have been 'encouraged' in their 'good enterprises', the advancement of maritime and nautical knowledge and finally, climaxing in the 'benefit of [the] Commonwealth'. In one of the early instances of the mercantilisation of national interest and the nationalisation of mercantile interests, the Charter makes the Company responsible to the nation and implicitly signals the need for the Company to see their work of trade not as individual but as national projects.

Related to the theme of national interests is the injunction that the Company should not interfere with the rights of any other nation in those trading places/countries. That is, the Company's actions should not produce any disputes between the queen of England and her European allies by seeking rights that would conflict with the rights of other nations. The allies who possess trading rights in the East would be, the Charter makes clear, Christian nations. The Charter states:

> The same trade be not undertaken nor addressed to any country, island, port, haven, city, creek, town or place, already in the lawful and actual possession of any such Christian prince or state, as this present is, or any time hereafter shall be in league or amity with us, or heirs or successors, and who doth not or will not accept such trade, but doth overtly state and publish the same to be utterly against his or their good will and liking. (8)

If a Christian king or an ally of England did not wish the Company to trade in a nation where he had interests, the Company should refrain from doing so. This point is emphasised later when the Charter says that the Company, which is licensed to permit individuals to trade, shall not, however, permit them to do so with countries whose trade rights are with a Christian prince or an ally, if the prince/ally does not 'like' it.

Clearly, the Charter demonstrates the monarchy's awareness of possible trading conflicts that would adversely impact the national interests. However, it is silent on whether the Company could compete with non-Christian kings who may be trade rivals. Or rather, it implies that the preferences of non-Christian princes—as to whether they want the Company to trade in their country or not—can be ignored, because the non-Christian's possession of the land does not count. In the process, the Charter categorises, as is expected of the times, the world into Christian and non-Christian segments.

The Corporate World(s) of/for Traders

The Charter permitted the Company to license individuals to engage in trade as well. Indeed, no individual could trade without this licence. (A Committee for Private Trade was created in 1660, by which time business was, so to speak, booming.) Emily Erikson writes about this distributed monopoly:

> the Company ceded several of its monopoly privileges to its own employees. These employees engaged in what was called the private trade, trade upon their own account and in their own interest, while in the employ of the Company. The private trade allowances both contributed to and were a part of a larger pattern of decentralized decision making in the English Company. (2)

The Charter, in empowering the committee/directors, also gave the licence to trade to the sons of the directors:

> Grant unto the said Governor and Company of Merchants of London, trading into the East Indies, and their successors, that they, and all that are or shall be of the said Company of Merchants of London, trading into the East Indies, and every one of them, and all the sons of them, at their several ages of one and twenty years or upwards… (7)

Thus, the Charter ensured the continuity of Company rights for families (the male line, at least). Further, as Nick Robins notes, 'semi-sovereign privileges to rule territories and raise armies certainly mark it [the Company] out as a corporate institution from another time' (2006, 5).

By restricting the right to East Indies trade to the London Company alone—this is the monopoly—the Charter also made the Company a world within a world, for the Company was exclusively a *London* firm, and no other British subject from any other English city was allowed to conduct trade. This would make the city of London the hub of England's financial network.

Then, there was the freedom of the Company to re-export the goods procured from the East Indies:

> The said Governor and Company of merchants of London, trading into the East Indies, than can be spent for the necessary use of the same in our realm, which of necessity must be transported to other countries, and there vended … it shall be lawful … to transport the same in English bottoms, freely out of this realm … without payment

> of any further custom, poundage, or any further subsidy, to us… (11–12)

The Charter also allows the Company to prepare and employ 'six good ships and six good pinnaces' 'fitted with ordnance and other munition' along with 'five hundred mariners, Englishmen' for their defence, shall 'quietly be permitted and suffered to depart … without any stay or contradiction' (14). However, if the kingdom requires, for either defence or offence, the services of additional ships, these ships and pinnaces must be returned to the crown, says the Charter.

The Charter also enjoins the administrative and military offices of the kingdom to extend their support to the Company:

> Commanding all and singular our admirals, vice-admirals, justices, mayors, sheriffs, escheators, constables, bailiffs, and all and singular other our officers, minister, liege men, and subjects whatsoever, to be aiding, favouring, helping and assisting unto the said Governor and Company … in executing and enjoying the premises, as well as on land as on sea, from time to time… (19–20)

The Charter was ensuring that the kingdom's offices recognised the importance of the Company, and what it was being set up to do. The Company was to be treated as a national project by the administrative, financial and juridical officers and structures. It was the making of a world of a special kind, to which the rest had to give sustenance and protection.

While there is no moral or ethical imperative being framed here in terms of conditions laid out for the other offices and officers of the realm, the Charter makes it clear that the Company is significant for the entire realm. Profits are necessary for the greater good of the realm. The Charter, therefore, plays it double-edged throughout: by insisting on ethical principles of not encroaching on another's rights (especially if they are Christian princes or allies) and speaking of financial and material gain from these transactions in the same breath. It binds the Company and the rest of the kingdom to these dual principles of making money and abiding by norms. This duality would be a marker of the policy directives to the Company for a long time: trying to balance the financial performance and maintain ethical standards, as Robins points out (120–121).

Another feature of this 'world within a world' of the Company of merchants was the global scope envisioned in the Charter. London's merchants were to have the right to trade in the geographically ambivalent space called the 'East', whose fullest extent and scope were left to the imagination, determination and choice of the merchant-adventurers. The 'adventure' component was not meant to indicate the sense of going out into an unknown world. As Robins notes:

> Capital costs were high in terms of both shipping and the bullion required to buy homebound goods.... Risks were extreme, both natural and political, with a high likelihood of the loss of some or all of the investment. (24)

When they did manage to reach the Indies, they had planned for and set up factories and trading posts as approved by the Charter. But, they discovered, neither the trade nor the factory settlements in Bengal, 'from the point of view of the East India Company' were 'secure during the decades before the military conquest of Hindusthan' (Sen 1998, 63). Thus, the Charter's cautionary tone and the repeated use of the word 'adventure' was to prove proleptic.[3] The 'adventure' then was a lot more than just a journey, it was about the risk of financial loss, and the possible loss of lives (the Lancaster voyages had lost plenty of men to scurvy and other conditions).

The emphasis on future discoveries and potential mentioned before was, I suggest, a geography-in-the-making of the world. That is, the Charter implicitly sets up the Company as a transnational, globally conquering trading body with a vast arsenal of rights of access for 15 years (in 1609, the Charter was renewed for an indefinite period). K.N. Chaudhuri says, 'The East India Company was the direct ancestor of the modern business firm, handling a multitude of trading products and operating in an international setting' (1978, 21).

The classification of the Company as a 'body corporate', i.e., a corporation, was founded on a Roman concept: *corpus politicum et corporatum* or *communitas perpetua*. This concept, Philip Stern argues, 'formed the bedrock for political and associational life in early modern England'. Stern writes:

> There were corporations for municipal government, domestic and regional trades, public works, ecclesiastical establishments and religious confraternities, universities and educational societies, charities, and, of course, for overseas English commerce, settlement, and colonization from Europe to the Atlantic, Russia to the Mediterranean and Africa. (2011, 7)

The corporate body was a form of governance:

> Whatever their immediate purposes and particular organization, all corporations shared a common purpose: to bind a multitude of people together into a legal singularity, an artificial person that could maintain common rights, police community standards and behavior, and administer over and on behalf of the collectivity. (7)

Yet, it was also a 'fellowship' and an association (Stern, 8). As a social form, it had its franchise, ceremony and rituals. For example, the Charter calls for the Company to have its own 'seal' (3) and outlines a procedure of regular meetings, elections and decision-making, and swearing-in rituals—a 'corporal oath', as the Charter puts it (4, 5 and elsewhere). But the larger point Stern makes is that such associations and body corporate(s) 'generated their allegiances and identities, compatible but also potentially in competition with others, including the Crown' (8). The EIC was a form of 'political community and polity',

> empowered and obligated to construct "Laws, Constitutions, Orders and Ordinances" to govern itself and those under its command, to administer oaths, and offer its "freedom," which essentially conferred on its holder a share of the Company's rights and privileges but also served as a form of allegiance and identity. (10)

And because it was a joint-stock company, the EIC was administered by its shareholders, with the structure replicated in its foreign government, too (11). It replicated an institutional culture, a 'delicate balance of strict hierarchy and consultative government, conditioned by an institutional culture defined and constantly reinforced by ritual, procedure, and ceremony' (11). For Stern, the Company was a political institution and shows 'a preoccupying concern with government that extended far beyond regulating trade and its "servants"' (12).

Stern writes of how the early Charter's terms, privileges and processes were expanded:

> The Company's charter, which encompassed all the trade and traffic between the Cape of Good Hope and the Strait of Magellan, translated into a claim to jurisdiction over all English subjects in Asia and the Eurasian populations resident in its growing network of settlements. Grant after grant from English monarchs progressively expanded this purview, giving the Company leave to establish fortifications, make law, erect courts, issue punishment, coin money, conduct diplomacy, wage war, arrest English subjects, and plant colonies. (12)

In other words, by creating a world within a world in the form of a corporate body, the Charter enabled the making of a form of political community and governance—which in turn laid the foundations of a colonial system in India. Giving the Company financial, procedural and judicial powers, allowing it to raise an army or mint its own currency (over the next 100 years or so, through later charters), and thus allowing it to build its own sovereignty.[4]

The Company was like a state, and the state in what would become 'British India' was a 'Company-State', as the title of Stern's book calls it.[5]

***

The Charter instantiates multiple aspirations and ambitions of the island nation. It signals the making of a corporate body licensed to roam the world seeking the best trade opportunities. It speaks of all-around support for the initiative and bestows the merchant-adventurer with enormous freedoms and powers—in the name of national interest and the interests of the Commonwealth.

Eventually, the Company's profits and contribution to the exchequer (calculated by several historians, especially K.N. Chaudhuri, 1978) makes it an integral part of the government's policy, attitude and aspirations for well over a century-and-a-half. The shift towards territorial conquest and determined colonisation that would become Company policy from the mid-18th century is, at the time of the Charter, some way off, but the aspirations embodied in the document, one speculates, lead to such a policy to facilitate greater profits, greater security for the traders and, of course, a better fulfilment of national interests.

INDIAN

CONSTITUTIONAL DOCUMENTS.

PART I.

GENERAL DOCUMENTS.

(1600-1858).

I. CHARTER GRANTED BY QUEEN ELIZABETH TO THE EAST INDIA COMPANY.

(Dated the 31st December, 1600.)

ELIZABETH, by the Grace of God, Queen of England, France, and Ireland, Defender of the Faith, &c. To all our officers, ministers, and subjects, and to all other people, as well within this our realm of England as elsewhere, under our obedience and jurisdiction, or otherwise, unto whom these our Letters Patents shall be seen, showed, or read, greeting. Whereas our most dear and loving Cousin, George, Earl of Cumberland, and our well-beloved subjects, Sir John Hart, of London, and others (here follow 214 other names which are omitted) have of our certain knowledge been petitioners unto us, for our Royal assent and licence to be granted unto them, that they, at their own adventures, costs, and charges, as well for the honour of this our realm of England, as for the increase of our navigation, and advancement of trade of merchandize, within our said realms and the dominions of the same, might adventure and set forth one or more voyages, with convenient number of ships and pinnaces, by way of traffic and merchandize to the East Indies, in the countries and parts of Asia and Africa and to as many of the islands, ports and cities, towns and places, thereabouts, as where trade and traffic may by all likelihood be discovered, established or had ; divers of which countries, and many of the islands, cities and ports thereof, have long since been discovered by others of our subjects, albeit not frequented in trade of merchandize. Know ye, therefore, that we, greatly tendering the honour of our nation, the wealth of our people, and the en couragement of them, and others of our loving subjects in their good enterprizes, for the increase of our navigation, and the advancement of lawful traffick to the benefit of our Commonwealth, have of our special grace, certain knowledge, and mere motion, given and granted and by these presents, for us, our heirs and successors, do give and grant unto our said loving subjects, before in these presents expressly named, that they and every of them from henceforth be, and shall be one body corporate and politick, in deed and in name, by the name of the Governor and Company of Merchants of London, trading into the East Indies, and them by the name of the Governor and Company of Merchants of London, trading into the East Indies, one body corporate and politick, in deed and in name, really and fully for us our heirs and successors, we do order, make, ordain, constitute, establish and declare, by these presents, and that by the same name of Governor and company of merchants of London, trading into the East Indies, they shall have succession, and that they and their successors, by the name of the Governor and Company of Merchants of London, trading into the East Indies, be and shall be, at all times hereafter, persons able and capable in law, and a body corporate and politick, and capable in law to have, purchase, receive, possess, enjoy and retain lands, rents, privileges, liberties, jurisdictions, franchises and hereditaments of whatsoever kind, nature, and quality so ever they be, to them and their successors. And also to give, grant, demise, alien, assign and dispose lands, tenements and hereditaments, and to do and execute all and singular other things, by the same name that to them shall or may appertain to do. And that they and their successors, by the name of the Governor and Company of Merchants of London, trading into the East Indies, may plead and be impleaded, answer and be answered, defend and be defended, in whatsoever courts and places, and before whatsoever judges and justices, and other persons and officers, in all and singular actions, pleas, suits, quarrels, causes and demands whatsoever, of whatsoever kind, nature or sort, in such manner and form, as any other, our liege people of this our realm of England, being persons able and capable in law, may or can have, purchase, receive, possess, enjoy, retain, give, grant, demise, alien, assign, dispose, plead and be impleaded, answer and be answered, defend and be defended, release and be released, do permit and execute. And that the said Governor and Company of Merchants of London, trading into the East Indies, and their successors, may have a common seal, to serve for all the causes and business of them and their successors. And that it shall and may be lawful to the said Governor and Company, and their successors, the same seal, from time to time, at their will and pleasure, to break, change, and to make new or alter, as to them shall seem expedient. And further, we will, and by these presents, for us, our heirs and successors, we do ordain, that there shall be from henceforth one of the same Company to be elected and appointed, in such form, as hereafter in these presents is expressed, which shall be called the Governor of the said Company, and that there shall be from henceforth twenty-four of the said Company, to be elected and appointed in such form, as hereafter in these presents is expressed, which shall be called the committees of the said Company, who, together with the Governor of the said Company for the time being, shall have the direction of the voyages, of or for the said Company, and the provision of the shipping and merchandizes thereto belonging, and also the sale of all merchandizes returned in the voyages, of or for the said Company, and the managing and handling of all other things belonging to the said Company and for the better execution of this our will and grant in this behalf we have assigned, nominated, constituted and made, and by these presents, for us, our heirs and successors, we do assign, nominate, constitute and make, the said Thomas Smith, Alderman of London, to be the first and present Governor of the said Company, to continue in the said office, from the date of these presents, until another of the said Company shall in due manner be chosen and sworn unto the said office, according to the ordinances and provisions hereafter in these presents expressed and declared, if the said Thomas Smith shall so long live; and also we have assigned, nominated and appointed, and by these presents, for us, our heirs and successors, we do assign, nominate, constitute and make, the said Paul Banning, Leonard Hollyday, John Moore, Edward Holmeden, Richard Staper, Thomas Cordell, William Garway, Oliver Style, James Lancaster, Richard Wiseman, Francis Cherry, Thomas Allabaster, William Romney, Roger How, William Chambers, Robert Sandye, John Eldred, Richard Wiche, John Hylord, John Middleton, John Comb, William Harrison, Nicholas

Ling and Robert Bell, to be the twenty-four first and present committees of the said Company, to Continue in the said office of committees of the said Company from the date of these presents, for one whole year next following. And further we will and grant, by these presents, for us, our heirs and successors, unto the said Governor and Company of Merchants of London, trading into the East Indies, and their successors, that it shall and may be lawful to and for the said Governor and Company, for the time being, or the more part of them, present at any publick assembly, commonly called the Court, holden for the said Company, the Governor of the said Company being always one, from time to time, to elect, nominate and appoint one of the said Company, to be deputy to the said Governor, which deputy shall take a corporal oath, before the Governor and five or more of the committees of the said Company for the time being, well, faithfully and truly to execute his said office of deputy to the Governor of the said Company, and after his oath, so taken, shall and may from time to time, in the absence of the said Governor, exercise and execute the office of Governor of the said Company, in such sort as the said Governor ought to do : and further we will and grant, by these presents, for us, our heirs and successors, unto the said Governor and Company of Merchants of London, trading into the East Indies, and their successors, that they or the greater part of them, whereof the Governor for the time being or his deputy to be one, from time to time, and at all times hereafter shall and may have authority and power, yearly and every year, on the first day of July, or at any time within six days after that day, to assemble and meet together, in some convenient place, to be appointed from time to time by the governor, or in his absence by the deputy of the said Governor for the time being, and that they being so assembled, it shall and may be lawful to and for the said Governor, or deputy of the said Governor, and the said Company for the time being or the greater part of them, which then shall happen to be present, whereof the Governor of the said Company or his deputy for the time being, to be one, to elect and nominate one of the said Company, which shall be Governor of the said Company for one whole year, from thence next following, which person, being so elected and nominated to be governor of the said company, as is aforesaid before he be admitted to the execution of the said office, shall take a corporal oath before the last Governor, being his predecessor or his deputy, and any six or more of the committees of the said Company for the time being, that he shall, from time to time, well and truly execute the office of Governor of the said Company, in all things concerning the same ; and that immediately after the said oath so taken, he shall and may execute and use the said office of Governor of the said Company, for one whole year, from thence next following : And in like sort we will and grant, that as well every one above-named to be of the said Company fellowship as all others hereafter to be admitted, or free of the said Company, shall take a corporal oath before the Governor of the said Company, or his deputy for the time being, to such effect, as by the said Governor and Company, or the more part of them, in any public court to be held from the said Company, shall be in reasonable manner set down and devised, before they shall be allowed, or admitted to trade or traffick, as a freeman of the said Company. And further we will and grant, by these presents, for us, our heirs and successors, unto the said Governor and Company of Merchants of London, trading into the East Indies, and their successors, that the said Governor, or the deputy of the said Governor, and the Company and their successors, for the time being, or the greater part of them, whereof the Governor, or the deputy of the Governor, from time to time, to be one, shall and may, from time to time, and at all times hereafter, have authority and power, yearly and every year, on the first day of July, or at any time within six days after that day, to assemble and meet together, in some convenient place, to be from time to time appointed, by the said Governor of the said Company, or in his absence, by his deputy : And that they being so assembled, it shall and may be lawful, to and for the said Governor or his deputy, and the Company for the time being, or the greater part of them, which then shall happen to be present, whereof the Governor of the said Company, or his deputy for the time being, to be one, to elect and nominate twenty-four of the said Company, which shall be committee of the said Company, for one whole year, from thence next ensuing, which person being so elected and nominated to be committees of the said Company, as aforesaid, before they be admitted to the execution of their said offices, shall take a corporal oath, before the Governor or his deputy, and any six or more of the said committees of the said Company, being their last predecessors for the time being, that they and every of them shall well and faithfully perform their said office of committees, in all things concerning the same, and that immediately after the said oath so taken, they shall and may execute and use their said offices of committees of the said Company, for one whole year, from thence next following; and moreover our will and pleasure is, and by these presents, for us our heirs and successors, we do grant unto the said Governor and Company of Merchants of London, trading into the East Indies, and to their successors, that when and as often as shall happen, the Governor of the said Company for the time being, at any time within one year, after that he shall be nominated, elected and sworn to the office of Governor of the said company, as is aforesaid, to die or to be removed from the said office, which governor, not demeaning himself well in his said office, we will to be removeable at the pleasure of the said Company, or the greater part of them, which shall be present, at any of their publick assemblies, commonly called their general court, holden for the said Company, that then and so often it shall and may be lawful, to and for the residue of the said Company for the time being, or the greater part of them, within convenient time after the death or removing of any such Governor, to assemble themselves in such convenient place as they shall think fit, for the election of the Governor of the said Company : And that the said Company, or the greater part of them, being then and there present, shall and may, then and there, before their departure from the said place, elect and nominate one other of the said company, to be Governor of the same Company, in the place or stead of him that so died or was so removed, which person, being so elected, and nominated to the office of Governor of the said company, shall have and exercise the said office for and during the residue of the said year, taking first a corporal oath as is aforesaid, for the due execution thereof ; and this to be done from time to time, so often as the case shall so require. And also our will and pleasure is, and by these presents, for us, our heirs and successors, we do grant unto the said Governor and Merchants of London, trading into the East-Indies, and to their successors, that when and as often as it shall happen, any of the committees of the said Company for the time being, at any time within one year, next after that they or any of them shall be nominated, elected, and sworn to the office of committees of the said Company, as is aforesaid, to die or be removed from the said office, which committees, not demeaning themselves well in their said office, we will to be removeable, at the pleasure of the said Governor and Company or the greater part of them, whereof the Governor of the said Company, for the time being, or his deputy for the time being, to be one that then and so often, it shall and may be lawful, to and for the said Governor and Company for the time being, or the greater part of them, whereof the Governor for the time being, or his deputy, to be one, within convenient time, after the death or removing of any of the said committees, to assemble themselves in such convenient place, as is or shall be usual and accustomed, for the election of the Governor of the said Company, or where else the Governor of the said Company for the time being, or his deputy, shall appoint : and the said Governor and Company, or the greater part of them, whereof the Governor for the time being, his deputy, to be one, being then and there present, shall and may then and there, before their departure from the said place elect and nominate one or more of the said Company, to be committees of the same Company, in the places and steads, place or stead, of him or them that so died, or were or was so removed, which person or persons. so elected and nominated to the office or offices of committee, or committees, of the said Company, shall have and exercise the said office and offices, during the residue of the said year, taking first a corporal oath as is aforesaid, for the due execution thereof, and this to be done from time to time, so often as the case shall require. And further we do, by these presents, for us, our heirs and successors, will and grant unto the said Governor and Company of Merchants of London, trading into the East Indies, and their successors, that they, and all that are or shall be of the said Company of Merchants of London, trading into the East Indies, and every of them, and all the sons of them, at their several ages of one and twenty years or upwards : And further, all such the apprentices, factors or servants of them, and of every of them, which hereafter shall be employed by the said Governor and Company, in the said trade of merchandize, of or to the East-Indies, beyond the seas, or any other the places aforesaid, in any part of the said East Indies, or other the places aforesaid, shall and may, by the space of fifteen years, from the feast of the birth of our Lord God last past, before the date hereof, freely traffick and use the trade of merchandize, by seas, in and by such ways and passages already found out and discovered, or which hereafter shall be found out and discovered, as they shall esteem and take to be fittest, into and from the said East-Indies, in the countries and parts of Asia and Africa, and into and from all the islands, ports, havens, cities, creeks, towns and places of Asia and Africa, and America, or any of them, beyond the cape of Bona Esperanza to the straits of Magellan, where any trade or traffick of merchandize may be used or had, and to and from every of them, in such order, manner, form, liberty and condition, to all intents and purposes, as shall be, from time to time, at any publick assembly or court, held by or for the said Governor and Company, by or between them of the said fellowship or Company of Merchants of London, trading into the East Indies, or the more part of them, for the time being, present at such assembly or court, the Governor, or his deputy, being always present at such court or assembly, limited and agreed, and not otherwise, without any molestation, impeachment, or disturbance, any statute, usage, diversity of religion or faith or any other cause or matter whatsoever, to the contrary notwithstanding: So always the same trade be not undertaken nor addressed to any country, island, port, haven, city, creek, town or place, already in the lawful and actual possession of any such Christian prince or state, as at this present is, or at any time hereafter shall be in league or amity with us, our heirs or successors, and who doth not or will not accept of such trade, but doth overtly declare and publish the same to be utterly against his or their good will and liking. And further our will and pleasure is, and by these presents, for us, our heirs and successors, we do grant unto the said Governor and Company of Merchants of London, trading into the East Indies, and to their successors, that it shall and may be lawful, to and for the said Governor and Company, and their successors, from time to time to assemble themselves, for or about any the matters, causes, affairs or businesses of the said trade, in any place or places, for the same convenient, during the said term of fifteen years, within our dominions or elsewhere, and there to hold court for the said Company, and the affairs thereof; and that also it shall and may be lawful, to and for them, or the more part of them, being so assembled, and that shall then and there be present, in any such place or places, whereof the Governor or his deputy for the time being, to be one, to make, ordain, and constitute such, and so many reasonable laws, constitutions, orders and ordinances, as to them, or the greater part of them, being then and there present, shall seem necessary and convenient, for the good government of the same Company, and of all factors, masters, mariners and other officers, employed or to be employed in any of their voyages, and for the better advancement and continuance of the said trade and traffick, and the same laws, constitutions, orders and ordinance, so made, to put in use and execute accordingly, ands at their pleasure to revoke or alter the same, or any of them as Octatian shall require ; and that the said Governor and Company, so often as they shall make, ordain or establish any such laws, constitutions, orders or ordinances, in form aforesaid, shall and may lawfully impose, ordain, limit and provide such pains, punishments and penalties, by imprisonment of Body, or by Fines and Amerciaments, or by all or any of them upon and against all Offenders, contrary to such laws, constitutions, orders and ordinances, or any of them as to the said Governor and Company for the time being, or the greater part of them, then and there being present, the said Governor, or his deputy, being always one, shall seem necessary, requisite and convenient, for the observation of the same laws, constitutions, orders and ordinances ; and the same fine and amerciaments shall and may levy, take and have, to the use of the said Governor and Company, and their successors, without the impediment of us, our heirs or successors, or of any the officers or ministers of us, our heirs or successors, and without any account thereof, to us, our heirs or successors, to be rendered or made ; all and singular which laws, constitutions, orders and ordinances, so as aforesaid to be made, we will to be duly observed and kept, under the pain and penalties therein to be contained ; so always as the said laws, orders, constitutions, ordinances, imprisonments, fines and amerciaments be reasonable, and not contrary or repugnant to the laws, statutes, or customs of this our realm. And for as much as the said Governor and Company of Merchants of London, trading into the East Indies, have not yet experienced of the kinds of commodities and merchandizes, which are or will be vendible, or to be uttered in the said parts of the East-Indies, and therefore shall be driven to carry to those parts, in their voyages outward, divers and sundry commodities, which are likely to be returned again to this our realm : we therefore of our especial grace, certain knowledge and mere motion, for the better encouraging of the said governor and Company of Merchants of London, trading into the said East Indies, and for the advancement of the said trade, do grant unto the said Governor and Company, and to their successors, that they and their successors, during the four first voyages, which they shall make, or set forth, for or towards the said East Indies, shall and may transport, and carry out of our realm of England, and the ports, creeks and havens thereof, all such and so much goods, and merchandizes, being goods and merchandizes lawfully passable and transportable out of this realm, and not prohibited to be transported by any law or statute of this realm, as shall be by them, their factors or assigns, shipped in any ship or ships, vessel or vessels, to be employed in any of the said four first voyages, free of custom, subsidy or poundage, or any other duties or payments, to us or our successors, due or belonging, for the shipping or transporting of the same, or any of them ; and yet nevertheless our will and pleasure is and we do, by these presents, straightly charge and command, that all and every such goods and merchandizes, so to be transported out of this realm, from time to time, during the said four first voyages, as is aforesaid, shall, from time to time, be duly entered by the customer, controller or other officer of such port, creek or place, where the same goods and merchandizes shall happen to be shipped and loaden, before such time as the same shall be shipped, or loaden, to be transported as is aforesaid : And also of our further especial grace, certain knowledge and mere motion, we do, for us, our heirs and successors, grant to and with the said Governor and Company of Merchants of London, trading into the East Indies, and their successors, that when and as often, at any time, during the said time and space of fifteen years, as any custom, poundage, subsidy, or other duties, shall be due and payable unto us, our heirs, or successors, for any goods, wares, or merchandizes whatsoever, to be returned out or from any the islands, ports, havens, cities, towns or places aforesaid, unto our port of London, or any of the havens, creeks, members or places to the same port belonging, that the customers and all other officers for the time being, of us, our heirs or successors, for or concerning receipts of customs, poundage, subsidies or other duties, unto whom it shall appertain, shall upon the request of the Governor and Company of the said Merchants of London, trading into the East Indies, or any their agents, factors or assigns give unto the said Governor and Company, their agents, factors or assigns, six months' time, for payment of the one half, and after those six months ended, other six months' time, for the payment of the other half, of their said customs, poundage, or other subsidy or duties, receiving good and sufficient bonds, with surety, to the use of us, our heirs and successors, for the true payment of the same accordingly; and upon receipt of the said Bonds, with surety, from time to time, to give unto the said Governor and Company of Merchants of London, trading into the East Indies, for the time being their agents, factors or assigns, their cocket or other warrant, to take out and receive on land the same goods, wares, or merchandizes, by virtue thereof, without any disturbance; and that also as often as at any time, during the said time of years, any goods, wares or merchandizes of the said Governor and Company, for the time being, laden from our port of London, or any the creeks, members or places to the same port belonging, to be transported to or towards any the islands, ports, havens, cities, towns or places aforesaid, shall happen to miscarry or be lost, before their safe arrival or discharge in the ports, for and to which the same shall be sent, that then and so often so much custom poundage, subsidies, or other duties, as they answered to us, for the same, before their going forth of our said ports, havens or creeks, shall, after due proof made, before the treasurer of England, for the time being, of the said loss, and the just quantity thereof, be, by virtue hereof, allowed to the said Governor and Company, their agents or factors, by warrant of thes aid treasurer, to the said customers or officers, in the next goods, wares or merchandizes, that the said Governor and Company, or their successors, shall or may ship, for or towards those parts, according to the true rates of the customs, poundage or subsidies, before paid for the goods, wares or merchandizes, so lost or miscarrying, or any part thereof. And for that, the said Governor and Company of merchants of London, trading into the East Indies, are like to bring to this our realm, a much greater quantity of foreign commodities, from the parts of the said East Indies, than can be spent for the necessary use of the same our realm, which of necessity must be transported into other countries, and there vended, we, for us, our heirs and successors, of our epecial grace, certain knowledge and mere motion, do grant to and with the said Governor and Company of Merchants of London, trading into the East Indies, and their successors, that at all times, from time to time, during the space of thirteen months, next after the discharge of any the same foreign commodities, so to be brought in, the subsidies, poundage, customs, and other duties for the same, being first paid or compounded for as aforesaid, it shall be lawful for the said Governor and Company, and their successors, or any other the natural subjects of this our realm, which may or shall buy the same of them, to transport the same in English bottoms, freely out of this realm as well ungarbled as garbled, without payment of any further custom, poundage, or any further subsidy, to us, our heirs or successors for the same; whereof the subsidy, poundage, customs or other duties, shall be so formerly paid or compounded for as aforesaid, and so proved; and the said customer or other officer or officers, to whom it shall in that behalf appertain, for the time being, by virtue hereof, shall, upon due and sufficient proof thereof, made in the custom-house of or belonging to the same port of London, give them sufficient cocket or certificate for the safe passing out thereof accordingly: And to the end no deceit be used herein, to us, our heirs or successors, certificate shall be brought from the collector of the customs, subsidy, poundage or other duties, inwards, of us, our heirs or successors, to the collector of the customs, subsidy, poundage or other duties, outward, of us, our heirs and successors, that the said goods, wares, and merchandizes, have, within the time limited, answered their due customs, subsidy, poundage or other duties, for the same inwards: And moreover, we of our further especial grace, certain knowledge and mere motion, have granted, and by these presents, for us, our heirs aud successors, do grant unto the said Governor and Company of Merchants of London, trading into the East Indies, that it shall and may be lawful for them, their factors or assigns, in their first voyage or fleet, which is now in preparing for their first adventure to the said East Indies, to transport out of this our ream of England, all such foreign coin of silver, either Spanish or other foreign silver, as they have procured, prepared and gotten, or shall procure, prepare or get, as likewise all such other coin of silver, as they have procured, or shall procure, to be coined in our mint, within our tower of London, out of such plate or bullion, as is or shall be provided, by the said Governor and Company of Merchants of London, trading into the East Indies, their factors or assigns before the going forth of the same fleet in this their first voyage, so as the whole quantity of coin, or monies to be transported, in this their said first voyage, do not exceed the value or sum of £30,000 sterling, and so as the sum of £6,000, at the least, parcel of the said sum of £30,000, be first coined in our mint, within our tower of London, before the same shall be transported as aforesaid, any law, statute, restraint or prohibition, in that behalf notwithstanding: And in like manner, of our like especial grace, certain knowledge and mere motion, we have granted, and by these presents, do for us, our heirs and successors, grant unto the said Governor and Company of Merchants of London, trading into the East Indies, and their successors, that it shall and may be lawful, to and for the said Governor and Company, and their successors, after the said first voyage, set forth yearly, for and during the residue of the said term of fifteen years, to ship and transport out of this our realm of England, or dominions of the same, in any their other voyages, to or towards any the parts, aforesaid, in form afore-mentioned, all such foreign coin of silver, Spanish or other foreign silver, or bullion of silver, as they shall, during the said term, bring or cause to be brought into this realm of England, from the parts beyond the seas, either in the same kind, sort, stamp or fashion, which it shall have when they bring it in, or any other form, stamp or fashion, to be coined within our mint, within our tower of London, at their pleasure ; so as the whole quantity of coin or monies, by them to be transported, in any their said voyages, during the residue of the said terms, do not exceed the value or sum of £30,000 in any one voyage ; and so as the sum of £6,000 at the least, parcel of the said sum or value of £30,000, so to be transported as aforesaid, be first coined, within our said tower of London, before the same shall be transported in any of the said voyages, any law, statute, restraint or prohibition, in that behalf, in anywise notwithstanding : And further we of our ample and abundant grace, mere motion and certain knowledge, have granted, and by these presents, for us, our heirs and successors, do grant unto the said Governor and Company of Merchants of London, trading into the East Indies, and their successors, that they and their successors, and their factors, servants and assigns, in the trade of merchandize, for them and on their behalf, and not otherwise, shall, for the said term of fifteen years, have, use, and enjoy, the whole entire and only trade and traffick, and the whole entire and only liberty, use and privilege of trading and trafficking, and using feat and trade of merchandize to and from the said East Indies, and to and from all the islands, ports, havens, cities, towns and places aforesaid, in such manner and form as is above mentioned ; and that they the said Governor and Company of Merchants of London, trading into the East Indies and every particular and several person, that now is or that hereafter shall be of that Company, or incorporation, shall have full and free authority, liberty, faculty, license and power, in form aforesaid, to trade and traffick to and from the said East Indies, and all and every the parts thereof, in form aforesaid, according to the orders, ordinances and agreements hereafter to be made and agreed upon, by the said Governor and Company of Merchants of London, trading into the East Indies, and their successors, or the more part of them, present at any court or publick assembly, of or for the said Company, the Governor of the said Company, or his deputy for the time being, being always present, at such court or assembly, and not otherwise : and for that the ships, sailing into the said East Indies, must take their due and proper times, to proceed in their voyages, which otherwise, as we well perceive, cannot be performed in the rest of the year following : Therefore we of our especial grace, certain knowledge and mere motion, for us, our heirs and successors, do grant, to and with the said Governor and Company of Merchants of London trading into the East Indies, and their successors, that, in any time of restraint, six good ships and six good pinnaces, well furnished with ordnance, and other munition for their defence, and five hundred mariners, Englishmen, to guide and sail in the same six ships and six pinnaces, at all times, during the said term of fifteen years, shall quietly be permitted and suffered to depart, and go in the said voyages, according to the purport of these presents, without any stay or contradiction, by us, our heirs or successors, or by the lord high admiral, or any other officer or subject of us, our heirs or successors, for the time being, in anywise, any restraint, law, statute, usage or matter whatsoever, to the contrary notwithstanding. Provided nevertheless, that if we shall, at any time within the said term of fifteen years, have just cause to arm our navy in warlike manner, in defence of our realm, or for offence of our enemies, or that it shall be found needful to join to the navy of us, our heirs or successors, the ships of our subjects, to be also armed for the wars, to such a number as cannot be supplied, if the said six ships and six pinnaces should be permitted to depart, as above is mentioned, then upon knowledge given, by us, our heirs or successors, or by our admiral to the said Governor and Company, about the 20th day of the month of July, or three months before the said Governor and Company shall begin to make ready the same six ships and six pinnaces, that we may not spare the said six ships and six pinnaces, and the mariners requisite for them, to be out of our realm during the time that our navy shall be upon the seas, that then the said Governor and Company shall forbear to send six such ships and six pinnaces, for their trade and merchandize, until that we shall revoke or withdraw our said navy from the said service : And we of our further royal favour, and of our especial grace, certain knowledge and mere motion, have granted, and by these presents, for us, our heirs and successors, do grant to the said Governor and Company of Merchants of London, trading into the East Indies, and to their successors that the said East Indies, nor the islands, havens, ports, cities, towns or places thereof nor any part thereof shall not be visited, frequented or haunted by any of the subjects of us, our heirs or successors, during the same term of fifteen years, contrary to the true meaning of these presents : And by virtue of our prerogative royal, which we will not in that behalf have argued, or brought in question we straightly charge, command and prohibit, for us, our heirs and successors, all the subjects of us, our heirs and successors, of what degree or quality soever they be, that none of them, directly or indirectly do visit, haunt, frequent or trade, traffick or adventure, by way of merchandize intoor from any of the said East Indies, or into or from any the islands, ports, havens, cities, towns or places aforesaid, other than the said Governor and Company of Merchants of London, trading into the East Indies, and such particular persons as now be, or hereafter shall be of that Company, their agents, factors and assigns during the said term of fifteen years, unless it be by and with such license and agreement of the said Governor and Company of Merchants of London, trading into the East Indies, in writing first had and obtained, under their common seal to be granted, upon pain that every such person or persons that shall trade or traffick into or from any of the said East Indies, other than the said Governor and Company of Merchants of London, trading into the East Indies, and their successors, shall incur our indignation, and the forfeiture and loss of the goods, merchandizes, and other things whatever, which so shall be brought into this realm of England, or any the dominions of the same, contrary to our said prohibition, or the purport or true meaning of these presents, as also the ship and ships with the furniture thereof, wherein such goods, merchandizes, or things shall be brought ; the one half of all the said forfeitures to be to us, our heirs and successors, and the other half of all and every the said forfeitures, we do, by these presents, of our especial grace, certain knowledge and mere motion, clearly and wholly for us, our heirs and successors, give, and grant unto the said Governor and Company of Merchants of London, trading into the East Indies: And further all and every the said offenders, for their said contempt, to suffer imprisonment during our pleasure, and such other punishment, as to us, our heirs or successors, for so high a contempt, shall seem meet and convenient, and not to be in anywise delivered, until they and every of them shall become bound unto the said Governor for the time being in the sum of £1,000 at the least, at no time then after, during this present grant, to sail or traffick, into any of the said East Indies, contrary to our express commandment in that behalf herein set down and published: And further, for the better encouragement of merchants, strangers or others, to bring in commodities into our realm, we for us, our heirs and successors, do grant unto the said Governor and Company of Merchants of London, trading into the East Indies, that they and their successors, may, from time to time, for any consideration or benefit, to be taken to their own use, grant or give license, to any the personor persons to sail, trade or traffick into or from any the said East Indies, so as such license be granted or given, before such goods, wares and merchandizes be laid on land, and so as such license be made by the said Governor and Company of Merchants of London, trading into the East Indies, for the time being, under their common seal: And further of our especial grace, certain knowledge and mere motion, we have condescended and granted, and by these presents, for us, our heirs and successors, we do condescend and grant unto the said Governor and Company of Merchants of London, trading into the East Indies, and their successors that we, our heirs and successors, during the said term of fifteen years, will not grant liberty, license or power to any person or persons whatsoever, contrary to the tenor of these our letters patents, to sail, pass, trade or traffick, to the said East Indies, or into or from the islands, ports, havens, cities, towns or places aforesaid, or any of them, contrary to the true meaning of these presents, without the consent of the said Governor and Company of Merchants of London, trading into the East Indies, or the most part of them: And our will and pleasure is, and hereby we do also ordain, that it shall and may be lawful, to and for the said Governor and Company of merchants of London, trading into the East Indies, or the more part of them, whereof the governor for the time being, or his deputy, to be one, to admit into and to be of the said Company, all such apprentices, to any of the said fellowship or Company, and all such servants and factors, of and for the said Company, and all such other, as to them, or the most part of them, present at any court, held for the said Company, the Governor, or his deputy, being one, shall be thought fit and agreeable, with the orders and ordinances to be made for the government of the said Company. Provided always, that if any of the persons, before named and appointed, by these presents, to be free of the said Company of Merchants of London, trading into the East Indies, shall not before the going forth of the fleet, appointed for this first voyage, from the port of London, bring in and deliver to the treasurer or treasurers appointed, or which, within the space of twenty days next after the date hereof, shall be appointed, by the said Governor and Company, or the more part of them, to receive the contributions and adventures, set down by the several adventurers, in this last and present voyage, now in hand, to be set forth, such sums of money as have been, by any of the said persons, by these presents, nominated to be of the said Company, expressed, set down and written in a book for that purpose, and left in the hands of the said Thomas Smith, Governor of the said Company, or of the said Paul Banning, Alderman of London, and subscribed with the names of the same adventurers, under their hands, and agreed upon to be adventured in the said first voyage, that then, it shall be lawful for the said Governor and Company, or the more part of them, whereof the said Governor or his deputy, to be one, at any their general court, or general assembly, to remove, disfranchise and displace him or them at their wills and pleasures. And the said Governor and Company, of Merchants of London, trading into the East Indies, for them and their successors, do, by these presents, covenant, promise and grant, to and with us, our heirs and successors, that they the said Governor and Company, and their successors, in all and every such voyage, as they at any time or times hereafter, during the said term, shall make out of this realm, by virtue of this our grant and letters patents, the first voyage only excepted, shall and will, upon every return which shall be made back again into this realm, or any of our dominions, or within six months next after every such return, bring into this our realm of England, from the said East Indies, or from some other parts, beyond the seas, out of our dominions as great or greater value in bullion of gold or silver, or other foreign coin of gold or silver, respectively, for every voyage, the first voyage only excepted, as shall be by force of these presents transported and carried out of this realm, by them or any of them, in any kind of silver abovesaid whatsoever, in any of the said voyages ; and that all such silver, as by virtue of this our grant and letters patents, shall be shipped or laden by the said Governor and Company or their successors, to be transported out of this realm, in any of the said voyages, shall from time to time, at the setting forth of every such particular voyage, be shipped and laden at the ports or havens of London, Dartmouth, or Plymouth, or at some of the same ports or havens, and at no other port or haven whatsoever, within this our realm, or the dominions thereof ; and that all and every such silver, as from time to time shall be shipped and loaden in the said ports of London, Dartmouth, or Plymouth, or any of them, to be by force of these presents transported out of this realm, as is aforesaid shall, from time to time, be duly entered by the customer, controller, collector or other officer to whom it shall appertain, of every such port or haven, where the same shall happen to be shipped or laden, in the Custom-Book belonging to the said port or haven, before such time as the same shall be shipped or laden, to be transported as is aforesaid, without any custom or subsidy, to be paid for the same ; and that in like manner, all and all manner of gold and silver whatsoever, which shall be brought into this realm, or any of our dominions, by the said Governor and Company, or any of them, according to the true meaning of these presents, shall likewise be, from time to time, duly entered by the customer, controller, or other officer of every such port, creek or place, where the same gold or silver shall happen to be unshipped, or brought to land, before such time as the same gold or silver or any part thereof, shall be unshipped or brought to land, as is aforesaid. Provided always, nevertheless, and our will and pleasure is, that these our letters patents, or any thing therein contained, shall not in any sort extend to give or grant any license, power or authority unto the said Governor and Company of Merchants of London, trading into the East Indies, or to any of them to undertake or address any trade unto any country, port, island, haven, city, creek, town, or place, being already in the lawful and actual possession of any such christian prince or state, as at this present is, or at any time hereafter shall be in league or amity, with us, our heirs or successors, and which doth not, or will not accept of such trade, but doth overtly declare and publish the same, to be utterly against his or their good-will and liking, any thing before in these presents contained, to the contrary thereof notwithstanding. Provided also, that if it shall, hereafter appear to us, our heirs or successors, that this grant or the continuance thereof, in the whole or in any part thereof, shall not be profitable to us, our heirs and successors, or to this our realm, that then, and from thenceforth, upon and after two years' warning, to be given to the said Company, by us, our heirs or successors, under our or their privy seal, or sign manual, this present grant shall cease, be void and determined, to all intents, constructions and purposes: And further of our especial grace, certain knowledge and mere motion we have condescended and granted, and by these presents for us, our heirs and successors, do condescend and grant to the said Governor and Company of Merchants of London, trading into the East Indies, and their successors that if at the end of the said term of fifteen years, it shall seem meet and convenient unto the said Governor and Company, or any the parties aforesaid, that this present grant shall be continued, and if that also it shall appear unto us, our heirs and successors, that the continuance thereof shall not be prejudicial or hurtful to thisour realm, but that we shall find the further continuance thereof profitable for us, our heirs and successors, and for our realm, with such conditions as are herein mentioned, or with some alteration or qualification thereof, that then we, our heirs or successors, at the instance and humble petition of the said Governor and Company, or any of them, to be made unto us, our heir and successors, will grant and make unto the said Governor and Company, or any of them, so suing for the same; and such other person and persons, our subjects, as they shall nominate and appoint, or shall be by us, our heirs or successors, newly nominated, not exceeding in number twenty-four, new letters patents, under the great seal of England, in due form of law, with the like covenants, grants, clauses and articles, as in these presents are contained, or with addition of other necessary articles, or changing of these into some other parts, for and during the full term of fifteen years, the next following; willing hereby and straightly charging and commanding all and singular our admirals, vice-admirals, justices, mayors, sheriffs, escheators, constables, bailiffs, and all and singular other our officers, ministers, liege men and subjects whatsoever, to be aiding, favouring, helping and assisting unto the said Governor and Company, and to their successors, and to their deputies, officers, factors, servants, assigns and ministers and every of them, in executing and enjoying the premises, as well on land as on sea, from time to time, when you or any of you shall thereunto be required, any statute, act, ordinance, proviso, proclamation or restraint, heretofore had, made, set forth, ordained, or provided, or any other matter, cause or thing whatsoever, to the contrary in any way notwithstanding ; although express mention of the true yearly value or certainty of the premises, or of any of them, or of any other gifts or grants, by us, or any of our progenitors, to the said Governor and Company of Merchants of London, trading into the East Indies, or to any of them, before this time made, in these presents is not made, or any statute, act, ordinance, provision, proclamation or restraint, to the contrary heretofore had made, ordained or provided, or any other thing, cause or matter whatsoever, in anywise notwithstanding. In witness whereof, we have caused these our letters to be made patents : Witness ourself, at Westminster, the thirty-first day of December, in three and fortieth year of our reign.

II. THE EAST INDIA COMPANY ACT, 1773.*

(13, Geo. 3, C. 63).

AN ACT FOR ESTABLISHING CERTAIN REGULATIONS FOR THE BETTER MANAGEMENT OF THE AFFAIRS OF THE EAST INDIA COMPANY, AS WELL IN INDIA AS IN EUROPE.

Preamble.

"Whereas the several Powers and Authorities granted by charters to the United Company of Merchants of England trading to the East Indies have been found, by experience, not to have sufficient Force and Efficacy to prevent various Abuses which have prevailed in the Government and Administration of the Affairs of the said United Company, as well at Home as in India, to the manifest Injury of the Publick Credit, and of the commercial interests of the said Company ; and it is therefore become highly expedient that certain further Regulations, better

* This Act is commonly known as "The Regulating Act."

2

IMPERIAL PROSPECTING

Robert Boyle had published 'General Heads for a Natural History of a Countrey, Great or Small' in the *Philosophical Transactions of the Royal Society* (1.11 [1665–1666], 186–89). The 'heads' included 'superterraneous', 'terrestrial' and 'subterraneous'. It called for attention to not only minerals and natural 'productions' of a region but also to the 'Stature, Shape, Colour, Features, Strength, Agility, Beauty (or the want of it) Complexions, Hair, Diet, inclinations, and Customs that seem not due to Education of the inhabitants and [the] Fruitfulnefs or Barrenness; their, hard or easy Labour [of women]'. Boyle also wished for information on the mineral wealth of the country:

> Among these *Subterraneal* observations may be taken notice of, what forts of Minerals of any kind they want, as well as what they have. *Then*, what Quarries the Country affords, and the particular conditions both of the Quarries and the Stones: As also, how the Beds of Stone lye, in reference to North and. South, *&c.*- What Clays and Earths it affords, as Tobacco-pipe clay, Marles [marl], Fullers-earths, Earths for Potters wares, Bolus's and other medicated Earths: What other Minerals it yields, as Coals, Salt-Mines, or Salt-springs, Allom, Vitrial, Sulphur, *&c.* What Metals the Country yields, and a description of the Mines, their number, situation, depth, signs, waters, damps, quantities of ore, goodness of ore, extraneous things and ways of reducing their ores into Metals. (189)

Aware of the fact that not every traveller could be knowledgeable enough to observe all of these, Boyle concluded with

> *Inquiries* about *Traditions* concerning all particular things, relating to that Country, as either peculiar to it, or at least, uncommon elsewhere. *Inquiries,* that require *Learning* or *Skill* in the Answerer: to which should be subjoined *Proposals* of ways, to enable men to give Answers to these more difficult inquiries. (189)

Boyle was implying that training may be required for those who were expected to answer the questions.

A year later, on more or less similar lines, Boyle published his 'Inquiries for Suratte' for other nations.

The 'Inquiries' are cast in a tradition of similar travel instructions. Albertus Meierius' *Certain Briefe and Speciall Instructions for Gentlemen, Merchants, Students, Souldiers, Marriners* appeared in 1589. Francis Bacon's

'Of Travel' appeared in 1625, and listed the things a traveller must note when in new and strange lands:

> The things to be seen and observed are, the courts of princes, especially when they give audience to ambassadors, the courts of justice … the churches and monasteries … the walls and fortifications of cities and towns … antiquities and ruins; libraries, colleges, disputations, and lectures … shipping and navies; houses and gardens of state and pleasure, near great cities; armouries; arsenals, magazine; exchanges; burses; warehouses; exercises of horsemanship, fencing, training of soldiers, and the like; comedies … treasuries of jewels and robes, cabinets and rarities; and, to conclude, whatsoever is memorable in the places where they go. (Bacon 1860 [1625], 12: 138)

Robert, Earl of Essex, Philip Sidney and William Davison published *Profitable Instructions* in 1633 in which they wrote:

> For your better information in the state of any Prince, or Country, it shall be necessary for you to observe,
>
> The Country.
>
> The People.
>
> The policy and government. (1633, unpaginated)

As for the country, the traveller was to record

> The situation & nature thereof; As whether it be
> Island, or continent; near, or far from the sea.
> Plaine, or hilly; full or scarce of Rivers. (Unpaginated)

Besides these, they were to also observe, the country's relations and location vis-à-vis its neighbours

> How it confineth with other Countries; and
> What these Countries are,
> What their strength and riches are.
> Wherein they consist.
> Whether friends or enemies. (Unpaginated)

The 'Inquiries', like his 'General Heads for a Natural History', lists the set of domains a traveller to the East Indies needs to conduct observations in, which include geographical and topographical features, cultural practices, fauna and flora, and the behaviour of the inhabitants.

Boyle notes that these 'Inquiries' have been sent with the travellers who had left for the East Indies, and some answers had already been received by him. But what he is looking for, he says in the headnote to the 'Inquiries', is 'confirmations of the truth of these things from several hands before they be relied on'. Boyle is clearly indicating the need for multiple authentications of the information received, as a way of establishing what counts as 'truth'. This itself has institutional and political contexts, as we shall see.

Structure and Content

The 'Inquiries' are in the form of 38 questions and focuses on the Indian subcontinent and what is now East Asia (Burma, Japan, Java-Sumatra, Philippines, Maluka). Several questions are to do not just with precious stones and the mineral wealth of these regions, but also ores like iron and geological formations (rocks and stones). There are questions about seasons. There are strange questions, perhaps derived from myths or exaggerated travellers' tales, about 'ignivomous' (literally fire-spitting) mountains that produce certain kinds of stones. There are questions about tides, wood, vegetables, snakes and other animals.

There are many questions about vegetables, plants and fruits (papayas, camphor, betel nuts, cinnamon), as well as products like musk. Questions about poisonous plants and animals abound, as well as queries about antidotes. There is a question about animal ethnology: whether the rhinoceros is antagonistic towards the elephant.

Some questions are to do with human productions, such as cloth dyes, varnishes and poisons.

Institutions and Processes

In 1661, the Royal Society, notes Rita Banerjee in her recent study, *India in Early Modern English Travel Writings,* 'constituted a committee composed of notable individuals like Viscount Brouncker, Sir Robert Murray, [Robert] Boyle, John Wilkins, John Evelyn, and Henry Oldenburg to frame suitable questions which would contribute to generating knowledge' (2021, 19). Banerjee adds:

> travel narratives collected information to answer these questions. The travel narrative had evolved from pilgrims' tales and semi-fictional stories of marvels into a genre which aided scientific knowledge-building by providing directed sample collection wherever possible, systematic classification of data, arrangement and ordering of specimens, and above all by emphasizing the importance of empiricism. And knowledge-building was not limited to the sphere of science and natural philosophy but extended to ethnography. (20)

The 'Inquiries' are a consequence of this decision and policy of the Royal Society.

By 1682, members of the Royal Society were also stockholders of the English East India Company (EIC), and India travellers like John Fryer were elected to the society as well. Boyle himself owned stocks in the EIC, and many aspiring natural philosophers setting out for the East corresponded with him and reported to him their findings about the weather, plants and animals, minerals, etc. (Ogborn 2007, xvii–xviii). These were, on occasion, discussed at the Royal Society:

> Their reports arrived in London with the valuable cargoes of cloth and spices, and with the Company's own letters and the accounts cast up for each of the factories. They were sometimes read at Royal Society meetings, and evaluated in ways that weighed the Company's own reputation in the scales of credit and credibility alongside questions of gentlemanly civility. (xviii)

Miles Ogborn offers an interpretation of this print culture that linked the Royal Society, the EIC and the factors in the East Indies. He argues that 'the history of Empire and the history of the book' are interlinked (2). It also means that documents like the 'Inquiries' played a major role in the shaping of the early Empire, even as a collaboration and co-production (between the Englishmen and the 'natives') produced these documents and information sources. That said, it would be another hundred years before the residents of the colonial territories became eligible for the Fellowship of the society, thereby directly linking imperial power with formal structures of knowledge (see Home 2002).

In Anna Winterbottom's study of the knowledge practices of the Royal Society, she argues that the 'early experiments' demonstrate 'the deep connection of the Royal Society's understanding of what constituted useful knowledge to the projects of colonisation and international trade—including the slave trade' (2016: 17–18). Winterbottom writes:

> Numerous examples, including that of the *bezoar* stone mentioned above, are concerned with testing the value of products from the Indies—camphor, cinnamon and nutmeg to name just a few others—or understanding Indian Ocean technologies, from writing to dyes to weights. (18)

The *bezoar* stone figures in the 'Inquiries' in question number 35. Then there is the question (number 10) of updated maps of the worlds beyond Japan.

The Society and the EIC, linked through this systematic organisation of knowledge, together create London as a Latourian 'centre of calculation' (1987). London, where both the EIC and the Society were located, becomes the place where knowledge in the form of responses to the 'Inquiries', accumulates and is interpreted by 'experts'. In other words, London becomes a capital for knowledge about the other countries and regions because of the work of organisations such as the Royal Society. The 'centre for calculation' also, over time, becomes the capital of the Empire. That is, the centring of knowledge production enables the city of London to become an imperial city, demonstrating the link between knowledge and power.

'Inquiries' and the English 'Observer'

Boyle begins by stating that the 'relations published in Samuel Purchas, Jan Huygen van Linschoten, and others, concerning those parts, have given occasion' to propose these questions. There are several points of interest in this statement, especially if read alongside the headnote where he says he seeks confirmation of information already received. In fact, such confirmation, he says, is 'altogether necessary'.

First, Boyle is establishing a lineage of enquiries, accounts and exploratory documentation of the East Indies. Samuel Purchas, famous for *Hakluytus Posthumus, or, Purchas His Pilgrims* (1625), was not a traveller but a compiler of travel accounts. (For students of English literature, the volume is famous for providing the source tale of 'Kubla Khan', Samuel Taylor Coleridge's famous poem.) This suggests not only a long history of travel but also travel reporting. The reference to Linschoten, the Dutch merchant-traveller and the author of *Itinerario* (1596)—which showcased maps of voyages into the East Indies—suggests a European lineage to travel and travel writing, too.

Second, the reference to 'truth' and 'confirmation' may well be a veiled reference to John Mandeville's collection of lies in his travelogue (1375, in the English version)—which was, as commentators note, a popular text through the Early Modern period (Moseley 2011). The problem of authenticity haunted the travel report, and Boyle, like others, was concerned about the reliability of the information being delivered in the narratives of distant places. The first question itself indicates this concern:

> Whether it be *true*, that diamonds and other precious stones, do grow again after three or four years, in the same places where they have been digged out? (15, emphasis added)

Third, the questions are about the 'observable' events and objects. This emphasis on the observable object stems from the Early Modern valorisation of the centrality of *experience*. In his account of the Royal Society, Peter Dear writes:

> When a Fellow of the Royal Society made a contribution to knowledge, he did so by reporting an experience ... the veracity of the report clearly depended on the original experience of a specified person on a particular occasion ... No hearsay evidence could be admissible.... An experience was linked to a particular time and place. Knowledge about the world was to be provided by a definite occurrence happening to a particular person. The resulting style of presentation allowed no clear

> distinction to be made between a 'natural historical' (in the modern sense) and an 'experimental' report; each was, in the same way, given as an experience defined in space and time by an actor, the observer. The credentials that established the actuality of the event were provided by surrounding the description by a wealth of circumstantial detail. All of this constituted the report of an experience, and the literary form itself represented a credential formerly supplied by references to an appropriate ancient, or by a different literary form—the commentary. (2015, 63–66)

Dear notes how the Royal Society marks in its approaches to knowledge production and dissemination a major shift from the weight of authority to the weight of experimentation, observation and experience (58). I suggest that when Boyle sends out the 'Inquiries' with the insistence on multiple sources of information, he is, in fact, implying that the weight of Purchas, Linschoten and other travellers and their reports, must be checked against the weight of later-day travellers and their observations. That is, without empirical confirmation through observation, the handed-down knowledge of the East Indies was not adequate. 'Authority', in this case, of older/predecessor texts and travellers, was diminished in favour of on-the-spot observations and documentation of experience.

Fourth, the significance of the traveller as eyewitness is underscored in the very texture of the 'Inquiries' and is in the tradition of the Royal Society, as Dear notes. Indeed, Dear's reading of the Royal Society's insistence on observation and experience—eyewitnessing—is a feature of almost every single East Indies travelogue of the 17th century.

Author Edward Terry states in his dedicatory note to *A Voyage to East-India*:

> For *my self I* was an *eye-witness* of much here related, living more than two years at the court of that mighty monarch the great Mughal. (1655: unpaginated Preface, emphasis added)

Thomas Herbert writes in his dedicatory note to the Earl of Pembroke:

> *My* desire to *see*, took away my sight, as it fares with those who are suddenly taken with a killing beauty, or gaze upon the sun. Yet some glimmerings *I* have *observed*, like an ill-sighted man, who sees with spectacles or perspectives. (1634, unpaginated Preface, emphasis added)

Ecclesiastical writer and traveller John Ovington defends the publication of his travelogue by declaring that he has described things that have 'escaped the observation of other travellers' (1696: unpaginated Preface). As argued elsewhere, 'each of the above images lays emphasis on personal experience' (Nayar 2008, 20).

The visualism in all the above implies intensive study rather than imagination, to adapt Stephen Bann's argument (1999, 9–17, 103). The word 'observe' flourishes in both its senses of 'seeing' and 'following an established programme' (Nayar, 20–21). The English observer who responds to these 'Inquiries' was the eyewitness, the seeing eye through which the region (East Indies) was not only perceived but also translated into 'evidence' (via the experience of *being there*) for the English back home. This seeing eye is not innocent, as Peter Burke warns us in his study of images as historical evidence, because it is already 'instructed' through the cultural training to look for certain objects and in certain ways (2001, 19). Most importantly, the 'Inquiries' position the traveller-observer in ways so as to privilege his—in this era, the traveller-explorer was male—vision and view(point). This 'ocularcentrism' (Jay 1998) was in many ways predetermined, as Joan-Pau Rubiés argues:

> After the fifteenth century, the pilgrim lost ground steadily to more secularized travellers—to the practical reporter with specific aims, and eventually to a first-person curious observer free from any obvious external sources of authority. (85)

The traveller, write Rubiés and Ollé, had to be 'a reliable witness' or 'an insightful interpreter of an exotic reality' (2016, 276).[1]

The 'Inquiries' imply that the observer may not be an expert to report unbiasedly on all these subjects. That is, these are *protocols of seeing and reportage* that make up for the lack of expertise. Barbara Shapiro writes about early travel reporting:

> Chorographic and travel literature assumed that under favorable conditions ordinary persons were capable of reporting the facts accurately and ordinary readers could understand and evaluate their reports. In most instances it was not necessary to be learned or expert to state what one had observed or witnessed. (1983, 64)

However, it was not deemed safe to leave it to the uninformed observer to provide reliable knowledge. Thus the 'Inquiries', were constructed as a frame of observation that enabled the traveller-observer to merely record what he had been asked, by the 'Inquiries', to record.

The 'Inquiries' call for the English observer to be a reliable witness who pays attention to specific objects and conditions in the places he visits. It provides a framework for observation, perhaps a means to avert the risk of a highly subjective observation and documentation of the East Indies. Admittedly, this is not the 'colonial' era yet. But, as Helga Quadflieg puts it:

> The writings of these Tudor and early Stuart travellers, therefore, can be analysed not only as examples of a particular kind of colonial discourse, but also as texts that are symptomatic of the changes in

> the perception of the world which took place in the sixteenth and seventeenth centuries and which constitute the 'modernity' of the early modern period. One aspect of this modernization is the increased differentiation between a public and a private sphere, and the necessity of establishing and defining one's individual place, function and identity in both sphere. (2016, 28)

Quadflieg flags the construction of the English observer and the 'native' observed here. In the case of the 'Inquiries', an imperious, empiricist and reliable observing English self is being constructed, and simultaneously, a study object (the East Indies) is placed before this self.

Objects of Study

As the list of questions in the 'Inquiries' indicates, the traveller was supposed to observe natural phenomena—from the quality of soil to topography to fauna and flora—as well as the cultural practices and behaviour of the inhabitants. For instance, one question addressed the properties of the datura herb:

> Whether the Indians can so stupefying herb, called *dutroa* or *datura*, that they make it lie for several days, months, and years, according as they design it, in a man's body, without doing him any hurt, and at the end they kill him, without missing an hours time? (418)

Or:

> Whether it be true, that upon the Coast of Coromandel, 16 deg. Northern Latitude, between Paleacote [Pallayakotai] and Masulipatan [Masulipatnam], 50 leagues in length (the hot winds blowing from the Land-ward from 8 in the Morning, till 4 in the Afternoon, with such a suffocating heat, that the Inhabitants are not able to endure it, without extraordinary helps and refreshments) every one daily for his provision of drink, hangs his Bottle, made of common pot-earth; and filled with Well-water, or other potable Liquor, upon some post, tree, or wall, in places, where the Sun and Wind are most piercing and leaving it there all the day long in the scorching heat and then taking it up about Evening at 4. of the Clock, the drink is more cool, than any depth of cellarage with us can make it? And whether, on the contrary, the bottles being suffered to continue in the air, as before, during the cool sea-gales, which in after the said hour, and continue all night, till 8 in the morning, to the refreshment of all creatures, the Liquors grow hot and unfit for drink? (416)

Such questions cover a wide variety of subjects, such as the climate, the seasons, local habits and products—especially of the medicinal/soporific kinds, among others. These questions are essentially chorographic in nature. Chorography and political reporting, notes Barbara Shapiro, were the key topics in early travel reportage (1983, 63–85). Chorography, writes Shapiro,

> was a rather peculiar early modern genre that combined history, geography, topography, natural history, antiquities, and genealogy with socioeconomic, political, and cultural description of a particular region. Typically, it followed a preexisting pattern of topics that included soil, climate, agricultural products, manufactures, rarities, monuments, architecture, and remains of antiquity and thus tended to focus on the description of 'things' available to the eye both of human and natural origin. (65)

The 'Inquiries' have questions that encompass much of the above inventory. It delineated the objects as well as the modes of study. Travel writing in the Early Modern period merged eyewitness and experiential reportage with chorographic description, writes Shapiro (70).

The 'Inquiries', we have noted, carried several questions on the natural wealth of the East Indies. The very first question was about diamonds (already cited). The next three are:

> Whether the Quarries of Stone near Fettipore [Fatehpore], not far from *Agra,* in the Mogol's dominions, may be cleft like Logs, and fawnlike Planks, to ceel [seal] Chambers and cover Houses therewith? Likewise, whether about *Jafanapatan,* on the Coast of Coromandel, there be a stone of the like nature, so as, setting a wedge upon it, one may cleave it with a Mallet as thick and as thin, as one pleaseth?
>
> Whether upon the same Coast of about Tuticorin and upon that of *Ceylon, at Manar,* and *at,* they fish pearls, as good as those about *Ormus*? Whether those Pearls are the better, the deeper they lie? What is the greatest depth, they are known to have been taken at? And whether it be true, that some of the Natives there, can stay under water half an hour, without any art?
>
> Whether the Iron in *Pegu* and *Japan,* be far better than ours—and if so, what is to be observed in the melting, forging, and tempering of it? (Boyle 415)

The emphasis on mineralogical and natural wealth, rather than the anthropological, was a typical feature of the era (Campbell 1988, 69–71). The mercantile and corporate interests triumph in the 'Inquiries', but these kinds of questions also indicate a nascent fantasy of acquiring, at some point, the Other's wealth—the query about the 'native divers' procuring the buried pearls gestures at something like this, to hazard a guess.

The climatological and mineralogical differences, where the East Indies' variety, quantity and quality are set distinctively from England's, was a form of chorographic Othering.[2] While not quite presented as a wilderness (where the wilderness was treated as the truly 'Other': Murdoch 1990; Helsinger 1997), the distinctive nature of minerals and precious (natural) products that were to be documented as objects of study, as the 'Inquiries' willed it, did set up the England/Other binary in the proto-colonial imagination.

In the process of developing the objects and modes of study for the subcontinent, the 'Inquiries' merges both, natural events/phenomena like climate and human events/actions. Thus, in the above questions, we see the emphasis on weather conditions *and* human responses to the conditions. In short, the subcontinent was subject to a well-organised examination, whose modalities were laid out in the form of the 'Inquiries'.

This attempt to organise knowledge and information from the East Indies into a systematic form assumed a scientific rather than a simple humanistic enquiry:

> The [Royal] Society created and disseminated 'articles of inquiry' that provided grounds on which travelers might organize their observations. Although these categories stemmed from and overlapped with those of Renaissance chorographers, which in turn were descended from Strabo and the ancients, the Society's efforts are often viewed as having a 'scientific' rather than a 'humanistic' flavor. (Shapiro, 73)

The purported scientism of the 'Inquiries', if we go with Shapiro's persuasive argument, looks forward to the forms of knowledge-making that would come to characterise British imperial discourses on India. The myth of unprejudiced and objective reporting and study would be perpetuated in later centuries, whether this is the Great Trigonometrical Survey of India or the ethnographic works of Herbert Risley and others.

The responses that the 'Inquiries' sought and received would acquire the status of 'facts', since they had been ostensibly empirically acquired and documented—through the protocols of information gathering and codification—for the learned society. In her study of the rise of the 'modern fact', Mary Poovey writes:

> The singular experiences or observed particulars that natural philosophers began to value in the seventeenth century were not evident, because they were neither signifiers or anything nor self-evidently valuable; only when such particulars were interpreted as evidence did they seem valuable enough to collect, because only then did they acquire meaning or even, I contend, identity as facts. (1998, 9)

The 'fact' is 'an epistemological unit of particular interest' (9–10). More importantly, Poovey argues that '"fact" moved from whatever is observed to being what is observed as evidence for some theory' (9).

There is no tangible or discernible 'theory' about the East Indies in the set of 38 questions that make up the 'Inquiries'. At this point—the mid-17th century—the East India Company has been in operation in the subcontinent for just over 50 years. However, a proto-colonial imaginary is at work and this is the 'theory' for which the observations and responses serve as evidence.

The proto-colonial imaginary moved, as I have argued elsewhere (2008), from the exploration of marvellous difficulty, variety and wonder to the *causes* of the variety, the marvellous and the strange. The 'Inquiries' represent an attempt to find causes and map cultural behaviour—whether of natural phenomena or human responses to storms and climate. That is, the proto-colonials did continue to see the subcontinent as a place of bewildering and exotic variety, but the 'Inquiries' represent, I suggest, an attempt to organise the variety and convert it into a manageable object of study. In the 'Inquiries', we see the beginnings of a categorical imperative, a classificatory paradigm, that would eventually organise the subcontinent into a governable variety, a managed/manageable marvellous.

The information so gathered could be thought of, based on what we now know as the history of the use of the term, as 'data'. In her painstaking examination of the first two centuries of the *Philosophical Transactions* (1665–1886), Chris Meyns writes:

> data retains an epistemic structure. It picks out that which is held fixed (the datum), while something else is being sought (the quaesitum). In the early decades of the Society's publication, when talk of data enters through the field of mathematics, both the nature of whatever can occupy the places of what was given or sought, as well as the relation between those two elements, were highly restricted. Both the sought and found were quantities, and the relation of the one to the other was one of determination (calculation). (2020, 525)

More importantly, Meyns notes: 'from a relation initially between things of the same kind (say, quantities), it [data] now may also relate two things of completely different kinds (say, observations and doctrines)' (525). Data such as that produced by the responses to the 'Inquiries' shaped imperial doctrines and were shaped by them.

***

The 'Inquiries for Suratte and other Parts of the East-Indies' constitute an epistemic structure that enabled and was enabled by the EIC, and form the first moments of the process that would eventually produce a vast imperial archive about India/the subcontinent. Formally instituted as a practice and a set of protocols for the English setting out to the East, the 'Inquiries' are a key document in an emerging attitude towards the future colony, a region in which some trading rights had been obtained.

What the 'Inquiries' initiated would culminate in massive works such as the series of reports from the Great Trigonometrical Survey of India, the Archaeological Survey of India and, of course, the Census of India. It is a slim document and, as seen in the preceding paragraphs, is best read alongside other such documents but also within a specific proto-colonial context in which knowledge-gathering about England's travels was still nascent.

Inquiries for Suratte,

and other parts of the East-Indies,

Though these Quæries have been already dispatcht for India, *and some of them even received an Answer, yet, because 'tis altogether necessary, to have confirmations of the truth of these things from several hands, before they be relyed on, it was thought fit, rather to publish the* Inquiries *alone, for a more certain and full Information, than now to joyn* such Answers *thereunto.*

The *Inquiries* are these; as the Relations publisht by *Purchas*, *Linschoten*, and others, concerning those parts, have given occasion to propose them.

1. Whether it be true, that Diamonds and other Pretious Stones, do grow again after three or four years, in the same places where they have been digg'd out?

2. Whether the Quarries of Stone near *Fettipore*, not far from *Agra*, in the *Mogol*'s Dominions, may be cleft like Loggs, and sawn like Planks, to ceel Chambers and cover Houses therewith? Likewise, Whether about *Sadrapatan*, on the Coast of *Coromandel*, there be a Stone of the like nature, so as, setting a Wedge upon it, one may cleave it with a Mallet as thick and as thin, as one pleaseth?

3. Whether upon the same Coast of *Coromandel*, about *Tutucorin*; and upon that of *Ceylon*, at *Manar*, and *Jafanapatan*, they fish *Pearls*, as good as those about *Ormus*? Whether those Pearls are the better, the deeper they lie? What is the greatest depth, they are known to have been taken at? And whether it be true, that some of the Natives there, can stay under Water half an hour, without any Art?

4. Whether the Iron in *Pegu* and *Japan*, be far better than ours; and if so, what is to be observed in the melting, forging, and tempering of it?

5. Whether in *Sumatra* there be a fountain, running a very Sanative Oyl? And whether the ignivomous Mountain in the same Island, do burn continually, and cast out stones so eaten out by the fire, that they swim?

6. What is the Opinion of the more Inquisitive Men in those parts, of *Amber-gris*? And whether the greatest quantities and masses of it are found about the Isle *Mauritius*?

7. Whether it be Winter on the East-side of the Mountain *Gates*, which comes from the North to Cape *Comorin*, whil'st it is Summer on the West-side, and so, *vice versa*?

8. Whether it be true, that upon the Coast of *Coromandel*, 16 deg. Northern Latitude, between *Paleacote* and *Maselupatan*, 50. Leagues in length (the hot winds blowing from the Land-ward from 8. in the Morning, till 4. in the Afternoon, with such a suffocating heat, that the Inhabitants are not able to endure it, without extraordinary helps and refreshments;) every one daily for his provision of drink, hangs his Bottle, made of common pot-earth, and filled with Well-water, or other potable Liquor, upon some Post, Tree, or Wall, in places, where the Sun and Wind are most piercing; leaving it there all the day long in the scorching heat; and then taking it up about Evening at 4. of the Clock, the Drink is more cool, than any depth of Cellerage with us can make it? And whether, on the contrary, the Bottles being suffered to continue in the Air, as before, during the cool Sea-gales, which come in after the said hour, and continue all Night, till 8. in the Morning, to the refreshment of all Creatures, the Liquors grow hot and unfit for drink?

9. Whether the *Tyde* near *Mindanao*, going from the *Molucca's* to the *Philippina's*, are so swift, that neither contrary Winds nor Anchors, can save a Ship from being carried away by it; and that it rises but about 3. or 4. feet? And whether the like be observed in the Bay of *Cambaja*, and in that between *Martaban* and *Pegu*? And particularly, Whether in the said *Bayes*, the Tides come in with that impetuosity and swiftness about the *Quarters* of the *Moon*, that the Watch-men from high Towers must with their Trumpets give warning to the people to retire; and that a Horse in his swiftest course, when such a Tide comes upon him, cannot out-run it: as *Isaac Vossius* observes, Lib. *De Motu*

Marium & Ventorum. c. 15. And what other particulars are obſervable upon all thoſe Coaſts, concerning the Tydes?

10. Whether there be any Diſcoveries newer, than the neweſt printed Maps, of the parts of the World *North-eaſt* of *Japan*? And whether *Japan* be truly an Iſland, or no?

11. What is the true way of making and colouring *China-Diſhes*; and how in *China* and *Japan*, they make the *Black-verniſh*?

12. With what Materials, and how they paint both upon Cloths, commonly call'd *Pintado's*, and likewiſe upon Canvas, *&c*?

13. Whether the *Lignum Aloes* be the Wood, or Root of a Tree? In what Countrey it is found? And how to know the beſt of the kind?

14. Whether the beſt *Tea* be that, which comes forth at the firſt of the Spring, and are the Top-leaves? In what manner 'tis dried; and whether the too haſty drying thereof hurts it?

15. Whether there grows a Wood in *Java*, that naturally ſmells like humane Excrement? And if ſo, what kind of ground it grows in?

16. Whether in the *Moluccque* Iſlands there be a *Red Wood*, which burns, ſparkles, and flames, without being conſumed; yet may be reduced to powder, by rubbing between ones fingers?

17. Whether near the Fort of *Ternate* there be a Plant, call'd by the Inhabitants *Catopa*, whence fall little Leaves, which are turned into Butter-flies?

18. Whether in *Pegu*, and other places of the *Eaſt-Indies*, they uſe a poyſon, that kills by ſmelling, and yet the poiſonous ſmell is hardly perceived?

19. Whether it be true, that the onely Antidote hitherto known, againſt the famous and fatal *Macaſſar*-poyſon, is *humane Ordure*, taken inwardly? And what ſubſtance that poyſon is made of?

20. Whether there be ſuch a Vegetable in *Java*, call'd *Mangas bravas*, that is ſo poiſonous, that it kills preſently, and for which no remedy hath been yet found?

21. Where the beſt *Calamba-wood*, or *Palo d' Aquila*, grows? Whether the *Palo d' Aquila* be much inferiour to *Calamba*; and

how they are distinguisht? Whether the later be the *Pith* of the former? Whence the best sort comes? Whether it be stored with a rich and cordial Balme, and that be the cause of its great rate, being much used in cases of decay of Spirits, and the lameness and impotency of Nerves?

22. Whether they draw an *Oyl*, resembling Oyl of *Camphire*, from the Roots of *Cinamon*-trees; and if so, how they draw it?.

23. Whether the Camphire of *Borneo* be not the Exsudation or Gum of a Tree?

24. Whether the *Indians* can so prepare that stupifying Herb, call'd *Dutroa* or *Datura*, that they make it lie several Dayes, Moneths, and Years, according as they design it, in a Mans Body, without doing him any hurt, and at the end kill him, without missing an hours time?

25. Whether the *Betele* hath such a contrariety to the *Durion*, that a few leaves of that, put to a whole Shop-full of *Durions*, will make them all rot suddenly? And whether those, that have surfetted on *Durions*, and thereby over-heated themselves, do, by laying a leaf or two of *Betele* upon their Breasts or Stomachs, immediately cure the Inflamations, and recover?

26. Whether the *Papayas*, which bear fruit like a Melon, do not bear, unless Male and Female (as the Vulgar distinguishes them) stand together?

27. Whether there be two sorts of the Tree, call'd *Arbor Triste*, one, by the Name of *Triste di Die*,.. the other, *Triste di Notte*; whereof the former sheds his flowers at the Rising, the other, at the Setting of the Sun? And whether the distilled water thereof (call'd *Aqua di Mogli* by the Portugals) may not be transported into these parts?

28. Whether one of those Trees, call'd *Arbre de Rays*, propagates it self into a whole Forrest, by shooting up, and letting fall Roots from all its branches into the ground, that spring up again, and so on? And whether there be any single ones of these Trees, that are above 50. feet in Diameter, as some affirm?

29. What particulars are observable in any other Plants of those parts?

30. Whether those *Shell-fishes*, that are in *these parts* plump and in season at the *Full Moon*, and lean and out of season at the *New*, are found to have contrary Constitutions in the *East-Indies*?

31. Whether the Animal, that yields the true *Muske*, be like a *Dear*, hornless, found in the High-Countrey between *Pegu* and *China*? And whether the *Muske* grows in Baggs, Blisters, or Swellings, which the Beast rubs off against Trees; it being affirmed to have been found in the Woods by the Scent? Whether true Muske, is discerned from false by its yellowness, when rubb'd upon ones hand, and by its keeping that Colour and the Scent?

32. Whether there be two sorts of *Gum-lack*, one produced by an Insect, a certain winged Ant; the other, the Exsudation of a Tree?

33. To inquire after the Fish call'd *Caballa*, said to be very powerful in stanching of blood?

34. Whether about *Java* there be Oysters, or other Shell-fishes, of that vast bigness, as to weigh 300. pounds?

35. Whether in *Malacca* there grows sometimes a stone in the stomack of a kind of *Porcupine*, call'd *Pedro Porco*, esteemed for its Cordial Vertue above *Bezoar*?

36. Whether there be found in the head of a certain Snake, a Stone, which laid upon a wound of any Venemous Creature, sticks fast to it, and draws away all the poyson; then being put in Milk, voids its poison, and turns the Milk blew; and then applied again, draws out the rest of the poison, that may be behind, till the wound be perfectly cleansed?

37. Whether the *Rhinoceros* have such an Antipathy against Elephants, as is commonly related?

38. Whether in the Island of St. *Helena*, the Tide be at the same time round in the several Coasts of it; and what is the hour of Full Sea, and what the age of the Moon at the time of Observation?

Inquiries for Persia.

1. WHat are chiefly the present Studies of the *Persians*; and what Kind of Learning they now excell in?

2. What other Trades or Practices, besides *Silk*-and *Tapistry*-making, they are skilled in?

3. VVhether, there being already good Descriptions in *Words* of the Excellent Pictures and Basse Relieves, that are about *Persepolis* at *Chimilnar*, yet none very particular; some may not be found sufficiently skill'd, in those parts, that might be engaged to make a Draught of the Place, and the Stories there pictured and carved?

4. How they make that Plaister, wherewith in those parts and in *India* they line their *Tanks* or *Cisterns*, and which, when dry, shines like Marble, and is much harder?

Other *Quaries*, concerning the Air, VVaters, Minerals, Vegetables, Animals, *&c.* peculiar to *Persia*, may be taken out of those *General Heads* of Inquiries, *for a Natural History of a Countrey*, printed in *Numb.* 11. and out of those *Articles* of *Inquiries concerning Mines*, publisht in *Numb.* 19. to which we refer the *Reader.*

As to the Inquiries proper for Turkey, *they also are already publick.* See *Numb.* 20.

Inquiries
For Virginia *and the* Bermudas.

1. COncerning the Varieties of *Earths*; 'tis said, there is one kind of a *Gummy* consistence, white and cleer: Another, white, and so light, that it swims upon water: Another, red, call'd *Wapergh*, like *Terra Sigillata.* Quære, what other considerable kinds are there? And to send over a parcel of each.

2. VVhat considerable Minerals, Stones, Bitumens, Tinctures, Drugs?

3. VVhat hot Baths, and of what Medicinal use?

4. VVhat is the Original of those large Navigable Rivers,

which empty themselves into the Bay of *Chesapeak*? And whether on the other side of that ridge of Mountains, from which they are supposed to proceed, there be not other Rivers, that flow into the *South-Sea*?

5. How the Silk-grasse is prepared?

6. To give a full account of that Vulnerary Root, called *Wichacan*: Of *Pocone*, a Root of a red juyce, a good tincture: Of *Musquaspenn*, a Root of a red tincture: Of the Plant *Maricock*, whose fruit is said to be fashion'd like a *Lemmon*, exceeding pleasant to the taste; of a blossom most beautiful: Of the *Chincomen*-Tree, whose fruit is said to have a huske like a *Chesnut*, luscious and hearty meat, both raw and boiled.

7. Whether there be in the *Bermudas* a Poison-weed, like our *Ivy*, whose leaves do by the touch cause Blisters? And a Reed, whose juyce or infusion causeth Vomit?

8. What kind of Trees those Barkes are taken from, that are used instead of Tile or Slate in the covering of their Houses, being cooler in Summer and warmer in Winter, than Stone?

9. To give a particular account of the Spider in the *Bermudas*, said to be large and beautiful for its colours; weaving a Web betwixt several Trees, which is affirmed to be for substance and colour like perfect raw Silk; so strong, that Birds, like Snites, are snared therein?

10. Whether Deer have there generally three or four Fawnes at a brood? And whether any of the Cattle transported from hence, becomes there more fruitful, than they were here?

11. Whether the Relation be true, of a *Glue* made of Harts-Horn, that will not dissolve in Water; and if so, how made?

12. Whether at the bottom of the Bay of *Cheasapeak* Northward, the Natives be still of such a *Gigantick* Stature, as has been reported? And, whether there be another people, not far from these, Eastwardly, of a *Dwarfish* Stature?

13. Whether round about the Coast of the *Bermudas*, the *Tydes* keep the same time; and at what a clock precisely 'tis *High-water* on the Dayes of *Full* and *New* Moon; and how high the Water rises then? And the like on the Coasts of *Virginia* and *Florida*?

For Guaiana *and* Brafil.

1. VVHether about *Urraba* near *Oronoque*, fome 8. degrees Northern Latitude, and about the Town *Darien*, Toads are prefently produced, by throwing a kind of Moorifh Water found there, upon the Floors of their Houfes? *Linfchoten*.

2. Whether it be true, that the Locuft of *Brafil*, call'd *Caayara*, changeth in the Spring-time of that Countrey into a Plant, and withers away, like a Plant? And whether in the fame Countrey, that kind of *Eruca*, call'd by the Portugals *Lagartas des Verias*, turns into a Bird, admirable for Colour and fwift flying; the change thereof being made fo leafurely, that one may for a while fee half of the Infect, and the other half of the Bird, which the Natives call *Guainumbi*, the Portugals *Pegafrel*. *Pifo*.

3. Whether upon the Leaves of that *Brafilian* Tree, call'd *Cereiba*, there is, in a Sun-fhiny day, found a *White Salt* in that quantity, that one may gather as much from two or three Leaves, as will well falt a good pot of Broth? *Pifo*.

4. Whether there be found about the mouth of the River of *Amazons*, a *green Argilla*, which, though very foft under water, yet, when expofed to the Air, grows almoft as hard as a Diamond; in fo much that the Natives make *Hatchets* of them, ftrong and fharp enough to cleave Wood; for which purpofe alfo thofe *Indians* are faid to have ufed it, before they got Iron-ones? And, whether this *Argilla*, become Stone, have a peculiar vertue againft the *Epilepfys*, when carried by the Patient? *Pelleprat* in his Relation of the *Iflands* and *Terra-firma* of the *Southern America*.

5. Whether the *Black Bees* in *Guaiana*, about the River *Orenoque*, make black Honey and Waxe? And whether they have no Stings, as the fame *Pelleprat* affirmeth?

The other Inquiries, ready for the other Countries above-named, are, to avoid tedioufnefs, referred to another opportunity.

3

IMPERIAL VULNERABILITY

John Zephaniah Holwell wrote his account on board a ship returning to Britain in 1757, a year after the events in Calcutta (present-day Kolkata). It appeared in print in 1758. But this was not the first account of the Black Hole. Partha Chatterjee notes that the first mention occurs 'in a letter written on July 3, 1756, some two weeks after Calcutta's fall, by an anonymous Frenchman of Chandannagar' (2012, 19).[1]

By this time, the Company had regained control of Calcutta and its properties and ensured the assassination of Siraj-ud-Daulah, the last independent nawab of Bengal.

Holwell was trained as a physician and came to India as a surgeon's assistant. Once in Bengal, he became a rich landowner, and eventually a member of the Company's council. He is known today principally for his account of the Black Hole incident, although he also produced other works on India.

The events leading to the Black Hole were as follows. Siraj-ud-Daulah, upon taking charge of the throne at Murshidabad, asked the Company to stop expanding Fort William. He was perhaps seeking to reduce their rights and privileges which, he believed, caused substantial losses in revenue for him. Negotiations and talks between the nawab and Roger Drake, governor at Fort William, did not fetch the former the desired results. Thwarted, the nawab's army attacked Calcutta on 16 June 1756. The officers in Fort William decided to abandon their posts and flee because they perceived the cause as lost, especially as ammunition ran low on the third day of the battle. Drake and others left the fort by boat. In his absence, Holwell was nominated as the governor. Defending the fort, Holwell and his army of 150 exhausted soldiers, finally surrendered on 20 June 1756. The nawab ordered that the Europeans were to be imprisoned in the fort itself, in a cell used previously by the English to inter drunk or unruly compatriots. This cell was the Black Hole, into which, by Holwell's account, 146 Europeans were pushed in, and 123 'smothered' to death (255).

Structure and Content[2]

The *Genuine Narrative* is in the form of a letter to William Davis dated 28 February 1757. In his address to the general reader, Holwell calls it a 'simple detail of a most melancholic event, delivered in the genuine language of sincere concern' (383). It was written, he says, on board a ship when he had the 'leisure to reflect' on the event that 'was too strongly impressed upon his memory' (383). Holwell also admits that the tone in many places is 'a little passionate', but that is because, he says in his defence, he had not intended it to be a public document. He goes on to add that the writing is not embellished in any way, since he is not a writer, and he simply 'trusted to his feeling, and endeavoured to express by his pen, the emotions of his heart' (384). Employing the modesty trope common to the genre of travel writing, wherein the traveller states that he did not wish to pen his account but the insistence of his friends—who persuaded him that it would be an unusual account—made him write it, Holwell records that he wrote it down at the 'request of his friends' (384).

Holwell then affirms that he had 'written with the strictest regard to veracity', the 'transactions of an extraordinary nature' (383–384). Holwell adds that the real events were 'so full of misery and horror' that no one could even imagine them, and would shock people (he mentions that wives, in particular, would not 'permit' such scenes). However, he states that the events are 'lessons to mankind' (384). He concludes this address with a moral lesson: that such events may befall others, too, and the narrative would instruct them that 'we ought never to despair' (384).

The main narrative reiterates the emotional nature of the narrative to follow, and wonders if his language is 'capable of raising an adequate idea of the horrors' he had witnessed (388). Then he proceeds with the narrative: of the nawab not honouring his word 'as a soldier' (389), the atrocities of the Indian guards in locking the Europeans up and mocking them, the scenes inside the cell as the imprisoned suffocated in the heat and experienced extreme thirst and dehydration. Throughout, he records his state of despair and determination.

The Trauma Narrative

Holwell's text is a trauma narrative, as Chatterjee argues (25). The recording of this trauma is in the form of an emphasis on the author's feelings and bodily sensations, as Kate Teltscher notes, at witnessing and experiencing the events of that night (1996, 32). Holwell is drawing on the tradition of sentimental literature of the time and his narrative is 'grafted' onto the older genre of survival literature (1996, 32).

Trauma is first writ upon the body, as Holwell's narrative underscores throughout. Holwell begins by specifying the suddenness with which they were forced into the cell, its dimensions and the visceral shock experienced by the Europeans. The cell was about 18 feet and had two windows, 'from which we could receive scarce any the least circulation of fresh air' (392). Holwell then describes the efforts made to obtain minimal relief—taking off their clothes, fanning themselves, squatting, etc. The prisoners try to force the door but in vain. Their thirst mounts and people begin to collapse and die from exhaustion.

The details in Holwell's narrative became so well known that they were also the subject of medical disquisitions, such as H.P. Bayon's 'John Zephaniah Holwell and the Black Hole of Calcutta' (1944). Bayon speculates on the nature of the deaths of the Europeans.

> When all the circumstances are considered, it may seem strange that so many could die from the lack of oxygen or breathing air. The floor space was 308 square feet, which gave scanty standing room; the corresponding breathing space must have been about 30 to 40 cubic feet per person; it is true that the expired moisture, settling in still air, would soon render the atmosphere unbearable. The night was said to have been particularly hot and close; it was the rainy season and the wet bulb temperature may well have been in the neighbourhood of 346 Centigrade.
>
> Had the prisoners kept perfectly still, more would have survived: but the unfortunate people crushed against the door in a vain attempt to burst it open and then tried to crowd to the windows for a breath of relatively fresh air.
>
> Then there is this to be considered; it has been ascertained that if human beings are closely confined in a room, the walls of which are near or above body-heat, so that little or no vital warmth can be absorbed, the temperature of the bodies will rise approximately by 10 C per hour. Once fever heat is reached, delirious conditions will follow, with convulsions, coma and death. This death by heat-stroke may not be a common occurrence because the walls are usually sufficiently cool to reduce the heat and condense steam; but in the "Black Hole" of Calcutta several adverse circumstances prevailed. (1944, 17)

However, despite the insistence on the bodily suffering and speculations around the process of death, as studied by Bayon in the text cited above, the corporeal aspects that are realistically described are subsumed under something else in Holwell's narrative, and that is the documentation of social entropy and the collapse of European 'values'. Trauma, as Holwell implies, was the experience of being a spectator to the dissolution of Englishness itself. This occurs when relief, such as it was, appears in the form of some meagre water supplies.

Holwell's trauma narrative, of course, foregrounds his own physical and emotional distress in the course of the night's imprisonment, but his greater trauma stems from the recognition of the white man's vulnerability and the loss of racial values and cultural training.

First, the Holwell narrative depicts suffering English soldiers. This was a different portrait of the Englishman, from the conquering, trading and capable one to a suffering, vulnerable and helpless one. Linda Colley writes about the captive Europeans in this period:

> individuals caught up bodily in zones of imperial contest, forced into protracted encounters where they were at the bottom, and other people who were generally not European, and not Christian, or white, had power of life or death over them … who got caught and caught out because of this [Britain's imperial] power's amalgam of incessant extroversion and aggression, and frequent and intrinsic vulnerability. (2004, 16–17)

Colley is pointing to the shift in the very nature of the imperialist in India. Holwell's narrative is an illustration of Colley's argument because the English at Calcutta, in the nawab's view, were overly aggressive and exploitative. Treating them as a part of the imperial apparatus, the nawab had engaged them first in battle and later imprisoned those he could find. Thus, the Company's aggression attracted action in Calcutta and was directed at the Company soldiers. In the process, the soldiers' vulnerability lay exposed: their leaders fled, their battle plans destroyed and their defeat imminent. But, beyond this, the English were also rendered vulnerable like any other prisoners of war: their bodies in the sightline of the nawab's army, and later incarcerated in the cell.

Secondly, the incarceration demolished the veneer of culture and stoicism of the English. Holwell records the downward slide in the quality of the Europeans' behaviour as the night progressed.

The Indian guard 'taking pity on us', writes Holwell, 'ordered the people to bring some skins of water'. The appearance of water, notes Holwell, induced 'universal agitation and raving' (395). He is appalled at what happens subsequently:

> many forcing their passage from the further part of the room, pressed down those in their way, who had less strength, and trampled them to death. (396)

He would repeat the observations: that 'every corporal or common soldier' had trod upon the dead at their feet as they made their way to the window for the water supply (396). Several of the prisoners, writes Holwell, had become 'ungovernable', being in an 'outrageous delirium' and 'few retaining any calmness (400). The Europeans fall apart:

> others who had yet some strength and vigour left, made a last effort for the windows, and several succeeded by leaping and scrambling over the backs and heads of those in the first ranks; and got hold of the bars, from which there was no removing them. (400–401)

As Chatterjee notes: 'for Holwell, it was unforgivable that native eyes should have been allowed to witness the descent of a group of Europeans into a state of natural savagery' (23). But for Holwell, it was horrific, too—because he witnessed a spectacle wherein the moral order and English character collapsed. The emphasis he lays on the selfish behaviour of the prisoners—trampling over each other, Lushington sucking the sweat off Holwell's sleeve, etc.—signals his discomfort at the 'new' European he is witness to.

Holwell's trauma narrative then is not only about the corporeal suffering he and his compatriots are subject to. The trauma that he documents is that of a witness who feels betrayed by the ugliness of his compatriots' behaviour.

Captivity and Cultural Difference

Chatterjee argues:

> For Holwell…. All he could do by way of retaliation was to transfer the attribute of "brutality" from his benighted compatriots to the amused Indian prison guards. (23)

Holwell ensures that the barbarism of the Europeans' behaviour is subsumed under the cruelties of the Indian guards. He begins this theme by noting the nawab's words of assurance—the promise of a soldier, as he records:

> he repeated his assurances to me, *on the word of a soldier,* that no harm should come to us; and indeed I believe his orders were only general. (389, emphasis in original)

The subsequent events give the lie to the nawab's words, although, as Chatterjee notes, Holwell does not blame the nawab directly for the behaviour of the men guarding the Europeans (21).

Holwell writes:

> Can it gain belief, that this scene of misery proved entertainment to the brutal wretches without? But so it was; and they took care to keep us supplied with water, that they might have the satisfaction of seeing us fight for it, as they phrased it, and held up lights to the bars, that they might lose no part of the inhuman diversion. (397)

This is what he terms a 'cruel scene' (397). Later, on the journey out of Calcutta, he provides another instance of the cruelties of the Indian soldiers. Holwell records:

> I urged the impossibility of my walking, covered as my legs were with boils, and several of them in the way of my fetters; and intreated, if I must go, that they would for the time take off my irons, as it was not in my power to escape from them; for they saw I was hardly able to stand. But I might as well have petitioned tygers, or made supplication to the wind. I was obliged to crawl. (409)

Holwell, like in other captivity narratives from the early years of the Raj (James Bristow, Henry Oakes, William Drake, Innes Munro) and the later ones from the Afghan wars and the 'Mutiny' (Vincent Eyre, Lady Sale, Julia Inglis), is keen on establishing a cultural difference between the Europeans and the Indians. While he admits, and mourns, the collapse of order, discipline and the 'English' character among the prisoners, he ensures that this collapse is attributed to the behaviour of the Indian wardens and guards. The imprisoned Europeans demonstrate selfishness in their will to survive, but the Indians, he suggests, were being unnecessarily harsh and indeed were seeing the suffering Europeans as a source of entertainment. Holwell paints a picture of helplessness (English) and unwarranted and wanton cruelties (Indian).

Thus, the imprisonment theme morphs into a larger theme of cultural difference, soldiering, soldiers' honour and ethical treatment of prisoners in Holwell's text. With this move, Holwell seeks to set up a model of behaviour, manners and character for both the English—who collapsed under pressure—and the Indians. It becomes, in other words, a device for establishing *identities*.

Andrea Tinnemeyer, examining 19th-century American captivity narratives, argues that the genre 'readily molds itself to the nation-building project' (xii). Similarly, Holwell's narrative, one could argue, becomes a cultural text that documents abstract notions of English character and morals, contrasting these with Indian character and Indian morals. Employing stereotypes like the barbaric Indian soldier enables a social imaginary around not just racial types, but also race relations (that is: how should the Indian soldier in particular, or Indians in general, be treated). As Teltscher argues, Holwell's account established a connection between the Black Hole and the battle of Palashi (Plassey) of 1757, the year from which the British Empire in India has generally been dated. As Teltscher puts it, 'the Black Hole massacre justifies British military intervention and the establishment of centuries of political and territorial control' (40).

Holwell's captivity narrative is constitutive then of a national imaginary of the besieged-but-brave Europeans/Englishmen engaged in an overwhelmingly one-sided battle with the barbaric Indians represented by the nawab's soldiery.

There is one more aspect of the Holwell text that demands attention. He writes:

> In the rank close behind me was an officer of one of the ships, whose name was Carey, who had behaved with much bravery during the siege, (his wife, a fine woman though country-born, would not quit him, but accompanied him into the prison, and was one who survived). (402)

And later, he would refer to Carey's wife thus:

> The rest, who survived the fatal night, gained their liberty, except Mrs. Carey, who was too young and handsome. The dead bodies were

> promiscuously thrown into the ditch of our unfinished ravelin, and covered with the earth. (406)

There was one woman—there may have been more, but Holwell mentions only Carey's wife—in the Black Hole. Her fate has been debated endlessly. Chatterjee cites Macaulay:

> the mysterious Mrs. Carey, now referred to as "one Englishwoman [who] had survived that night," was, according to Macaulay, "placed in the harem of the Prince at Moorshedabad". (163)

There are other references that Chatterjee cites to indicate that she married again and lived in Calcutta till 1801 (265–266), and notes that a Warren Hastings snuffbox carries her portrait. Chatterjee writes:

> Victoria Memorial Hall in Calcutta displays to this day a snuffbox that is said to have belonged to Warren Hastings and bears a little gilded portrait of "Mrs. Carey, a survivor of the Black Hole." There is rich irony in the knowledge that Mrs. Carey, allegedly sent to the nawab's harem in Murshidabad, also found her way on to Hastings's snuffbox. (266)

Now, Holwell's narrative only implies the consequences she faced with his statement 'the rest, who survived the fatal night, gained their liberty, Mrs. Carey, who was too young and handsome' (406). What are we to infer from the above comment? Implied, I suggest, in Holwell's vague and cagey lines on Carey's wife, is the *untold* and *untellable* horror of real or imagined masculine violence on a European woman, who was both 'young' and 'handsome'. We now know that the white woman was the centrepiece of an English national discourse of racial purity, national identity and national pride (Sharpe 1993, McClintock 1994).[3] In the non-narrated story of her fate lies the imagining of horror around the English woman. Holwell, by making her fate *ob-scene* (off the main scene) literally foregrounds for his readers back in England the worst possible events that *could* or *did* befall her.

Prisoner Self-Fashioning

Admittedly, in the case of Europeans, Holwell can hold himself up as a quasi-heroic figure when all around him the Europeans are misbehaving and losing their self-control and character. Holwell uses the genre of the captivity narrative to craft a particular self and identity for himself, as a morally upright Englishman. This self-fashioning produces many layers to the *character* of Holwell the prisoner.

To begin with, Holwell seeks to calm down the agitated prisoners:

> Observing every one giving way to the violence of passions, which I foresaw must be fatal to them, I requested silence might be preserved, whilst I spoke to them, and in the most pathetic and moving terms

> which occurred, I begged and intreated, that as they had paid a ready obedience to me in the day, they would now for their own sakes, and the sakes of those who were dear to them, and were interested in the preservation of their lives, regard the advicc I had to give them. I assured them, the return of day would give us air and liberty; urged to them, that the only chance we had left for sustaining this misfortune, and surviving the night, was the preserving a calm mind and quiet resignation to our fate; intreating them to curb, as much as possible, every agitation of mind and body, as raving and giving a loose to their passions could answer no purpose, but that of hastening their destruction. (392–393)

Here, Holwell depicts himself as employing and embodying the very voice of reason: he tries to present to his fellow prisoners, a case for remaining calm and ensuring their survival. In the process he presents himself as their opposite: they are given to the passions and he, while empathetic towards them, is stoic and calm.

Holwell is also prepared for death, he claims:

> I had seen this common migration [from life to death] in too many shapes, and accustomed myself to think on the subject with too much propriety to be alarmed at the prospect, and indeed felt much more for my wretched companions than myself. (393)

This is a philosophically inclined Holwell that we see. Having accepted the inevitability of death, Holwell also declares that he 'feels' much more for the others—presumably those who had not come to terms with death—than for himself, implying a certain empathy. He would underscore his empathy and sympathy for his fellow prisoners on other occasions:

> I hitherto felt little pain or uneasiness, but what resulted from my anxiety for the sufferings of those within.... Think, if possible, what my heart must have suffered at seeing and hearing their distress, without having it in my power to relieve them... (395)

Through such modes, Holwell presents at once a detached 'observer self' and a deeply empathetic self.

Then, he also seeks, as can be seen from the above passages, to demonstrate leadership. Advising and instructing the other prisoners, pleading with them and appealing to them, Holwell reinforces the need for strong leadership. Acutely aware that he has been bestowed with the charge of heading what was left of the English army, Holwell seeks to impose discipline on a group of suffering and unruly soldiery. While he fails on most occasions to 'improve' them, given their situation, Holwell manages to communicate to the readers that he was a natural leader of men and that he had the best interests of 'his' men at heart.

Holwell also presents himself as resilient and resourceful. As Chatterjee puts it, the lesson Holwell seeks to communicate is 'the value of mental self-discipline and informed moral judgment in coping with unanticipated disaster' (25).

Holwell records:

> But from the water I found no relief; my thirst was rather increased by it; so I determined to drink no more, but patiently wait the event; and kept my mouth moist from time to time by sucking the perspiration out of my shirt-sleeves… (398)

He then discovers someone else is stealing his perspiration:

> one of my miserable companions on the right of me, in the expedient of allaying my thirst by sucking my shirt-sleeve. He took the hint, and robbed me from time to time of a considerable part of my store; though after I detected him, I had ever the address to begin on that sleeve first, when I thought my reservoirs were sufficiently replenished; and our mouths and noses often met in the contest. This plunderer, I found afterwards, was a worthy young gentleman in the service, Mr. Lushington, one of the few who escaped from death… (399)

Here, Holwell tempers his self-portrait as a resilient, tenacious and moral creature by admitting to his selfishness. This humanises the stoic Englishman, conveying to us that despite his best efforts, he lapses into the behaviour of ordinary mortals.

If self-fashioning is improvisation, then Holwell certainly fits the definition with his resourcefulness in making the best use possible of their nightmarish situation. Always making sure he underscores *character*, Holwell does not play a helpless victim: he plays, instead, a victim of circumstance who falls back on his own resources, his faith and his character to help him survive. Although careful not to present himself as beyond pain and suffering by highlighting moments of acute discomfort and selfishness, Holwell's self-portrait is of the enduring Englishman, a model prisoner who seeks to survive but also to lead *by example*. Accepting his fate and yet fighting it, as he depicts the events, Holwell becomes the fighting, gritty Englishman, the very epitome of the best English character.

Holwell's self-fashioning through his self-critical lens turned on his behaviour is more or less consonant with convict writings wherein the institution of the prison seeks to

> construct individuals' awareness of their identities by subjecting the 'incarcerated characters to self-inspection through the use of letters, diaries, autobiographies, and confessions'. (Sean Grass, cited in Anne Schwann, unpaginated)

For Anne Schwann, reading women convict writings, more than subjectivity, their

> stories often moved beyond concerns with individual psychology and redemption, instead becoming emblematic of intersubjectivity and collective experiences. (Schwann, unpaginated)

In Holwell's case, he casts his subjectivity and fashions himself in comparison with that of his fellow inmates, ensuring that we as readers *see* how he is different from them.

With such a move, Holwell also presents himself as an observer of human behaviour. This changes his own status, from being just a prisoner to a *knower*. I adapt here Sarah Colvin's argument about prison writings:

> Prisoners appear in culture not as knowers, but as known (stereotypes) or unknowable (exotic beings). They are thereby dehumanised. Seeing "prison writing" as a field provides a basis for recognising the human experience it transports as knowledge. It becomes readable not only as literature but as "history and documentary" that, among other things, does the important work of illuminating "a collective ethos founded on denial and exclusion" (Colvin 2021, 24)

By drawing himself as an observer who does not quite approve or like what he observes, Holwell implies that even during a crisis, he remains the curious and quester-for-knowledge Englishman—a role that the English in India performed in earnest right from the early 17th century. The prison then becomes the site of knowledge, a laboratory in and from which Holwell observes and documents human—both English and Indian—behaviour.

***

Holwell's account of the Black Hole became an energising myth of the British Empire, as critics have documented. In documenting the barbaric native and the stoic-if-suffering Englishman, Holwell crafted effective binaries of racial types and racial behaviour that in turn enabled an imperial discourse. As a prison narrative, Holwell inaugurates a genre itself for Raj writing.

A GENUINE NARRATIVE OF THE DEPLORABLE DEATHS OF THE ENGLISH GENTLEMEN, and Others, who were suffocated in the BLACK-HOLE in FORT-WILLIAM, at CALCUTTA, in the Kingdom of BENGAL; in the Night succeeding the 20th Day of JUNE, 1756.

In a LETTER to a FRIEND,

By J. Z. HOLWELL, Esq;

——— —*Quæque ipse miserrima vidi,*
Et quarum pars magna fui. Quis talia fando,
Myrmidonum, Dolopumve, aut duri miles Ulyssei
Temperet a lachrymis? Virg. Æneid. Lib. ii.

LONDON:
Printed for A. MILLAR in the STRAND.
MDCCLVIII.
(Price One Shilling.)

[iii]

TO THE

READER.

THE following narrative will appear, upon perufal, to be a fimple detail of a moft melancholy event, delivered in the genuine language of fincere concern, in a letter to a friend; from whom the greateft kindneffes had been received, and in whom the greateft confidence was placed. It was written on board the veffel in which the author returned from the Eaft-Indies, when he had leifure to reflect, and was at liberty to throw upon paper, what was too ftrongly im-

A 2 preffed

preſſed upon his memory, ever to wear out. If therefore it appears in ſome places, a little paſſionate; in others, ſomewhat diffuſe; and through the whole, tinctured with that diſpoſition under which it was written; the occaſion, and the nature of the performance, will ſufficiently excuſe what might have been conſidered as imperfections, if it had been intended for the public view; and which may perhaps be conſidered in another light, now, that through a train of unforeſeen accidents, it comes to appear in print.

The ſubject being of a very mixed nature, and ſomething more than a bare relation of private calamity, rendered many people curious to ſee it, when it was once known, that ſuch a paper exiſted; and as there was nothing contained in it, that required either much ſecrecy, or circumſpection; it has been freely communicated to ſeveral, and amongſt thoſe, to ſome perſons of the firſt diſtinction; who thought it might gratify public expectation, more eſpecially if it appeared in the ſame natural, and undiſguiſed dreſs, in which they had ſeen it; for truth, and more eſpecially ſo affecting a truth, ſtands little in need of ornament, and appears to more advantage, the leſs it is aſſiſted by the arts of writing, to which the author being a ſtranger, he truſted to his feeling, and endeavoured to expreſs by his pen, the emotions of his heart. He the more readily yielded to this requeſt of his friends, from the following motives, which as they wrought much upon him, may poſſibly have ſome weight with you.

It is ſomewhat rare, to find tranſactions of an extraordinary nature, delivered circumſtantially by thoſe who are not only acquainted with, but were alſo actors in them; whilſt the matter is freſh in their minds, and conſequently when they are fitteſt, to give a clear, connected, and impartial account. This therefore having been his original intention, though for the ſatisfaction only of a private friend; yet when called upon to make it public, it appeared to him a very perſuaſive argument, as he was conſcious to himſelf, that he had written it with the ſtricteſt regard to veracity, in every point, and to diſburthen his thoughts of that load of affliction, which would have been as intolerable as the misfortune itſelf, if both had not been qualified by the remembrance of that mercy by which he was delivered, and which ſeemed to claim a grateful return of public acknowledgement, for ſo peculiar a deliverance.

He was farther moved, by the conſideration that there are ſome ſcenes in real life, ſo full of miſery and horror, that the boldeſt imagination would not dare to feign them, for fear of ſhocking credibility. He thought ſuch ſcenes as theſe could not be permitted, by a wiſe, a beneficent being, but for the ſake of their becoming leſſons to mankind; and he therefore thought, that this intention could never be better anſwered, than by conſenting to render them public; that by this means, a door of hope, and of confidence may be opened, to ſuch as may hereafter, fall under like tryals, by giving them an inſtance (and ſure a ſtronger cannot well be given) that we ought never to deſpair, when innocence and duty have been the cauſes of our diſtreſs.

A LETTER FROM J. Z. HOLWELL, Esq; TO W^M. DAVIS, Esq;

From on board the SYREN-SLOOP, the 28th of February, 1757.

DEAR SIR,

THE confusion which the late capture of the East-India company's settlements in Bengal must necessarily excite in the city of London, will, I fear be not a little heightened by the miserable deaths of the greatest part of those gentlemen, who were reduced to the sad necessity of surrendering themselves prisoners at discretion in Fort William.

By narratives made public you will only know, that of one hundred and forty-ſix priſoners, one hundred and twenty-three were ſmothered in the Black-Hole priſon, in the night of the 20th of June, 1756. Few ſurvived capable of giving any detail of the manner in which it happened; and of theſe I believe none have attempted it: for my own part, I have often ſet down with this reſolution, and as often relinquiſhed the melancholy taſk, not only from the diſturbance and affliction it raiſed a-freſh in my remembrance, but from the conſideration of the impoſſibility of finding language capable of raiſing an adequate idea of the horrors of the ſcene I eſſayed to draw. But as I believe the annals of the world cannot produce an incident like it in any degree or proportion to all the diſmal circumſtances attending it, and as my own health of body and peace of mind are once again, in a great meaſure, recovered from the injuries they ſuffered from that fatal night, I cannot allow it to be buried in oblivion; though ſtill conſcious, that however high the colouring my retentive memory may ſupply, it will fall infinitely ſhort of the horrors accompanying this ſcene. Theſe defects muſt, and I doubt not, will be aſſiſted by your own humane and benevolent imagination; in the exerciſe of which I never knew you deficient, where unmerited diſtreſs was the object.

The ſea-air has already had that ſalutary effect on my conſtitution I expected; and my mind enjoys a calm it has been many months a ſtranger to, ſtrengthened by a clear chearful ſky and atmoſphere, joined to an unuſual pleaſant gale, with which we are paſſing the equinoctial. I can now, therefore, look back with leſs agitation on the dreadful night I am going to deſcribe; and with a grateful heart ſincerely acknowledge, and deeply revere that Providence, which alone could have preſerved me through that and all my ſucceeding ſufferings and hazards.

Before I conduct you into the Black-Hole, it is neceſſary you ſhould be acquainted with a few introductory circumſtances. The Suba ‡ and his troops were in poſſeſſion of the fort before ſix in the evening. I had in all three interviews: the laſt in Durbar || before ſeven, when he repeated his aſſurances to me, *on the word of a ſoldier*, that no harm ſhould come to us; and indeed I believe his orders were only general. That we ſhould for that night be ſecured; and that what followed was the reſult of revenge and reſentment in the breaſts of the lower Jemmaatdaars †, to whoſe cuſtody we were delivered, for the number of their order killed during the ſiege. Be this as it may, as ſoon as it was dark, we were all, without diſtinction, directed by the guard over us, to collect ourſelves into one body, and ſit down quietly under the arched Veranda or piazza, to the

‡ Suzajud-Dowla, viceroy of Bengal, Bakar, and Orixa. || In council. † An officer of the rank of Serjeant.

weſt of the Black-Hole priſon, and the barracks to the left of the court of guard; and juſt over againſt the windows of the governor's eaſterly apartments. Beſides the guard over us, another was placed at the foot of the ſtairs at the ſouth end of this Veranda, leading up to the ſouth-eaſt baſtion, to prevent any of us eſcaping that way. On the parade (where you will remember the two twenty-four pounders ſtood) were alſo drawn up about four or five hundred gun-men with lighted matches.

At this time the factory was in flames to the right and left of us; to the right the Armory and Laboratory; to the left the Carpenters' yard: though at this time we imagined it was the Cotta-ware-houſes ‡. Various were our conjectures on this appearance; the fire advanced with rapidity on both ſides; and it was the prevailing opinion, that they intended ſuffocating us between the two fires: and this notion was confirmed by the appearance, about half an hour paſt ſeven, of ſome officers and people with lighted torches in their hands, who went into all the apartments under the eaſterly curtain to the right of us; to which we apprehended they were ſetting fire, to expedite their ſcheme of burning us. On this we preſently came to a reſolution, of ruſhing on the guard, ſeizing their ſcymitars, and attacking the troops upon the parade, rather than be thus tamely roaſted to death. But to be ſatisfied of their intentions, I advanced, at the requeſt of Meſſrs. Baillie, Jenks, and Revely, to ſee if they were really ſetting fire to the apartments, and found the contrary; for in fact, as it appeared afterwards, they were only ſearching for a place to confine us in; the laſt they examined being the barracks of the court of guard behind us.

Here I muſt detain you a little, to do honour to the memory of a man, to whom I had in many inſtances been a friend, and who, on this occaſion, demonſtrated his ſenſibility of it in a degree worthy of a much higher rank. His name was Leech, the company's ſmith, as well as clerk of the pariſh; this man had made his eſcape when the Moors entered the fort, and returned juſt as it was dark, to tell me he had provided a boat, and would enſure my eſcape, if I would follow him through a paſſage few were acquainted with, and by which he had then entered. (This might eaſily have been accompliſhed, as the guard put over us took but very ſlight notice of us.) I thanked him in the beſt terms I was able; but told him it was a ſtep I could not prevail on myſelf to take, as I ſhould thereby very ill repay the attachment the gentlemen and the garriſon had ſhewn to me; and, that I was reſolved to ſhare their fate, be it what it would: but preſſed him to ſecure his own eſcape without loſs of time; to which he gallantly replied, that "then he was reſolved to ſhare mine, and would not leave me."

To myſelf and the world I ſhould ſurely have ſtood excuſed in embracing the overture abovementioned, could I have conceived what immediately followed; for I had ſcarce time to make him an anſwer, before we obſerved part of the guard drawn up on the parade, advance to us with the officers who had been viewing the rooms. They ordered us all to riſe and go into the barracks to the left of the court of guard. The barracks, you may remember, have a large wooden platform for the ſoldiers to ſleep on, and are open to the weſt by arches and a ſmall parapet-wall, correſponding to the arches of the Veranda without. In we went moſt readily, and were pleaſing ourſelves with the proſpect of paſſing a comfortable night on the platform, little dreaming of the infernal apartment in reſerve for us. For we were no ſooner all within the barracks, than the guard advanced to the inner arches and parapet-wall; and, with their muſkets preſented, ordered us to go into the room at the ſouthermoſt end of the barracks, commonly called the Black-Hole priſon; whilſt others from the Court of Guard, with clubs and drawn ſcymitars, preſſed upon thoſe of us next to them. This ſtroke was ſo ſudden, ſo unexpected, and the throng and preſſure ſo great upon us next the door of the Black-Hole priſon, there was no reſiſting it; but like one agitated wave impelling another, we were oblig-ed to give way and enter; the reſt fol-lowed like a torrent, few amongſt us, the ſoldiers excepted, having the leaſt idea of the dimenſions or nature of a place we had never ſeen: for if we had, we ſhould at all events have ruſhed upon the guard, and been, as the leſſer evil, by our own choice cut to pieces.

Amongſt the firſt that entered, were myſelf, Meſſieurs Baillie, Jenks, Cooke, T. Coles, Enſign Scot, Revely, Law, Buchanan, &c. I got poſſeſſion of the window neareſt the door, and took Meſ-ſieurs Coles and Scot into the window with me, they being both wounded (the firſt I believe mortally). The reſt of the abovementioned gentlemen were cloſe round about me. It was now about eight o'clock.

Figure to yourſelf, my friend, if poſſible, the ſituation of a hundred and forty ſix wretches, exhauſted by continual fatigue and action, thus crammed together in a cube of about eighteen feet, in a cloſe ſultry night, in Bengal, ſhut up to the eaſtward and ſouthward (the only quarters from whence air could reach us) by dead walls, and by a wall and door to the north, open only to the weſtward by two windows, ſtrongly barred with iron, from which we could receive ſcarce any the leaſt circulation of freſh air.

What muſt enſue, appeared to me in lively and dreadful colours, the inſtant I caſt my eyes round and ſaw the ſize and ſituation of the room. Many unſucceſsful attempts were made to force the door; for having nothing but our hands to work with, and the door opening inward, all endeavours were vain and fruitleſs.

Obſerving every one giving way to the violence of paſſions, which I foreſaw muſt be fatal to them, I requeſted ſilence might be preſerved, whilſt I ſpoke to them, and in the moſt pathetic and moving terms, which occurred, "I begg'd and intreated, that as they had paid a ready obedience to me in the day, they would now for their own ſakes and the ſakes of thoſe, who were dear to them, and were intereſted in the preſervation of their lives, regard the advice I had to give them. I aſſured them, the return of day would give us air and liberty; urged to them, that the only chance we had left for ſuſtaining this misfortune, and ſurviving the night, was the preſerving a calm mind and quiet reſignation to our fate; intreating them to curb, as much as poſſible, every agitation of mind and body, as raving and giving a looſe to their paſſions could anſwer no purpoſe, but that of haſtening their deſtruction."

This remonſtrance produced a ſhort interval of peace, and gave me a few minutes for reflection: though even this pauſe was not a little diſturbed by the cries and groans of the many wounded, and more particularly of my two companions in the window. Death, attended with the moſt cruel train of circumſtances, I plainly perceived muſt prove our inevitable deſtiny: I had ſeen this common migration in too many ſhapes, and accuſtomed myſelf to think on the ſubject with too much propriety to be alarmed at the proſpect, and indeed felt much more for my wretched companions than myſelf.

Amongſt the guards poſted at the windows, I obſerved an old Jemmautdaar near me, who ſeemed to carry ſome compaſſion for us in his countenance; and indeed he was the only one of the many in his ſtation, who diſcovered the leaſt trace of humanity. I called him to me, and in the moſt perſuaſive terms I was capable, urged him to commiſerate the ſufferings he was a witneſs to, and preſſed him to endeavour to get us ſeparated, half in one place, and half in another; and that he ſhould in the morning receive a thouſand Rupees for this act of tenderneſs. He promiſed he would attempt it, and withdrew; but in a few minutes returned, and told me it was impoſſible. I then thought I had been deficient in my offer, and promiſed him two thouſand: He withdrew a ſecond time, but returned ſoon, and (with I believe much real pity and concern) told me, it was not practicable; that it could not be done but by the Suba's order, and that no one dared awake him.

During this interval, though their paſſions were leſs violent, their uneaſineſs encreaſed. We had been but few minutes confined before every one fell into a perſpiration ſo profuſe, you can form no idea of it. This conſequently brought on a raging thirſt, which ſtill increaſed, in proportion as the body was drained of its moiſture.

Various expedients were thought of to give more room and air. To obtain the former, it was moved to put off their cloaths: This was approved, as a happy motion, and in a few minutes I believe every man was ſtripped (myſelf, Mr. Court, and the two wounded young gentlemen by me excepted) for a little time they flattered themſelves with having gained a mighty advantage; every hat was put in motion to produce a circulation of air, and Mr. Baillie propoſed that every man ſhould ſit down on his hams: as they were truly in the ſituation of drowning wretches, no wonder they caught at every thing that bore a flattering appearance of ſaving them. This expedient was ſeveral times put in practice, and at each time many of the poor creatures, whoſe natural ſtrength was leſs than others, or had been more exhauſted and could not immediately recover their legs, as others did when the word was given to RISE, fell to riſe no more: for they were inſtantly trod to death, or ſuffocated. When the whole body ſat down, they were ſo cloſely wedged together, that they were oblig-ed to uſe many efforts, before they could put themſelves in motion to get up again.

Before nine o'clock every man's thirſt grew intolerable, and reſpiration diffi-cult. Our ſituation was much more wretched than that of ſo many miſer-able animals in an exhauſted receiver; no circulation of freſh air ſufficient to continue life, nor yet enough diveſted of its vivifying particles to put a ſpeedy period to it.

Efforts were again made to force the door, but in vain. Many inſults were uſed to the guard to provoke them to fire in upon us (which as I learned af-terwards, were carried to much greater lengths, when I was no more ſenſible of what was tranſacted). For my own part, I hitherto felt little pain or uneaſineſs, but what reſulted from my anxiety for the ſufferings of thoſe within. By keeping my face between two of the bars, I obtained air enough to give my lungs eaſy play, though my perſpiration was exceſſive, and thirſt commencing. At this period, ſo ſtrong a urinous volatile effluvia came from the priſon, that I was not able to turn my head that way, for more than a few ſeconds at a time.

Now every body, excepting thoſe ſituated in and near the windows, began to grow outrageous, and many dilirious: "WATER, WATER," became the general cry. And the old Jemmautdaar, beforementioned, taking pity on us, ordered the people to bring ſome ſkins of water, little dreaming, I believe, of its fatal effects. This was what I dreaded. I foreſaw it would prove the ruin of the ſmall chance left us, and eſſayed many times to ſpeak to him privately to forbid its being brought; but the clamour was ſo loud, it became impoſſible. The water appeared. Words cannot paint to you the univerſal agitation and raving the ſight of it threw us into. I had flattered myſelf that ſome, by preſerving an equal temper of mind, might outlive the night; but now the reflection, which gave me the greateſt pain, was, that I ſaw no poſſibility of one eſcaping to tell the diſmal tale.

Until the water came, I had myſelf not ſuffered much from thirſt, which inſtantly grew exceſſive. We had no means of conveying it into the priſon, but by hats forced through the bars; and thus myſelf and Meſſieurs Coales and Scot (notwithſtanding the pains they ſuffered from their wounds) ſupplied them as faſt as poſſible. But thoſe, who have experienced intenſe thirſt, or are acquainted with the cauſe and nature of this appetite, will be ſufficiently ſenſible it could receive no more than a momentary alleviation; the cauſe ſtill ſubſiſted. Though we brought full hats within the bars, there enſued ſuch violent ſtruggles, and frequent conteſts to get at it, that before it reached the lips of any one, there would be ſcarcely a ſmall tea-cup full left in them. Theſe ſupplies, like ſprinkling water on fire, only ſerved to feed and raiſe the flame.

Oh! my dear Sir, how ſhall I give you a conception of what I felt at the cries and ravings of thoſe in the remoter parts of the priſon, who could not entertain a probable hope of obtaining a drop, yet could not diveſt themſelves of expectation, however unavailing! And others calling on me by the tender conſiderations of friendſhip and affection, and who knew they were really dear to me. Think, if poſſible, what my heart muſt have ſuffered at ſeeing and hearing their diſtreſs, without having it in my power to relieve them: For the confuſion now became general and horrid. Several quitted the other window (the only chance they had for life) to force their way to the water, and the throng and preſs upon the window was beyond bearing; many forcing their paſſage from the further part of the room, preſſed down thoſe in their way, who had leſs ſtrength, and trampled them to death.

Can it gain belief, that this ſcene of miſery proved entertainment to the brutal wretches without? But ſo it was; and they took care to keep us ſupplied with water, that they might have the ſatisfaction of ſeeing us fight for it, as they phraſed it, and held up lights to the bars, that they might loſe no part of the inhuman diverſion.

From about nine to near eleven, I ſuſtained this cruel ſcene and painful ſituation, ſtill ſupplying them with water, though my legs were almoſt broke with the weight againſt them. By this time I myſelf was very near preſſed to death, and my two companions, with Mr. William Parker (who had forced himſelf into the window) were *really* ſo.

For a great while they preſerved a reſpect and regard to me, more than indeed I could well expect, our circumſtances conſidered; but now all diſtinction was loſt. My friend Baillie, Meſſrs. Jenks, Revely, Law, Buchanan, Simſon, and ſeveral others, for whom I had a real eſteem and affection, had for ſome time been dead at my feet; and were now trampled upon by every corporal or common ſoldier, who, by the help of more robuſt conſtitutions, had forced their way to the window, and held faſt by the bars over me, till at laſt I became ſo preſſed and wedged up, I was deprived of all motion.

Determined now to give every thing up, I called to them, and begged, as the laſt inſtance of their regard, they would remove the preſſure upon me, and permit me to retire out of the window, to die in quiet. They gave way; and with much difficulty I forced a paſſage into the center of the priſon, where the throng was leſs by the many dead, (then I believe amounting to one-third) and the numbers who flocked to the windows: for by this time they had water alſo at the other window.

In the Black-Hole there is a platform * corresponding with that in the barracks: I travelled over the dead, and repaired to the further end of it, just opposite the other window, and seated myself on the platform between Mr. Dumbleton and captain Stevenson; the former just then expiring. I was still happy in the same calmness of mind I had preserved the whole time; death I expected as unavoidable, and only lamented its slow approach, tho' the moment I quitted the window my breathing grew short and painful.

Here my poor friend Mr. Edward Eyre came staggering over the dead to me, and with his usual coolness and good nature, asked me how I did? but fell and expired before I had time to make him a reply. I laid myself down on some of the dead behind me, on the platform; and, recommending myself

* This platform was raised between three and four feet from the floor, open underneath; it extended the whole length of the east side of the prison, and was above six feet wide.

to heaven, had the comfort of thinking my ſufferings could have no long duration.

My thirſt grew now inſupportable, and difficulty of breathing much increaſed; and had not remained in this ſituation, I believe, ten minutes, when I was ſeized with a pain in my breaſt, and palpitation of my heart, both to the moſt exquiſite degree. Theſe rouſed and obliged me to get up again; but ſtill the pain, palpitation, thirſt, and difficulty of breathing increaſed. I retained my ſenſes notwithſtanding, and had the grief to ſee death not ſo near me as I hoped; but could no longer bear the pains I ſuffered without attempting a relief, which I knew freſh air would and could only give me. I inſtantly determined to puſh for the window oppoſite to me; and by an effort of double the ſtrength I ever before poſſeſſed, gained the third rank at it, with one hand ſeized a bar, and by that means gained the ſecond, though I think there were at leaſt ſix or ſeven ranks between me and the window.

In a few moments my pain, palpitation, and difficulty of breathing ceafed; but my thirft continued intolerable. I called aloud for "WATER FOR GOD'S SAKE:" had been concluded dead; but as foon as they heard me amongft them, they had ftill the refpect and tendernefs for me, to cry out, "GIVE HIM WATER, GIVE HIM WATER!" nor would one of them at the window attempt to touch it until I had drank. But from the water I found no relief; my thirft was rather increafed by it; fo I determined to drink no more, but patiently wait the event; and kept my mouth moift from time to time by fucking the perfpiration out of my fhirt-fleeves, and catching the drops as they fell, like heavy rain from my head and face: you can hardly imagine how unhappy I was if any of them efcaped my mouth.

I came into the prifon without coat or waiftcoat; the feafon was too hot to bear the former, and the latter tempted the avarice of one of the guards, who robbed me of it when we were under the Veranda. Whilſt I was at this ſecond window, I was obſerved by one of my miſerable companions on the right of me, in the expedient of allaying my thirſt by ſucking my ſhirt-ſleeve. He took the hint, and robbed me from time to time of a conſiderable part of my ſtore; though after I detected him, I had ever the addreſs to begin on that ſleeve firſt, when I thought my reſervoirs were ſufficiently repleniſhed; and our mouths and noſes often met in the conteſt. This plunderer I found afterwards was a worthy young gentleman in the ſervice, Mr. Luſhington, one of the few who eſcaped from death, and ſince paid me the compliment of aſſuring me, he believed he owed his life to the many comfortable draughts he had from my ſleeves. I mention this incident, as I think nothing can give you a more lively idea of the melancholy ſtate and diſtreſs we were reduced to. Before I hit upon this happy expedient, I had, in an ungovernable fit of thirſt, attempted drinking my urine; but it was ſo intenſely bitter there was no enduring a ſecond taſte, whereas no Briſtol water could be more ſoft or pleaſant than what aroſe from perſpiration.

By half an hour paſt eleven the much greater number of thoſe living were in an outrageous delirium, and the others quite ungovernable; few retaining any calmneſs, but the ranks next the windows. By what I had felt myſelf, I was fully ſenſible what thoſe within ſuffered; but had only pity to beſtow upon them, not then thinking how ſoon I ſhould myſelf become a greater object of it.

They all now found, that water, inſtead of relieving, rather heightened their uneaſineſſes; and, "AIR, AIR," was the general cry. Every inſult that could be deviſed againſt the guard, all the opprobrious names and abuſe that the Suba, Monickchund &c, * could be

* Rajah Monickchund, appointed by the Suba governor of Calcutta.

loaded with, were repeated to provoke the guard to fire upon us, every man that could, ruſhing tumultuouſly towards the windows with eager hopes of meeting the firſt ſhot. Then a general prayer to heaven, to haſten the approach of the flames to the right and left of us, and put a period to our miſery. But theſe failing, they whoſe ſtrength and ſpirits were quite exhauſted, laid themſelves down and expired quietly upon their fellows: others who had yet ſome ſtrength and vigour left, made a laſt effort for the windows, and ſeveral ſucceeded by leaping and ſcrambling over the backs and heads of thoſe in the firſt ranks; and got hold of the bars, from which there was no removing them. Many to the right and left ſunk with the violent preſſure, and were ſoon ſuffocated; for a now a ſteam aroſe from the living and the dead, which affected us in all its circumſtances, as if we were forcibly held with our heads over a bowl full of ſtrong volatile ſpirit of hartſhorn, until ſuffocated; nor could the effluvia of the one be diſtinguiſhed from the other, and frequently, when I was forced by the load upon my head and ſhoulders, to hold my face down, I was obliged, near as I was to the window, inſtantly to raiſe it again to eſcape ſuffocation.

I need not, my dear friend, ask your commiſeration, when I tell you, that in this plight, from half an hour paſt eleven till near two in the morning, I ſuſtained the weight of a heavy man, with his knees in my back, and the preſſure of his whole body on my head. A Dutch ſerjeant, who had taken his ſeat upon my left ſhoulder, and a Topaz * bearing on my right; all which nothing could have enabled me long to ſupport, but the props and preſſure equally ſuſtaining me all around. The two latter I frequently diſlodged, by ſhifting my hold on the bars, and driving my knuckles into their ribs; but my friend above

* A black Chriſtian ſoldier: uſually termed ſubjects of Portugal.

ſtuck faſt, and as he held by two bars, was immoveable.

When I had bore this conflict above an hour, with a train of wretched reflections, and ſeeing no glimpſe of hope on which to found a proſpect of relief, my ſpirits, reſolution, and every ſentiment of religion gave way. I found I was unable much longer to ſupport this trial, and could not bear the dreadful thoughts of retiring into the inner part of the priſon, where I had before ſuffered ſo much. Some infernal ſpirit, taking the advantage of this period, brought to my remembrance my having a ſmall claſp penknife in my pocket, with which I determined inſtantly to open my arteries, and finiſh a ſyſtem no longer to be born. I had got it out, when heaven interpoſed and reſtored me to freſh ſpirits and reſolution, with an abhorrence of the act of cowardice I was juſt going to commit: I exerted a-new my ſtrength and fortitude; but the repeated trials and efforts I made to diſlodge the inſufferable incumbrances upon me at laſt quite exhauſted me, and towards two o'clock, finding I muſt quit the window, or ſink where I was, I reſolved on the former, having bore, truly for the ſake of others, infinitely more for life than the beſt of it is worth.

In the rank cloſe behind me was an officer of one of the ſhips, whoſe name was Carey, and who had behaved with much bravery during the ſiege, (his wife, a fine woman tho' country-born, would not quit him, but accompanied him into the priſon, and was one who ſurvived.) This poor wretch had been long raving for water and air; I told him I was determined to give up life, and recommended his gaining my ſtation. On my quitting, he made a fruitleſs attempt to get my place; but the Dutch ſerjeant who ſat on my ſhoulder ſupplanted him.

Poor Carey expreſſed his thankfulneſs, and ſaid, he would give up life too; but it was with the utmoſt labour we forced our way from the window, (ſeveral in the inner ranks appearing to me dead ſtanding *.) He laid himſelf down to die: and his death, I believe, was very ſudden; for he was a ſhort, full, ſanguine man: his ſtrength was great, and I imagine, had he not retired with me, I ſhould never have been able to have forced my way.

I was at this time ſenſible of no pain and little uneaſineſs: I can give you no better idea of my ſituation than by repeating my ſimile of the bowl of ſpirit of hartſhorn. I found a ſtupor coming on apace, and laid myſelf down by that gallant old man, the reverend Mr. Jervas Bellamy, who lay dead with his ſon the lieutenant, hand in hand, near the ſouthermoſt wall of the priſon.

When I had lain there ſome little time, I ſtill had reflection enough to ſuffer ſome uneaſineſs in the thought, that I ſhould be trampled upon, when dead, as I myſelf had done to others. With ſome difficulty I raiſed myſelf, and gained the platform a ſecond time, where I pre-

* Unable to fall by the throng and equal preſſure round.

ſently loſt all ſenſation: the laſt trace of ſenſibility that I have been able to recollect after my laying down, was my ſaſh being uneaſy about my waſte, which I untied and threw from me.

Of what paſſed in this interval to the time of my reſurrection from this hole of horrors, I can give you no account; and indeed, the particulars mentioned by ſome of the gentlemen who ſurvived, (ſolely by the number of thoſe dead, by which they gained a freer acceſſion of air, and approach to the windows) were ſo exceſſively abſurd and contradictory, as to convince me, very few of them retained their ſenſes; or at leaſt, loſt them ſoon after they came into the open air, by the fever they carried out with them.

In my own eſcape from abſolute death the hand of heaven was manifeſtly exerted: the manner take as follows. When the day broke, and the gentlemen found that no intreaties could prevail to get the door opened, it occurred to one of them, (I think to Mr. ſecretary Cooke) to make a ſearch for me, in hopes I might have influence enough to gain a releaſe from this ſcene of miſery. Accordingly Meſſrs. Luſhington and Walcot undertook the ſearch, and by my ſhirt diſcovered me under the dead upon the platform. They took me from thence; and imagining I had ſome ſigns of life, brought me towards the window I had firſt poſſeſſion of.

But as life was equally dear to every man, (and the ſtench ariſing from the dead bodies was grown intolerable) no one would give up his ſtation in or near the window: ſo they were obliged to carry me back again. But ſoon after captain Mills (now captain of the company's yatcht) who was in poſſeſſion of a ſeat in the window, had the humanity to offer to reſign it. I was again brought by the ſame gentlemen, and placed in the window.

At this juncture the Suba, who had received an account of the havock death had made amongſt us, ſent one of his Jemmautdaars to inquire if the Chief survived. They shewed me to him; told him I had appearance of life remaining, and believed I might recover if the door was opened very soon. This answer being returned to the Suba, an order came immediately for our release; it being then near six in the morning.

The fresh air at the window soon brought me to life; and a few minutes after the departure of the Jemmautdaar, I was restored to my sight and senses. But oh! Sir, what words shall I adopt to tell you the whole that my soul suffered at reviewing the dreadful destruction round me? I will not attempt it; and indeed, tears, (a tribute I believe I shall ever pay to the remembrance of this scene, and to the memory of those brave and valuable men) stop my pen.

The little strength remaining amongst the most robust who survived, made it a difficult task to remove the dead piled up against the door; so that I believe it was more than twenty minutes before we obtained a passage out for one at a time.

I had ſoon reaſon to be convinced the particular inquiry made after me, did not reſult from any dictate of favour, humanity, or contrition; when I came out, I found myſelf in a high putrid fever, and, not being able to ſtand, threw myſelf on the wet graſs without the Veranda, when a meſſage was brought me, ſignifying I muſt immediately attend the Suba. Not being capable of walking, they were obliged to ſupport me under each arm, and, on the way, one of the Jemmautdaars told me, as a friend, to make a full confeſſion where the treaſure was buried in the fort, or that in half an hour I ſhould be ſhot off from the mouth of a cannon *. The intimation gave me no manner of concern; for, at that juncture, I ſhould have eſteemed death the greateſt favour the tyrant could have beſtowed upon me.

Being brought into his preſence, he ſoon obſerved the wretched plight I was in, and ordered a large folio volume, which lay on a heap of plunder, to be brought

* A ſentence of death, common in Indoſtan.

brought for me to ſit on. I endeavoured two or three times to ſpeak, but my tongue was dry and without motion. He ordered me water. As ſoon as I got ſpeech, I began to recount the diſmal cataſtrophe of my miſerable companions. But he ſtopt me ſhort, with telling me, he was well informed of great treaſure being buried, or ſecreted, in the fort, and that I was privy to it; and if I expected favour, muſt diſcover it.

I urged every thing I could to convince him there was no truth in the information; or that if any ſuch thing had been done, it was without my knowledge. I reminded him of his repeated aſſurance to me, the day before; but he reſumed the ſubject of the treaſure, and all I could ſay ſeemed to gain no credit with him. I was ordered priſoner under Mhir Muddon, General of the Houſhold Troops.

Amongſt the guard which carried me from the Suba, one bore a large Moratter battle-ax, which gave riſe I imagine to Mr. Secretary Cooke's belief and report to the fleet, that he ſaw me carried out, with the edge of the ax towards me, to have my head ſtruck off. This I believe is the only account you will have of me, until I bring you a better myſelf. But to reſume my ſubject: I was ordered to the camp to Mhir Maddon's quarters, within the outward ditch, ſomething ſhort of Omychund's garden (which you know, is above three miles from the fort) and with me Meſſieurs Court, Walcot, and Burdet. The reſt, who ſurvived the fatal night, gained their liberty, except Mrs. Carey, who was too young and handſome. The dead bodies were promiſcuouſly thrown into the ditch of our unfiniſhed ravelin, and covered with the earth.

My being treated with this ſeverity, I have ſufficient reaſon to affirm, proceeded from the following cauſes. The Suba's reſentment for my defending the fort, after the governor, &c. had abandoned it; his prepoſſeſſion touching the treaſure; and thirdly, the inſtigations of

Omychund * in reſentment for my not releaſing him out of priſon, as ſoon as I had the command of the fort: a circumſtance, which in the heat and hurry of action, never once occurred to me, or I had certainly done it; becauſe I thought his impriſonment unjuſt. But that the hard treatment I met with, may truly be attributed in a great meaſure to his ſuggeſtions and inſinuations, I am well aſſured, from the whole of his ſubſequent conduct; and this further confirmed to me, in the three gentlemen ſelected to be my companions, againſt each of whom he had conceived particular reſentment; and you know Omychund can never forgive.

We were conveyed in a Hackery † to the camp the 21ſt of June, in the morning, and ſoon loaded with fetters, and ſtowed all four in a ſeapoy's tent, about four feet long, three wide, and about three high; ſo that we were half *in*, half *out*: All night it rained ſeverely.

* A great Gentoo merchant of Calcutta.

† A coach drawn by oxen.

ly. Diſmal as this was, it appeared a paradiſe compared with our lodging the preceding night. Here I became covered from head to foot with large painful boils, the firſt ſymptom of my recovery; for until theſe appeared, my fever did not leave me.

On the morning of the 22d, they marched us to town in our fetters, under the ſcorching beams of an intenſe hot ſun, and lodged us at the Dock-head in the open ſmall Veranda, fronting the river, where we had a ſtrong guard over us, commanded by Bundo Sing Hazary, an officer under Mhir Muddon. Here the other gentlemen broke out likewiſe in boils all over their bodies (a happy circumſtance, which as I afterwards learned, attended every one who came out of the Black-Hole).

On our arrival at this place, we ſoon were given to underſtand, we ſhould be embarked for Muxadabad *, where I think you have never been; and ſince I have brought you thus far, you may as well

* The capital of Bengal.

well take this trip with us likewiſe. I have much leiſure on my hands at preſent; and, you know, you may chuſe your leiſure for peruſal.

We ſet out on our travels from the Dock-head the 24th in the afternoon, and were embarked on a large Wollack*, containing part of Bundo Sing's plunder, &c. She bulged a-ſhore a little after we ſet off, and broke one of her floor timbers: however they puſhed on, tho' ſhe made ſo much water ſhe could hardly ſwim. Our bedſtead and bedding were a platform of looſe unequal bamboos laid on the bottom timbers: ſo that when they had been negligent in bailing, we frequently waked with half of us in the water. We had hardly any cloaths to our bodies, and nothing but a bit of mat, and a bit or two of old gunny-bag, which we begged at the Dock-head to defend us from the ſun, rains, and dews. Our food only rice, and the water along-ſide, which you know: is neither very clean, nor very palatable in the

rains:

* A large boat.

mains: but there was enough of it without ſcrambling.

In ſhort, Sir, though our diſtreſſes in this ſituation, covered with tormenting boils, and loaded with irons, will be thought, and doubtleſs were, very deplorable; yet the grateful conſideration of our being ſo providentially a remnant of the ſaved, made every thing elſe appear light to us. Our rice and water-diet, deſigned as a grievance to us, was certainly our preſervation: for could we (circumſtanced as we were) have indulged in fleſh and wine, we had died beyond all doubt.

When we arrived at Hougly fort, I wrote a ſhort letter to Governor Biſdom (by means of a pencil and blank leaf of a volume of Archbiſhop Tillotſon's ſermons, given us by one of our guard, part of his plunder) adviſing him of our miſerable plight. He had the humanity to diſpatch three ſeveral boats after us, with freſh proviſions, liquors, cloaths, and money; neither of which reached us. But, "Whatever is, is right."

Our rice and water were more ſalutary and proper for us.

Matter ridiculous and droll abundantly occurred in the courſe of our trip. But theſe I will poſtpone for a perſonal recital, that I may laugh with you, and will only mention, that MY hands alone being free from impoſthumes, I was obliged for ſome time to turn nurſe, and feed my poor diſtreſſed companions.

When we came oppoſite to Santipore, they found the Wollack would not be able to proceed further, for want of water in the river; and one of the guard was ſent a-ſhore to demand of the Zemindar * of that diſtrict, light boats to carry priſoners of ſtate under their charge to Muxadabad. The Zemindar, giving no credit to the fellow, muſtered his guard of pykes, beat him, and drove him away.

This, on the return of the Burkandaſs, raiſed a moſt furious combuſtion. Our Jemmautdaar ordered his people to arms, and the reſolution was to take the Zemindar and carry him bound a priſoner to Muxadabad. Accordingly they landed with their fire-arms, ſwords, and targets; when it occurred to one miſchievous mortal amongſt them, that the taking me with them, would be a proof of their commiſſion, and the high offence the Zemindar had committed.

Being immediately lugged a-ſhore, I urged the impoſſibility of my walking, covered as my legs were with boils, and ſeveral of them in the way of my fetters; and intreated if I muſt go, that they would for the time take off my irons, as it was not in my power to eſcape from them; for they ſaw I was hardly able to ſtand. But I might as well have petitioned tygers, or made ſupplication to the wind. I was obliged to crawl: They ſignified to me, it was now my buſineſs to obey, and that I ſhould remember, I was not then in the Kella of Allynagore *. Thus was I marched in a ſcorching ſun, near noon, for more than a mile and half; my legs running in

* The name given to Calcutta, by the Suba, after the capture.

n a ſtream of blood from the irritation of my irons, and myſelf ready to drop every ſtep with exceſſive faintneſs and unſpeakable pain.

When we came near the Cutcherry of the diſtrict, the Zemindar with his pykes, was drawn up ready to receive us; but as ſoon as they preſented me to him as a priſoner of ſtate, eſtimated and valued to them at four lack of rupees*, he confeſſed himſelf ſenſible of his miſtake, and made no further ſhew of reſiſtance. The Jemmautdar ſeized him, and gave orders to have him bound and ſent to the boat: but on his making further ſubmiſſion, and promiſing to get boats from Santipore to ſend after us, and agreeing to pay them for the trouble he had cauſed, he was releaſed, and matters accommodated.

I was become ſo very low and weak by this cruel travel, that it was ſome time before they would venture to march me back; and the "ſtoney-hearted villains," for their own ſakes, were at laſt obliged to carry me part of the way, and ſupport me the reſt, covering me from the ſun with their ſhields. A poor fellow, one of our Under-Gomaſtaus of Santipore, ſeeing me at the Cutcherry, knew me, and, with tears in his eyes, preſented me with a bunch of plantains, the half of which my guard plundered by the way.

We departed from hence directly, in expectation of boats following us, but they never came; and the next day (I think the laſt of June) they preſſed a ſmall open fiſhing-dingy, and embarked us on that, with two of our guard only; for in fact, any more would have ſunk her. Here we had a bed of bamboos, ſomething ſofter, I think, than thoſe of the great boat; that is, they were ſomething evener, but were ſo diſtreſſed for room, that we could not ſtir without our fetters bruiſing our own, or each others boils; and were in woeful diſtreſs indeed, not arriving at Muxadabad until the 7th of July in the afternoon. We were all this while expoſed to one regular ſucceſſion of heavy rain, or intenſe ſun-ſhine, and nothing to defend us from either.

But then don't let me forget our bleſſings: for by the good-nature of one of our guard, Shaike Bodul, we now and then latterly got a few plantains, onions, parched rice, with Jaggree *, and the bitter green, called Curella: all which were to us luxurious indulgences, and made the rice go down deliciouſly.

On the 7th of July, early in the morning, we came in ſight of the French factory. I had a letter prepared for Mr. Law the Chief, and prevailed with my friend Bodul, to put to there. On the receipt of my letter, Mr. Law, with much politeneſs and humanity, came down to the water-ſide, and remained near an hour with us. He gave the Shaike a genteel preſent for his civilities, and offered him a conſiderable reward and ſecurity, if he would permit us to land for an hour's refreſhment: but he replied, his head would pay for the indulgence. After Mr. Law had given

us

* Molaſſes.

us a ſupply of cloaths, linen, proviſions, liquors, and caſh, we left his factory with grateful hearts and compliments.

We could not, as you may imagine, long reſiſt touching on our ſtock of proviſions; but however temperate we thought ourſelves, we were all diſordered more or leſs by this firſt indulgence. A few hours after I was ſeized with a painful inflammation in my right leg and thigh.

Paſſing by our fort and factory at Coſſimbuzar, raiſed ſome melancholy reflections amongſt us. About four in the afternoon we landed at Muxadabad, and were conducted to, and depoſited in an open ſtable, not far from the Suba's palace in the city.

This march, I will freely confeſs to you, drew tears of diſdain and anguiſh of heart from me: thus to be led like a felon, a ſpectacle to the inhabitants of this populous city! My ſoul could not ſupport itſelf with any degree of patience; the pain too ariſing from my boils, and inflammation of my leg, added not a little, I believe, to the depreffion of my fpirits.

Here we had a guard of Moors placed on one fide of us, and a guard of Gentoos on the other; and being deftined to remain in this place of purgatory, until the Suba returned to the city, I can give you no idea of our fufferings. The immenfe crowd of fpectators, who came from all quarters of the city to fatisfy their curiofity, fo blocked us up from morning till night, that I may truly fay we narrowly efcaped a fecond fuffocation, the weather proving exceeding fultry.

The firft night after our arrival in the ftable, I was attacked by a fever; and that night and the next day, the inflammation of my leg and thigh greatly increafed: but all terminated the fecond night in a regular fit of the gout in my right foot and ankle; the firft and laft fit of this kind I ever had. How my irons agreed with this new vifitor I leave you to judge; for I could not by any intreaty obtain liberty for fo much as that poor leg. Dur-

During our reſidence here, we experienced every act of humanity and friendſhip from Monſ. Law and Mynheer Vernet, the French and Dutch Chiefs of Coſſimbuzar, who left no means uneſſayed to procure our releaſe. Our proviſions were regularly ſent us from the Dutch Tankſall * in Coriemabad; and we were daily viſited by Meſſrs. Roſs and Ekſtone, the Chief and Second there; and indeed received ſuch inſtances of commiſeration and affection from Mynheer Roſs, as will ever claim my moſt grateful remembrance.

The whole body of Armenian merchants too were moſt kind and friendly to us; particularly Aga Manuel Satoor: we were not a little indebted to the obliging good-natured behaviour of Meſſrs. Haſtings and Chambers, who gave us as much of their company as they could. They had obtained their liberty by the French and Dutch Chiefs becoming bail for their appearance. This ſecurity was often tendered for us, but without effect.

* The Dutch mint near Muxadabad.

The 11th of July the Suba arrived in the city, and with him Bundoo Sing, to whoſe houſe we were removed that afternoon in a Hackery; for I was not able to put my foot to the ground. Here we were confirmed in a report which had before reached us, that the Suba, on his return to Houghly, made inquiry for us when he releaſed Meſſieurs Watts and Collett, &c. with intention to releaſe us alſo; and, that he had expreſſed ſome reſentment at Mhir Muddon for having ſo haſtily ſent us up to Muxadabad. This proved a very pleaſing piece of intelligence to us; and gave us reaſon to hope the iſſue would be more favourable to us than we expected.

Though we were here lodged in an open Bungulo only, yet we found ourſelves relieved from the crowd of people which had ſtifled us at the ſtable, and once more breathed the freſh air. We were treated with much kindneſs and reſpect by Bundoo Sing, who generally paſſed ſome time or other of the day with us, and feaſted us with hopes of been ſoon releaſed.

The 15th we were conducted in a hackery to the Kella §, in order to have an audience of the Suba, and know our fate. We were kept above an hour in the ſun oppoſite the gate, whilſt here we ſaw ſeveral of his miniſters brought out diſgraced, in the cuſtody of Soota-purdars, and diſmiſſed from their employs, who but a few minutes before we had ſeen enter the Kella in the utmoſt pomp and magnificence.

Receiving advice, that we ſhould have no audience or admittance to the Suba that day, we were depoſited again at our former lodgings, the ſtable; to be at hand, and had the mortification of paſſing another night there.

The 16th in the morning an old female attendant on *Allyverdy Cawns Begum* ‡, paid a viſit to our Shaike, and

§ The ſeat of the Suba's reſidence in the city of Muxadabad.

‡ The dowager princeſs grandmother of Surajud Dowla.

diſcourſed half an hour with him. Overhearing part of the converſation to be favourable to us, I obtained the whole from him; and learned, that at a feaſt the preceding night, the *Begum* had ſollicited our liberty, and that the Suba had promiſed he would releaſe us on the morrow. This, you will believe, gave us no ſmall ſpirits; but at noon all our hopes were daſhed by a piece of intelligence from Bundoo Sing, implying, that an order was prepared, and ready to paſs the ſeal, for returning us in irons to Rajah Monickchund, governor of Allynâgore, the name the Suba had given to Calcutta.

I need not tell you what a thunderclap this proved to us in the very height of our flattering expectations; for I was, as to myſelf, well convinced I ſhould never have got alive out of the hands of that rapacious harpy, who is a genuine Hindoo †, in the very worſt acceptation of the word; therefore, from that moment gave up every hope of liberty.

† Hindoo or Gentoo.

Men in this ſtate of mind are generally pretty eaſy: it is hope which gives anxiety. We dined and laid ourſelves down to ſleep; and for my own part I never enjoyed a ſounder afternoon's nap.

Towards five the Shaike waked me with notice, that the Suba would preſently paſs by to his palace of Mooteejeel. We rouſed, and deſired the guard would keep the view clear for us. When the Suba came in ſight, we made him the uſual Salaam; and when he came abreaſt of us, he ordered his litter to ſtop, and us to be called to him. We advanced; and I addreſſed him in a ſhort ſpeech, ſetting forth our ſufferings, and petitioned for our liberty. The wretched ſpectacle we made, muſt, I think, have made an impreſſion on a breaſt the moſt brutal; and if he is capable of pity or contrition, his heart felt it then. I think it appeared in ſpight of him in his countenance. He gave me no reply: but ordered a Sootapurdar and Chubdaar, immediately to ſee our irons cut off, and to conduct us wherever we choſe to go, and to take care we received no trouble nor inſult; and having repeated this order diſtinctly, directed his retinue to go on. As ſoon as our legs were free we took boat, and proceeded to the Tank-fall, where we were received and entertained with real joy and humanity.

Thus, my worthy friend, you ſee us reſtored to liberty, at a time when we could entertain no probable hope of ever obtaining it. The foundation of the alarm at noon was this: Moneloll, the Suba's Dewan, and ſome others, had in the morning taken no ſmall pains to convince the Suba, "That, notwithſtanding my loſſes at *Allynagore*, I was ſtill "poſſeſſed of enough to pay a conſiderable ſum for my freedom; and adviſed the ſending me to *Monickchund*, "who would be better able to trace out "the remainder of my effects." To this I was afterwards informed the Suba replied. "It may be; if he has any "thing left, let him keep it: his ſufferings have been great; he ſhall have "his liberty." Whether this was the reſult of his own ſentiments, or the conſequence of his promiſe the night before to the old *Begum*, I cannot ſay; but, believe, we owe our freedom partly to both.

Being myſelf once again at liberty, it is time I ſhould releaſe you, Sir, alſo from the unpleaſing travel I have led you in this narrative of our diſtreſſes, from our entrance into that fatal Black-Hole. And, ſhall it after all be ſaid, or even thought, that I can poſſibly have arraigned or commented too ſeverely on a conduct which alone plunged us into theſe unequalled ſufferings? I hope not.

I am,

DEAR SIR,

Your moſt faithful and

obedient humble Servant,

J. Z. HOLWELL.

LIST of the SMOTHERED in the BLACK-HOLE Prison (exclusive of Sixty-nine, consisting of Dutch and English Serjeants, Corporals, Soldiers, Topaz's, Militia, Whites, and Portugueze) whose Names I am unacquainted with, making on the whole, One hundred and twenty-three Persons.

Of Counsel.

E. Eyre
Wm. Baillie } Esqs;

The Rev. Jervas
Bellamy.

Gentlemen in the Service.

Messrs. Jenks
Revely
Law
Coales, Ens. Mil.
Valicourt
Jebb
Toriano
E. Page
S. Page
Grub
Street.

Messrs. Harod
P. Johnstone
Ballard
N. Drake
Carse
Knapton
Gosling
Bing
Dod
Dalrymple.

Military Captains.

Clayton
Buchanan

Witherington

Lieutenants.

Bishop
Hays
Blagg

Simson
Bellamy.

Ensigns.

Paccard
Scot
Hastings
C. Wedderburn
Dumbleton, Ens. Mil.

Serjeants, &c.

Serjeant Major
Quarter-Master Serjeant
Abraham, Cartwright, Bleau — Serjeants of Militia.

Sea Captains.

Hunt
Osburne
Purnell, survived the night, but died next day.
Messrs. Carey
Stephenson
Guy
Porter
W. Parker
Caulker
Bendall
Atkinson
Leech, &c. &c.

LIST of those who SURVIVED the BLACK-HOLE Prison.

Messrs. Holwell
Court
Secretary Cooke
Lushington
Burdet
Ens. Walcott
Mrs. Carey
Capt. Mills
Capt. Dickson
Mr. Moran
John Meadows and 12 Military and Militia Blacks and Whites, some of whom recovered when the door was open.

THE END.

4

IMPERIAL CARTOGRAPHY

One of the founders of the Royal Geographical Society, James Rennell, as the surveyor general to the EIC (1767), focused on the Indian subcontinent, Asia Minor and Africa in his geographical accounts—of which he authored many. His works on India were very specific. Other than the best-known *Bengal Atlas* (1799) and *Memoir of a Map of Hindoostan* (1788), he also wrote accounts of the Ganga and Brahmaputra (from surveys conducted in the 1760s and included in the *Memoir*). Later, he would also write major works of oceanography (the Atlantic) and hydrography (the Nile). His survey of Bengal (1765–1771) was the first extensive survey undertaken by the British in the subcontinent.

Often described as the 'father of Indian geography', Rennell's work altered the tradition of geography writing. Robert Mayhew writes of this shift in the nature of geography writing:

> we see the emergence of a different conception of geographical authorship, in which the geographer is an individual writing a series of related works about one area, based on their own fieldwork. This contrasts with the early-modern conception, where a geography book is a one-off summary of geographical knowledge, functioning as a ground-work for other and more significant forms of enquiry, and built by the collation of a miscellany of texts by travellers. (2000: 195)

The imperial foundations of Rennell's geographical work are beyond dispute. In his *Memoir*, he underscores the centrality of geographical knowledge to war and the safety of the British in India. Rennell writes of the 'natural situation of Bengal':

> It is on the west only, that any enemy is to be apprehended, and even there the natural barrier is strong; and with its population and resources, aided by the usual proportion of British troops, in addition to the sepoy establishment, Bengal might bid defiance to all that part of Hindustan, which might find itself inclined to become its enemy. Even in case of invasions, the country beyond the Ganges would be exempt from the ravages of war… (cxv)

Structure and Content

Rennell opens not with geographical accounts but a history of the Mughal empire and the Marathas. He then moves on to an account of the European 'conquests' (his term) and rivalries on the subcontinent. He offers a 'geographical division of Hindoostan into provinces or states' in the Mughal period, focusing on Akbar's reign. Rennell follows this up with the 'present division of Hindoostan', which he describes thus:

> The present division of it, as far as respects the principal states, or the powers that have appeared on the political theatre since the establishment of the British influence.
>
> The British nation possesses, in full sovereignty, the whole *soubah* of Bengal, and the greatest part of Bahar [Bihar]. (cviii)

He then gives a table of the area under British control in square miles, the revenues generated, the demographics (tribes and others), a history of the various regions and their kings, wars and internecine rivalries and a 'chronological table of emperors'.

The section titled 'memoir' is divided into sea coasts and islands, the Bengal region, the Indus region, the region between the Krishna and Ganga-Indus, the peninsula south of the Krishna and the region between Hindustan and China. A 'table of distances in Hindoostan' brings up the concluding section.

Rennell includes an account of the Ganga and Brahmaputra rivers as an appendix, and a postscript on the 'geography of the countries contiguous to the lower part of the course of the River Indus'.

A Ruin Geography

Rennell, after describing the Bengal possessions, writes that the land now 'enjoyed a greater share of tranquillity than any other part of India' ever since it came into British possession (cv). Such a statement is an integral part of the ruin rhetoric of the English writings of the late 18th and early 19th centuries.

What Rennell does is map a ruin geography of the subcontinent and trace the causes to its many wars, rebellions and territorial squabbles. The geographical account of territory morphs into a political cause-effect rhetoric through such a ruin geography common to the English writings of the period. Thus, we see George Forster writing in 1798:

> It would be difficult to discover, that this place [Raj Mahal] had been, so lately, the principal city of a powerful and opulent chief. (1798, 1: 13)

William Petrie, deposing before the Committee of Secrecy, says of Tanjore (now Thanjavur):

> [Tanjore] one of the most flourishing, best cultivated, populous districts in Hindostan ... but its decline has been so rapid ... it would

> now be difficult to trace the remains of its former opulence. (*Fourth Report of the Committee of Secrecy*, House of Commons 1782b, 705)

Or here is Jemima Kindersley on Pondicherry (now Puducherry):

> I cannot help figuring to myself the situation of its inhabitants during the siege, their prosperity destroyed, their houses laid waste, widows bewailing the loss of their husbands, and mothers of their children! But they had this consolation, that … they fell into the hands of a merciful enemy; the English, ever merciful as brave, never showed it more than on this occasion. Private property was as much as possible secured. (Kindersley 1777, 74–75)

In the context of a flourishing rhetoric of ruin, it is not surprising to see Rennell writing:

> Of the state of the internal government of Hindoostan, a judgment may be formed, by the punishment inflicted on the Mewatti, or the Banditti tribe, which inhabit the hilly tract, within 25 miles of Delhi. In 1265, 100,000 of these wretches were put to the sword: and a line of forts was constructed along the foot of their hills. Rebellions, massacres, and barbarous conquests, make up the history of this fair country (which, to an ordinary observer, seems destined to be the paradise of the world) the immediate effect of the mad ambition of conquering more than can be governed by one man for the whole empire being portioned out to rapacious governors, who domineering over the governed, until their spirits were sufficiently debased… (xlix)

Again, as a geographer linking lands, climates and dispositions, Rennell writes:

> throughout the known parts of the world, despotism prevails most in the warm climates. The Patan, Mogul, and Tartarian conquerors in Hindoostan and China, however hardy at first, have, in a course of ages, sunk into the same state of effeminacy with their subjects: and, in their turn, have, with them, received a new master. Let those who are in the habit of complaining of the severity of a northern climate, reflect, that whatever physical evils it may produce, it matures the great qualities of the mind; and renders its inhabitants pre-eminent among their species: while a flowery poet, or a more flowery historian, is the most eminent production of the tropical regions. (l)

The climate not only destroys the emotional and mental states of the natives but also those foreigners who come to conquer or reside in India.[1] Rennell would go so far as to identify prosperity with potential ruin when he speaks of Pune:

> An overgrown capital, full of rich inhabitants, and a general depository of wealth, however pleasant it may be, as it respects polished society,

> and the elegancies of life; yet from the greatness of its extent, and other circumstances, incapable of defence, must be considered a political evil in a state… (134–135)

Elsewhere, comparing the histories and maps produced by Mughal and other sources, Rennell writes of ruined cities (149). The Rajput territories, records Rennell, are in ruins. 'They are reduced to their present low state, merely by the depredations of Mahratta settlements…' (cxxxi–cxxxii).

Kanauj, writes Rennell, 'is now reduced to the size of a middling town' (54). He adds later that the 'principal cities of Hindoostan', as mentioned by 'Thevenot, Bernier, Tavernier, P.de la Valle' have 'very considerably declined … owing to the almost continuous wars and revolutions' (57). Agra, he writes, is 'reduced very low' although it was never such a great city: 'even for an Indian city, very ill built' (66). And, of course, Rennell would attribute, like several of his contemporaries, the ruin of Indian cities to Muslim invasions (151).

By underscoring the sad, ruined state of the subcontinent's many principalities and regions, Rennell was gesturing at the *need* to restore peace and prosperity—and since the local kings and even the Mughals had failed, the only solution and hope was the Company. Further, the ruin is not the result of natural disaster, but the product of civil strife and wars—that is, human-induced. Implicit in these representations is the idea (and ideology) that the subcontinent has been ruined due to its poor governance, indifferent rulers and an unruly civil society. To restore the land to a prosperous and peaceful region requires an administration that was fair, just and tough,—that is, the British.

A 'New' Map of India

While Rennell may have produced a more detailed map of the subcontinent, it was *not* the first map of the region. There were significant surveys preceding Rennell's: William Frankland and later Robert Barker's of 24 Parganas (1758), Bartholemew Plaisted's survey of the river and coasts near Chittagong (1761), Hugh Cameron's of the 24 Paraganas (1761), De Gloss' of Burdwan (1761), Plaisted's of Meghna River (1765) and Balasore (1766). The period was, in Baijayanti Chatterjee's words, a 'cartographic watershed' in the history of India, as evidenced by the surveys and maps.

Many of the European surveys, including Rennell's, made use of pre-existing, Mughal maps.

Kapil Raj notes:

> far from being a geographical *tabula rasa*, terrestrial surveying, measuring, and representation were common in South Asia, constantly developing through processes of circulation and the negotiated

> adaptation of embodied skills and instruments, intimately linked with the culture and economics of pre-colonial regimes. In this respect, the development and uses of terrestrial surveying in South Asia were not very different from those in contemporary Britain. (72; Chatterjee 2021)

Neither was Rennell's map a pioneering, solo effort. Indeed, *Memoir* carries enough evidence for the English appropriation of earlier maps.

Rennell informs us, scrupulously, of the sources of his information. The Europeans who aided in and formed the bedrock of much of his raw data are listed in the Preface—David Anderson, Jonathan Scott, Mr Wilkins etc. (viii). Besides these, he relied on an 'MS account of the country of the Rajpoots … by P. Wendell' (ix) and William Dalrymple (ix), Jean-Baptiste d'Apres de Mannevillette (x), the marches of M. Buffy (xi). D'Anville's maps are also cited (x). However, he also asserts that the 'whole mass of geographical matter that respects India [is] probably in the hands of people who are ignorant of its value' (xi).

Rennell also admits that he has relied heavily on data and maps from the Mughal surveys and records, specifically the *Ain-i-Akbari*. Rennell writes:

> In the division of Hindoostan into *Soubahs*, &c. I have followed the mode adopted by the Emperor Acbar, as it appeared to me to be the most permanent one: for the ideas of the boundaries are not only impressed on the minds of the natives by tradition, but are also ascertained in the *Ayeneh Acbaree*; a register of the highest authority. (vi)

Rennell, then, acknowledges the superior data-collection techniques and accuracy of the Mughal surveys, and the *Ain-i-Akbari* is cited throughout the *Memoir*. The southern regions of the subcontinent, however, he writes, were not covered by the *Ain-i-Akbari* in a thorough manner (the 'standard being found wanting', as he puts it, vi). Later, Rennell also calls for travellers to contribute, in an early instance of crowdsourced data, to the surveys:

> It should be a rule for every traveller to use, not only the measures, but the denomination of the country he passes through, for then we are likely to possess a better scale, than his judgment can furnish us with. (173)

The task of mapping India, then, is not the surveyor general's alone, but of all travellers, in a move that is reminiscent of Robert Boyle's instructions and 'inquiries' for travellers to India (examined in the early chapter).

Kapil Raj writes:

> although Rennell did personally conduct some terrestrial surveys (mainly around the delta region), he relied largely on the route marches of soldiers and surveyors, both British and Indian. From their journals

> and travel accounts, as well as those of other Asian and European travellers and missionaries, he began compiling his map of Bengal and then of the whole of the Subcontinent. (76)[2]

While Raj's is a well-taken point about collaboration and received information that Rennell then codified into an acceptable form (for the European reader, trader and soldier), there is a specific paragraph in the same *Memoir's* Preface that gestures at something more than either a collaboration or borrowings. Rennell writes:

> It must be observed, that since the empire has been dismembered, a new division of its provinces has also taken place; by which means, some *soubahs* now form a part of the dominion of three or more princes; and very few are preserved entire. (vi)

I suggest that Rennell, by offering a history of the changes in land and territorial ownership—the 'dismembered' Mughal empire—is signalling the absence of a coherent empire, sovereign and demographics. He is signalling, if not a *terra nullius*, a territory that is masterless and ownerless, and perhaps ripe for a new conqueror—the Company.

Eventually, extensive survey projects such as Rennell's would climax in the Great Trigonometrical Survey of India (1802–1843). The mapping of the subcontinent, as Matthew Edney argues in his magisterial *Mapping an Empire*, gave a concrete shape to the colony in the British imagination: it defined, delineated and drew India for their consumption and understanding:

> Rennell's maps provided the definitive image of India for the British and European public. It is in his highly influential maps that we find the establishment of India as a meaningful, if still ambiguous, geographical entity. (1997, 9)

One more point needs to be made, not about maps but about the rise to prominence of another imperial device: the globe. Sumathi Ramaswamy in her *Terrestrial Lessons* notes how the globe, created by the Europeans, circulated as an integral part of the education system for the colonised. This was 'cartographic evangelism', 'an enthusiastic emissary of the new useful knowledge centred on atlases, maps, and globes whose mastery was deemed critical to the improvement, even salvation of the native' (2017, xix). Geography as a discipline was taught in schools and produced—like the student-imparted moral training (see the chapter on Macaulay's Minute)—a colonial subject:

> They [maps and globes] served the world up to the learning child—metropolitan and native—in a particular manner, reminding both of their respective place on the surface of an Earth dominated by Europe (and by extension, by Christianity, even in non-denominational books). (167)

That is, the maps and globes, initiated by Rennell and the cohort of surveyors, were not just instruments of coordinating a nascent Empire's territorial acquisitions and administrative units, or of communicating to European/ English audiences a sense of the colony and Britain's imperial reach. It was also, over the next century, training the colonial subject to identify with the Empire and their location *within* it.

Political Geography/Politics of Geography

Rennell's *Memoir* is not simply a cartographic account of the subcontinent. While it does map the land and its features, Rennell also invests considerable political significance in what he observes and describes, thereby embodying it in his texts as a politics of geography and not just political geography. From the very title, wherein he conflates the land 'Hindustan' with the Mughal empire, he establishes what Edney calls a 'conceptual equivalency' between the subcontinent and the Mughal empire (11).

First, Rennell in his Preface draws the linkage between imperial wars and imperial–geographical knowledge when he writes

> The war with Hyder Ally and Tippoo Sultan, his successor, has produced much new geographical matter, in various parts of the peninsula, by the marches of the different armies, and their detachments; particularly that of Col. Fullarton, in the southern provinces and Coimbettore. These are the most material acquisitions to the present Map, as they, in effect regulate a considerable part of the general outline, and determine the proportions of some of the principal members of it. (iv–v)

It is important to note that Rennell's first mapping project was commissioned by Robert Clive as an accompanying illustration to Robert Orme's *History of the Military Transactions of the British Nation in Indoostan from the Year 1745* (1782), once again demonstrating the link between imperial wars and cartographic knowledge. As Baijayanti Chatterjee argues, the reason why Rennell, D'Apres, D'Anville and others were so assiduously engaged in the cartographic project was because 'the region had been transformed into a theatre of war between the French and the English East India Companies' (2021, unpaginated).

Elsewhere, Rennell expresses his astonishment that 'it is remarkable … the English have been more inattentive than other European nations, to the natural advantages of situation [by which he means topography and natural barriers], in their foreign settlements' (59). He also notes that the cost of making a permanent outpost at Calcutta 'may have been equal to two millions sterling' (59).

Second, Rennell has this to say about the absence of accurate measures and calculations:

> Much less can any absolute dependence be placed on lines of bearing and distance taken from maps, whose history and construction is not before us. (26)

The map-making and calculations were not within British hands, neither was the territory and so the details cannot be relied upon. Rennell, therefore, makes a case for political control of the territory to facilitate geographical knowledge. So long as the native kings, such as Hyder Ali, retain possession of the land, there will be ruin but also only meagre and inaccurate geographical knowledge. Passages such as the above must be read in conjunction with the ideas Rennell has of imperial expansion elsewhere in the work:

> I believe there are many who think that the British might have extended their possessions in Hindoostan, *ad libitum*: however, one of the greatest of our Indian statesmen, Lord Clive, thought that the Bengal provinces and the circars, together with a moderate tract of land round Madras, and the island of Salsette, near Bombay, were fully equal to the measure of good policy, and to our powers of keeping possession. (cv)

Rennell is categorical that marking territory and its potential is the geographer's principal contribution to his country. While admitting that being a 'tributary state' whose 'supreme ruling power, resides at the distance of half of the circumference of the globe' produces 'evils', he hopes that the 'advantages of military protection' will produce a better government, agricultural production and manufactures (cvi). Imperial control will produce, Rennell writes, 'improvement', although he is also cautious to add that

> the grand object for which the Bengal provinces are held, militates against the ease and happiness of their inhabitants: for there can be no inducement to increase a national income for the purpose of finally enriching another nation. (cv)

It is this ambivalence towards colonial conquest that leads Robert Mayhew to say: '[Rennell] advocated a limited empire in India, not total domination' (200). The map, like the globe, was to be an instrument of unification by conquest, by the civilisational mission (which hinged on, of course, detailed knowledge of the colonised subjects, in which, again, the map plays a role) and represents an Enlightenment ideology of 'encirclement' and universal cartographics (Cosgrove 2001, 195–199).

Third, Rennell's surveys—of which the *Memoir* and its maps are only one—were necessitated by the collapse of the Mughal authority in the subcontinent and the EIC obtaining diwani rights. Further, the navigation and transportation potential of the land had to be documented if the imperial expansion was to proceed. Thus, Rennell would compare the

Mughals' riverine navigation projects through both, an examination of the *Ain-i-Akbari* and his own surveys. He writes:

> The text … and the different positions in the map … do not allow us to comprehend the whole scope of Feroze's plan of inland navigation. By a slight inspection of the map, it will appear that this project would, if the ground admitted of its being successfully put into exaction, be one of the greatest undertakings of the kind that ever was projected; that of cutting thought the isthmus of Suez, only excepted. (73–74)

Navigation, so central to trade but also to the imposition of political authority, is Rennell's clear emphasis here. In the process of making such analogies and comparisons, Rennell is also indicating a future imperial process and structures: navigation, borders, transportation, communications and mapping.

Fourth, Rennell addresses the problem of imposing political authority on a land where much of the inner territories were unmapped. For example, he writes of the Mewar region's tribes and communities who are beyond the reach of the law:

> [a] nursery for thieves and robbers, that parties of Mewatti are taken into pay by the Chiefs of upper Hindoostan, for the purpose of distressing the countries which are made the seat of war. (cxx)

Banditry and lawlessness, as a direct challenge to any authority, including that of the EIC, was only one aspect of Rennell's argument. Elsewhere, he writes of the difficulty in ascertaining the boundaries of princely states and native kingdoms and therefore the impossibility of determining taxation and revenues. About the Malwa region, for example, Rennell writes:

> The Paishwah, or his representatives, possess also many other districts in the NE … the territories subject to Poonah, are separated, or rather insulated, in an extraordinary manner … any considerable Jaghiredar may withhold the government's share of the revenues, and convert it to his own use … it will appear impossible to discriminate the possessions of the Paishwah, and more than those of his Jaghiredars, on the map…. Nor is it less difficult to ascertain the sum of the revenue of this state, than to particularize the extent of the districts, from whence it is collected…. If the provinces possessed by this state, were to be rated in the same proportion as in the time of Aurungzebe, the net revenue would be about 8 crores of rupees or 8 million sterling. (cxxvii–cxxviii)

Rennell's interest is in the revenues of each region and he is frustrated when he is unable to ascertain this. For example, about the Hyderabad/Nizam territory, he writes 'it has not been in my power to obtain even a tolerably exact account of the sum of the Nizam's revenue, or of his military establishment' (cxxxvi).

Later, we understand why his interest is piqued and anger aroused:

> The revenue of the [Carnatic] Nabob is stated at about a million and a half sterling, per annum: out of which, he pays a subsidy of 160,000 l[akhs] to the East India Company towards the expence [sic] of their military establishment. The evils attendant on the improvident conduct of the Nabob, were severely felt, during the late war, and ought to be cautiously guarded against, in future. (cxxxvii)

Thus, the measurement and mapping of the land go hand in hand with the assessment of revenues, the expenses of each state and the Company's share in the revenues.

Fifth, the emphasis on noting the state of fortifications in every city, either from maps or surveys, is a feature of Rennell's text. It recalls instructions issued in Early Modern texts, such as Francis Bacon's 'Of Travel' (1625) where the traveller was expected to make a note of the defence mechanisms of cities and towns:

> The things to be seen and observed are, the courts of princes, especially when they give audience to ambassadors, the courts of justice … the churches and monasteries … the walls and fortifications of cities and towns … antiquities and ruins; libraries, colleges, disputations, and lectures … shipping and navies; houses and gardens of state and pleasure, near great cities; armouries; arsenals, magazine; exchanges; burses; warehouses; exercises of horseman-ship, fencing, training of soldiers, and the like; comedies … treasuries of jewels and robes, cabinets and rarities; and, to conclude, whatsoever is memorable in the places where they go. (Bacon 1860: 138)

When writing of the Madras (now Chennai) region, Rennell speaks of the better quality of its fortifications that could 'prevent a surprise from the enemy's horse; an evil to which every open town in the Carnatic is subject' (183). This improved quality, he writes, was a Company measure:

> Madras was settled by the English about the year 1640 and was hardly defensible, until the destruction of Fort St. David in 1758, pointed out the necessity of it. It is not perhaps one of the best fortresses in the possession of the English nation… (183)

Thus, Rennell maps the Mughal, Maratha, Sikh and other Indian forts and fortifications but also the British conquests, improvements and dismantling of these in what is akin to a military geography of the land.

By compiling distances, revenues, borders and demographics, the Rennell projects can also be considered the preliminary moves towards a standardised procedure for the construction of what would be a modern 'state'. I return to Edney here and his argument via Eric Hobsbawm:

> One benefit for applying the lessons of the British mapping of India to Europe is to highlight the role of the systematic surveys in the territorial definition of the modern state…. A necessary ingredient in this process was the establishment of a sense of territorial uniformity that allowed *all* of a state's territory to be treated in the same manner, regardless of obvious and compelling regional variations. A significant element in the formation of the modern state was, accordingly, the proliferation after 1750 of systematic territorial and statistical surveys. The application of the same techniques and scales of enquiry to each and every district meant that the resultant maps and statistical tables all contained the same sorts of information and were constructed and tabulated in the same manner. They therefore obscured, or denied, local nuances and particular circumstances. The systematic surveys provided the information required by increasingly centralized states and, more fundamentally, they constituted each state's representation of its territorial self. (35–36, emphasis in original)

If we examine Rennell's memoir we see the integration of data on borders (princely states, Company possessions, Mughal territories), revenues, distances, locations (latitudes and longitudes), people (communities), the general health of the region (prosperous or not), history, among others. By compiling this same data for the entire subcontinent (and beyond), Rennell was providing a grid for administrative purposes so that, as Edney argues, policies could be framed across the entire subcontinent. This would make the various 'possessions' into an integrated empire.

***

By providing textual access to the land and its people—since a large portion of the *Memoir* is devoted to the history of the subcontinent—Rennell (and later the Great Trigonometrical Survey) was marking an epistemological conquest of the subcontinent. Encyclopaedic in scope, the maps and surveys introduced and then consolidated a 'geographical reality' called India (Edney 17). The maps and surveys were a 'territorial archive' (35).

This reality was also founded on the notion of a scientifically organised, 'proven' and calculated methodology which invested the cartographic and survey process with scientific objectivity characteristic of the era's Enlightenment discourse and imaginary. When Rennell corrects and rectifies the extant maps from other European and Mughal texts as well, he implicitly signals the power and authority of British science. In short, the entire survey process enabled the British to construct themselves simultaneously as intrepid explorers, committed scientists and efficient administrators—because the map and the survey, as embodied in Rennell's *Memoir* and other works, was an icon of British science and efficiency.

The maps represent the integration of various fragments, whether of the Mughals or the Marathas, whether Golkonda or the 'Carnatic', into a textual—and eventually political and financial—unit for the Company to administer. That is, the maps merged and organised the territory for a single administrative unit's functions and ordering systems: the Company could now tabulate, predict and control revenues, the movement of goods and people, and administer the places more efficiently for their imperial ends.

MEMOIR

OF A

MAP OF HINDOOSTAN;

OR THE

MOGUL EMPIRE

WITH

AN INTRODUCTION, ILLUSTRATIVE OF THE GEOGRAPHY AND PRESENT DIVISION OF THAT COUNTRY:

AND

A MAP OF THE COUNTRIES SITUATED BETWEEN THE HEADS OF THE INDIAN RIVERS, AND THE CASPIAN SEA:

ALSO,

A SUPPLEMENTARY MAP,

Containing the improved Geography of the Countries contiguous to the HEADS of the INDUS.

BY JAMES RENNELL, F. R. S.

LATE MAJOR OF ENGINEERS, AND SURVEYOR-GENERAL IN BENGAL.

————The flow'r and choice
Of many provinces from bound to bound,
From ARACHOSIA, from CANDAOR east,
And MARGIANA, to the HYRCANIAN cliffs
Of CAUCASUS————
From SAMARCHAND by OXUS, Temir's throne,
To AGRA and LAHOR of Great Mogul,
Down to the GOLDEN CHERSONESE——
And utmost Indian Isle TAPROBANE. MILTON.

TO WHICH IS ADDED,

AN APPENDIX, CONTAINING AN ACCOUNT OF THE GANGES AND BURRAMPOOTER RIVERS.

THE THIRD EDITION.

WITH A SECOND SUPPLEMENTARY MAP,
CONTAINING THE NEW GEOGRAPHY OF THE PENINSULA OF INDIA;
AND AN EXPLANATORY MEMOIR.

LONDON:

PRINTED BY W. BULMER AND CO.
FOR THE AUTHOR; AND SOLD BY G. NICOL, BOOKSELLER TO HIS MAJESTY, PALL-MALL.
MDCCXCIII.

1793

PREFACE

TO THE FIRST EDITION.

As almost every particular relating to Hindoostan, is become an object of popular curiosity, it can hardly be deemed superfluous to lay before the Public an improved System of its Geography. Indeed, the flattering reception that was given to my former work, on the same subject, has, in a manner, made that an object of duty, which was originally an object of choice: for the public having condescended to receive the imperfect information afforded them in 1782, I felt an indispensible obligation on me to render that information more perfect, whenever I might possefs the means of accomplishing it. I hesitated only at the measure of subjecting them to an additional tax, so recently after the payment of the former one.

A large collection of materials of various kinds, having been added to my former stock, I have been enabled to produce a work of a more perfect kind than the former; and have therefore drawn it on a larger scale: the surface of the present Map, exceeding that of the former one, in the proportion of 2 and a quarter to 1. The scale of this Map, is one inch and a half to an equatorial degree: and the quantity of land represented in it, is about equal to one half of Europe. It is contained in four large sheets, which may either be joined together for the purpose of bringing the whole into one point of view, or bound up separately, in an Atlas; as may suit the fancy or convenience of the purchaser.

By the aid of a series of observations of latitude and longitude, taken by Capt. Huddart, along the Malabar coast, or western coast of India, the form of the peninsula, &c. is now brought very near to the truth: and the eastern coast, by the observations of Col. Pearse, is much improved, in the distribution of its parts, although its general form has undergone but little alteration. A measured line has also been drawn from the Bengal provinces to Nagpour, in the very centre of India: which has not only established an important geographical point, in a part where it was most wanted; but has been the means of furnishing a great deal of matter towards filling up the vacant intervals on three sides of that point. Lastly, the war with Hyder Ally and Tippoo Sultan, his succefsor, has produced much new geographical matter, in various parts of the peninsula, by the marches of the different armies, and their detachments; particularly that of Col. Fullarton, in the southern provinces and Coimbettore. These are the most material acquisitions to the present Map, as they, in effect regulate a considerable part of the general outline, and determine the proportions of some of the principal members of it. But of the kind of materials, which without affecting the general proportions of the Map, serve the purpose of filling up the void spaces in it, there will be found very great abundance. In particular, Guzerat, and the Rajpoot provinces, have undergone very considerable improvement ; as well as the Panjab country and Sindy. The upper part of the course of the Ganges, to the cow's mouth, or cavern through which the Ganges paſses ; and the course of the Gogra river to its fountains ; are both inserted from the work of M. Bernoulli. In short, additions and corrections are diſseminated over the whole map : and, in general, if we except the south part of Berar, the western part of the peninsula, and the countries bordering on the river Indus, and the Panjab, the Map is filled up in such a degree, as to have no considerable blanks in it.

As Mr. Forster's route from India to Ruſsia furnished some new ideas, and elucidated many former paſsages, I judged it proper to expreſs his route to the Caspian sea, on a separate map ; and at the same time to add to it, the countries contiguous to Hindoostan on the north and north-west ; so as to include Samarcand, and the marches of Alexander from the borders of the Caspian sea, to the river Jaxartes (the modern Sihon, or Sirr).

In the division of HINDOOSTAN into soubahs, &c. I have followed the mode adopted by the Emperor ACBAR, as it appears to me to be the most permanent one: for the ideas of the boundaries are not only impreſsed on the minds of the natives by tradition, but are also ascertained in the AYIN ACBAREE ; a register of the highest authority. But for the lower parts of the DECCAN, and the peninsula in general, this standard being wanting, I had recourse to the best information I could get, which was not, indeed, of the most perfect kind : and therefore I directed my attention principally to the state of the modern divisions in those quarters ; the imprefsing a clear idea of which, is one principal aim of the work.

It must be observed, that since the empire has been dismembered, a new division of its provinces has also taken place ; by which means, some soubahs now form a part of the dominions of three or more princes; and very few are preserved entire. These modern divisions are not only distinguished in the Map by the names of the present pofsefsors; but the colouring also is entirely employed in facilitating the distinctions between them. So that the modern divisions appear, as it were, in the *fore ground* ; and the ancient ones in the *back ground*; one illustrating and explaining the other.

Considering the vast extent of India, and how little its interior parts have been visited by Europeans, till the latter part of the last century, it ought rather to surprise us, that so much geographical matter should be collected during so short a period ; especially where so little has been contributed towards it by the natives themselves, as in the present case. Indeed, we must not go much farther back than thirty-five years, for the matter that forms the basis of this Map. And it must not be forgotten, that the East-India Company have caused a mathematical survey to be made, at their own expence, of a tract equal in extent to France and England taken together ; besides tracing the outline of near 2000 miles of sea coast, and a chain of islands in extent 500 miles more.*

In general, I have acknowledged in the course of the Memoir, the afsistance that I have received from the different Gentlemen, who have obligingly furnished me with the materials, therein discufsed. But there were other kinds of afsistance afforded, where no opportunities of acknowledgment occurred; such as the furnishing of useful hints, and correcting of errors, into which I had unavoidably fallen, through ignorance of local circumstances, or historical facts; or misconceptions of the meaning of authors, whom I had consulted. The Gentlemen to whom I stand particularly indebted on this score, are, Mr. Francis Rufsell, Mr. David Anderson, and Mr. James Anderson;† Capt. Jonathan Scott,

* Whatever charges may be imputable to the Managers for the Company, the neglect of useful Science, however, is not among the number. The employing of Geographers, and Surveying Pilots in India; and the providing of astronomical instruments, and the holding out of encouragement to such as should use them; indicate, at least, a spirit somewhat above the mere consideration of Gain: but above all, the establishment of an office at home, for the improvement of hydrography and navigation, and their judicious choice of a superintendant for it, reflects the highest honour on their administration; and ought to convince us, that in a free country, a body of subjects may accomplish, what the State itself despairs even to attempt. For, however surprising it may appear, it is neverthelefs true, that the first maritime nation in the world, has no good chart to direct its fleets towards its own coasts: nor even a criterion, by which the public may be enabled to judge, of the merit of any hydrographical production whatsoever. So that the soundings on the coast of Bengal, are better known than those in the British Channel; of which, no tolerable chart exists, even at this day. During the late war, an East-India ship owed her safety to the knowledge obtained from a chart of the mouths of the Ganges (made, and published by order of the Company) into one of which she escaped from two French cruizers, and afterwards came into the Hoogly river by the inland navigation. We had just become masters of the hydrography of America, when we lost the sovereignty of it. I hope no one will think ominously of our Indian pofsefsions from this circumstance: but even if he does, he may make himself easy on the score of Great Britain.

† To Mr. James Anderson, I am, in particular, indebted, for the account of the derivation of the term MAHRATTA, and for that of the ancestry of Sevajee: as also for the

Mr. Wilkins, Mr. Middleton, Col. Popham, and the late Col. Camac; all of the Bengal establishment: Mr. Bensley, and Mr. Inglis, both of the East-India direction: Mr. Marsden, Mr. John Sulivan, and Mr. Callander; severally of the establishments of Fort Marlborough, Madras, and Bombay: and Mr. Dryander.

To Lord Mulgrave I am indebted for a copy of Mr. Forster's route from Jummoo to the Caspian sea: as well as for his Lordship's very ready communication of every species of information, that could be of service to the work in question.

The routes of Mr. Smith, and of General Goddard acroſs the continent, from the Jumnah river to Poonah and Surat, contain much useful matter; and have been the means of determining a number of geographical points.

A MS. account of the country of the Rajpoots, and other provinces, on the south, and S W of Agra; together with a map, both of them composed by P. Wendell, in 1779, were of very great use in describing the geography of those parts. And to render the MS. more valuable, there has been added to it, Mr. James Anderson's account of the changes that have taken place since that period, in consequence of Sindia's attacks, and negotia-

subject matter of the notes that accompany those articles. And to him, and to his brother, Mr. David Anderson (each of whom, at different times, resided in a public capacity with Madajee Sindia) I owe the most valuable part of the information, respecting the geographical division of the Mahratta States, and their tributaries.

tions. The former was communicated by Col. Popham, and the latter by the Right Hon. Charles Greville.

Mr. Dalrymple, to whom I made my acknowledgments for the afsistance afforded me, in the course of my former work, has, on the present occasion, not only procured for me every new material that fell under his notice, but instructed me how to procure others, and to draw information from various sources, that I was before ignorant of. To his valuable, and perhaps unequalled, collection of MS. charts, and of voyages and travels, I have also had accefs, on all occasions; and I wish to be understood to speak with the utmost sincerity, when I say, that without this afsistance, my performance must have been extremely imperfect: or in other words, that Mr. Dalrymple is entitled to the thanks of the public, in a positive degree; although my share of those thanks, may be only comparative.

Although the new translation of the AYIN ACBAREE may have in part superseded the value of the extracts furnished me on the former occasion by Sir Charles Boughton Rouse; as the translation contains the whole subject in a connected form; and was also a task which none but a person who devoted his whole time to it, could effect; yet I am by no means unmindful of my former obligations to this Gentleman.

I have borrowed, largely, from M. D'Apres' New *Neptune Orientale*, for the sea coasts and islands: and also, though in a smaller degree, from M. D'Anville's maps of Asia and India published in 1751 and 1752. When it is considered that this excellent Geographer had scarcely any materials to work on for the inland parts of India, but some vague itineraries, and books of travels, one is really astonished to find them so well described as they are. It is with regret that I find myself obliged to differ in opinion from him concerning some positions in ancient Geography: I mean, that of Palibothra, in particular; and some few others. I have generally avoided all disquisitions of this kind, from a conviction of the general obscurity of the subject; and which even an intimate knowledge of the Indian languages would not enable me to clear up: for the similitude between ancient and modern names, is very fallacious, unlefs strongly corroborated by situation. But we cannot well refuse our afsent to the opinion that Ptolemy meant the *Suttuluz*, or *Setlege* by the *Zaradrus*; the *Rauvee* by the *Rhuadis*, or *Adaris*; and the *Chunaub* by the *Sandabalis*: because not only the names, but the positions have an affinity to each other. And yet this is a part of Ptolemy, which M. D'Anville discredits the most: but the reason was, that M. D'Anville himself was unacquainted with the true names of those rivers.

M. Bufsy's marches in the Deccan afford *data* for fixing the positions of many capital places there; particularly Hydrabad, Aurungabad, Bisnagur and Sanore. But still there are plans of some of his marches wanting, which, could they be procured, would throw much light on the geography of the peninsula, and the Deccan: such as that from Pondicherry to Cuddapah, Adoni, and Hydrabad; that from Aurungabad to Nagpour; and the campaign towards Poonah. There are also existing, itineraries kept by very intelligent people, who have travelled from Pondicherry, direct to Delhi; but I know not how to set about procuring them. The public records at Goa, I am informed, contain a vast fund of geographical knowledge; and yet we are more in the dark, concerning the country on that side of the peninsula, than we are with respect to the centre of the Deccan.

Could the whole mafs of geographical matter that respects India (much of which, is probably in the hands of people who are ignorant of its value) be collected, I make no doubt but that very complete maps of the several provinces of it, might be constructed, on scales large enough for any ordinary purpose.

It is intended by this Memoir to particularize the several authorities from whence the positions in the Map are drawn; together with the manner of comparing them, in cases where they disagreed; as also the manner of combining them, when more than one circumstance was required to establish a position. By this means, the authority for each particular, may be known to those who have curiosity enough to inquire after it: and the defective parts being thus pointed out, some future Geographer may be stimulated to seek for better materials. It may also tempt those who are already in pofsefsion of such materials, when they are apprised of their use, to contribute them to the public stock. Any communications of the kind will be thankfully received; and a proper use made of them.

There will be found, at the end of the work, distinct Indexes, referring to the matter of the Memoir, and to the names of countries and places in the Map. The great waste of time occasioned by searching after particular situations, in maps of any extent, renders an index as necefsary an appendage to a large map, as to a large book. For an index will, in the first instance, inform the reader whether the place sought after, be in the map, or not. If in the map, he is directed to it with as much facility, as to a passage in a book, from an ordinary index. And if it be not there, although he may, indeed, blame the map for its deficiency, he must allow that it does not rob him of his time, by encouraging fruitlefs researches. There are also added, Tables of Distances between the principal cities and towns of Hindoostan; and a small map, which brings into one view the respective positions of all the places mentioned in the Tables.

As there does not exist at present, under any form whatsoever, a connected abstract of Indian history, it is a very difficult task for any reader, although pofsefsed of inclination and leisure, to make himself acquainted with the principal events that form the ground-work of the history of that country: and particularly those which laid the foundation of the British power there. The many valuable tracts on this subject, that have appeared at different times, are so disjointed in point of chronology, that no idea of general history can be obtained from them: nor can the chasms be readily filled up. I have therefore been tempted to compile a sort of chronological table of events, from the æra of the first Mahomedan conquests, to the final dissolution of the Mogul empire: and wish the reader to understand, that what is offered to his perusal under that form, is intended as a mere sketch; and that, chiefly with a view to render so dry and so unentertaining a subject as the geography of a country, somewhat more interesting, by accompanying it with an account of the principal events and revolutions, to which the country has given birth. I am but too conscious of the deficiency of this part of my performance. Besides, many of the events are related so differently by different people, who pretend to an equal knowledge of the circumstances of them, that it will be no matter of surprise if I am found (by those whose knowledge of eastern languages has gained them access to authentic records) to be often mistaken. In whatsoever case this may happen, I make no doubt but that I shall experience the exercise of their candour, as to the motives by which I was actuated, when I adopted any particular opinion, or mode of relation. The present disputes concerning some recent historical facts in this and the neighbouring countries, shew how extremely difficult it is to come at the truth, even when the researches after it, are made under every favourable circumstance that can possibly attend them.

MARCH 1st, 1788.

PREFACE

TO THE SECOND EDITION.

SINCE the publication of the first edition, much valuable matter, serving both to correct, and to extend, the geography of India, and the countries bordering on it, to the north-west; has been transmitted to me. I have, in consequence, inserted in the body of the Map, such of the new matter, as it was poſsible to aſsimilate with the old; namely, Capt. Reynolds's route through Malwa; and from Surat to Tippoo's frontier, through Baglana, and the western part of the Deccan. But on the north-west of Delhi, the new materials not only differed as widely from the old, as they excelled them in point of authority; but were also extended through a tract, far beyond the limits of the General Map: so that the corrections could no otherwise be accomplished with effect, than by inserting them in a separate map. Accordingly, a new map, on a scale similar to that of the General one, and forming an appendage, or supplement to it; has been constructed: and contains generally, the countries situated between Delhi, Candahar, Badakshan, and the two Thibets: including, of course, all the upper branches of the Indus, and the valley of Cashmere. This new piece of geography (with the exception of that part of it, between Delhi and the Panjab) has been formed of materials most obligingly communicated by Capt. Kirkpatrick, of the Bengal establishment; and of which materials, a detailed account will be found in its place. And the part which forms the exception, is taken from a MS. map, as obligingly communicated by Colonel Polier: and which is no lefs valuable, from its supplying the deficiency of the other materials, than from the importance, and novelty of its subject.

Having detected a very considerable error, in the relative positions of the two Bucharias, as they stand in our best maps; and having also made a great alteration in the course of the principal branch of the Indus, towards its source; I have re-constructed the map of the countries, situated between the Ganges and the Caspian sea, in order to correct these errors, and to insert other positions, founded on the result of much investigation and inquiry. For the accommodation of the purchasers of the first edition, these additional Maps, as well as the letter-prefs of the Third Section, which relates to them; will be sold separately.

Having been formerly misled, by Mr. Tiefentaller's representation of the course of the Ganges, between Hurdwar and Sirinagur; I have now corrected it, according to the report of some English gentlemen, whose curiosity led them to the foot of mount *Himmaleh*. As Mr. Daniel was amongst the number, we may expect to receive from his pencil, correct drawings of the lower fall of the Ganges (at Hurdwar), and of the romantic scenes in its neighbourhood.

NOVEMBER 22d, 1791.

PREFACE

TO THE THIRD EDITION.

THE present edition, both of the Memoir and Map, does not differ in any respect, from the last. But since the Memoir was printed, very great changes have taken place, in the political division of the Peninsula of India: and the late war, which gave occasion to this change, has produced a great many valuable materials, for correcting the natural, as well as the political, geography of the Peninsula. A new, and much improved Map of this tract, has therefore been constructed; in the course of which, all the new authorities have been consulted: and it is accompanied by a short Memoir, explanatory of the construction, and political consequence, of the tract represented. This new piece, is in its nature, an appendage to the Memoir of the Map of Hindoostan: and the letter-preſs of both, being printed uniformly, may conveniently be bound up together, by those who choose it: but the Map, from its size, cannot very conveniently be folded into the book.

A further number of copies, of the Third Section, and of the two Maps belonging to it, have been printed, for the accommodation of the purchasers of the first edition of this work.

JANUARY 21st, 1793.

CONQUESTS *of* EUROPEAN POWERS, *since the Downfall of the* MOGUL EMPIRE.

AMONG the new powers that arose on the downfall of the Mogul empire, we must not forget to mention the French and English. As for the Portuguese, their power had past its meridian before this period: besides, their views being (apparently) confined altogether to traffic, they wisely made choice of insular situations; such as Goa, Bombay, Salsette, Diu, &c.; and never appear to have poſseſsed any very considerable extent of territory, although they kept on foot a large army of Europeans. The Dutch system was nearly the same: and their prosperity, in a great measure, grew out of the misfortunes of the Portuguese; who having fallen under the dominion of Spain, became obnoxious as well to the jealousy of rivalship, as to the revenge of the Hollanders.

The French power was but of short duration, but remarkably brilliant. It was a bright meteor, that dazzled at first, but which soon burnt itself out, and left their East-India Company in utter darkneſs. It commenced during the government of M. Dupleix at Pondicherry, in 1749. The French having aſsisted a soubah of the Deccan in mounting the throne, attended his future steps with an army, and established an influence in his councils that promised to be permanent; but which vanished very early, by the mere breath of court intrigue: for while M. Buſsy, at the head of the French army, was at Sanore, in the western quarter of the peninsula (in 1756), a quarrel with the minister of the soubah, effected the dismiſsion of the French. They were then compelled to retreat through an enemy's country for near 300 miles, until they reached

Hydrabad; where they fortified themselves, and waited for a reinforcement from Masulipatam, their nearest settlement; which was upwards of 200 miles from Hydrabad. Great ability was discovered by M. Bufsy, on this memorable occasion: an account of which, as well as of M. Bufsy's warfare and negociations in general, will be found at large, in Mr. Orme's invaluable History of the Military Transactions of the British Nation, in Hindoostan. At Hydrabad, the quarrel was compromised: and the following year (1757) and part of the next, was spent by M. Bufsy in reducing the refractory rajahs, or zemindars, in the northern circars; and in afsisting the soubah in the execution of his own plans. But in the midst of these transactions, he was suddenly recalled into the Carnatic, by M. Lally; who determined to collect the whole force of the French, within that quarter: so that the soubah was left at full liberty to accede to the proposals of the English. Lally was also accused of being jealous of the fame of M. Bufsy.

The circars, the fruits of M. Bufsy's wars and negociations in the Deccan (and which had been obtained in 1753), yet remained to the French: but Colonel Clive, who was at this time Governor of Bengal, with that promptitude and decision which so strongly marked his character, seized on them, with a force from Bengal, in 1759; although they were defended by a much superior force; and the French were deprived of resources to carry on the war in the Carnatic. So that Lally failed to accomplish the purposes for which the French interest in the Deccan had been relinquished; namely, that of expelling the English from the Carnatic: for, on the contrary, the French not only lost all their pofsefsions in that quarter, but in every other part of India. Thus, their political existence may be said to begin, in 1749; and to end in 1761, by the capture of their principal settlement, Pondicherry. They appear to have been the first European power, that trained the natives of India to regular discipline;* as well as the first who set the example of acquiring territorial poſseſsions, of any great extent, in India: in which they have been so succeſsfully followed by the English.

THE expedition of the British troops into Tanjore, in 1749, was the first warfare in which they were engaged, against the forces of an Indian prince: and it proved unsucceſsful, as to its main object; which was, the restoration of a deposed king, or rather rajah, of Tanjore, who had applied for aſsistance to the governor of Fort St. David. The price of this aſsistance, was to be the fort and territory of Devicottah, situated at the mouth of the Coleroon, or principal branch of the Tanjore river; and this fort, notwithstanding their want of succeſs in the cause of the deposed rajah, the Company's troops, aided by the fleet under Admiral Boscawen, took poſseſsion of, after a short siege. In the following year they were called on, by the circumstances of the times, to take part in the disputed succeſsion to the nabobship of Arcot, in opposition to the French: who (as has been before observed) had taken the lead, both in the affairs of the Carnatic, and of the Deccan. We have also observed, that Nizam-al-Muluck, soubah of the Deccan, had placed Anwar o'dien in the nabobship of Arcot (in 1743); and that the death of the same Nizam, in 1748, had occasioned a considerable change in the politics of the Deccan; in which the French engaged so deeply. Chunda Saib was the person whom the French wished to raise to the government of Arcot: and the expulsion of the family of Ánwar o'dien, was a neceſsary step towards it. These contests, which had been carried on with great credit to the British arms, were put an end to, by the interference of the two East-India

* I am far from being well informed concerning the early history of the Portuguese in India: but by a paſsage in Mr Orme's Historical Fragments, page 175, it would appear that they had not, in 1683, trained the natives to regular discipline. He says, "The Viceroy of "Goa took the field (against Sambajee, with 1200 Europeans, and 25,000 *natives of his own territory*." From the confined limits of the Portuguese territories, we may conclude that these were the ordinary inhabitants only.

Companies, in Europe, in 1754: and Mahomed Ally, son of Anwar o'dien (who had fallen in the course of the war), was left in posfefsion of the Carnatic: or, at least, of that portion of it which had been recovered to him by the British arms. The particulars of these wars will be found in Mr. Orme's History, volume the first.

War breaking out in Europe in 1756, the truce was reduced to a very short period. The first object of the British councils, was to wrest the northern circars out of the hands of the French; in order to deprive them of the means of paying their army. The second was to drive M. Bufsy's force out of the Deccan, by means of an alliance with the Nizam, or Soubah. Both of these projects were at this time defeated; the first by the miscarriage of dispatches to India; the second, by the capture of Calcutta, the chief British settlement in Bengal, in June, 1756: which induced the necefsity of relinquishing every plan of hostility in the Deccan and Carnatic, in order that a force might be spared, sufficient to accomplish the recovery of so important a settlement as Calcutta; on which the whole trade to Bengal depended.

Aliverdy Cawn, Nabob of Bengal, died in 1756, and was succeeded by his grandson Surajah Dowlah. This young man either was, or pretended to be, irritated at the conduct of the English within his dominions; and was probably jealous of the rising power of Europeans in general, in other parts of India. He determined to expel the English (at least) from Bengal: and accordingly took their fort at Calcutta, and compelled those among them, who were not made prisoners, to retire. In the following year, an armanent from Madras, under Admiral Watson and Colonel Clive, not only recovered the settlement of Calcutta, but brought the nabob to terms. The sword, however, being thus drawn, no permanent security could be expected on the side of the intruders, unlefs supported by power: which could not be obtained, while a nabob, inimical to their interests, pofsefsed the whole power of the kingdom. Suspicions on both sides soon brought matters to a crisis: and Jaffier Ally Cawn, an omrah in high trust and favour with the nabob, was negociated with; and, on condition of their afsisting him in his views towards the throne, engaged to be their future *ally and confederate*; for, so much were matters changed by the late efsay of their strength, and by the genius and good fortune of Clive, that *protection* would ill exprefs the current expectation of the British. The famous battle of Plafsey, fought in June, 1757, and in which Jaffier aided the accomplishment of their wishes, by standing neuter, laid the foundation of the future power of the British nation in Bengal and Hindoostan. From that time they became the arbiters of the succefsion of the nabobship of Bengal; which speedily led to the pofsefsion of the powers of government: for Cofsim Ally, who had been placed in the room of Jaffier, disliking his situation, resolved to hazard a change at all events; and this brought on a war, which ended in the expulsion of Cofsim, and left the Bengal provinces in the pofsefsion of the English, who restored Jaffier to the nabobship. He had been deposed, on a charge of imbecility, in 1760, and was now restored, in 1763. Cossim retired to Sujah Dowlah, Nabob of Oude, and prevailed on him to espouse his cause. Sujah had distinguished himself in the celebrated battle of Pannipput, in 1761; and is reported to have had a considerable share in turning the fortune of the day, at the very moment when victory inclined towards the Mahrattas. Whether he over-rated his own talents for war, or mistook the military character and resources of the British, he, however, engaged too rashly in the war; and the consequences were, a total defeat of his forces, joined with Cofsim Ally's, at Buxar, in 1764: and this was followed by the lofs of all his territories, during that and the following year.

Those, whose belief has been staggered by the accounts of the conquests made on the Indians and Persians, by the Grecian, Patan, and Mogul armies, may reconcile their doubts by attending to the events of their own days; in which a handful of French troops effected revolutions in the Deccan: and another of British, made an entire conquest of Bengal, Bahar, and Oude, in little more than two campaigns. Each of those conquerors, both ancient and modern, after gaining certain advantages, pursued them by means of levies raised in the conquered countries themselves; and thus rendered the vanquished, subservient to the final reduction of their own country. This was even the case of Alexander, who set out with 35,000 men, and left India, with 120,000. Such measures could only be pursued in countries, where the habit of changing their governors, had rendered the governed indifferent to the choice of them. Even the whole number of the combatants on the side of the British, did not exceed 7000, at the battle of Buxar: and of these 1200 might be Europeans. The battle of Plafsey was gained with an army of about 3000 men; of whom 900 only were Europeans.

Lord Clive, who reafsumed the government of Bengal, in 1765, found matters in the state I have just represented. He seized the opportunity of taking pofsefsion of the Bengal provinces; the Nabob Jaffier Ally having recently died; and obtained from the nominal Mogul, Shah Aulum (who, together with his nominal vizier, Sujah Dowlah, had, as before related, thrown themselves on the generosity of the British); a grant of the duanny, or administration of the revenues of Bengal, Bahar, and Orifsa; on condition of paying the Mogul 26 lacks of rupees per annum (260,000l.). Thus a territory producing at that time, at least a million sterling, per annum, after every expence was defrayed, and containing at least ten millions of inhabitants, was gained to the Company, on the side of Bengal: together with the northern circars, valued at near half a million more, and for which a grant was also obtained. Sujah Dowlah had all his territories restored to him, except the provinces of Corah and Allahabad, which were retained for the Mogul; together with the fortrefs of Allahabad, which was afsigned to him, as a proper place of residence.

Although the English were thus firmly and peaceably established in Bengal, in 1765, yet within two years afterwards, they were engaged in a very arduous contest in the peninsula, with Hyder Ally, the sovereign of Mysore, leagued with the Nizam or Soubah of the Deccan. Hyder's history is now so well known to the generality of readers in Europe, by means of the several publications that have lately appeared,* that it will be unnecefsary to give any thing more than a short abstract of it, here.

Hyder Ally was a soldier of fortune, and the son of a person who served in quality of *Killadar*, or governor of a small fortrefs, to one of the kings of Mysore. He is said to have acquired the rudiments of war in the French camps: and in the year 1753, distinguished himself, as their auxiliary, in the plains of Tritchinopoly. About ten years afterwards, being then at the head of the Mysore army, he dethroned his sovereign, and governed under the title of Regent. Soon after, he extended his dominions on every side, the Carnatic excepted: the fine province of Bednore (or Biddanore) and the Patan nabobships of Cuddapah, Canoul, &c. besides some Mahratta provinces towards the river Kistnah; and the country of the Nairs, and other small states on the Malabar coast, were added to his original pofsefsions; until at last he was at the head of a state, in extent equal to Great Britain, and producing a grofs revenue of four millions sterling. The civil broils and revolutions in the western Mahratta state, particularly in latter times, allowed Hyder to aggrandize himself at its expence; but he, neverthelefs, received some severe checks from that quarter. He was not arrived at the height of his power, when the war between him and the English broke out, in 1767: but his power was such as to alarm his neighbours, and a resolution was taken to attack him. The Mahrattas under Maderow, entered Hyder's country on the side towards Visiapour; and the Nizam, joined by a de-

* Capt. Robson's, and M. M. L. D T.'s Lives of Hyder Ally, &c. &c.

tachment of British troops, moved from Hydrabad towards the frontier of Mysore, soon after. Hyder first contrived to buy off the Mahrattas with a large sum of money, and the restitution of some of the places he had taken from them. Next, he negociated with the Nizam, and had the addrefs, not only to detach him from the English, but to draw him over to his party: so that the English detachment was compelled by necefsity to retire to the Carnatic; on the frontiers of which their grand army was now afsembling. Besides the whimsical character of the Nizam, several other circumstances might conspire towards the determining him to act in the manner he did. The grant of the northern circars, and the emancipation of the Carnatic from any dependence on the Deccan, both of which were obtained from the Mogul, by the English, could not but be very mortifying to the Nizam; as having the appearance of a forcible partition of his territories. The circars, however, came into their hands (as we have seen) by conquest from the French, to whom they were originally granted by a former soubah of the Deccan: so that the grant from the Mogul was merely nominal: besides, the Nizam had been prevailed on to acquiesce in the measure, by an offer on the part of the English, of five lacks of rupees (50,000l.) per annum, by way of tribute or quit rent. As to his superiority in the Carnatic, it had ever been nominal; yet Hyder, who now meditated the conquest of it, was glad to obtain from the Nizam, a grant, or sunnud, for the nabobship of it: and from this time, at least, he considered Mahomed Ally as his rival. It is proper to observe, that in the days of Mahomed Ally's distrefs, when he pofsefsed only a small part of the Carnatic, he had engaged to cede the fortrefs of Tritchinopoly, a most important post in the southern division of it, to the king of Mysore, for afsistance then afforded him: but this engagement never being performed, Hyder, as might be expected, adopted the claims and resentments of the prince, whose throne he had taken pofsefsion of; and never lost sight of his title to Tritchinopoly. Had the engagement been fulfilled, it would have had the effect of separating for ever, from the nabobship of the Carnatic, the provinces of Tanjore, Madura, and the rest of the southern provinces.

The war that immediately followed, was productive of some sharp battles on the common frontiers of the Carnatic and Mysore: besides which, a strong detachment of the British army seized on Hyder's province of Coimbettore, a fertile district on the south of Mysore, and commanding a ready way to Hyder's capital, Seringapatam. This was the first war in which the British arms had met with any steady opposition from a prince of the country; for in the affair of Tanjore, in 1749, their arms were triumphant in the end, by the taking of Devicottah, their proper object. The war was continued with various succefs, during the year 1767, 1768, and part of 1769; when Hyder, with a strong detachment of chosen troops, chiefly horse, giving the British army the slip, came within seven miles of Madras, and dictated a peace to the government of that place. This peace was disreputable to the British councils only: since the hands of the Commander in Chief (General Joseph Smith) were tied up, at the very moment, the most favourable for striking a blow; and when Hyder, fearing the general's approach, could purchase his security no other way than by intimidating government into the measure of laying their commands on the general, not to advance; by which measure he might pofsibly have cut Hyder and his detachment to pieces.

The Nizam, very early in the war, had been detached from Hyder's alliance; chiefly by the strong measure of sending a detachment from Bengal, into the heart of Golconda; which made him tremble for his capital, Hydrabad.

The peace left matters much in the same state as before the war: and whatever credit Hyder might have gained by the conclusion of it, was done away by the total defeat which he suffered, in 1771, from the Mahratta army, within a few miles of his capital; into which he escaped with great difficulty, with a small remnant of his army; and afterwards defied the attacks of his numerous enemies, who pofsefsed neither the skill, nor the ordinary requisites for a siege. Hyder waited in patience, until the enemy by desolating the country, were compelled to leave it. A few years of peace not only restored matters to their former state, but improved both his revenues and his army, to a degree beyond probability; and at the same time, the distractions that prevailed among the Mahrattas, enabled him to extend his territories at their expence. Such are the effects of firmnefs, perseverance, and economy.

It may be asked, how the Mahrattas, who are represented as so inferior in point of discipline to Hyder's troops, came to defeat him? It is accounted for by the vast superiority in numbers of the Mahratta army (chiefly horse), which surrounding Hyder's troops, cut off their supplies of provisions, and compelled them to retire towards their capital; through an open country, the most favourable to the attacks of cavalry. Hyder's army was formed into one vast hollow square, and marched, closely surrounded by the Mahrattas; when the advanced front of the square making too hasty a step, separated from the others; and the Mahrattas, pushing through the openings thus made, threw Hyder's whole army into irreparable disorder.

We have spoken before concerning the treaty made with the Nabob of Oude, and the mutual advantages derived to both parties; but particularly to the British, from the mode of defence adopted for Oude, considering it as a common frontier to both states: as also concerning the departure of the Mogul, in 1771; which threw the Corah, &c. provinces, into the hands of Sujah Dowlah.

It may be supposed, that the opposition made to the Mahrattas, when they attempted to take pofsefsion of those provinces in 1772, must have created some disgust. Indeed the British government had long considered the Mahrattas, in the general scope of their designs, as inimical to its interests. In 1773, the Mahrattas crofsed the Ganges to invade the Rohilla country. A brigade of the

British army marched to the western frontier of that country, and drove the Mahrattas acrofs the river. For this protection, the Rohilla chiefs had stipulated to pay Sujah Dowlah forty lacks of rupees (it must be observed that the British army moved, only as his allies): but when this efsential service was performed, the payment of the money was evaded This breach of treaty led to the invasion and conquest of the Rohilla country, the following year, 1774. A considerable tract of land in the Dooab, was also conquered from the Jats, and other adventurers; by which the boundary of Oude was advanced westward within 25 miles of Agra; north-westward, to the upper part of the navigable course of the Ganges; and south-westward, to the Jumnah river. In the following year (1775), on the death of Sujah Dowlah, and the accefsion of his son Azuph, a new treaty was made with the British government, by which the quantum of the subsidy for the use of the brigade was increased; and the province of Benares, which produced a clear revenue of 240,000l. per annum, was ceded to the Company.

The war with the Poonah, or western Mahrattas, of which we have already spoken (in page lxxxvii), occasioned the march of a brigade acrofs the continent to the side of Bombay and Surat, in 1778-9. This is, perhaps, the most brilliant epoch of the British military history in India. The brigade, which consisted of lefs than 7000 men, all native troops, commanded by European officers, marched from the banks of the Jumnah to the western sea, in despite of the Mahrattas, whose empire they traversed almost the whole way. The French war breaking out at this time, and Hyder Ally expecting a communion of interests with the French, he; in the autumn of 1780, broke into the Carnatic with 100,000 troops; and those, both of foot and horse, the very best of their kind that had ever been disciplined by a native of India. His succefs in cutting to pieces Col. Baillie's detachment, and the consequent retreat of the Carnatic army, occasioned the British interests in that quarter to be given up for lost, in the opinion of most people in Europe. Happily, Mr. Hastings and Sir Eyre Coote thought otherwise: and there was sent from Bengal, to the relief of the Carnatic, a brigade of about 7000 men; together with ample supplies of money and provisions. Until the arrival of these troops and supplies, the British poſseſsed nothing more in the Carnatic, than the ground occupied by their camps and fortreſses. Under Sir Eyre Coote, Hyder was succeſsfully combated during two campaigns; at the end of which (October, 1782) he found the poſseſsion of his object, the Carnatic, at so great a distance, that he appeared to be sincerely desirous of peace. So vast an army as he brought into the field, could not long be supported in it, by the revenues of Mysore alone; and the Carnatic was quite exhausted. Anticipation of revenue in Asiatic governments, has an immediate destructive effect; and cannot often be repeated. Hyder therefore saw the neceſsity of quitting his ambitious projects; and probably would never have pursued them, had he not expected a more early and effectual co-operation on the side of the French; with whose aſsistance he hoped to effect our expulsion, in a campaign or two. But he became, perhaps, more jealous of the French than of the English; and had the peace of Paris left the Carnatic in his hands, instead of Mahomed Ally's, the French would eventually have been on a worse footing than they are now likely to be: for he certainly never intended that they should aſsume any character in it, beyond that of merchants; although their object was the obtaining of a territorial revenue; without which, they well know, no European power can easily effect any thing against another, already in poſseſsion of one. In this disposition of mind, Hyder died soon*

* The character of the late Hyder Ally appearing to me to be but little understood in this part of the world, I have ventured to attempt an outline of it. His military succeſs, founded on the improvement of discipline; attention to merit of every kind; conciliation of the different tribes that served under his banners; contempt of state and ceremony, except what naturally arose from the dignity of his character; and his consequent economy in personal expences (the different habits of which, form the chief distinction of what is called Character

after; and was succeeded by his son Tippoo, who seemed determined to prosecute the war. It was supposed that an attack of Tippoo's provinces, on the west of India, would, by giving an immediate entry into the most valuable part of his dominions, draw him from the Carnatic: and although there could be little doubt of its producing this effect, yet that part of the plan, which regarded the retreat, or security of the troops afterwards, does not appear to have been so well concerted. The deplorable end of this detachment,* which was commanded by General Matthews, is too well known. At last, Tippoo finding that the Mahrattas, his natural enemies, were at peace with the English, and consequently at liberty to pursue their ancient enmities; and moreover that the French had left him; he condescended, though reluctantly, to make peace: and matters were restored nearly to the condition they were in, before the commencement of hostilities. This peace was signed in March, 1784, at Mangalore.

During the whole course of Sir Eyre Coote's warfare with Hyder Ally, it appeared, that nothing decisive could be accomplished, while the latter poſseſsed so large a body of excellent cavalry, together with draught cattle so superior to ours, that his guns were always drawn off, and their retreat covered, although his army was beaten. The inconveniences arising from the want of a sufficient body of cavalry, may, perhaps, be incurable; but with early and proper attention, we might surely have our choice of draught cattle.

among ordinary princes) together with his minute attention to matters of finance, and the regular payment of his army; all these together, raised Hyder as far above the princes of Hindoostan, as the great qualities of the late Pruſsian monarch raised him above the generality of European princes: and hence I have ever considered Hyder as the FREDERICK of the East. Cruelty was the vice of Hyder: but we are to consider that Hyder's ideas of mercy, were regulated by an Asiatic standard; and it is not improbable that he might rate his own character for moderation and clemency, as far above those of Tamerlane, Nadir Shah, and Abdalla, as he rated his discipline above theirs.

Sir Eyre Coote survived Hyder only about five months. It is a remarkable circumstance that the commanders in chief of two armies, opposed to each other, should both die natural deaths, within so short a space of time.

* In April, 1783.

We have slightly mentioned a general confederacy of the powers of Hindoostan, against the British. The Nizam or Soubah of the Deccan, having taken disgust at the conduct of the Madras government towards him, in 1779; determined on a very deep revenge. This was no lefs than to engage all the principal powers of Hindoostan and the Deccan to join in a confederacy to expel the British. The Poonah Mahrattas were already engaged, and Hyder preparing; there remained the Nizam himself, and the Berar Mahratta.* Each party was to pursue a particular scheme of attack, suited to his local position and means. Hyder was of course, to attack the Carnatic: the Nizam, the circars: the Poonah Mahrattas were to keep the Guzerat army, under Goddard, employed; and the Berar Mahratta was to invade and lay waste the Bengal and Bahar provinces. It has been the fate of most of the grand confederacies that we meet with in history, that they have terminated rather in mutual blame, than mutual congratulation. The truth is, that they are seldom, if ever, pursued with the same unity of action, and energy, that are displayed by single states. Some are more deeply interested than others: one fears that another will be too much aggrandized; and a third is compelled to take part, contrary to his wishes. In the present case, the Poonah Mahratta and Hyder were each pursuing their proper, original plans, which had no reference to the particular object of the confederacy: the projector (the Nizam) had probably no intention ever to act at all: and the Berar Mahratta, appeared to act on compulsion: for although the Berar army *did* march, it was contrived that it should never arrive at the projected scene of action. Be it as it will, it was an awful moment for the British interests in India. The speedy pacification of the Nizam, and the money advanced to the Berar army at Cattack (call it by what denomination we may, subsidy, or

* It has been said, that Nudjuff Cawn, who in latter times erected for himself a principality in the soubah of Agra, made a fifth party in this confederacy. Of this circumstance, I am not sufficiently informed.

loan) were means very opportunely used by the Bengal government. Indeed the whole conduct of the war was such as reflected the highest honour on that government: and when we succefsively were made acquainted with the news of the capitulation of the whole Bombay army in 1779; of the total annihilation of the flower of the Madras army in 1780; the approach of the Berar army towards Bengal in 1781 (which seemed to preclude all pofsibility of relieving the Carnatic by a brigade from Bengal), together with the grand confederacy: I say, when the news of all these misfortunes and threatening appearances reached Europe, every one had made up his mind to the certain lofs of some capital settlement, or to the mutiny of one of the grand armies, for want of pay: and many persons thought that they saw the total destruction of the British influence and power in India. How then were we surprised, to find, that notwithstanding all these miscarriages, we were able, soon after, not only to face, but to seek the enemy in every quarter: and to hear of victories gained by the British armies, when we expected that even the very ground they fought on, had been abandoned to our enemies!

The establishment of the British power in the Mogul empire, has given a totally different aspect to the political face of that country, from what it would have worn, had no such power ever existed. No one can doubt that the Mahrattas, had they been left to pursue their plans of conquest, would have acquired Corah and Allahabad in 1772, as well as the Rohilla country in 1773: and afterwards they might have over-run, at their leisure, the province of Oude, and its dependencies. The British interference prevented this. On the other hand, Hyder might have kept pofsefsion of the Carnatic. Some may be tempted to ask whether Hyder might not be as good a sovereign as Mahomed Ally; or the Mahrattas, as Azuph Dowlah? Whatsoever may be the answers to these questions, they have no reference to the British politics; which require that Hyder or Tippoo, should not pofsefs the Carnatic, in addition to

Mysore: and that the Mahrattas should not poſseſs Oude, or Rohilcund.

I believe there are many who think that the British might have extended their poſseſsions in Hindoostan, *ad libitum:* however, one of the greatest of our Indian statesmen, Lord Clive, thought that the Bengal provinces and the circars, together with a moderate tract of land round Madras,* and the island of Salsette, near Bombay, were fully equal to the measure of good policy, and to our powers of keeping poſseſsion. Nor have his succeſsors *acted* otherwise: for our wars since his time, have not been wars of conquest for ourselves; though erroneously represented as such. The late war in India may convince such persons, as require conviction on the subject, that conquests made either on Tippoo, or the Mahrattas, could not be preserved with such an army as the revenues of the conquered tracts would support. We got poſseſsion of Bengal and the circars, under circumstances particularly favourable: such as may never occur again.

The Bengal provinces which have been in our actual poſseſsion near 23 years (that is, from the year 1765, to the present, 1788), have, during that whole period, enjoyed a greater share of tranquillity than any other part of India; or indeed, than those provinces had ever experienced since the days of Aurungzebe. During the above period of 23 years, no foreign enemy has made any incursion into any part of them, nor has any rebellion happened in any of the provinces (the very inconsiderable one of the zemindar of Jungleterry, in 1774, excepted).† Previous to the establishment of our influence, invasions were frequent, particularly by the Mahrattas: and one province or other was ever in rebellion; owing to a want of energy in the ruling power; an ill paid,

* That is, the Carnatic being already the property of another. No one can doubt but that it would be more for our advantage to have the largest part of the Carnatic in our own hands, than in those of Mahomed Ally; although the whole revenue of it should be laid out in its defence. But the Carnatic is our weak side, in more respects than one.

† The province of Benares, in which a rebellion happened in 1781, is distinct from the Bengal provinces. It was ceded to the British, as has been observed above, in 1775.

and mutinous army; or an excefs of delegated power. Those who know what miseries are brought on a country, by its being the seat of war, will know how to appreciate the value of such a blefsing, as that of having the horrors of war removed to a distance from our habitations. There are, doubtlefs, evils that are inseparable from the condition of a tributary state, where the supreme ruling power resides at the distance of half the circumference of the globe: but these are, I hope, amply balanced by the advantages of military protection: and it is a fact not to be controverted, that the Bengal provinces have a better government, and are in a better state, as to agriculture and manufactures, than any other of the Asiatic countries, China alone excepted. But this state is doubtlefs very susceptible of improvement, even under a despotic government: though it unfortunately happens, that the grand object for which the Bengal provinces are held, militates against the ease and happinefs of their inhabitants: for there can be no inducement to increase a national income for the purpose of finally enriching another nation.

The state into which Hindoostan has fallen, since the downfall of the Mogul empire, is materially different from what it was, before it was united under the Mahomedan conquerors. It was then parcelled out into several moderate kingdoms, which appear to have preserved a degree of balance among themselves: but now, Hindoostan and the Deccan may be said to consist of six principal states, which hold as tributaries, or feudatories, all the inferior ones; of which there are many. The reader will not be at a lofs to know that the two Mahratta states, the Nizam, Tippoo, the Seiks, and the British, are those I mean: for whatever verbal distinctions may be made, a compulsive alliance is at least a dependant, if not in fact, a tributary situation.

I have ran over the events of the late war in India, with a brevity which may probably be deemed censurable, considering their importance and variety. But I reflected that the accounts of those events are in every body's hands; and that every day produces some fresh matter, illustrative of them. The history of events that have happened, and that have also been recorded, in our own times, may be referred to, by the aid of memory; their connexion or dependency traced; and their chronology ascertained: but it was necefsary to bring the events of a remoter period more within the view of the reader; the public records of those times being lefs copious, as the scenes recorded were lefs interesting to public curiosity.

5

IMPERIAL EYEWITNESSING

Nothing perhaps exercised the English imagination and constructed outrage as much as the practice of sati/suttee.[1] Suttee and female infanticide, in fact, were the two crucial themes within the civilisational and moral imperialist discourse of the late 18th and early 19th centuries, and anticipated the widow remarriage, women's education and 'age of consent' debates of the 19th century.

Documentation of the practice in British records is aplenty, not to mention the parliamentary debates that then coalesced into William Bentinck's initiative of banning sati in 1829. The bulk of the material circulating in the periodical press in England purported to be eyewitness accounts and took the form of a personalised report that recorded the 'shock' of the observer. We see instances like this in such accounts:

> It was impossible to hear the woman, had she groaned, or even cried aloud, on account of the mad noise of the people, and it was impossible for her to stir or struggle, on account of the bamboos, which are held down upon them like the levers of a press. We made much objection to their using these bamboos, and insisted it was using force to prevent the woman getting up, when the fire burnt her. But they declared it was only done to keep the pile from burning down. We could not bear to see more, but left them, exclaiming loudly against the murder, and full horror at what he had seen. (Nayar 2013, 19)

The above appeared in *The Weekly Entertainer* of 25 June 1804.

Based on such accounts in weeklies and periodicals, activists wrote commentaries that called for immediate action against the social evil as a part of England's duty towards the blighted heathen, of which James Peggs' *India's Cries to Humanity* (1830) was well known. Visual texts also appeared. For example, the woman being led to the funeral pyre of her husband as a sati was the subject of William Skelton's engraving after William Hodges's account in *Travels in India, During the Years 1780, 1781, 1782, and 1783* (1793).

British attitudes towards sati changed with their own changing status, argues Arvind Sharma:

> As traders they had largely been spectators on the Indian scene, now they became actors. In due course this change of status showed a change of attitude towards *sati*. Whereas the earlier attitude had been one of passive reaction, of observation and criticism, it could now be one of active intervention, of prevention and abolition. (1988, 6)

But it was not easy for the Englishman to *witness* sati. Claudius Buchanan wrote in 1813: 'unless an Englishman comes casually upon the scene, he never can, generally speaking, see a burning. The only expedient is, to desire your Hindoo servants to mention when they hear that one is about to take place' (iii–iv). William Ward the missionary claimed he was an eyewitness to many such instances in his *An Account of the Writings, Religion and Manners of the Hindoos*, and elsewhere documented 250 satis in Bengal alone (1822, 3: 308–41).

Joseph Wilson's account appeared in *The Weekly Miscellany* in January 1778.

Structure and Content

John Wilson submitted and published a letter written by one Joseph Wilson, who purportedly witnessed a sati in Bengal. The letter, dated 1 March 1777, is treated as authentic, as is the report by the eyewitness. John Wilson suggests that this report is evidence that contradicts the claim made by one William Guthrie in his *Geographical Grammar* that sati as a practice has disappeared from India (15).[2]

The Joseph Wilson letter opens with the statement that he took notes 'of all that had passed' and pronounces the authenticity of the narrative: 'you may depend upon the following narration to be strictly true'. He gives the date and location of the incident (2 September 1776 in the bazaar at 'Cansbang') thus underscoring the I-was-there trope commonplace in travel accounts. He also gives the name of the woman, Jananca, and her husband, Otran Gose (15).

The account, covering a day and a night, opens with the husband's death and the woman's preparations for sati. She summons her friends and was 'very merry', he writes (15). It is however not clear how Joseph Wilson witnessed the events inside the Gose [Ghose?] household—events that *preceded* the sati, which he, of course, claims he had witnessed. After the man dies, the son comes to Joseph Wilson and asks for permission to have the funeral pyre in the bazaar, close to Wilson's house.

Wilson claims the woman should not be forced to commit sati, and the son assures him that it was an honour for the entire family that his widowed mother had decided to do so, and that there was no pressure on her. In fact, says the son, he had assured his mother that he would give her 'two rupees a month for life' (16). When the procession arrived at the venue, the woman issued 'several orders to the people in making the pile' (16). Wilson states that he approached her and queried whether she was doing this of 'her own free will and consent' (16). She assures him this was the case, and thanks him for permitting the sati. She also requests that she not be opposed by Wilson and tells him that if he does oppose her, she would 'make away with herself' (16).

Wilson then describes the rituals wherein she worships the husband's dead body. The widow then 'mounted the pile without help' (16). The fire is lit and 'both were burnt to ashes in less than an hour' (17). Wilson comments:

> I believe she soon died, for she never moved, though there was no weight upon her but what she might have easily overset, had she any inclination. It was an entirely voluntary act, and she was as much in her senses as ever she was in her life. (17)

Wilson concludes with: 'the above, I assure you, is a true account of what I saw' (17).

The Voluntary Sati

Wilson's emphasis on the woman's agency holds centre stage in his account. The claim that he had approached the woman and she had assured him that she would, if prevented from the sati, one day take her own life, is meant to indicate that there was no pressure on her to martyr herself on the husband's pyre. He also draws the portrait of the widow as one cheerful to the last, again reinforcing her choice and agency in undertaking this act.

The sati, then, is a woman who has chosen to make this ultimate sacrifice and die horrifically, along with her husband. Wilson assures us that she is determined to do so because she has promised that she would die, no matter that the English gentleman may thwart her *now*. The statement that she refused the offered economic support by her son, as Wilson reports, serves to amplify the choice she made—to be *not* dependent on her family/son for her widowed life.

There is also the report that her sati would be a matter of honour for the family—a comment Wilson claims the son makes. With this, Wilson is also locating himself in the private sphere of the household into which, as an outsider, he ought not to step in: it is a matter of *family* honour. The woman then is heroic: she is upholding the family honour because, after all, it is the woman's task and responsibility to do so. For the white man, this voluntary and courageous act inscribes the widow within the established trope of the woman as a placeholder of tradition and honour—and this is one he is not willing to question or abrogate. In Paul Courtright's summary:

> In the imagined India of Western experience and interpretation, *sati* came to stand for the whole of Hinduism as an irrational, perverse, and heroic religious orientation to life. (1995, 185)

Taken together, Wilson implies steely determination and a certain heroism to the woman's acts: she is cheerful, she is determined and she is independent to the last. By focusing on her ability to be cheerful, to issue orders so as to ensure the correctness of the ritual, and her refusal to cry out or step out of the engulfing flames, Wilson draws the portrait of a courageous woman. She could have, he says, thrown off the weight on her 'had she any inclination'. Then, by reiterating that 'she was as much in her senses as ever she was in her life', Wilson takes away the possibility of doubt that the widow was traumatised by grief or had been psychologically manipulated into sati. It was, in Wilson's view, a conscious, deliberate and completely sensible act.

Here, Ania Loomba's argument, made via Romila Thapar's work, that 'the *sati*, like the warrior, dies positively for something, instead of negatively to escape a miserable life', appears relevant because of Wilson's focus on the widow's insistence on independence. As Loomba puts it: 'such a comparison obviously deflects attention from the miserable fate that awaited, and still threatens most Indian widows' (1993, 210). Wilson does not question whether the amount of two rupees was indeed offered by the son as a form of maintenance fund, or whether the amount was sufficient for his widowed mother to lead a dignified and independent life. Wilson thus assumes that the woman's decision was taken despite the offer of protection and support, and therefore, implicitly, she has asserted her agency. This is the 'idealisation of the burning widow', as Loomba puts it (210).

The tone of admiration in Wilson's account is just an undercurrent, but it exists nevertheless, and emblematises the (Western) male's fantasy of genuine female devotion (Loomba 210). The Indian not only did not need rescue (least of all by the Englishman), she issues a threat that she would take her life if he thwarted her and thus commits herself to the husband in life and in death, embodying, thereby, the perfect wife.[3] Wilson implicitly underscores the (Hindu/Brahmin) woman's *desire* and *will* to die along with her husband. Sati, in Wilson's reading, is voluntary.

At no point does Wilson wonder whether this agency he ascribes to the widow is in any way constrained and if she is acting in severely restricted conditions. He also, in the process, eschews presenting her as any kind of *victim* (as commentators have shown, colonial discourse on sati was organised into two poles: the widow as victim and the widow as agential, as heroines or as pathetic victims. See Mani, 162). Whether her calmness and determination were born of a fear of bringing her family into disrepute is not a question that arises in Wilson's mind, of course (Mani, 164).

The Eyewitness

There is no voice of the sati herself, as numerous critics have noted in their readings of the colonial discourse on the subject (Spivak 1988). This means the telling of the sati tale or event was entirely the (white) man's doing, and hence the emphasis of Wilson on his being-thereness.

The Englishman as authoritative *eyewitness* and *author* was ensured by the very condition of colonial dominance: this was the voice of rationality, of the law and keen empirical observation. The quantum of details given in Wilson's account is meant to serve as indexes to the authenticity of what he narrates. As Lata Mani has argued, 'the bulk of the narrative is given over to a scrutiny of the widow, her demeanour, and her actions' (161). Wilson observes the widow's cheerful demeanour, her steely will and the confidence with which she orders the ritual processes. Later, he records her calmness in ascending the funeral pile. This is almost a psychological evaluation of the 'victim' by an impartial observer. When Wilson concludes that she was in her senses, the psychological profile is complete.

This account of Wilson's close observation and the significance of personal 'eye witnessing' are modes of verification and validation. In Wilson's case, this is compounded by the authority of the note taking, which casts Wilson in the role of ethnographer and observer. In the process, the woman/widow becomes the subject of the Englishman's gaze. The note taking, which he mentions at the very beginning of his letter, assures us that the widow and the events that follow are not the products of his imagination but rather the products of an intensive study. The study and its published version's structure imply the quest for an (imperial) understanding of the nature of the act and the ordering of the events into a suitable narrative.

The study and its report follow a specific pattern: contexts (time, setting), background (the names of the protagonists, the husband's dying), process (from the son's request to Wilson, the widow's own exchange with Wilson, the various rituals and ceremonies, to the burning on the pyre) and finally the eyewitnesses' *concluding* remarks or 'findings'. This last includes the statements about the widow's sanity and the voluntariness of her act. With this, Wilson has ordered the event into a systematic narrative form.

The eyewitness performed another crucial role, one stemming from the colonial recognition that sati was a religious ritual and hence sacred and off-limits for colonial interventions. One notes Wilson's emphasis that he insisted the act had to be voluntary and that he would not accept forced burning/murder. Thus, his role at the sati was merely to ensure the process was voluntary on the part of the widow. The British were not, as individuals or in the form of their legal system, competent to discuss Hindu rituals. Therefore, people like Wilson—whose permission was sought for the sati, as he records, implying he was a man of consequence and authority in the area—could only observe the ritual. In case there were signs that she did not wish to die, the white man/observer would intervene and enable the sati to get off the pyre (Tschurenev 2004, 76).

That is, Wilson has to balance the religious aspect of sati, which he encounters in the form of the son appealing to him, the rituals he (over)sees, with the modern, secular view of the woman's agency. Here, Courtright's argument about the frames of interpreting sati resonates with the victim/agent binary of the sati-woman:

> [Sati] exposes the rupture between two incommensurate views of reality. On the one side is a religious view in which lives travel from incarnation to incarnation, and self-sacrificial actions have effects that go well beyond the immediate circumstances in which they are produced. On the other side is a modern view according to which individuals "make themselves" in social environments that are more or less hospitable to a person's self-fulfillment. In the former view, sati is the ideal heroic and sacred action; in the latter, it is a paradigm of powerlessness. (1994, 29)

In the case of the colonial eyewitnesses, their horror at the spectacle and their contempt at Hindu rituals was also, often, tempered by their awe at the woman's courage, even going so far as to call them 'superhuman' (Courtright 1994, 46).

English Presence

Wilson insinuates that he was prepared to intervene in the ritual if the widow demonstrated anything less than voluntariness. In this insinuation, one which would gather strength from the early decades of the next century, we can see the anterior moments of what Clare Midgley terms 'evangelical manhood' (2000, 110). Midgley writes of an

> eighteenth-century literary tradition of the sati as a tragic victim rescued by a chivalrous British man reshaping it to create in Heber the ideal of evangelical manhood: sensitivity combined with steadfastness and moral authority. (110)

Wilson does not explicitly state his chivalrous intentions here but he claims he informs the son: 'I should take care that no force was used to burn her against her will' (16). He also claims he enquired with the widow herself whether 'it was her own free will and consent' (16). One draws by inference the theme of chivalry and evangelical manhood but also of the English authority of the 'man-on-the-spot' (Tidrick 1990): at that point, the Englishman is the sole authority to determine whether the woman has voluntarily embraced sati.

In other words, we only have Wilson's statements about the true nature of the woman, her intentions and contexts that *produce* her as not just a bereaved widow but as a keeper of the family honour, a sati. He is present to ensure that the process is in accordance with the principle of free will, but he also respects the ritual as a part of the custom followed by the family and the community.

When Wilson pays attention to every stage of the ritual process, he not only fashions himself as an ethnographic observer but also as a quasi-judicial presence ensuring that everything that is going on is in accordance with custom and tradition. Now, where this tradition may have contradicted the principle of free will and the woman's agency, this contradiction was resolvable—at least in the way Wilson presents the events—only by the Englishman. The woman's determination to go ahead with the sati, Wilson decides, was entirely in consonance with custom. He confirms this later when she is getting ready. In short, Wilson also functions as a custodian of the native's custom and tradition. As Mani puts it in her study: 'what was at stake was not women but tradition', and this is what the Englishman is guarding (153). Here, it is not made clear whether Wilson *knows* the Indian/Hindu tradition and custom. His scholarship on the practice of sati is not mentioned. He affirms from the widow and the family that their decision and the practice is indeed founded on custom, *and he takes their word for it.*

The Englishman fashions himself as an authority then, and the adjudicator on the ritual and process. Taking the words of the family and the sati herself as indisputable, and adding the weight of his (white man's) words in the form of the document, Wilson *becomes* a guardian of Indian/Hindu textual traditions and custom. Here Wilson looks forward to the great sati debates of the early 19th century.

Wilson as the voice of interpretive authority is anterior to William Bentinck and the advocates of the sati ban where Bentinck as governor general sought to affirm that the practice was as prescribed by the shastras.[4] To this end, he consulted religious scholars to seek clarity on the scriptural evidence. The question was put to the pundits of the Nizamut Adawlut and the answer received was as follows:

> *As it sometimes happens among persons professing the Hindoo religion, that upon the death of a man his widow becomes a suttee, i.e. burns herself with the body of her deceased husband, you are therefore asked, whether a woman is enjoined by the Shaster voluntarily to burn herself with the body of her husband, or is prohibited; and what are the conditions prescribed by the Shaster on such occasions? You are desired to give an answer in the course of fifteen days. 4th March 1805.*
>
> Answer. Having duly considered the question proposed by the court, I now answer it to the best of my knowledge:—Every woman, of the four casts (Brahmin, *khetry*, *bues* and *soodur*) is permitted to burn herself with the body of her husband, provided she has not infant children, nor is pregnant, nor in a state of uncleanness, nor under the age of puberty; in any of which cases she is not allowed to burn herself with her husband's body.
>
> But a woman who has infant children, and can procure another person to undertake the charge of bringing them up, is permitted to burn.
>
> It is contrary to law, as well as to the usage of the country, to cause any woman to burn herself against her wish, by administering drugs to stupefy or intoxicate her.

> When women burn themselves, they pronounce the *sunkulp*, and perform other prescribed ceremonies previously to burning.
>
> This rests upon the authority of *Anjira, Vijasa* and *Vrihapati, mooni.*
>
> (Parliamentary Papers, Vol. 18, No. 749, 1821, cited in Nayar 2013, 98–99, emphasis in original)[5]

Thus it came about that when sati was banned, the governor general in the Council of Fort St George, Madras wrote to the Court of Directors on 12 February 1830:

> Having received from the Supreme Government a copy of the Regulation enacted by the Governor General in Council, for declaring the practice of Suttee to be illegal, we carefully examined all the texts of Hindoo Law which bear upon this subject… (Parliamentary Papers, No. 550, 1830, cited in Nayar 2013, 415)

But this validation of what the scriptures say does not suffice, for the task and responsibility of ensuring the actual process fits the scriptures is assigned to the man on the spot. M.H. Turnbull of Fort William issued orders to the effect that, if there has been a sati, the local police officers and/or magistrate had to enquire and determine whether the widow had indeed 'attained the age of puberty, viz., her 16th year', whether she was pregnant, menstruating or was nursing an infant', before permitting the sati (Parliamentary Papers, No. 749, 1821, cited in Nayar, 111–115).

The debate around the practice, as Mani persuasively argues, was primarily infused with an interest in defining the tradition—and had little to do with the woman *per se* (see also Nair 1994). The Englishman, by his acts of *personal and embodied* interpretation, bestowed the events with legal approval and in the process affirmed the sanctity of the Hindu practice. Wilson's action thus looks forward to the Turnbull injunction that the local police officer had to 'enquire and determine' whether the widow had acquired the legal age and whether she was qualified for sati.

Following Kathryn Tidrick's argument, I suggest that well before the furious sati debate of the later decades, Wilson was, in his account, casting himself in the role of a paternalist guardian. In addition to the authority of interpretation that he ascribes to himself (which, as noted before, would be formalised in the form of Turnbull's orders), he also takes on the role of a moral guardian. He leads by personal example, offering to 'free' the widow if she was being forced to commit sati. In Tidrick's words, 'the evangelical belief in the changing power of personal example became conflated, in the political sphere, with a belief in its power to control' (4). And this conflation is precisely what Wilson's tract presents: in the event of the sati, he is a political authority who interprets the ritual's legal aspects and affirms its legitimacy and a moral guardian who personally supervises the event. He is both the white male authority figure and the protective leader who leads by personal example. He collaborates with the native custom when he endorses it, and yet he represents the grand majesty of the Company's rule when he verifies the spirit and substance of the custom and satisfies himself that it is legitimate.

The question of legitimacy would, over the next few decades, also appear in the form of the educational philosophy imparted to the Englishmen who were to come out to India as administrators. They had to be 'imperial minded', as Rosanne Rocher terms it (1993, 219). This educational philosophy that trained the would-be administrator included not just an emphasis on the acquisition of orientalist learning but on specific moral attitudes towards the subjects they would eventually govern. For example, as early as 1803, the cadets for the administrative services had to address topics such as this:

> The suicide of Hindoo widows by burning themselves with the bodies of their deceased husbands is a practice repugnant to the natural feelings, and inconsistent with moral duty. (Rocher 1993, 218)

Rocher notes that the administrators, despite their intentions and training, came with

> cultural and other blinders; it did not exempt them from experiencing difficulties in understanding foreign concepts and from interpreting them through the lens of their own culture and of the dominant thought processes of their times. (219)

The Rocher argument is about the 19th-century English administration but, I suggest, it is prefigured in the Wilson stance towards the events of sati that he witnessed. Wilson wishes to understand the custom, validate it and ensure its proper execution. The 'man on the spot' may be morally perturbed by what he sees and shocked at the cultural differences, but he continues to remain steadfast in his task of ensuring the correctness of ritual protocol and of monitoring the woman's demeanour and (ostensible) willingness to go through with the sati.

***

The Wilson text looks forward to several of the 19th-century debates and concerns regarding sati. In the process, it signals the quest for knowledge of local practices—the note taking!—and the need to understand the culturally different customs.

The text also presents the Englishman as a moral authority and as the person entitled and empowered to interpret the proceedings. He embodies, in other words, epistemic and legal authority. Sati then becomes the site for a larger colonial discourse to operate.

It is important to note that the colonial discourse on sati was not uniform. While many of the normative debates were informed by case studies from Bengal, the discourse was different in the case of the princely states. Because the 'political configurations of the princely states meant that the, albeit refracted, voices of the Indian elite penetrated the official colonial discourse in this area more frequently than was the case in Bengal' (Major 2011, 10). Thus, writes Andrea Major:

> When dealing with sati in the princely states, colonial discourse on the subject underwent subtle, but significant changes, including a reinsertion of elements of heroism and female agency, as sati was repositioned as a Rajput rather than a Bengali issue. (6)[6]

THE

ANNUAL REGISTER,

OR A VIEW OF THE

HISTORY, POLITICS,

AND

LITERATURE,

For the YEAR 1777.

LONDON:

Printed for J. Dodsley, in Pall-Mall, 1778.

to his bed, and in a few days died; leaving his friend Mr. Robe to enjoy the fruits of his mirth.'

Authentic Account of the Burning of a Gentoo *Woman, at her own request, at* Azumabad.

IT being asserted by Mr. Guthrie, in his Geographical Grammar, p. 536, and some other authors, that the custom of the Gentoo women burning themselves with their deceased husbands was disused in India, I desire you would insert the following Extract of a Letter from Mr. Joseph Wilson, at Azumabad, (lately called Cansbang) in the kingdom of Bengal, by which it appears that custom is yet kept up and practised. I give it in his own words.

March 1, 1777. Yours,
Broomhead. JOHN WILSON.

" I WAS last September an eye witness to a Gentoo woman burning with her husband; and as I stood by all the time, and took notes of all that passed, you may depend upon the following narration to be strictly true; I mean the ceremonies that were used by these people, who had always got their bread by their labour, and indeed were so very poor, that the son was obliged to go from house to house to beg fire-wood to burn them with: the richer people are more curious, and have their piles made of a sweet-scented wood called Sandal, and much larger than the people I am speaking of can possibly afford.

" *The Account of* Jananca, *Wife of* Otram Gose, *who was burnt alive with her Husband,* Sept. 2, 1776, *at the Head of the Bazaar at* Cansbang.

" AS soon as her husband was given over by the Doctor, she sent for a Bramin, and declared her intentions to burn herself, son, and daughter, (which was the whole of the family together,) which some neighbours endeavoured as much as possible to dissuade her from, but all to no purpose, and from that time refused eating any thing, except a few plantains and betel-nuts. She sent for all her friends, who staid with her all night, and with whom she was very merry. In the morning the man died, and his son came to me to ask leave to burn his father and mother in the Bazaar (or market-place), as it belongs to the plantation, and is close to my house. I told him very well; but that I should take care no force was used to make her burn against her will. He told me he was so far from forcing, that he had offered her two rupees a month for life; but yet could not help saying it would reflect an honour on his family for his mother to burn. The man was scarce cold before he and his wife were carried upon men's shoulders, she sitting by him; and having provided herself with some couries (small shells which go current for money here), she distributed them amongst the populace, together with rice fried in butter and sugar very plentifully, as she passed from her house to the place of burning; where, when she arrived, they had not begun to make the pile: so she was set down, together with her dead husband, and gave several orders to the people in making the pile, and was ſo far from being in the leaſt afraid, that ſhe rejoiced much. I went up to her, and aſked her if it was her own free will and conſent? She told me it was, and that ſhe was much oblig-ed to me for giving her liberty to burn in that place, and deſired I would not offer to oppoſe it, as ſhe would certainly make away with herſelf, was ſhe prevented. She ſat there, talking with her friends and neighbours, till the pile was ready, which was above an hour, and then went a little diſtance off, where the deceaſed was alſo carried, and were both waſhed with Ganges water, and clean cloaths put on them. The ſon of the deceaſed then put a painted paper crown, or cap, on his father's head, of the ſame kind as is uſual for them to wear at their marriages; and a Bramin woman brought four lamps burn-ing, and put one of them into the woman's hand, and placed the other three round her upon the ground: all the time ſhe held the lamp in her hand, the Bramin wo-man was repeating ſome prayers to her; which when finiſhed, ſhe put a garland of flowers round her head, and then gave the ſon of the deceaſed, who was ſtanding cloſe by, a ring made of graſs, which ſhe put upon one of his fingers, and an earthern plate full of boiled rice and plantains mixed up together, which he immediately offered to his deceaſed father, put-ting it three times to his mouth, and then in the ſame manner to his mother, who did not taſte it. The deceaſed was ſupported all this time, and ſet upon his breech cloſe by his wife, who never ſpoke after this, but made three ſelams to her huſband, by putting her hands upon the ſoles of his feet, and then upon her own head. The deceaſed was then carried away and laid upon the pile, and his wife immediately followed, with a pot under her arm, containing 21 cou-ries, 21 pieces of ſaffron, 21 pons for betel-nut, and the leaf made up ready for chewing; one little piece of iron, and one piece of ſandal-wood. When ſhe got to the pile, ſhe looked a little at her huſband, who was lying upon it, and then walked ſeven times round it; when ſhe ſtopped at his feet, and made the ſame obeiſance to him as before. She then mounted the pile without help, and laid herſelf down by her huſband's ſide, putting the pot ſhe carried with her cloſe to her head; which as ſoon as done, ſhe claſped her huſ-band in her arms; and the ſon, who was ſtanding ready with a wiſp of ſtraw lighted in his hand, put the blaze of it three times to his father and mother's mouths, and then ſet the pile on fire all round, whilſt the populace threw reeds and light wood upon them; and they were both burnt to aſhes in leſs than an hour. I believe ſhe ſoon died, for ſhe never moved, though there was no weight upon her but what ſhe might have eaſily overſet, had ſhe had any inclina-tion. It was intirely a voluntary act, and ſhe was as much in her ſenſes as ever ſhe was in her life. I forgot to mention that ſhe had her forehead painted with red paint, which ſhe ſcraped off with her nails, and diſtributed amongſt her friends, and alſo gave them chewed betel out of her mouth, for which favours every one ſeem-ed very ſolicitous. The above, I aſſure you, is a true account of what I ſaw.

Account of the Inhabitants of Wallachia, *by Baron* Inigo Born.

THEIR manner of living is extremely rough and ſavage. They want religion, arts and ſciences. Their children are from their firſt infancy waſhed every day in the open air, in warm water, and then ſwathed in coarſe linen or woollen cloth. The difference of the ſeaſons and the weather makes herein no difference. From the fifth to the twelfth or fourteenth year of their age they are left with the herds and flocks to attend them; however, the girls are taught in the ſame time waſhing, baking, ſpinning, making needle-work, weaving, and ſo on. From the fourteenth year they are brought up and employed in huſbandry. Kukuruz, or maiz, is their chief object of agriculture. However, they ſow likewiſe oats, barley, and wheat. They diſtil from the fruits of trees, which they plant in great plenty, a ſort of brandy, called rakie, which they are very fond of. Their meat is as ſimple as their dreſs. Biſcuit of coarſe grinded maiz, baked under aſhes, which they call malai, ſome fleſh, milk, cheeſe, beans, and other vegetables, are their common food. Their dreſs is various; but generally it conſiſts of the following articles. The men wear long white woollen trowſers, as the Hungarians, but wider; ſoles of raw ſkin tied about the feet inſtead of ſhoes; a ſhirt open on the breaſt; a woollen jacket or coat, tight around the waiſt, with long ſleeves, and a fur cap, or bonnet, for the head. The women have long ſhirts down to the ancles; a brown variegated ſtriped petticoat open on both ſides, and tied with a girdle; a waiſtcoat or garment of coarſe cloth, ſomewhat ſhorter than the ſhirts, and an annular bolſter ſtuffed with hair or ſtraw upon their head, which they cover with a woven cloth. The girls go bare-headed. Their ornaments conſiſt of ear-rings of white or yellow braſs, of coloured glaſs, beads, pearls, glaſs, feathers, and pieces of money faſtened to a ſtring and tied round the head and neck. This ornament makes a ringing, ſo that a fine dreſſed Raize, or Wallachian girl, may very often be heard ſooner than ſeen. They marry very young; and there are married couples, the man not above fourteen; the wife even not twelve years of age. Some manual arts ſeem to be peculiar to them. Scarce any where you will find a cartwright or a weaver; every Wallachian being a cartwright, and every woman a weaver. No woman is ſeen going about without ſome work in hand. What they bring to ſale they carry on their heads. If they have a child to nurſe, it is carried in the ſame manner. The ſpindle is ſticking in their girdle, and all the way they are ſpinning. All their neceſſaries are worked up by themſelves. Scarce any tradeſmen nor any beggars are ſeen among them. What can I ſay to you of their religion? They confeſs the non-united Greek religion, *Græci ritus non unitorum*. But in fact, they have ſcarce more religion than their domeſtic animals, except repeated faſtings, which almoſt take up half

6

IMPERIAL LITERARY

William Jones arrived as a judge of the Supreme Court, Fort William, Calcutta (Kolkata as it was called then) in 1783. He came with a sense of the greatness of the subcontinent's civilisation but was also certain that this same civilisation had stagnated and the people needed to be governed by an absolute power.

Jones, fascinated by Hinduism, Islam, the languages and cultures of the subcontinent, began writing commentaries on these subjects within a year of his arrival, inaugurating his oeuvre, so to speak, with 'Hymn To Camdeo'. This was also the year (1784) that the Asiatick Society would be founded and Jones would provide the motto (still inscribed on a plaque inside the building on Park Street, Calcutta):

> The bounds of investigations will be the geographical limits of Asia, and within these limits its enquiries will be extended to whatever is performed by man or produced by Nature. (cited in Franklin 2011, 19)

At the Asiatick he would, over the years, deliver several 'Discourses', of which the 'Third' would become famous for his account of Sanskrit (by this time Jones had acquired a working knowledge of the language). Jones had a remarkable facility for languages, having come to India with Latin, Greek, French, Italian, German, Persian, Hebrew, Arabic, Spanish and Chinese. He could also write poetry in several of these, besides reading these kinds of literature in the original and even translating from them. He went on to acquire Sanskrit, Turkish, Hindi, and a working knowledge of Pali, Pahalvi, Coptic, Welsh, Syriac, Dutch, Russian and Swedish. The biography of John Shore, who was Lord Teignmouth, cited by Franklin Edgerton in his entry on Jones in *Portraits of Linguists*, stated that Jones knew 28 languages (2002, 10). His library in 1784, as a recent account shows, had 118 Arabic, Persian and Urdu manuscripts, 69 Sanskrit manuscripts and 9 Chinese manuscripts (Lawrence 2021).

Jones was an integral part of the Orientalist regime of Warren Hastings, whose focus on understanding the subcontinent was an instrumentalist one, guided more by the exigencies of colonial rule than the need to broaden Western/European/English epistemes. Jones's talent for languages and his vigorous pursuit of textual materials—from the *Ain-i-Akbari* to the *Laws of Manu* and *Shakuntala*—from the subcontinent enabled the colonial regime, still nascent in terms of an empire, to fit themselves into both, the vacuum left behind by the disappearing Mughals *and* the legacy of rulers like Akbar.

To this end, Jones, with encouragement from Hastings, sought to provide a compendium of Hindu laws so that the British could govern India through their own laws. Here Jones was continuing the tradition of Nathaniel Halhed, who published the *Code of Gentoo Laws* in 1776 when he, Jones, published *Institutes of Hindu Law: or, the Ordinances of Menu* [sic] in 1796.

Jones published his translation of the Sanskrit epic with the title *Sacontalá, or the Fatal Ring*, on 8 October 1789, and it was priced at 12 sicca rupees (30 shillings). It would have an immeasurable impact on Europe, as we shall see, in the next century. It was advertised as follows:

> A work so perfectly novel, curious, and interesting, and the purchase of which amounts only to the price of a play ticket, will no doubt have a large sale; more particularly as the liberal and humane translator has appropriated the amount, free from all expence [sic], to the relief of insolvent debtors. (cited in Franklin 252).

Shakuntala, however, was not Jone's first foray into Eastern poetry or poetics. In his volume *Poems, Consisting Chiefly of Translations from the Asiatick Tongues* (1772), he had appended two essays, of which one was the famous 'On the Poetry of the Eastern Nations'. Here he offers a commentary on Arab poetry and examines the works of major poets like Hafiz. He would declare that 'it is certain … that the poets of *Asia* have as much genius as ourselves' (Jones 2009, ii). After stating the natural beauties of the Arab lands—'*Aden*, in the Eastern dialects, is precisely the same word with *Eden*… a *settled abode*, its second, *delight*, *softness* or *tranquillity*'—Jones announces that both the beautiful and the sublime are available in the land and in its poetry. He then proposes that the Arabs who

> are such admirers of *beauty*, and as they enjoy such ease and leisure, they must naturally be susceptible of *that passion*, which is the true spring and source of agreeable poetry; and we find, indeed, that *love* has a greater share in their poems than any other passion… (77, emphasis in original)

Jones goes on to add that 'this delicacy of their lives and sentiments has insensibly affected their language, and rendered it the softest, as it is one of the richest, in the world' and pronounces, when comparing Hafiz to Shakespeare, what could well be his defining judgement: 'Eastern imagery is not so different from the *European* as we are apt to imagine' (76, 82). Then he comes to his major conclusion: a method to revive European poetry through assimilation, translation and adaptation of the Eastern poets:

> I must once more request, that, in bestowing these praises on the writings of *Asia*, I may not be thought to derogate from the merit of the *Greek* and *Latin* poems, which have justly been admired in every age; yet I cannot but think that our *European* poetry has subsisted too long

> on the perpetual repetition of the same images, and incessant allusions to the same fables: and it has been my endeavour for several years to inculcate this truth, That, if the principal writings of the Asiaticks, which are reposited in our publick libraries, were printed with the usual advantage of notes and illustrations, and if the languages of the Eastern nations were studied in our places of education, where every other branch of useful knowledge is taught to perfection, a new and ample field would be opened for speculation; we should have a more extensive insight into the history of the human mind, we should be furnished with a new set of images and similitudes, and a number of excellent compositions would be brought to light, which future scholars might explain, and future poets might imitate. (85)

Shakuntala, then, would be the manifestation of his own *programmatic* commentary in 'On the Poetry of Eastern Nations'.

A few years after *Shakuntala*, Jones would return to some of these themes and poets in his 'On the Mystical Poetry of the Persians and Hindus' (1792), in which he would translate some of his favourite authors and list the others. Here, turning to Jaydev's *Gitagovinda*, Jones writes that in Hindu poetry, we can 'find the same emblematical theology, which Pythagoras admired and adopted' (1824, Vol. II: 150). In the words of Michael Franklin,

> Jones sought similitude between West and East, and part of this overarching project was to stress the compatibility of Hindu and Islamic mysticism … though fascinated by the dramatic Otherness of India, Jones has found similitude everywhere… (214, 257)

Structure and Content

A brief Preface is followed by a page of Prologue before the text of the play starts.

The Preface tells us how Jones came to Kalidasa's play—on the recommendation of a 'very sensible Brahman, Radhakanta' (2021, 2). He then narrates how he procured a 'correct copy' of the text and, 'assisted by [his] teacher Ramalochana', began translating it (2).

Jones translated the text first into Latin because, as he puts it, that language 'bears so great a resemblance to Sanskrit' and because 'it is more convenient than any modern language for a scrupulous interlineary version' (2). It is from the Latin that Jones then translates *Shakuntala* into English. He adds:

> I then turned it word for word into English, and afterwards, without adding or suppressing any material sentence, disengaged from the stiffness of a foreign idiom, and prepared the faithful translation of the Indian drama. (2)

He also offers comments on the antiquity of Indian drama ('immemorially ancient in the Indian empire'). He declares:

> it was carried to great perfection in its kind, when Vicramáditya, who reigned in the first century before Christ, gave encouragement to poets, philosophers, and mathematicians, at a time when the Britons were as unlettered and unpolished as the army of Hanumat [sic]: nine men of genius, commonly called the nine gems, attended his court, and were splendidly supported by his bounty; and Cálidás is unanimously allowed to have been the brightest of them. (3–4)

Jones famously referred to Kalidasa as 'the Shakespeare of India' (4) before going on to state that 'Indian theatre would fill as many volumes as that of any nation in ancient or modern Europe' (5). He also speculates on the popularity of Kalidasa's play:

> The play of Sacontalá must have been very popular when it was first represented; for the Indian empire was then in full vigour, and the national vanity must have been highly flattered by the magnificent introduction of those kings and heroes in whom the Hindus gloried... (5–6)

Jones concludes with a plea that more Englishmen should learn Sanskrit and translate Kalidasa. He would like to turn to other kinds of (Eastern/ Indian) texts himself:

> It is my anxious wish that others may take the pains to learn Sanscrit, and may be persuaded to translate the works of Cálidás: I shall hardly again employ my leisure in a task so foreign to my professional (which are, in truth, my favourite) studies; and have no intention of translating any other book from any language, except the Law Tract of Menu, and the new Digest of Indian and Arabian laws... (7–8)

The Reception of *Sacontalá*

Jones's translation received favourable reviews. A reviewer wrote in the *Analytical Review* of August 1790:

> This Indian drama, translated by Sir William Jones, if we may credit common fame, will undoubtedly be thought not only by the man of taste, but by the philosopher, a precious *morceau*; for whilst the latter has the opportunity of tracing human passions clothed in a new modification of manners, the former will be immediately gratified by the perusal of some pathetic scenes, and beautiful poetic similes. (361)

The reviewer concludes with praise for the 'elegant translation' for its

> poetic delineation of Indian manners, and the artless touches of human nature, which come home to the human bosom in every climate.... The morality is pure, and the refinement, conspicuous throughout, never degenerating into affectation, an interesting simplicity of manners is uniformly preserved. (373)

A reviewer in the *Monthly Review* of February 1791 says the play

> irresistibly calls forth the tender feelings ... the affecting parts here are the natural parts: every one has felt similar sensations; and every one must be pleased with having them recalled to his imagination. (124)

It adds that the play 'must give pleasure to every reader of taste; and, in particular, to all who are curious in their inquiries concerning ancient oriental literature' (137).

The *Blackwood's Edinburgh* (October 1819–March 1820) review began with:

> Will our readers turn from those fierce, wild and turbulent passions ... as they have been exhibited to them in English and German drama and, going back with us, 'into a long recess of years,' wander for a while among the still and sacred groves of India, and indulge in the fantastic but splendid visions of her allegoric mythology. (417)

The review emphasised the 'half-human, half-divine' nature of the characters, but rejects Jone's adulation of Kalidasa as the Shakespeare of India, arguing that 'neither the human mind nor the human life did ever so exist in India, as to create such kind of faculties as those of Shakespeare'. The reviewer is not very happy at the 'high mythological character' of the play but admits that 'it is delightful to sink away into those old green and noiseless sanctuaries'.

In the next century, Jones's *Sacontalá* would have 46 translations in 12 different languages.

Constructing India via Translation

Jones was, despite his eagerness to establish both the similarity and difference of Eastern (in his writings, this includes the Middle East and the subcontinent, Persian texts and Hindu mysticism) literature through his commentaries and translations, generating an Other to Europe. Translation, as postcolonial commentators argue, was a method of Othering where the source text/culture was deemed not only the Other but also secondary to the European one. Susan Bassnett writes:

> translation was effectively used in the past as an instrument of colonial domination, a means of depriving the colonized peoples of a voice. For in the colonial model, one culture dominated and the others were

> subservient, hence translation reinforced that power hierarchy. (2002, 4)

Along similar lines, Tejaswini Niranjana argues about the colonial power relations that inform translations:

> Translation as a practice shapes, and takes shape within, the asymmetrical relations of power that operate under colonialism. What is at stake here is the representation of the colonized, who need to be produced in such a manner as to justify colonial domination, and to beg for the English book by themselves.... Translation thus produces strategies of containment. By employing certain modes of representing the other which it thereby also brings into being translation reinforces hegemonic versions of the colonized. (1992, 2)

More specifically about Jones, Niranjana says:

> Jones was responsible for the most influential introduction of a textualized India to Europe ... he contributes to a historicist, teleological model of civilization that, coupled with a notion of translation presupposing transparency of representation, helps construct a powerful version of the "Hindu" that later writers of different philosophical and political persuasions incorporated into their texts in an almost seamless fashion.
>
> The most significant nodes of Jones's work are (a) the need for translation by the European, since the natives are unreliable interpreters of their own laws and culture; (b) the desire to be a lawgiver, to give the Indians their "own" laws; and (c) the desire to "purify" Indian culture and speak on its behalf. (12–14)

Jones's translation then serves not only as a gateway into the East/the subcontinent but also serves as the definitive, authoritative interpretation of the region and its texts. In other words, the translation became the authorised version of ancient Indian texts, their poetics and even the cultures from which the texts drew. In fact, in his essay, 'On the Mystical Poetry of the Eastern Nations', about his translation of *Gitagovinda*, Jones admitted to have 'omit[ted] only those passages, which are too luxuriant and too bold for an European taste' (10). It was not, therefore, simply a translation from one language into another as much as the creation of a specific interpretive frame by the Orientalist-colonial through which the subcontinent's textual tradition and its cultures would hereafter be viewed. Indian/Hindu culture was what Jones and the Europeans defined it as, and this was the authorised culture/text that would be 'taught' to the British administrators and officers, and the 'emergent middle-class Indian ... to imprint on his mind the interpretation given to it by Orientalist scholarship' (Thapar 2010, 218). In S.N. Mukherjee's words,

> [Jones] embodies the dichotomy of attitudes of some of the British officers in India; many were radicals at home and were attracted by India, by her 'glorious past' and her 'simple people', yet they had to uphold an authoritarian rule. Jones epitomizes this dichotomy in his life and works. (1968, 3; Franklin 272)

Edward Said argued that Jones set out 'to rule and to learn' and 'to subdue the infinite variety of the Orient' (1979, 78). However, this view of Orientalist translation of literary texts and its integral features, such as exoticism, as inextricably linked to cultural hegemony and imperial domination—such critiques mostly emerging in the wake of Said's work—has also been hotly contested (for instance, see Figueira 1991). Despite such defences, it remains hard to ignore the fact that events and actions like the Permanent Settlement of Bengal could only have been possible because they had been rendered legitimate through the codification of Hindu and Islamic codes of property and the law, all of which had been made available through the work of Orientalists like Jones, Wilkins and Halhed. As Siraj Ahmed observes in his study of Jones's jurisprudence and legal tracts in translation:

> Eighteenth century British Orientalism's chief aim and achievement was to provide a textual basis for Indian law, property law in particular indeed in a form that would become absolutely seminal for the subsequent development of Indian history and historiography. In doing so, Orientalism helped the East India Company simplify India's otherwise profoundly complicated, heterotopic, and fluid system of property ownership and sovereignty. In other words, Orientalism used its putative authority on all subjects Indian to legitimize the Company's attempts to fix, to control, and so to centralize revenue appropriation which the Permanent Settlement brought to logical culmination. (2009, 173)

Dorothy Matilda Figueira argues that the translations (Jones's and later, Georg Forster's) of *Shakuntala* encouraged the Europeans to 'seek the broader path in their interests, and brought them into contact with the common spiritual and aesthetic movements of the time' (12). It had other effects, she writes: 'it enabled the re-evaluation of various national literatures, it raised questions about the project and remit of translations'. In the process, she also notes how Jones made stylistic 'distortions' to the text as a result of which, she argues, several passages become 'Biblical in tone by bringing in the question of the soul' (82), and locates multiple 'cultural prejudices in mistranslating ... impose a value judgement and tie Shakuntala (the character) to a vision of etiquette which is wholly Western' (124). Figueira's view regarding the mistranslations is echoed in a different key by Romila Thapar, who argues that Jones's wish to

> convince his readers of the greatness of Indian civilisation ... led him to tone down some of what he thought were the more erotic passages, which he assumed would unnecessarily result in English hostility towards the Sanskrit classics. (2010, 199–200)

Michael Dodson echoes Figueira when he writes:

> European-produced translations of these texts might serve to reinforce the dominance of a European aesthetic sensibility through a process of 'naturalisation', in which the culturally specific is 'sanitised', subordinated to a European norm, thereby inherently limiting the 'artistic achievement' of the colonised.... On the other hand, literary translations from Sanskrit might also foreground the 'otherness' of Indian texts and cultural norms through a strategy of 'foreignisation'; that is, by registering for the European reader differences in language and cultural content. (118)

That is, the Orient was rendered both familiar and exotic, sanitised for European taste and its otherness preserved.

The Pundits, Jones and Imperial Knowledge

That Orientalist scholarship was an indispensable tool of imperial dominance is now a truism stated ad infinitum. Dodson writes:

> early orientalist knowledge, preconceptions, and methodologies, constructed largely during the late eighteenth century, were partially utilised by constructive orientalists within a specific project of colonial education underwritten largely by liberal conceptions of civilisational hierarchy, the attendant concerns for 'improvement' and 'progress', as well as for the justification of empire. (88)

Jones in his Preface tells us how he sought advice from Radhakanta Sarman regarding Indian drama, and Radhakanta referred him to Kalidasa's *Shakuntala*.

The nature of the relationship between Jones and the pundits has been extensively debated. Kate Teltscher, for example, is categorical in her reading of the John Flaxman memorial of Jones in Oxford, 'arguing that the posture of the three pundits and Jones indicate the triumph of the British imperialist's expertise' over 'indigenous knowledge', represented by the pundits (200). Others such as Rosane Rocher have proposed that a 'bicultural' exchange and interaction marks the relationship of Jones and the pundits (1993, cited in Hatcher 2005). But, Rocher writes,

> The way British orientalists related to pandits was highly ambiguous: they initially depended entirely on pandits for information and for instruction in Sanskrit, yet they sought to exercise control over them.

> This relationship was all the more complicated since the pandits themselves were uncertain of how to respond to this new breed of rulers. Bengali pandits did not respond immediately to British requests for instruction in Sanskrit and information about Indian culture, nor to offers of employment with the courts. (cited in Hatcher 2005, 690)

Jones, on the one hand, enjoyed his interactions with the pundits, and on the other, he was also suspicious of them (Rocher, cited in Hatcher 691). Brian Hatcher argues:

> it is worth noting that men like Jones and Wilkins at times tended to view their pandit associates more as the embodiment of an ancient ideal than as living collaborators. (693)

Indigenous scholarship was subject to the colonial, Christian and other forms of knowing/knowledge making. Writes Hatcher:

> local scholars were not merely victims of classicist philology, but suffered also from the imagination of Christian evangelicals and Utilitarian administrators, both of whom agreed that the pandit was a major impediment to the quick and efficient 'improvement' of native learning. (694)

Radhakanta's affiliation with Jones was made officially possible because the governor general agreed that Jones could 'appoint as many of the most respectable Maulavies and Pundits of this Country as [Jones might] think necessary to give [him] effectual Assistance' (cited in Rocher 1989, 631). In his 'On the Literature of the Hindus', a text which was 'communicated by Govardhan Caul' and translated by Jones, Jones writes:

> Encouraged by the mildness of our government and manners, [the Indian scholars] are at least as eager to communicate their knowledge of all kinds, as we can be to receive. (1807, Vol. IV: 113)

It is because of such affiliations that Hatcher concludes that

> Colonial history includes a cast of thousands of actual pandits, who occupy almost every conceivable ideological and social position and whose stories diverge and intermingle in the most surprising ways. (719)

There is one more dimension to the Jones–pundit collaboration in the production of *Sacontalá* (as well as later works). The native scholars were not all Brahmins. One of Jones's teachers was a non-Brahmin, Ramalochan. Garland Cannon offers this information:

> Jones sought a tutor at Nadia in 1785, at a time when the Brahmanic faculty were on vacation. The choice was a pleasant *vaidya,* who was not attending the seasonal Durga ceremonies because he was not a Brahman: "[Ramalocana] has taught grammar and ethics to the most

> learned Brahmins, and has no priestly pride, with which his pupils in general abound". (1990, 229)

Partially in response to the charges of imperial hegemony as the *only* possible relationship between Jones and the pundits, commentators like Rocher and Franklin propose a more dialogic model of intercultural connections and exchanges. Franklin writes:

> In consulting Radhakanta Sarman as to which of the Indian plays was 'most universally esteemed', Jones was enlisting Brahmanical authority, a cultural hegemony that can scarcely be seen as 'western'. Alternatively, in translating *Shakuntala* with the help of a non-Brahman scholar Jones was arguably fostering an anti-Brahmanical stance. (Franklin 272)

While it seems incredible to assume that there was no imperial agenda or unequal power relations in the Jones–pundits relationship, to assume that all knowledge formation led directly to genocidal and conquistadorial acts is also equally incredible for it brings into play the same binary operations and stereotyping that the postcolonial discourse accuses the West of doing.

Sanskrit, European Romanticism and India

Jones argued that Europeans would benefit from reading Sanskrit texts, even the medical tracts, in his '*On the Literature of the Hindus*'. He makes specific mention of the tracts on law and inheritances, such as Manu's and others, claiming that these are subjects that are 'so interesting to the British government' (1807, Vol. IV: 109).

In his famous 3rd Discourse ('On the Hindus') at the Asiatick Society of Bengal, 2 February 1786, Jones said:

> The *Sanscrit* language, whatever be its antiquity, is of a wonderful structure; more perfect than the *Greek*, more copious than the *Latin*, and more exquisitely refined than either, yet bearing to both of them a stronger affinity, both in the roots of verbs and in the forms of grammar, than could possibly have been produced by accident; so strong indeed, that no philologer could examine them all three, without believing them to have sprung from some common source, which, perhaps, no longer exists: there is a similar reason, though not quite so forcible, for supposing that both the *Gothick* and the *Celtick*, though blended with a very different idiom, had the fame origin with the *Sanscrit;* and the old *Persian* might be added to the same family, if this were the place for discussing any question concerning the antiquities of *Persia*. (28–29)

Jones's sweeping comparisons of traditions, aesthetics, languages and literature was building similarities and differences simultaneously. As Dodson puts it:

> Jones' discussion of the relationship between Sanskrit, Greek, and Latin was to support a specific historiographical agenda; namely, the conversion of the study of language into a discipline from which historical 'truth' might be elicited. (2007, 28)

With his translation of Kalidasa, he demonstrated these as well, and the impact was such that Europe itself became a fan of the character, the play and ancient Indian culture embodied in Jones's interpretive translation. It would become, in Raymond Schwab's words, a 'Shakuntala era' (1984, 57). As the *Calcutta Review* put it in 1851, till Jones translated Kalidasa, 'the literary public of the West was not even aware that the Hindus had a national drama' (97).

Often deemed to be the harbinger of both, Orientalism and German romanticism's interest in and passion for the Other, Jones's version of Kalidasa's heroine became a household name for European authors. Goethe's invocation of the name in verse is well known:

> If you want the spring's blossoms and the fruits of the maturer year,
> What is seductive and creates joy, or what is satisfying and nourishing,
>
> If you want to encompass Heaven and Earth in one single name,
>
> Then I name you, Sacontala, and everything is said. (Cited in Franklin 251)

This kind of response constructed Jones's status as a mediator of Indian/ Sanskrit/Hindu culture to the West, offering access to hitherto unknown riches of language and literature. The German romantics, like Johann Gottfried von Herder, were given their own version, by George Forster, and this, writes Franklin, was a more 'rapturous response':

> With no empire, German Romantics might feel genuinely cosmopolitan, free from imperial anxiety, more in tune with the *Weltgeist*. Yet their reaction to the heroine may be seen as a perfect example of imperial rhetoric whereby a colonized land is allegorized as a female body. India **was** Sakuntalā, without italics, but with bold sensual emphasis, in an elaborate fantasy of seduction. (259, emphasis in original)

This fascination meant, as Schwab has argued, that European classicism itself, in the 1790s–1830s period, was 'enhanced by Sanskrit' (53). Via the Forster translation into German, argues Schwab, Europe redefined humanity, human history and aesthetics itself. It 'constructed an Indic fatherland for the human race in its infancy' (59). The portrait of Shakuntala as a child of nature (in the Jones translation) captured the German/European imagination so that 'the Shakuntala of the play became the ideal Indian woman encapsulating the beauty of womankind' (Thapar 2010, 208). She became, argues Thapar, the very contrast to the woman of the neoclassical 'crafted women' (208). (Novalis, a key figure in German romanticism, named his fiancée 'Shakuntala' after he read the work.)

Hindu philosophies, too, entered the European romantic imagination through such translations, although, as Thapar notes, the possibility that the readings and translations might have been 'coloured' by European perceptions of the texts was not considered (210). The translation also fed the stereotype of the Indian as childlike and frozen in some golden era of the past. The emphasis on the Indian as childlike and closer to nature (in Jone's translation) was indubitably a racialised European imaginary, for it located the Indian at the lower end of the civilisational spectrum as primitive, pre-modern and implicitly distant from the modern European. This binary is instituted as early as 1791 in a review of Jones's translation where the author says:

> The peculiar manners and customs—indeed the uncommon expressions and metaphors, the wild imagery, the incredible effects of supernatural agency, as they perplex, and even distract the mind, are unfavourable to that disposition, which admits, without examining, all the milder emotions; and which gives immediate way to its feelings, without once thinking of employing judgment, or exerting reason. Much of this drama, which would at once dissolve an Indian into tears, must by us, be coolly investigated: to him it is simple, to us it is obscure: it speaks to his passions, it addresses our understandings: it is levelled against his heart, while with us it affects only the head: he melts at once into rapture, while we, after tracing the meaning of what is hidden, feel scarcely any other emotion than that of surprise. (*Monthly Review* [1791], 124)

The play appealed to the emotions of the Indians, and was designed, suggests the reviewer, to do so because 'reason' and 'understanding' are not features of the natives' make-up. The 'simplicity' of the text that appeals to the 'simple' mind of the native is also mentioned in the *Analytical Review*'s review of the play (already cited).

Another unexpected role for Jones's text and the play itself was in the context of India's renaissance. A view first offered by S.N. Mukherjee in *Sir William Jones: A Study in Eighteenth-Century British Attitudes to India* (1968), the text was a key factor in the Indians' perception of itself:

> His Sakuntala had a profound effect in India. By saving Kalidasa from the medieval commentators he ushered in what has been called 'an Indian Renaissance'. (3)

***

The debate around the complicity of William Jone's scholarship with the colonial enterprise and its contribution to cultural imperialism and dominance continues in the wake of the studies of his translations, commentaries and other works. Linguist, poet, translator, lawyer and statesman, Jones, as the most significant Orientalist of the British Empire, enabled the 'orientalising' of Europe, providing the German and other romanticists with a body of work from which to launch their own variants. Jones's *Sacontalá* is, therefore, the cornerstone of both, the imperial edifice in India and the European literary and cultural renaissance.

SACOONTALA;

OR,

THE FATAL RING:

AN

INDIAN DRAMA.

Á L I D Á S.

TRANSLATED FROM THE ORIGINAL SANSCRIT AND PRÁCRIT.

L O N D O N:

Printed for EDWARDS, Pall Mall;

By J. COOPER, No. 31, Bow Street, Covent Garden,

WITH HIS NEW-INVENTED INK.

M.DCC.XC.

PREFACE.

IN one of the letters which bear the title of EDIFYING, though moſt of them ſwarm with ridiculous errours, and all muſt be conſulted with extreme diffidence, I met, ſome years ago, with the following paſſage: "In the north of "India there are many books, called Nátac, which, as "the Bráhmens aſſert, contain a large portion of ancient "hiſtory without any mixture of fable;" and having an eager deſire to know the real ſtate of this empire before the conqueſt of it by the Savages of the North, I was very ſolicitous, on my arrival in Bengal, to procure acceſs to thoſe books, either by the help of tranſlations, if they had been tranſlated, or by learning the language in which they were originally compoſed, and which I had yet a ſtronger inducement to learn from its connection with the adminiſtration of juſtice to the Hindus; but when I was able to converſe with the Bráhmens, they aſſured me that the Nátacs were not hiſtories, and abounded with fables; that they were extremely popular works, and conſiſted of converſations in proſe and verſe, held before ancient Rájás in their publick aſſemblies, on an infinite variety of ſubjects, and in various dialects of India: this definition gave me no very diſtinct idea; but I concluded that they were dialogues on moral or literary topicks; whilſt other Europeans, whom I conſulted, had underſtood from the natives that they were diſcourſes on dancing, muſick, or poetry. At length a very ſenſible Bráhmen, named Rádhácánt, who had long been attentive to Englifh manners, removed all my doubts, and gave me no lefs delight than furprife, by telling me that our nation had compofitions of the fame fort, which were publickly reprefented at Calcutta in the cold feafon, and bore the name, as he had been informed, of plays. Refolving at my leifure to read the beft of them, I afked which of their Nátacs was moft univerfally efteemed; and he anfwered without hefitation, Sacontalá, fupporting his opinion, as ufual among the Pandits, by a couplet to this effect: "The ring of Sacontalá, in which "the fourth act, and four ftanzas of that act, are emi-"nently brilliant, difplays all the rich exuberance of Cá-"lidáfa's genius." I foon procured a correct copy of it; "and, affifted by my teacher Rámalóchan, began with tranflating it verbally into Latin, which bears fo great a refemblance to Sanfcrit, that it is more convenient than any modern language for a fcrupulous interlineary verfion: I then turned it word for word into Englifh, and afterwards, without adding or fuppreffing any material fentence, difengaged it from the ftiffnefs of a foreign idiom, and prepared the faithful tranflation of the Indian drama, which I now prefent to the Publick as a moft pleafing and authentick picture of old Hindu manners, and one of the greateft curiofities that the literature of Afia has yet brought to light.

Dramatick poetry muft have been immemorially ancient in the Indian empire: the invention of it is commonly afcribed to Bheret, a fage believed to have been infpired, who invented alfo a fyftem of mufick which bears his name; but this opinion of its origin is rendered very doubtful by the univerſal belief, that the firſt Sanſcrit verſe ever heard by mortals was pronounced in a burſt of reſentment by the great Válmic, who flouriſhed in the ſilver age of the world, and was author of an Epick Poem on the war of his contemporary, Ráma, king of Ayódhyà; ſo that no drama in verſe could have been repreſented before his time; and the Indians have a wild ſtory, that the firſt regular play, on the ſame ſubject with the Rámáyan, was compoſed by Hanumat or Pávan, who commanded an army of Satyrs or Mountaineers in Ráma's expedition againſt Lancà: they add, that he engraved it on a ſmooth rock, which, being diſſatisfied with his compoſition, he hurled into the ſea; and that, many years after, a learned prince ordered expert divers to take impreſſions of the poem on wax, by which means the drama was in great meaſure reſtored; and my Pandit aſſures me that he is in poſſeſſion of it. By whomſoever or in whatever age this ſpecies of entertainment was invented, it is very certain, that it was carried to great perfection in its kind, when Vicramáditya, who reigned in the firſt century before Chriſt, gave encouragement to poets, philologers, and mathematicians, at a time when the Britons were as unlettered and unpoliſhed as the army of Hanumat: nine men of genius, commonly called the nine gems, attended his court, and were ſplendidly ſupported by his bounty; and Cálidás is unanimouſly allowed to have been the brighteſt of them.—A modern epigram was lately repeated to me, which does ſo much honour to the author of Sacontalá, that I cannot

forbear exhibiting a literal verſion of it: " Poetry was
" the ſportful daughter of Válmic, and, having been edu-
" cated by Vyáſa, ſhe choſe Cálidás for her bridegroom
" after the manner of Viderbha: ſhe was the mother of
" Amara, Sundar, Sanc'ha, Dhanic; but now, old and
" decrepit, her beauty faded, and her unadorned feet ſlip-
" ping as ſhe walks, in whoſe cottage does ſhe diſdain to
" take ſhelter?"

All the other works of our illuſtrious poet, the Shakeſpeare of India, that have yet come to my knowledge, are a ſecond play, in five acts, entitled Urvasí; an heroick poem, or rather a ſeries of poems in one book, on the Children of the Sun; another, with perfect unity of action, on the Birth of Cumára, god of war; two or three love tales in verſe; and an excellent little work on Sanſcrit Metre, preciſely in the manner of Terentianus; but he is believed by ſome to have reviſed the works of Válmic and Vyáſa, and to have corrected the perfect editions of them which are now current: this at leaſt is admitted by all, that he ſtands next in reputation to thoſe venerable bards; and we muſt regret, that he has left only two Dramatick Poems, eſpecially as the ſtories in his Raghuvanſa would have ſupplied him with a number of excellent ſubjects.— Some of his contemporaries, and other Hindu poets even to our own times, have compoſed ſo many tragedies, comedies, farces, and muſical pieces, that the Indian theatre would fill as many volumes as that of any nation in ancient or modern Europe: all the Pandits aſſert that their plays are innumerable; and, on my firſt inquiries concerning them, I had notice of more than thirty, which they conſider as the flower of their Nátacs, among which the Malignant Child, the Rape of Uſhá, the Taming of Durváſas, the Seizure of the Lock, Málati and Mádhava, with five or ſix dramas on the adventures of their incarnate gods, are the moſt admired after thoſe of Cálidás. They are all in verſe, where the dialogue is elevated; and in proſe, where it is familiar: the men of rank and learning are repreſented ſpeaking pure Sanſcrit, and the women Prácrit, which is little more than the language of the Bráhmens melted down by a delicate articulation to the ſoftneſs of Italian; while the low perſons of the drama ſpeak the vulgar dialects of the ſeveral provinces which they are ſuppoſed to inhabit.

The play of Sacontalá muſt have been very popular when it was firſt repreſented; for the Indian empire was then in full vigour, and the national vanity muſt have been highly flattered by the magnificent introduction of thoſe kings and heroes in whom the Hindus gloried; the ſcenery muſt have been ſplendid and beautiful; and there is good reaſon to believe, that the court at Avanti was equal in brilliancy during the reign of Vicramáditya, to that of any monarch in any age or country.—Duſhmanta, the hero of the piece, appears in the chronological tables of the Bráhmens among the Children of the Moon, and in the twenty-firſt generation after the flood; ſo that, if we can at all rely on the chronology of the Hindus, he was nearly contemporary with Obed, or Jeſſe; and Puru, his moſt celebrated anceſtor, was the fifth in deſcent from

Budha, or Mercury, who married, they ſay, a daughter of the pious king, whom Viſhnu preſerved in an ark from the univerſal deluge: his eldeſt ſon Bheret was the illuſtrious progenitor of Curu, from whom Pándu was lineally deſcended, and in whoſe family the Indian Apollo became incarnate; whence the poem, next in fame to the Rámáyan, is called Mahábhárat.

As to the machinery of the drama, it is taken from the ſyſtem of Mythology, which prevails to this day, and which it would require a large volume to explain; but we cannot help remarking that the deities introduced in the Fatal Ring are clearly allegorical perſonages. Maríchi, the firſt production of Brahmà, or the Creative Power, ſignifies light, that ſubtil fluid which was created before its reſervoir, the Sun, as water was created before the ſea; Caſyapa, the offspring of Maríchi, ſeems to be a perſonification of infinite ſpace, comprehending innumerable worlds; and his children by Aditi, or his active power, (unleſs Aditi mean the primeval day, and Diti, his other wife, the night) are Indra, or the viſible firmament, and the twelve Adityas, or Suns, preſiding over as many months.

On the characters and conduct of the play I ſhall offer no criticiſm; becauſe I am convinced that the taſtes of men differ as much as their ſentiments and paſſions, and that, in feeling the beauties of art, as in ſmelling flowers, taſting fruits, viewing proſpects, and hearing melody, every individual muſt be guided by his own ſenſations and the incommunicable aſſociations of his own ideas. This only I may add, that if Sacontalá ſhould ever be acted in

India, where alone it could be acted with perfect knowledge of Indian dreſſes, manners, and ſcenery, the piece might eaſily be reduced to five acts of a moderate length, by throwing the third act into the ſecond, and the ſixth into the fifth; for it muſt be confeſſed that the whole of Duſhmanta's converſation with his buffoon, and great part of his courtſhip in the hermitage, might be omitted without any injury to the drama.

It is my anxious wiſh that others may take the pains to learn Sanſcrit, and may be perſuaded to tranſlate the works of Cálidás: I ſhall hardly again employ my leiſure in a taſk ſo foreign to my profeſſional (which are, in truth, my favourite) ſtudies, and have no intention of tranſlating any other book from any language, except the Law Tract of Menu, and the new Digeſt of Indian and Arabian laws; but, to ſhow that the Bráhmens at leaſt do not think polite literature incompatible with juriſprudence, I cannot avoid mentioning, that the venerable compiler of the Hindu Digeſt, who is now in his eighty-ſixth year, has the whole play of Sacontalá by heart, as he proved when I laſt converſed with him, to my entire conviction: leſt, however, I ſhould hereafter ſeem to have changed a reſolution which I mean to keep inviolate, I think it proper to ſay, that I have already tranſlated four or five other books, and among them the Hitópadéſa, which I undertook, merely as an exerciſe in learning Sanſcrit, three years before I knew that Mr. Wilkins, without whoſe aid I ſhould never have learned it, had any thought of giving the ſame work to the Publick.

7

IMPERIAL EDUCATION

By the time Thomas Babington Macaulay submitted his Minute of 2 February 1835, the debate between Anglicists and Orientalists was already underway. British officials, groups of Indian students and others such as Ram Mohan Roy had presented, through various appeals, letters, commentaries and petitions, their views regarding the role and extent of English education for colonial subjects. The Anglicists argued that English-language education was essential for Indians since their own languages were inadequate for knowledge production, and all native language works/education could be ignored. The Orientalists argued that native language work was admirable, and any 'Western' knowledge system could only be grafted on to this, the native one.

Macaulay swung the debate in favour of the Anglicists when William Bentinck, the governor general, accepted the Minute in its entirety (Ghosh 1995). Hence, as numerous postcolonial scholars have argued, English education in India is dated to 1835 and this one document, although the debates, petitions, tracts and opinions that laid the foundation of the Minute go further back, into the late 18th century. As Lynn Zastoupil and Martin Moir note:

> Macaulay's minute, while brilliant rhetorically, conveys a very incomplete and partisan impression of the complex and important arguments advanced by various participants, British and Indian alike, in a controversy whose roots extended back into the eighteenth century. (1999, ix)

The debate continued to rage post 1835 and Macaulay–Bentinck, with Trevelyan's *On the Education of the People of India* (1838), letters, minutes and 'notes' from H.H. Wilson (1835), Brian Hodgson (1837, 1843), James Prinsep (1835), Lord Auckland (1836) and others, petitions and appeals from the Sanskrit College (Calcutta), and Hindu/Muslim representatives from Calcutta and other places (1835, 1836, etc.).

As a document, Macaulay's Minute, all of 10 pages, possesses enormous rhetorical power but also enables us to see how English imperial discourse, replete with racialised stereotypes and colonial attitudes, operated.

Structure and Content

Macaulay starts with a criticism of the Committee of Public Instruction and post-1813 British attitudes towards education in the colony. He cites the 1813 Charter Act, which states that the government would create a fund

> for the revival and promotion of literature, and the encouragement of the learned natives of India, and for the introduction and promotion of a knowledge of the Sciences among the inhabitants of the British Territories. (Nayar 2020, 55)

Unfortunately, says Macaulay, the committee had assumed that the act's sense of 'literature' 'can have meant only Arabic and Sanscrit literature'. Macaulay's main point is that

> they never would have given the Honorable appellation of 'a learned native' to a native who was familiar with the poetry of Milton, the metaphysics of Locke, and the Physics of Newton; but that they meant to designate by that name only such persons as might have studied in the sacred books of the Hindoos all the uses of Cusa-Grass, and all the mysteries of absorption into the Deity. (55)

Later, Macaulay expands on the idea of learning, or more specifically, what 'learning' means for the colonial subject.

He makes historical analogies with England's own past—the relevance and role of Greek and Latin texts in the nation's education and therefore its 'progress'. Then he shifts to the economics of educating the natives, noting:

> The grants which are made from the Public purse for the encouragement of literature differ in no respect from the grants which are made from the same purse for other objects of real or supposed utility. (56)

To fund the non-useful arts, says Macaulay, is unacceptable.

In the process, he underscores that there is no 'utility' in teaching the Indians from within their own traditions, which he dismisses as full of irrelevant, irrational and outdated information. He spends considerable space dismissing the Sanskrit tradition of learning, making what is now notorious comparisons with English texts, literature and rationality.

Macaulay paints the English/Western education model as devoted to rationality, utility and sensibility in contrast to the Indian/Sanskrit/Arabic one. Education, therefore, has to be devoted to those sciences and arts that inculcate, in Macaulay's view, rational values and thought.

Genealogies

There are two genealogies at work in Macaulay's Minute: one, the genealogy of his own work and two, those that he traces as the origins of English culture itself. I shall address each in turn.

Macaulay was *not* the initiator of the debate on English education. As Elmer Cutts put it in his 1953 essay, 'evangelical agitation and pressure for more than half a century before 1835 formed the basic background to Macaulay's minute' (824). Macaulay's Minute had interesting antecedents in the form of the educational debates—the Muslim community's petition and Warren Hastings's Minute of 1781, Jonathan Duncan's 1792 letter seeking a Sanskrit College in Calcutta and, of course, Ram Mohan Roy's famous 1823 'Letter to Lord Amherst'. These could very well be read as the cornerstones of the Anglicist–Orientalist debate into which Macaulay's Minute added the closing remarks with his own 1835 Minute.

Duncan argued that founding a Sanskrit college would have two advantages: it would 'endear' (his term) the British to the natives by 'our exceeding in our attention towards them & their Systems' and enabling the training of native by

> preserving and disseminating a knowledge of the Hindoo Law, and proving a Nursery of future Doctors and Expounders thereof to assist the European Judges in the due regular, and uniform administration of its genuine Letter and Spirit to the body of the people. (2020, 13)

Duncan advocates a concerted effort to collect ancient Indian treatises:

> Collecting Complete Treatises (altho' such as are well known to have existed) on the Hindoo Religion, Laws, arts or Sciences … a precious Library of the most ancient and Valuable General Learning and Tradition now perhaps existing in any part of the Globe. (12)

This effort, he argues, will cost 'only a small and Comparative expence [sic] to Government' (12–13). Thus, Duncan was advocating the building of a textual archive and educating the Indians in their own languages, primarily Sanskrit.

In the same year, and in contrast to Duncan's stance, Charles Grant, in *Observations on the State of Society Among the Asiatic Subjects* of *Great Britain, Particularly With Respect To Morals*, called for English education of the natives. He argued that 'the Hindoos err, because they are ignorant'. In order to dispel their ignorance, he said, 'light and knowledge' are indispensable. The task is to 'impart our superior lights', i.e., English/Western education (2020, 16). For this, Grant proposed, 'the communication of our knowledge shall be made by the medium of our own language'. Grant insisted that the English *language* had to be first imparted and then followed by other fields of English knowledge:

> make them acquainted with our easy literary compositions, upon a variety of subjects; and let not the idea hastily excite derision, *progressively* with the simple elements of our arts, our philosophy and religion. These acquisitions would silently undermine, and at length subvert, the fabric of error… (17, emphasis in original)

Grant admits that 'to introduce the language of the conquerors, seems to be an obvious means of assimilating the conquered people to them', but believes it would in the long run help Indians. He thus calls for establishing 'places of gratuitous instruction in reading and writing English' (18). He also suggests making English the language of administration so that 'the interest of the natives would induce them to acquire it' (18). His closing argument is: 'undoubtedly the most important communication which the Hindoos could receive through the medium of our language, would be the knowledge of our religion…' (20).

Roy, in his 'Letter', first admits that the establishment of a Sanskrit College 'evinces the laudable desire of Government to improve the natives of India by education' (2020, 2). Roy then declares that when the British government set out a budget for improving the educational levels of the Indians, some of the Indians such as himself,

> were filled with sanguine hopes that this sum would be laid out in employing European gentlemen of talents and education to instruct the natives of India in mathematics, natural philosophy, chemistry, anatomy, and other useful sciences… (2)

It was such knowledge, he argues, that has 'raised them [the Europeans] above the inhabitants of other parts of the world' (2). Roy then proceeds to argue against the Sanskrit College which would, he notes, 'impart such knowledge as is already current in India' (2). Adopting the utilitarian stance, Roy dismisses such knowledge that would 'load the minds of youth with grammatical niceties and metaphysical distinctions of little or no practicable use to the possessors or to society'. Sanskrit as a language is hard to acquire too, says Roy, and therefore 'the learning concealed under this almost impervious veil is far from sufficient to reward the labour of acquiring it' (2). Speaking the language of the civilisational mission, Roy argues that if the improvement of the colonial native subjects was the aim of the British government, then

> no improvement can be expected from inducing young men to consume a dozen of years of the most valuable period of their lives in acquiring the niceties of the Byakarun or Sanskrit grammar…. Nor will youths be fitted to be better members of society by the vedantic doctrines, which teach them to believe that all visible things have no real existence; that as father, brother, etc., have no actual entity … the Sanskrit system of education would be the best calculated to keep this country in darkness… (3)

Turning to a historical analogy to make his point, Roy argues that it is because of Baconian science that England has progressed:

> If it had been intended to keep the British nation in ignorance of real knowledge, the Baconian philosophy would not have been allowed to

> displace the system of the schoolmen, which was the best calculated to perpetuate ignorance… (3)

Roy concludes with a plea for a similar training programme, asking the British government to:

> promote a more liberal and enlightened system of instruction; embracing mathematics, natural philosophy, chemistry, anatomy, with other useful sciences, which may be accomplished with the sum proposed by employing a few gentlemen of talents and learning educated in Europe, and providing a college furnished with the necessary books, instruments, and other apparatus. (3)

It is in this context of the appropriate approach to the 'improvement' of the native subject that Macaulay weighs in on the side of English education, and indeed his Minute captures the differing stances admirably because it draws on both.

Like Charles Grant, Macaulay rejects Hinduism *in toto*, and attributes much of the 'evils' of the subcontinent to the religion. Linking the teaching of Sanskrit and Arabic to the reinforcement of the falsities of Hinduism, Macaulay writes of the recommendations of the Committee for Public Instructions to encourage and fund Sanskrit and Arabic:

> We are to teach false history, false astronomy, false medicine, because we find them in Company with a false religion … can we reasonably or decently bribe men, out of the revenues of the state, to waste their youth in learning how they are to purify themselves after touching an Ass, or what texts of the Vedas they are to repeat to expiate the crime of killing a goat? (2020, 62)

It would be, writes Macaulay, 'giving artificial encouragement to absurd history, absurd metaphysics, absurd physics, absurd theology', if the government were to fund Sanskrit and Indian languages. For Macaulay, then, to fund learning in the Indian languages was to tacitly endorse Hinduism and what he calls its 'absurdities'. He writes of the irrational nature of Sanskrit texts and their 'truths':

> medical doctrines which would disgrace an English farrier, astronomy which would move laughter in girls at an English boarding school, history abounding with kings thirty feet high and reigns thirty thousand years long, and geography made of seas of treacle and seas of butter. (58)

He returns to this 'nature' of Sanskrit texts when he writes that its 'literature inculcates the most serious errors on the most important subjects', and therefore is not 'reconcilable with reason, with morality' (62).

Sanskrit and Arabic—it is not clear why Macaulay sees only these two as representing all of the subcontinent's intellectual traditions—are, in his view, hollow traditions. Then, given his interest in history, Macaulay would dismiss the historical and topical information in Sanskrit/Arabic texts:

> all the historical information which has been collected from all the books written in the Sanscrit language is less valuable than what may be found in the most paltry abridgements used at preparatory Schools in England. (58)

Endorsing Roy and the Anglicists, Macaulay argues that the 'improvement' of the peoples of India was only possible through the introduction of English education. Very important for this, he agrees, is the need for English as a language. Building implicitly on Roy's formulations on the ease of acquiring English, and its necessity, Macaulay offers as historical analogy, the acquisition of Greek and Latin in England (and this is the *second* strand of genealogy implicit in the Minute):

> Had our ancestors acted as the Committee of Public Instruction has hitherto acted, had they neglected the language of Thucydides and Plato, and the language of Cicero and Tacitus—had they confined their attention to the old dialects of our own island, had they printed nothing and taught nothing at the universities but chronicles in Anglo Saxon and romances in Norman French—would England ever have been what she now is? (59)

Thus, it is the Hellenic legacy that has enabled England, and it would be English that would empower India. As another example, Macaulay turns to Russia. Stating that Russia now has a 'large educated class', Macaulay traces its source:

> Not by flattering national prejudices:—not by feeding the mind of the young Muscovite with the old women's stories which his rude fathers had believed:—not by filling his head with lying legends about St. Nicholas:—not by encouraging him to study the great question, whether the world was or not created on the 13th of September:—not by calling him 'a learned native' when he had mastered all these points of knowledge. But by teaching him those foreign languages in which the greatest mass of information had been laid up, and thus putting all that information within his reach. The languages of western Europe civilised Russia. (59)

As a conclusion, Macaulay declares: 'I cannot doubt that they will do for the Hindoo what they have done for the Tartar' (59).

Macaulay contrasts the legacies of the British with that of the Indians. Expanding 'English' into 'European' Macaulay writes:

> I am quite ready to take the Oriental learning at the valuation of the orientalists themselves. I have never found one among them who could deny that a single shelf of a good European library was worth the

> whole native literature of India and Arabic. The intrinsic superiority of the western literature is indeed fully admitted by those Members of the Committee who support the Oriental plan of education. (57)

Macaulay is no longer speaking of *English* traditions, arts or learning but of Europe itself as a comprehensive and comprehensible unit, descended from the Hellenic and instrumental in transforming all of Europe.

Later, Macaulay returns to the genealogy of the English-speaking peoples:

> It [the English language] abounds with works of imagination not inferior to the noblest which Greece has bequeathed to us, with models of every species of eloquence, with historical compositions which, considered merely as narratives, have seldom been surpassed, and which, considered as vehicles of ethical and political instruction, have never been equalled, with just and lively representations of human life and human nature—with the most profound speculations on metaphysics, morals, Government, jurisprudence, trade, with full and correct information respecting every experimental science which tends to preserve the health, to increase the comfort, or to expand the intellect of man. Whoever knows that language has ready access to all the vast intellectual wealth which all the wisest nations of the earth have created and hoarded in the course of ninety generations. (58)

Native Needs, Colonial Economies

Echoing Roy, Macaulay writes:

> We are withholding from them the learning which is palatable to them. We are forcing on them the mock learning which they nauseate. (60)

The natives, he states, have discovered the need for English education and the necessity to reject their own systems of learning. Referring to a petition from ex-students of the Sanskrit College, Macaulay has this to say:

> The Petitioners stated that they had studied in the college ten or twelve years, that they had made themselves acquainted with Hindoo literature and Science, that they had received certificates of proficiency. And what is the fruit of all this? 'Notwithstanding such testimonials,' they say, 'we have but little prospect of bettering our condition without the kind assistance of your Honorable Committee, the indifference with which we are generally looked upon by our Countrymen leaving no hope of encouragement and assistance from them.' They therefore beg that they may be recommended to the Governor-General for places under the Government—not places of high dignity or emolument, but such as may just enable them to exist. 'We want means,' they say, 'for a decent living, and for our progressive improvement, which, however,

> we cannot obtain without the assistance of Government, by whom we have been educated and maintained from childhood'. (60–61)

Thus, the demand for English education came from the 'natives' themselves—and this was, for Macaulay, the clinching argument.

Macaulay made the case for English education very simple: the Indians clamour for it because they need it. Here Macaulay inscribes the logic of native need within that of economies of Empire and improvement. Hence Macaulay emphasises the expense of educating the Indians and the cost to the exchequer. He writes of the absurdity of paying the colonial subject for studying Sanskrit or Arabic (in the form of special provisions for madrassas or the Sanskrit College):

> The people of India do not require to be paid for eating rice when they are hungry, or for wearing woollen cloth in the cold season. To come nearer to the case before us; the children who learn their letters and a little elementary arithmetic from the Village Schoolmaster are not paid by him. He is paid for teaching them. Why then is it necessary to pay people to learn Sanscrit and Arabic? Evidently because it is universally felt that the Sanscrit and Arabic are languages the knowledge of which does not compensate for the trouble of acquiring them. (60)

As Zastoupil and Morin put it:

> The emerging logic of political economy was at work here: what people find useful or valuable they will gladly pay for (no one has to be paid to eat rice or wear warm clothes in cold weather); therefore, education undertaken only with the promise of a stipend must be patently useless. (1999, 34)

After speaking of the petition submitted by the ex-students of the Sanskrit College, Macaulay writes:

> These are surely the first petitioners who ever demanded compensation for having been educated gratis, for having been supported by the public during twelve years, and then sent forth into the world well furnished with literature and science. They represent their education as an injury which gives them a claim on the Government for redress – as an injury for which the stipends paid to them during the infliction were a very inadequate compensation. And I doubt not that they are in the right. They have wasted the best years of life in learning what procures for them neither bread nor respect.... Bounties and premiums, such as ought not to be given even for the propagation of Truth, we lavish on false texts and false philosophy.... What we spend on the Arabic and Sanscrit colleges is not merely a dead loss to the cause of truth. It is bounty-money paid to raise up champions of error. It goes to form a nest not merely of helpless place-hunters but of bigots prompted alike

> by passion and by interest to raise a cry against every useful scheme of education. (61)

Even the Indians themselves, argues Macaulay, do not want this education:

> we are forced to pay our Arabic and Sanscrit students while those who learn English are willing to pay us … we cannot find in all our vast empire a single student who will let us teach him those dialects, unless we will pay him. (60)

Macaulay then turns to other expenses incurred in educating the colonial subjects, the costs of textbooks and instructional materials:

> The committee have thought fit to lay out above a lac of rupees in printing Arabic and Sanscrit books. Those books find no purchasers. It is very rarely that a single copy is disposed of. Twenty three thousand volumes, most of them folios and quartos, fill the libraries or rather the lumber rooms of this body. The Committee contrive to get rid of some portion of their vast stock of Oriental literature by giving books away. But they cannot give so fast as they print. About Twenty thousand rupees a year are spent in adding fresh masses of waste paper to a hoard which, one should think, is already sufficiently ample. During the last three years about sixty thousand rupees have been expended in this manner. The sale of Arabic and Sanscrit books, during those three years has not yielded quite one Thousand rupees. In the mean time, the School book society is selling seven or eight thousand English volumes every year, and not only pays the expenses of printing but realizes a profit of twenty per Cent. on its outlay. (61–62)

Macaulay also concludes the essay with an economic argument, one that resonates, ironically, even today in terms of the *use* value of education, the mere granting of degrees without skills and the drain on the exchequer. The Committee on Public Instruction, says Macaulay, seems to be devoted to

> raising up a breed of scholars who find their scholarship an incumbrance and blemish, who live on the public while they are receiving their education, and whose education is so utterly useless to them that, when they have received it, they must either starve or live on the public all the rest of their lives. (64)

It is an education that does not prepare the student for living: they cannot afford a living, in fact, especially if this education is in Sanskrit or Arabic. Implicitly, English education is economically empowering.[1]

The 'Imperishable Empire'

Macaulay's concern with *how* India was to be governed and how Indians were to be made colonial subjects dates further back in time and is a framework for the Minute. On 10 July 1833, Macaulay spoke on the India Bill in the English parliament. He said:

> It is scarcely possible to calculate the benefits which we might derive from the diffusion of European civilisation among the vast population of the East. It would be, on the most selfish view of the case, far better for us that the people of India were well governed and independent of us, than ill governed and subject to us; that they were ruled by their own kings, but wearing our broadcloth, and working with our cutlery, than that they were performing their *salams* to English collectors and English magistrates, but were too ignorant to value, or too poor to buy, English manufactures. To trade with civilised men is infinitely more profitable than to govern savages. That would, indeed, be a doting wisdom, which, in order that India might remain a dependency, would make it an useless and costly dependency, which would keep a hundred millions of men from being our customers in order that they might continue to be our slaves.
>
> Are we to keep the people of India ignorant in order that we may keep them submissive? Or do we think that we can give them knowledge without awakening ambition? Or do we mean to awaken ambition and to provide it with no legitimate vent? Who will answer any of these questions in the affirmative? Yet one of them must be answered in the affirmative, by every person who maintains that we ought permanently to exclude the natives from high office. I have no fears. The path of duty is plain before us: and it is also the path of wisdom, of national prosperity, of national honour....
>
> It may be that the public mind of India may expand under our system till it has outgrown that system; that by good government we may educate our subjects into a capacity for better government; that, having become instructed in European knowledge, they may, in some future age, demand European institutions. Whether such a day will ever come I know not. But never will I attempt to avert or to retard it. Whenever it comes, it will be the proudest day in English history. To have found a great people sunk in the lowest depths of slavery and superstition, to have so ruled them as to have made them desirous and capable of all the privileges of citizens, would indeed be a title to glory all our own. The sceptre may pass away from us. Unforeseen accidents may derange our most profound schemes of policy. Victory may be inconstant to our arms. But there are triumphs which are followed by no reverse. There is an empire exempt from all natural causes of decay. Those triumphs are the pacific triumphs of reason over barbarism; that empire is the imperishable empire of our arts and our morals, our literature and our laws. (Macaulay, 'Government of India', unpaginated)[2]

In short, Macaulay argued that educating the Indians on English lines would ensure the continuity of the British Empire because the Indians would be 'Englished', so to speak, and stay within the frames of 'civilisation' as defined, determined and tutored by the British long after the British leave. This idea of the 'imperishable Empire' is not simply about English education as a formal system and practice but more about cultural training and indoctrination. The 'imperishable empire' is the transformation of the colonial subjects into approximations of the white man, separated from their roots and cultures. To this end, he suggests that it was Greek and Latin that enabled the cultural improvement of the English people (as already cited). Whether this implies, by the same logic, that the British Isles were an outpost of, or clone of, the ancient Greek Empire(s) is a moot point!

This 'imperishable Empire' is to be built, then, on the foundation of English education. Anticipating the argument that such training in the English language may be difficult for the colonial subject to acquire, Macaulay writes:

> an intelligent English youth, in a much smaller number of years than our unfortunate pupils pass at the Sanscrit college, becomes able to read, to enjoy, and even to imitate not unhappily the compositions of the best Greek authors. Less than half the time which enables an English youth to read Herodotus and Sophocles ought to enable a Hindoo to read Hume and Milton. (2020, 63)

Once this education is acquired, argues Macaulay, their entry into the 'imperishable Empire' is assured because

> In India, English is the language spoken by the ruling class. It is spoken by the higher class of natives at the seats of Govt. It is likely to become the language of commerce throughout the seas of the East. (58)

The 'imperishable Empire' is made of colonial subjects who have a tradition of their own, but have been schooled in English/European ways of thinking and so will serve the British government in its work on the subcontinent:

> We must at present do our best to form a class who may be interpreters between us and the millions whom we govern – a class of persons Indian in blood and colour, but English in tastes, in opinions, in morals and in intellect. (63)

The purpose of English was, as Narayana Chandran puts it, the

> training of native clerks for the English offices of the colony [and] the trained native clerk, the 'Baboo', the 'writer' [who would], would train his successors in English for specific (administrative) purposes (Chandran 2009, 302)

But this class, Macaulay believes, will also serve the local cultures and languages:

> To that class we may leave it to refine the vernacular dialects of this Country, to enrich those dialects with terms of science borrowed from the western nomenclature, and to render them by degrees fit vehicles for conveying knowledge to the great mass of the population. (63)

This means the English-educated Indian would serve as a conduit for Western rationality, science, aesthetics and thinking in general to enter the large mass of people when these are infused into the vernacular. Macaulay sees the class of English-educated Indians as empowering the vernacular languages and cultures—but in the form of hybridised, Westernised domains infused with the thought of the Western world.

***

Macaulay settled the Anglicist-Orientalist debate and in the process enabled a social experiment/engineering on a massive scale in the form of English education. In the postcolonial era, the debate around the 'master's language', the professionalisation of English, the impact it has had on the consumption of knowledge and domains such as literary studies, and the 'transactions' English has had with Indian languages have been studied extensively (Trivedi 1995, Evans 2002, Vishwanathan 2015, Chandran 2018, among others). And yet, notes Chandran, despite the original 'purpose' the British administrators had for English in India, it grew 'outward' with

> the English-educated Indians enlarging the scope of this language by becoming writers not only of receipts and bills of lading but, nearly a hundred years later, of literary works of noticeable strength and public acclaim. (2009, 302)

It enables the managerial class to obtain and retain power:

> It [English] is used 'specifically' by an Olympian bureaucracy to obfuscate public reason and occlude larger social involvement. The other use for which English is widely harnessed in India is more lowly and plebian. We have the lower rungs of baboodom, the routinely underpaid and badly treated secretarial staff, for whom English is specifically and bluntly utilitarian. Lacking the command of both English and executive power, they revel in the offensive officialese of the colony, specimens of which are easily collected from governmental orders, public notices, and gazette records of India's state and central governments. (Chandran 2009, 303)

Others highlight the 'alternative hegemonies' English has enabled for the traditionally marginalised sections of Indian society in terms of social mobility (Mukherjee 2009).[3]

SPEECHES
BY LORD MACAULAY
with his Minute on
INDIAN EDUCATION

Selected with an Introduction
and Notes by
G. M. YOUNG

OXFORD UNIVERSITY PRESS
LONDON : HUMPHREY MILFORD

Thomas Babington, Lord Macaulay

Born, Rothley Temple, Leicestershire,
October 25, 1800.

Died, Holly Lodge, Campden Hill, Kensington,
December 28, 1859.

Macaulay's Speeches, corrected by himself, were first published in 1854. *In 'The World's Classics' the present selection, made by Mr. G. M. Young, together with Macaulay's Minute on Indian Education* (1835), *was first published in* 1935.

Minute of the 2nd of February, 1835

As it seems to be the opinion of some of the gentlemen who compose the Committee of Public Instruction, that the course which they have hitherto pursued was strictly prescribed by the British Parliament in 1813, and as, if that opinion be correct, a legislative act will be necessary to warrant a change, I have thought it right to refrain from taking any part in the preparation of the adverse statements which are now before us, and to reserve what I had to say on the subject till it should come before me as a member of the Council of India.

It does not appear to me that the Act of Parliament can, by any art of construction, be made to bear the meaning which has been assigned to it. It contains nothing about the particular languages or sciences which are to be studied. A sum is set apart 'for the revival and promotion of literature and the encouragement of the learned natives of India, and for the introduction and promotion of a knowledge of the sciences among the inhabitants of the British territories.' It is argued, or rather taken for granted, that by literature, the Parliament can have meant only Arabic and Sanscrit literature, that they never would have given the honorable appellation of 'a learned native' to a native who was familiar with the poetry of Milton, the Metaphysics of Locke, and the Physics of Newton; but that they meant to designate by that name only such persons as might have studied in the sacred books of the Hindoos all the uses of cusa-grass, and all the mysteries of absorption into the Deity. This does not appear to be a very satisfactory interpretation. To take a parallel case; suppose that the Pacha of Egypt, a country once superior in knowledge to the nations of Europe, but now sunk far below them, were to appropriate a sum for the purpose of 'reviving and promoting literature, and encouraging learned natives of Egypt,' would anybody infer that he meant the youth of his pachalic to give years to the study of hieroglyphics, to search into all the doctrines disguised under the fable of Osiris, and to ascertain with all possible accuracy the ritual with which cats and onions were anciently adored? Would he be justly charged with inconsistency, if, instead of employing his young subjects in deciphering obelisks, he were to order them to be instructed in the English and French languages, and in all the sciences to which those languages are the chief keys?

The words on which the supporters of the old system rely do not bear them out, and other words follow which seem to be quite decisive on the other side. This lac of rupees is set apart, not only for 'reviving literature in India,' the phrase on which their whole interpretation is founded, but also for 'the introduction and promotion of a knowledge of the sciences among the inhabitants of the British territories,'—words which are alone sufficient to authorise all the changes for which I contend.

If the Council agree in my construction, no legislative act will be necessary. If they differ from me, I will prepare a short Act rescinding that clause of the Charter of 1813, from which the difficulty arises.

The argument which I have been considering, affects only the form of proceeding. But the admirers of the Oriental system of education have used another argument, which, if we admit it to be valid, is decisive against all change. They conceive that the public faith is pledged to the present system, and that to alter the appropriation of any of the funds which have hitherto been spent in encouraging the study of Arabic and Sanscrit, would be down-right spoliation. It is not easy to understand by what process of reasoning they can have arrived at this conclusion. The grants which are made from the public purse for the encouragement of literature differed in no respect from the grants which are made from the same purse for other objects of real or supposed utility. We found a sanatarium on a spot which we suppose to be healthy. Do we thereby pledge ourselves to keep a sanatarium there, if the result should not answer our expectation? We commence the erection of a pier. Is it a violation of the public faith to stop the works, if we afterwards see reason to believe that the building will be useless? The rights of property are undoubtedly sacred. But nothing endangers those rights so much as the practice, now unhappily too common, of attributing them to things to which they do not belong. Those who would impart to abuses the sanctity of property are in truth imparting to the institution of property the unpopularity and the fragility of abuses. If the Government has given to any person a formal assurance; nay, if the Government has excited in any person's mind a reasonable expectation that he shall receive a certain income as a teacher or a learner of Sanscrit or Arabic, I would respect that person's pecuniary interests—I would rather err on the side of liberality to individuals than suffer the public faith to be called in question. But to talk of a Government pledging itself to teach certain languages and certain sciences, though those languages may become useless, though those sciences may be exploded, seems to me quite unmeaning. There is not a single word in any public instructions, from which it can be inferred that the Indian Government ever intended to give any pledge on this subject, or ever considered the destination of these funds as unalterably fixed. But had it been otherwise, I should have denied the competence of our predecessors to bind us by any pledge on such a subject. Suppose that a Government had in the last century enacted in the most solemn manner that all its subjects should, to the end of time, be inoculated for the small-pox:

would that Government be bound to persist in the practice after Jenner's discovery? These promises, of which nobody claims the performance, and from which nobody can grant a release; these vested rights, which vest in nobody; this property without proprietors; this robbery, which makes nobody poorer, may be comprehended by persons of higher faculties than mine.—I consider this plea merely as a set form of words, regularly used both in England and in India, in defence of every abuse for which no other plea can be set up.

I hold this lac of rupees to be quite at the disposal of the Governor-General in Council, for the purpose of promoting learning in India, in any way which may be thought most advisable. I hold his Lordship to be quite as free to direct that it shall no longer be employed in encouraging Arabic and Sanscrit, as he is to direct that the reward for killing tigers in Mysore shall be diminished, or that no more public money shall be expended on the chanting at the cathedral.

We now come to the gist of the matter. We have a fund to be employed as Government shall direct for the intellectual improvement of the people of this country. The simple question is, what is the most useful way of employing it?

All parties seem to be agreed on one point, that the dialects commonly spoken among the natives of this part of India, contain neither literary nor scientific information, and are, moreover, so poor and rude that, until they are enriched from some other quarter, it will not be easy to translate any valuable work into them. It seems to be admitted on all sides, that the intellectual improvement of those classes of the people who have the means of pursuing higher studies can at present be effected only by means of some language not vernacular amongst them.

What then shall that language be? One-half of the Committee maintain that it should be the English. The other half strongly recommend the Arabic and

Sanscrit. The whole question seems to me to be, which language is the best worth knowing?

I have no knowledge of either Sanscrit or Arabic. —But I have done what I could to form a correct estimate of their value. I have read translations of the most celebrated Arabic and Sanscrit works. I have conversed both here and at home with men distinguished by their proficiency in the Eastern tongues. I am quite ready to take the Oriental learning at the valuation of the Orientalists themselves. I have never found one among them who could deny that a single shelf of a good European library was worth the whole native literature of India and Arabia. The intrinsic superiority of the Western literature is, indeed, fully admitted by those members of the Committee who support the Oriental plan of education.

It will hardly be disputed, I suppose, that the department of literature in which the eastern writers stand highest is poetry. And I certainly never met with any Orientalist who ventured to maintain that the Arabic and Sanscrit poetry could be compared to that of the great European nations. But when we pass from works of imagination to works in which facts are recorded, and general principles investigated, the superiority of the Europeans becomes absolutely immeasurable. It is, I believe, no exaggeration to say, that all the historical information which has been collected from all the books written in the Sanscrit language is less valuable than what may be found in the most paltry abridgments used at preparatory schools in England. In every branch of physical or moral philosophy, the relative position of the two nations is nearly the same.

How, then, stands the case? We have to educate a people who cannot at present be educated by means of their mother-tongue. We must teach them some foreign language. The claims of our own language it is hardly necessary to recapitulate. It stands pre-eminent even among the languages of the west. It abounds with works of imagination not inferior to the noblest which Greece has bequeathed to us; with models of every species of eloquence; with historical compositions, which, considered merely as narratives, have seldom been surpassed, and which, considered as vehicles of ethical and political instruction, have never been equalled; with just and lively representations of human life and human nature; with the most profound speculations on metaphysics, morals, government, jurisprudence, and trade; with full and correct information respecting every experimental science which tends to preserve the health, to increase the comfort, or to expand the intellect of man. Whoever knows that language has ready access to all the vast intellectual wealth, which all the wisest nations of the earth have created and hoarded in the course of ninety generations. It may safely be said, that the literature now extant in that language is of far greater value than all the literature which three hundred years ago was extant in all the languages of the world together. Nor is this all. In India, English is the language spoken by the ruling class. It is spoken by the higher class of natives at the seats of Government. It is likely to become the language of commerce throughout the seas of the East. It is the language of two great European communities which are rising, the one in the south of Africa, the other in Australasia; communities which are every year becoming more important, and more closely connected with our Indian empire. Whether we look at the intrinsic value of our literature, or at the particular situation of this country, we shall see the strongest reason to think that, of all foreign tongues, the English tongue is that which would be the most useful to our native subjects.

The question now before us is simply whether, when it is in our power to teach this language, we shall teach languages in which, by universal confession, there are no books on any subject which deserve to be compared to our own; whether, when we can teach European science, we shall teach systems which, by universal confession, whenever they differ from those of Europe, differ for the worse; and whether, when we can patronise sound Philosophy and true History, we shall countenance, at the public expense, medical doctrines, which would disgrace an English farrier,—Astronomy, which would move laughter in girls at an English boarding school,—History, abounding with kings thirty feet high, and reigns thirty thousand years long,—and Geography, made up of seas of treacle and seas of butter.

We are not without experience to guide us. History furnishes several analogous cases, and they all teach the same lesson. There are in modern times, to go no further, two memorable instances of a great impulse given to the mind of a whole society,—of prejudices overthrown,—of knowledge diffused,—of taste purified,—of arts and sciences planted in countries which had recently been ignorant and barbarous.

The first instance to which I refer, is the great revival of letters among the Western nations at the close of the fifteenth and the beginning of the sixteenth century. At that time almost every thing that was worth reading was contained in the writings of the ancient Greeks and Romans. Had our ancestors acted as the Committee of Public Instruction has hitherto acted; had they neglected the language of Cicero and Tacitus; had they confined their attention to the old dialects of our own island; had they printed nothing and taught nothing at the universities but Chronicles in Anglo-Saxon, and Romances in Norman-French, would England have been what she now is? What the Greek and Latin were to the contemporaries of More and Ascham, our tongue is to the people of India. The literature of England is now more valuable than that of classical antiquity. I doubt whether the Sanscrit literature be as valuable as that of our Saxon and Norman progenitors. In some departments,—in History, for example, I am certain that it is much less so.

Another instance may be said to be still before our eyes. Within the last hundred and twenty years, a nation which had previously been in a state as barbarous as that in which our ancestors were before the crusades, has gradually emerged from the ignorance in which it was sunk, and has taken its place among civilised communities.—I speak of Russia. There is now in that country a large educated class, abounding with persons fit to serve the state in the highest functions, and in no wise inferior to the most accomplished men who adorn the best circles of Paris and London. There is reason to hope that this vast empire, which in the time of our grandfathers was probably behind the Punjab, may, in the time of our grandchildren, be pressing close on France and Britain in the career of improvement. And how was this change effected? Not by flattering national prejudices: not by feeding the mind of the young Muscovite with the old women's stories which his rude fathers had believed: not by filling his head with lying legends about St. Nicholas: not by encouraging him to study the great question, whether the world was or was not created on the 13th of September: not by calling him 'a learned native,' when he has mastered all these points of knowledge: but by teaching him those foreign languages in which the greatest mass of information had been laid up, and thus putting all that information within his reach. The languages of Western Europe civilised Russia. I cannot doubt that they will do for the Hindoo what they have done for the Tartar.

And what are the arguments against that course which seems to be alike recommended by theory and by experience? It is said that we ought to secure the co-operation of the native public, and that we can do this only by teaching Sanscrit and Arabic.

I can by no means admit that when a nation of high intellectual attainments undertakes to superintend the education of a nation comparatively ignorant, the learners are absolutely to prescribe the course which is to be taken by the teachers. It is not necessary, however, to say any thing on this subject. For it is proved by unanswerable evidence that we are not at present securing the co-operation of the natives. It would be bad enough to consult their intellectual taste at the expense of their intellectual health. But we are consulting neither,—we are withholding from them the learning for which they are craving, we are forcing on them the mock-learning which they nauseate.

This is proved by the fact that we are forced to pay our Arabic and Sanscrit students, while those who learn English are willing to pay us. All the declamations in the world about the love and reverence of the natives for their sacred dialects will never, in the mind of any impartial person, outweigh the undisputed fact, that we cannot find, in all our vast empire, a single student who will let us teach him those dialects unless we will pay him.

I have now before me the accounts of the Madrassa for one month,—the month of December, 1833. The Arabic students appear to have been seventy-seven in number. All receive stipends from the public. The whole amount paid to them is above 500 rupees a month. On the other side of the account stands the following item: Deduct amount realized from the out-students of English for the months of May, June and July last, 103 rupees.

I have been told that it is merely from want of local experience that I am surprised at these phenomena, and that it is not the fashion for students in India to study at their own charges. This only confirms me in my opinion. Nothing is more certain than that it never can in any part of the world be necessary to pay men for doing what they think pleasant and profitable. India is no exception to this rule. The people of India do not require to be paid for eating rice when they are hungry, or for wearing woollen cloth in the cold season. To come nearer to the case before us, the children who learn their letters and a little elementary Arithmetic from the village school-master are not paid by him. He is paid for teaching them. Why then is it necessary to pay people to learn Sanscrit and Arabic? Evidently because it is universally felt that the Sanscrit and Arabic are languages, the knowledge of which does not compensate for the trouble of acquiring them. On all such subjects the state of the market is the decisive test.

Other evidence is not wanting, if other evidence were required. A petition was presented last year to the Committee by several ex-students of the Sanscrit College. The petitioners stated that they had studied in the college ten or twelve years; that they had made themselves acquainted with Hindoo literature and science; that they had received certificates of proficiency: and what is the fruit of all this! 'Notwithstanding such testimonials,' they say, 'we have but little prospect of bettering our condition without the kind assistance of your Honorable Committee, the indifference with which we are generally looked upon by our countrymen leaving no hope of encouragement and assistance from them.' They therefore beg that they may be recommended to the Governor General for places under the Government, not places of high dignity or emolument, but such as may just enable them to exist. 'We want means,' they say, 'for a decent living, and for our progressive improvement, which, however, we cannot obtain without the assistance of Government, by whom we have been educated and maintained from childhood.' They conclude by representing, very pathetically, that they are sure that it was never the intention of Government, after behaving so liberally to them during their education, to abandon them to destitution and neglect.

I have been used to see petitions to Government for compensation. All these petitions, even the most unreasonable of them, proceeded on the supposition that some loss had been sustained—that some wrong had been inflicted. These are surely the first petitioners who ever demanded compensation for having been educated gratis,—for having been supported by the public during twelve years, and then sent forth into the world well furnished with literature and science. They represent their education as an injury which gives them a claim on the Government for redress, as an injury for which the stipends paid to them during the infliction were a very inadequate compensation. And I doubt not that they are in the right. They have wasted the best years of life in learning what procures for them neither bread nor respect. Surely we might, with advantage, have saved the cost of making these persons useless and miserable; surely, men may be brought up to be burdens to the public and objects of contempt to their neighbours at a somewhat smaller charge to the state. But such is our policy. We do not even stand neuter in the contest between truth and falsehood. We are not content to leave the natives to the influence of their own hereditary prejudices. To the natural difficulties which obstruct the progress of sound science in the East, we add fresh difficulties of our own making. Bounties and premiums, such as ought not to be given even for the propagation of truth, we lavish on false taste and false philosophy.

By acting thus we create the very evil which we fear. We are making that opposition which we do not find. What we spend on the Arabic and Sanscrit colleges is not merely a dead loss to the cause of truth; it is bounty-money paid to raise up champions of error. It goes to form a nest, not merely of helpless place-hunters, but of bigots prompted alike by passion and by interest to raise a cry against every useful scheme of education. If there should be any opposition among the natives to the change which I recommend, that opposition will be the effect of our own system. It will be headed by persons supported by our stipends and trained in our colleges. The longer we persevere in our present course, the more formidable will that opposition be. It will be every year reinforced by recruits whom we are paying. From the native society left to itself, we have no difficulties to apprehend; all the murmuring will come from that oriental interest which we have, by artificial means, called into being, and nursed into strength.

There is yet another fact, which is alone sufficient to prove that the feeling of the native public, when left to itself, is not such as the supporters of the old system represent it to be. The Committee have thought fit to lay out above a lac of rupees in printing Arabic and Sanscrit books. Those books find no purchasers. It is very rarely that a single copy is disposed of. Twenty-three thousand volumes, most of them folios and quartos, fill the libraries, or rather the lumber-rooms, of this body. The Committee contrive to get rid of some portion of their vast stock of oriental literature by giving books away. But they cannot give so fast as they print. About twenty thousand rupees a year are spent in adding fresh masses of waste paper to a hoard which, I should think, is already sufficiently ample. During the last three years, about sixty thousand rupees have been expended in this manner. The sale of Arabic and Sanscrit books, during those three years, has not yielded quite one thousand rupees. In the mean time the School-book Society is selling seven or eight thousand English volumes every year, and not only pays the expenses of printing, but realises a profit of 20 per cent. on its outlay.

The fact that the Hindoo law is to be learned

chiefly from Sanscrit books, and the Mahometan law from Arabic books, has been much insisted on, but seems not to bear at all on the question. We are commanded by Parliament to ascertain and digest the laws of India. The assistance of a law Commission has been given to us for that purpose. As soon as the code is promulgated, the Shasters and the Hedaya will be useless to a Moonsiff or Sudder Ameen. I hope and trust that before the boys who are now entering at the Madrassa and the Sanscrit college have completed their studies, this great work will be finished. It would be manifestly absurd to educate the rising generation with a view to a state of things which we mean to alter before they reach manhood.

But there is yet another argument which seems even more untenable. It is said that the Sanscrit and Arabic are the languages in which the sacred books of a hundred millions of people are written, and that they are, on that account, entitled to peculiar encouragement. Assuredly it is the duty of the British Government in India to be not only tolerant, but neutral on all religious questions. But to encourage the study of a literature admitted to be of small intrinsic value, only because that literature inculcates the most serious errors on the most important subjects, is a course hardly reconcileable with reason, with morality, or even with that very neutrality which ought, as we all agree, to be sacredly preserved. It is confessed that a language is barren of useful knowledge. We are to teach it because it is fruitful of monstrous superstitions. We are to teach false History, false Astronomy, false Medicine, because we find them in company with a false religion. We abstain, and I trust shall always abstain, from giving any public encouragement to those who are engaged in the work of converting natives to Christianity. And while we act thus, can we reasonably and decently bribe men out of the revenues of the state to waste their youth in learning how they are to purify themselves after touching an ass, or what text of the Vedas they are to repeat to expiate the crime of killing a goat?

It is taken for granted by the advocates of Oriental learning, that no native of this country can possibly attain more than a mere smattering of English. They do not attempt to prove this; but they perpetually insinuate it. They designate the education which their opponents recommend as a mere spelling book education. They assume it as undeniable, that the question is between a profound knowledge of Hindoo and Arabian literature and science on the one side, and a superficial knowledge of the rudiments of English on the other. This is not merely an assumption, but an assumption contrary to all reason and experience. We know that foreigners of all nations do learn our language sufficiently to have access to all the most abstruse knowledge which it contains, sufficiently to relish even the more delicate graces of our most idiomatic writers. There are in this very town natives who are quite competent to discuss political or scientific questions with fluency and precision in the English language. I have heard the very question on which I am now writing discussed by native gentlemen with a liberality and an intelligence which would do credit to any member of the Committee of Public Instruction. Indeed it is unusual to find, even in the literary circles of the continent, any foreigner who can express himself in English with so much facility and correctness as we find in many Hindoos. Nobody, I suppose, will contend that English is so difficult to a Hindoo as Greek to an Englishman. Yet an intelligent English youth, in a much smaller number of years than our unfortunate pupils pass at the Sanscrit college, becomes able to read, to enjoy, and even to imitate, not unhappily, the compositions of the best Greek Authors. Less than half the time which enables an English youth to read Herodotus and Sophocles, ought to enable a Hindoo to read Hume and Milton.

To sum up what I have said, I think it clear that we are not fettered by the Act of Parliament of 1813; that we are not fettered by any pledge expressed or implied; that we are free to employ our funds as we choose; that we ought to employ them in teaching what is best worth knowing; that English is better worth knowing than Sanscrit or Arabic; that the natives are desirous to be taught English, and are not desirous to be taught Sanscrit or Arabic; that neither as the languages of law, nor as the languages of religion, have the Sanscrit and Arabic any peculiar claim to our engagement; that it is possible to make natives of this country thoroughly good English scholars, and that to this end our efforts ought to be directed.

In one point I fully agree with the gentlemen to whose general views I am opposed. I feel with them, that it is impossible for us, with our limited means, to attempt to educate the body of the people. We must at present do our best to form a class who may be interpreters between us and the millions whom we govern; a class of persons, Indian in blood and colour, but English in taste, in opinions, in morals, and in intellect. To that class we may leave it to refine the vernacular dialects of the country, to enrich those dialects with terms of science borrowed from the Western nomenclature, and to render them by degrees fit vehicles for conveying knowledge to the great mass of the population.

I would strictly respect all existing interests. I would deal even generously with all individuals who have had fair reason to expect a pecuniary provision. But I would strike at the root of the bad system which has hitherto been fostered by us. I would at once stop the printing of Arabic and Sanscrit books, I would abolish the Madrassa and the Sanscrit college at Calcutta. Benares is the great seat of Brahmanical learning; Delhi, of Arabic learning. If we retain the Sanscrit college at Benares and the Mahometan college at Delhi, we do enough, and much more than enough in my opinion, for the Eastern languages. If the Benares and Delhi colleges should be retained, I would at least recommend that no stipends shall be given to any students who may hereafter repair thither, but that the people shall be left to make their own choice between the rival systems of education without being bribed by us to learn what they have no desire to know. The funds which would thus be placed at our disposal would enable us to give larger encouragement to the Hindoo college at Calcutta, and to establish in the principal cities throughout the Presidencies of Fort William and Agra schools in which the English language might be well and thoroughly taught.

If the decision of his Lordship in Council should be such as I anticipate, I shall enter on the performance of my duties with the greatest zeal and alacrity. If, on the other hand, it be the opinion of the Government that the present system ought to remain unchanged, I beg that I may be permitted to retire from the chair of the Committee. I feel that I could not be of the smallest use there—I feel, also, that I should be lending my countenance to what I firmly believe to be a mere delusion. I believe that the present system tends, not to accelerate the progress of truth, but to delay the natural death of expiring errors. I conceive that we have at present no right to the respectable name of a Board of Public Instruction. We are a Board for wasting public money, for printing books which are of less value than the paper on which they are printed was while it was blank; for giving artificial encouragement to absurd history, absurd metaphysics, absurd physics, absurd theology; for raising up a breed of scholars who find their scholarship an encumbrance and a blemish, who live on the public while they are receiving their education, and whose education is so utterly useless to them that when they have received it they must either starve or live on the public all the rest of their lives. Entertaining these opinions, I am naturally desirous to decline all share in the responsibility of a body, which, unless it alters its whole mode of proceeding, I must consider not merely as useless, but as positively noxious.

8

IMPERIAL CONTROL

Often called 'Thuggee Sleeman' for his efforts at rooting out the thuggee, Sleeman wrote extensively on the bandit communities of northern India. His *Rambles and Recollections of an Indian Official* (1844) carried a chapter on thugs and poisoners. He also published *Ramaseeana*, a 'vocabulary' of the language of the thugs (1836) and filed various reports with the government on the 'thuggee problem' and the campaigns against them. In 1839 he published the two-volume book-length study of thugs, in which he also added a section on the *pindaris* (volume I). Indeed, the very 'edifice of Thuggee' was constructed around the biography and figure of Sleeman himself, argues Máire Ní Fhlathuin (2001, 70). Sleeman was appointed the general superintendent who was entrusted with the task of suppressing the gangs of thugs.

Sleeman was not, however, the first to document the thugs. John Shakespeare published 'Observations Regarding Badheks and T'hegs' in the *Asiatic Researches* of 1820. Richard Sherwood, J.A.R. Stevenson, H.H. Spry and others had published similar accounts in places like the *Journal of the Royal Asiatic Society* and *The Phrenological Journal and Miscellany*, besides book-length works, studying the community of thugs and their depredations. Philip Meadows Taylor published his *Confessions of a Thug* in 1839. Much of the 19th-century and later perceptions of the thuggee stem from Sleeman's works. His writing in the periodicals enabled the public discourse around thuggee and was a part of the propaganda engineered by his department: 'the T[hugee] D[epartment] fed the press sensational details of thug activities, and their own successes against them, in order to argue for increased resources for themselves' (Fhlathuin 2004, 127).

For the British, thuggee was linked to all that was evil in Indian religion, particularly Hinduism. It was a form of ritual murder, committed by groups of people who travelled with unsuspecting traders and others on the highways and, at an opportune moment, strangled them to death. Closely aligned with the thugs were the 'poisoners' who employed poisons such as *datura* to kill their victims, also during a highway journey. For the British, these murders were committed under the auspices of Hindu gods such as Kali, for the thugs sought to propitiate the goddess.

From the 1830s, a concerted campaign by Sleeman, Philip Meadows Taylor and specific departments set out to identify and arrest the thugs, often employing former thugs as informers. By the mid-1830s, when the anti-thuggee campaign was already underway, legislation enabled the conviction of individuals caught for poisoning and robbery. This act, and the work of Sleeman and others, enabled the colonial state to construct the thuggee as religious in origin and organised as a community's practice. As early as 1839, Sleeman was able to announce the end of the thuggee as an organised criminal practice: 'In most parts of central India, Bundelcund, Boglecund, and from Allahabad to the Himalayah, Thuggee now scarcely exists' (I: 73).

Kim Wagner cautions us that the thug was not entirely a colonial construction:

> there *was* a social reality in terms of Indian banditry, which the British in turn misrepresented. It would be naïve to assume that the sources offer a direct access to the past, but it is equally naïve to assume that they do not in any way reflect the past from which they emerged. (2009, 8, emphasis in original. Also see Brown 2002, 82–83)[1]

Other commentators focus on the colonial construction of the thug as a monster and argue that the social reality of the thuggee is irrelevant in the face of the fact that all documentation on the phenomenon is solely colonial and hence must be read as an imperial discourse that created a reality (Bhattacharya 2020).[2] Yet others such as Parama Roy argue that the thuggee archive demonstrates two readings of the practice: the thugs as a unique community, set apart from other law-abiding citizenry, and thugs as natural to native society, fostered and encouraged by the society's values (Roy 1998, Chapter 2).

The history of the thuggee and the historiography around it, are 'incompatible', as an early and pioneering essay by Steward Gordon shows, in terms of how historians perceived their motivations, community/caste identities, the nature of their victims and finally, their political and geographic setting (1969, 404–405).

Structure and Content

Much of the content of the two volumes is, Sleeman writes in his 'Preface', from *Ramaseeana* and the works of others such as Richard Sherwood (who wrote about the thugs in 1816).

The first volume is divided into 'Early History', 'Difficulties Attending To the Suppression of Thuggee', 'Measures of the Government for Its Suppression', 'Captain Sleeman's Account', 'Disclosures of Informers in Conversation With Captain Sleeman'. The second volume opens with 'Disclosures of Informers', the *Ramaseeana*, and reproduces official papers from the prosecution and trials of the thugs.

The 'Early History' attempts to trace the origins of the name 'thug'. Sleeman then documents their religious affiliations and practices, their marriages and family systems, Hindu and Muslim thugs, their mode of operations, and others subjects.

> The Phansigars, or stranglers, are thus designated from the Hindustani word *phansis*, a noose. In the more northern parts of India, these murderers are called Thugs signifying deceivers: in the Tamul language, they are called *Ari Tulucar*, or Mussulman noosers: in Canarese, *Tanti Caleru* implying thieves, who use a wire or cat-gut noose: and in Telagu, *Warla Wahndlu* or *Warlu Vayshay Wahndloo* meaning people who use the noose. (13–14)

He gives the regional distribution of the thugs. He describes their ability at disguise and spends considerable time elaborating their modes of assassination, including their devices (ropes and nooses, kerchiefs). Sleeman is intensely curious about the religious affiliations of the thugs and discusses their Hindu and Muslim origins. Turning to their language, Sleeman proposes that the thugs employ a language, both verbal and gestural, that is secretive and restricted to the community (32).

Sleeman notes that despite their widespread carnage,

> I have heard of no instance in which a European was murdered by Phansigars. The manner in which they are accustomed to travel in India, is perhaps sufficient to exempt them from danger; added to which, apprehension of the consequences of strict inquiry ana search, should an European be missing, may be supposed to intimidate the *Phansigars*… (40)

He speaks of their 'moral insensibility' (43) and cites travellers like John Thavenot (travelling in India in 1666–1667) to document the history of their depredations over the ages. Women travellers were not, however, violated or murdered, notes Sleeman later (79)—a claim disproved by one of the interviews he conducts in which an informer admits that women have been killed by thugs (144).

Sleeman then turns to the British government's efforts to suppress thuggee but first notes that even though the government was not governed by the same superstitions, the conditions were not conducive to a serious effort to curb the practice (56–57). Indeed, Sleeman even states that the government was *not* keen to acknowledge such practices:

> Even had they [the officers of the government] been fully aware of it, the existence of such an evil as Thuggee over the whole of the British provinces, was by no means agreeable to the government, it would have contradicted their repeated assertions and representations … the proceedings of government have almost warranted a belief that they would prefer the existence of an evil, provided it were not generally

> known, even to the discovery of a remedy, if this should tend to produce a considerable sensation and excite inquiry. (I: 57–58)

He also notes that when the British government handed over captured thugs to the local native chiefs, they would be let off after a bribe (63) and notes that the criminals flourished because of the connivance of the landlords (93). Sleeman outlines the legal procedures—from arrest to deposition to approvers—instituted to convict the arrested thugs, noting with considerable delight that of the 2,000 who had been caught, about 300 turned approvers and about 1,400 sentenced to death/transportation (74). Sleeman then gives details of the several anti-thuggee campaigns in various parts of India.

There are fascinating accounts/transcripts of the conversations between the informers and Sleeman which make up the latter half of volume I. Sleeman elicits information about the caste configurations of the thuggee gangs, their area and modes of operations.

Volume II begins where volume I ends, with the accounts from informers in the form of interviews. Sleeman then includes the *Ramaseeana* here—which takes up the bulk of the second volume. He then reproduces correspondence of the British authorities dealing with the prosecution of the thugs and select trial proceedings.

Naming and Controlling

Wagner notes that while some indigenous sources do use the word 'thag' to signify a swindler and robbers who won the trust of the travellers and then strangled them, the British themselves 'never clearly defined their use of the word even when they perceived it as a fixed identity and made it a formal criminal category within the judicial system' (2009, 4). Thugs were recast as 'dacoits' after 1840, and 'dacoits' became 'criminal tribes' after 1870.

Identifying criminals and crimes was central to the colonial state's operations. David Arnold writes:

> Of greatest concern to the colonial authorities were those forms of crime, violence and protest that threatened either the general security of property or, more especially, the colonial power's authority and control. Perceptions of which crimes and which criminals were most dangerous changed over time. (1985, 83)

Eventually, of course, entire communities and castes would be identified and labelled as 'criminal tribes' through the enactment of a law in 1871. The Act of 1871 declared that the aim was 'to provide for the registration, surveillance and control of certain tribes', a process begun with Sleeman and the campaign against thuggee. Indeed, as Anand Yang points out, 'Punctuating the 1871 deliberations, which led to the enactment of the

Criminal Tribes' Act, were references to the earlier campaign against the thugs' (115).

The campaign against thuggee was driven by the recognition that the thugs were beyond imperial dominion and control. For the British to ensure their continuous and cohesive power over the land, such pockets of vagrant, unidentifiable groups of resisters (violent at that) could not be allowed to exist. In short, the surveil-and-exterminate movement against thuggee was an instantiation of imperial expansion. Mark Brown summarises the anxiety and campaign around thuggee thus:

> The 'discovery' of thuggee thus ought to be viewed in the wider context of British efforts to *know* the subjects of their governance and to identify threats to their rule. In such circumstances it might be more profitable, therefore, to read the discovery of thuggee and the campaign against it as indicative of a crisis of governance—a kind of moral panic—reflecting deeply felt British anxieties about their tenure on the subcontinent. (2002, 81–82, emphasis in original)

That is, the anti-thuggee campaigns, as they came to be called, were a part of the Company Raj's attempt to establish paramountcy.

Thus, the detailed accounts of identifying the religious and community affiliations of the thugs in Sleeman (and other accounts from the period: see Wagner 2007) were an integral part of the surveillance and classificatory system of the Empire. Information gathering through multiple modes—including, in Sleeman's case, the depositions and interviews—was also, as C.A. Bayly has argued (1999), an essential aspect of the colonial system. Dozens and dozens of reports were filed by Sleeman and other officers. But this was not all. As Fhlathuin observes:

> The key moment in the campaign, however, happened when these communications were taken out of the narrow circle of official and bureaucratic correspondence and moved into the public domain. (2004, 126–127)

Fhlathuin shows how the *Calcutta Literary Gazette* and the *Bengal Hurkaru* publishing 'the circulation of news of thugs' activities and TD actions against them' (128) enabled the public to be 'convinced of the reality of the Thugi menace' (129). The Sleeman texts, in both official and public domains, commitment to documenting the actions of the anti-thuggee campaign was an integral part of this mechanism. Contributing to the demonisation of the thugs, Sleeman's narratives borrowed from different genres and their conventions.

Turning to the victims of the thugs, Sleeman invokes the conventions of the sentimental novel as he paints two contrasting portraits: the distraught victim and the merciless killer.

> Since I undertook this duty, numbers have flocked to me to inquire after the fate of those whom they had long lost. Often in my court I have seen them listening with unobtrusive grief to a circumstantial detail of the murder of their parents, brothers or children from the mouths of these cold-blooded and merciless assassins, while the tears stole down their cheeks; and taking from my stores of recovered property some sad token in arms, dress, or ornaments, of the melancholy truth to take home to the widows and children of the murdered, who might otherwise doubt their tale of sorrow, and entertain some lingering but unavailing hope of their return. (I: 116)

The overwrought victim is here the centrepiece of Sleeman's description as he seeks to paint a remorseless perpetrator.

Sleeman speaks of 'thug families' (I: 17), suggesting that entire families are given to the profession. Even women, he claims, assisted in the murders. About the Phansigars he writes:

> They are often accompanied by children of ten years of age and upwards, who, while they perform menial offices, are initiated into the horrid practices of the Phansigars… (I: 18)

He then describes how the children are initiated into the profession over the years:

> Phansigars bring up all their male children to the profession, unless bodily defects prevent them from following it. The method observed in initiating a boy is very gradual. At the age often or twelve years, he is first permitted to accompany a party of Phansigars. One of the gang, generally a near relation, becomes his ustad or tutor, whom the child is taught to regard with great respect, and whom he usually serves in a menial capacity, carrying a bundle, and dressing food for him. Frequently the father acts as the preceptor to his son. In the event of being questioned by travellers whom he may meet, the boy is enjoined to give no information other than that they are proceeding from some one place to another. He is instructed to consider his interest as opposed to that of society in general and to deprive a human being of life is represented as an act merely analogous and equivalent to that of killing a fowl or a sheep. (I: 31)

Sleeman is gesturing at the inhuman nature of the family structure, too, by presenting the thuggee parenting system as one in which even the young are initiated into the barbaric ritual of killing. He also implies that for such a boy who has been told that taking human life is 'equivalent to that of killing a fowl or a sheep', the prospect of adulthood is a prospect of a murdering and pillaging life.

This collectivisation of crime was a key aspect of colonial control, as entire communities and groups could be defined as 'criminal' although, as Stewart Gordon points out,

> they came from dozens of different castes. Hindus and Moslems ate, slept, and worked together in some bands. Many of the men arrested were not members of long-standing criminal families, but were recruited later in life. Also, murder and robbery was not necessarily a hereditary occupation… (1969, 406–407)

Along with identifying sources of collective crimes, the colonial state also identified and persuaded several of the perpetrators to turn approvers and informers. Sandria Freitag writes of this system:

> Previously-convicted thugs were offered suspension of their sentences in return for testimony identifying other members of their gang and detailing the crimes committed by the gang. Often this was the only direct evidence against accused thugs, and the especially created "Thuggee and Dacoity Department" … sought out corroborative evidence and testimony of even insignificant details to make its veracity convincing. (1985, 147)[3]

In the early years (1790s–1820), one of the earliest Englishmen to encounter thuggee, Thomas Perry, the magistrate at Etawah, noted that

> by destroying all living testimony to the fact ... [the perpetrators] precluded the possibility of any complaints being preferred ... and consequently in no[t] one of the cases which has been reported to the office has any individual been directly implicated. (cited in Lloyd 2006, 3)

Tom Lloyd writes:

> Without witnesses to the attacks, or even formal complaints from relatives of the victims, the sole proof of the prisoners' guilt was their testimonies… (3)

But the approvers and informers also revealed the flaws in the system. For example, they confessed to bribing the local policemen. Nasir, one such approver, in the course of an interrogation, admits:

> I was obliged to give the chief officer at Kutungee a fine horse, and some other valuable articles that I had picked up on this expedition, as I found he was an old acquaintance of mine, and well disposed towards us as long as he was well conciliated in this way. I had got far off with my gang before the Subah's party came up after the rest. (Sleeman, II: 7)

They also reveal modes of operation and techniques of concealment such as the following:

> Shiekh Ahmed is the wisest man I know. He has great wealth, but he keeps it concealed in the woods. When danger approaches, he scatters his gang, and wanders alone with his wife till it is past or till he finds another secure abode, when he transfers his wealth to the woods about it. (II: 17)

In other cases, they recalled their depredations with pride, and in some cases, with sorrow when, for instance, young children died at their hands or because of their actions. In Ferinseea's narrative, we encounter this episode, which reveals the 'human' side of the thugs:

> We fell in with five Sikhs, and when we set out before daylight in the morning, Hursooka, who had been already on three expeditions, was ordered to take the bridle and keep the boy in the rear out of sight and hearing. The boy became alarmed, and impatient, got away from Hursooka, and galloped up at the instant the *Jhimee*, or signal for murder was given. He heard the screams of the men, and saw them all strangled. He was seized with a trembling, and fell from his pony; he became immediately delirious, was dreadfully alarmed at the sight of the turbans of the murdered men, and when any one touched or spoke to him, talked about the murders and screamed exactly like a boy talks in his sleep, and trembled violently if any one spoke to him or touched him. We could not get him on, and after burying the bodies, Aman and I, and a few others, sat by him while the gang went on. We were very fond of him, and tried all we could to tranquillize him, but he never recovered his senses, and before evening he died. I have seen many instances of feelings greatly shocked at the sight of the first murder, but never one so strong as this. (I: 128)

Genealogies, Religion and Crime

Edward Said's influential argument that the West sought to establish the Orient as a fixed, unchanging and timeless entity (1983) is borne out by Sleeman's text as well. In the Preface, thuggee is described as a 200-year-old practice (6), and Sleeman would also date it to 200 years in the past (I: 83). Later, trying to attempt a genealogy, Sleeman writes:

> I am still inclined to think that the vagrant bands, who, in the sixteenth century infested the roads, as above described, between Delhi and Agra, came from some wild tribe and country of the kind: and I feel myself no doubt, that from these vagrant bands are descended the seven clans of Mahommudun Thugs … who, by the common consent of all Thugs throughout India, whether Hindoos or Mahommuduns, are admitted to be the most ancient, and the great original trunk upon

which all others have at different times and in different places been grafted... (I: 82)

Sleeman here not only paints a picture of an antiquarian movement but also traces a 'root', so to speak, of the variations and divergences. This enables him to suggest that nothing in India has changed. Ancient practices, even barbaric ones, persist because, as Sleeman would observe elsewhere in the same work, India offers a 'congenial soil' in which thuggee

> flourished with rank luxuriance for more than two centuries, till its roots had penetrated and spread over almost every district within the limits of our dominions. (I: 83)

It also implies that India remains stuck in its antiquated customs and, therefore, represents the primitive stages of human civilisation, wherein such barbaric practices are the norm. As Gordon would comment about Sleeman's views: 'Thugs were assumed to be an ubiquitous, permanent, and immutable feature of Indian life' (405).

Indeed, Sleeman believed that even after thuggee had been put down, the chances of its revival were high because of the nature of religious beliefs in India:

> The old Thug Associations which have been now effectually put down in all parts of India ... would assuredly rise up again, and flourish under the assurance of religious sanctions and the strong and almost irresistible, disposition of the loose characters of the lowest class in India ... and new [associations] would be everywhere formed were the strengths of the special police, employed in the suppression, hastily reduced or its vigilance relaxed... (cited in Freitag, 148)

Genealogy interests Sleeman because he wishes to classify the thugs as Muslim or Hindu. This is the way a conversation with an informer proceeds:

> Q.—You are a Musulman?
>
> Sahib.—Yes, and the greater part of the Thugs of the south are Musulmans.
>
> Q.—And you still marry; inherit; pray; eat and drink according to the Koran; and your
>
> Paradise is to be the paradise promised by Mahommud?
>
> Sahib.—Yes, all, all.
>
> Q.—Has Bhowanee been any where named in the Koran?
>
> Sahib.—Nowhere.
>
> Here a musulman Thug from Hindustan interposed, and said, he thought *Bhowanee* and Fatima, the daughter of Mahommud, and wife Aisha were one and the same person; and that it was Fatima who

> invented the use of the *roomal* to strangle the great demon *Rukut-beej-dana*… (I: 124)

Throughout the work, Sleeman also makes the argument that thuggee is a natural consequence of the religious and idolatrous country that is the subcontinent. Thus, thuggee is endemic in India because the culture is given over to such barbaric activities, argues Sleeman. Aligning religious and criminal identities is a key focus of Sleeman's work. He writes:

> Though the Phansigars are almost all Mussulmans, they have nevertheless universally adopted, on certain occasions, the idolatrous worship Hindu deities Cali or *Marriaitta* (the goddess of small pox of the Carnatic) is regarded as their tutelary deity, and is the object of their adoration. (I: 26, also 44–45, 47–48 and elsewhere)

In order to paint them as primitive communities, Sleeman details their religious rituals and superstitions, their belief in omens and their festivities after a successful killing. He observes:

> Ridiculous as their superstitions must appear, they are not devoid of effect. They serve the important purposes of cementing the union of the gang; of kindling courage and confidence; and, by an appeal to religious texts deemed infallible, of imparting to their atrocities the semblance of divine sanction. (I: 29–30)

Their faith merely endorses their lack of conscience, implies Sleeman. Indeed, Sleeman shifts the focus of banditry away from the economic to religious bases. The thugs did not murder and rob for pecuniary gains, he argues:

> What constitutes the most odious feature in the character of these murderers is, that prodigal as they are of human life, they can rarely claim the benefit of even the palliating circumstance of strong pecuniary temptation. They are equally strangers to compassion and remorse—they are never restrained from the commission of crimes by commiseration for the unfortunate traveller—and they are exempted from the compunctive visitings of conscience, which usually follow, sooner or later, the steps of guilt. (I: 42–43)

The emphasis on the conscience-less thug is very evident in the above passage. In the prefatory note to the informer depositions, Sleeman writes:

> The perfect frankness of the disclosures, the coolness with which the most atrocious villanies are confessed and justified by an appeal to their superstitions; and the coincidence of the stories of different informers with respect to facts and motives, form one of the most singular chapters in the history of the human character. (I: 119)

In order to demonstrate the lack of conscience, Sleeman probes the motives and compulsions that drive the thugs, asking Sahib Khan:

> How can you murder old men and young children without some emotion of pity—calmly and deliberately, as they sit with you and converse with you…? (I: 126)

To this, Sahib Khan ostensibly replied:

> From the time the omens have been favourable, we consider them as victims thrown into our hands by the deity to be killed; and that we are the mere instruments in her hands to destroy them: that if we do not kill them, she will never be again propitious to us, and we and our families will be involved in misery and want … we sleep and eat just the same unless we are afraid of being discovered. (I: 126)

Later, Sleeman would try to establish a causal connection between the captured thug's religious identity and his profession. In his questioning of Nasir, Sleeman poses the following question:

> Do you ever recollect any misfortune arising from going on when a hare crossed the road before you? (I: 119)

And Nasir admits 'yes'. To which Sleeman then asks:

> And you think these signs are all mandates from the deity, and if properly attended to, no harm can befall you? (120)

And Nasir replies:

> Certainly; no one doubts it; ask any body. How could Thugs, have otherwise prospered? (120)

Sleeman probes further, and the exchange goes like this:

> Sleeman: "But if there was such a deity as *Bhowanee* and she were your patroness, how could she allow me and others to seize and punish so many Thugs?"
>
> Nasir: "I have a hundred times heard my father and other old and wise men say, when we had killed a sweeper and otherwise infringed their rules, that we should be some day punished for it; that the European rulers would be made the instruments to chastise us for our disregard of omens, and neglect of the rules laid down for our guidance."
>
> Sleeman: "And you really believe that *Bhowanee* sends these signs to warn you of your danger, and guide you to your booty?"
>
> Nasir: "Can we—can any body doubt it? Did she not in former days when our ancestors attended to rules, bury the bodies for us, and save us the trouble; and remove every sign by which we could be traced ?" (I: 120)

Sleeman's questions were directed at demonstrating the religious foundations of thuggee—which fit in with the colonial discourse of attributing all evils on the subcontinent to religion, superstition and outdated beliefs. It is this fanatic adherence to a faith that causes the thug to lose his conscience, Sleeman argues:

> All who have followed the trade of murder with the prescribed rites and observances, were acting under the immediate orders and auspices of the Goddess Devee, Durga, Kalee or Bhawanee, as she is indifferently called and consequently, there is not one who feels the slightest remorse for the murders which he may, in the course of his vocation, have perpetrated or assisted in perpetrating. (I: 79)

Structurally, the arrangement of Sleeman's text is interesting. He offers a detailed commentary on the Phansigars and thugs noting, in particular, their idolatry, superstitions and religious beliefs.

> The frequent association of the most abject superstition, with the deepest guilt, has been often noticed. The justness of the observation is exemplified in the conduct of most, perhaps of all classes of Indian delinquents, and remarkably so in that of the Phansigars. Their system, indeed, seems to be founded on the basis of superstition. They pay the most servile regard to omens; and they never leave their abodes to go on an expedition, without a previous persuasion, derived from modes of divination in use among them, that it will be attended with success. Though the Phansigars are almost all Mussulmans, they have nevertheless universally adopted, on certain occasions, the idolatrous worship of Hindu deities. (Sleeman I: 26)

Sleeman here has offered a thesis about the nature of the thuggee. The depositions by Nasir and other approvers/informers follow later in the work, almost as though they are the evidence for Sleeman's claims and observations in the first part of the book. In other words, his arguments are substantiated by the responses given by Nasir and others to interrogation later in the work, neatly following the rhetorical claim-and-proof structure.

The Sleeman text seeks to establish thugs as cold-blooded murderers driven by bloodlust alone. He reiterates that murder was the focus, and economic gain was only a secondary motive. This interpretation has been contested as early as 1969 when Gordon notes from the thug depositions that

> plunder was the main motivation.... The accused men took to the roads, not in search of just any traveller, but specifically looking for banker's agents, treasure-carriers, rich traders, and wealthy mercenary soldiers or pilgrims. Routes were chosen where booty was expected,

> and bodies of victims were especially severely mutilated when anticipated booty was not found. (407)

The interrogation itself was designed to extract certain kinds of answers that would substantiate the colonial's claims because the thug's life depended on what he revealed to the white man. As Wagner argues, 'the approver had to conform to a fixed model in order to be granted a pardon: he had to verify the official perception of thuggee in order to be believed' (2007, 20). This fixed model was of course the colonial construction of the thuggee that was driven primarily by economic factors but which the British redefined and categorised as a religious practice. Gordon concludes, highlighting Sleeman's role:

> It was the writing of William Sleeman and the Evangelical, crusading tone of the British Indian administration of the 1830's that played up these locally-organized, small-scale marauding groups (given the name "Thugs" by the British) into a hideous, widespread religious conspiracy, somehow typical of India and Indian "national character". We cannot and will not know the nature of the "Thugs" or any other marauding group of the eighteenth century until we return them to a historical and geographic setting, and view them in the context of the ongoing structure and processes of power. (429)

***

Sleeman's account of the thuggee is perhaps the best known in a vast corpus of personal memoirs, legal documents and histories on the subject. With regional variations, the banditry did exist across many parts of the subcontinent. The colonial state, as it sought to extend its control into all domains of the subject population's life, especially through the apparatus of the law (studied, most notably, by Radhika Singha), ensured that thuggee became a context for its interventions.

The linkage of the thugs with the local zamindars and power structures—a feature Sleeman dwells upon—was reciprocal in terms of roles: the zamindars provided the thugs and their families affiliation and protection. In turn, the thugs shared a part of their loot with the zamindars: so there was 'a pattern of continuing relationships between accused Thugs and local zamindars' (Gordon, 406). Be that as it may, for the colonial state, thuggee was an opportunity to strengthen its interventionary and regulatory actions, as Sleeman's text shows. The thug became the exact symbol the colonial ruler wanted: a barbaric, remorseless, murderous and fanatic Indian populace.

THE THUGS OR PHANSIGARS OF INDIA:

COMPRISING A

HISTORY OF THE RISE AND PROGRESS

OF THAT

EXTRAORDINARY FRATERNITY OF ASSASSINS;

AND A

DESCRIPTION OF THE SYSTEM WHICH IT PURSUES, AND OF THE MEASURES WHICH HAVE BEEN ADOPTED BY THE SUPREME GOVERNMENT OF INDIA FOR ITS SUPPRESSION.

Compiled from Original and Authentic Documents published

BY CAPTAIN W. H. SLEEMAN,

SUPERINTENDENT OF THUG-POLICE.

PHILADELPHIA:

CAREY & HART.

1839.

The frequent association of the most abject superstition, with the deepest guilt, has been often noticed. The justness of the observation is exemplified in the conduct of most, perhaps of all classes of Indian delinquents, and remarkably so in that of the Phansigars. Their system, indeed, seems to be founded on the basis of superstition. They pay the most servile regard to omens; and they never leave their abodes to go on an expedition, without a previous persuasion, derived from modes of divination in use among them, that it will be attended with success. Though the Phansigars are almost all Mussulmans, they have nevertheless universally adopted, on certain occasions, the idolatrous worship of Hindu deities. *Cali* or *Marriatta* (the goddess of small pox of the Carnatic) is regarded as their tutelary deity, and is the object of their adoration. She is usually invoked by them under the name of *Javi* or *Ayi* and of *Tuljapuri*.† Before

* The property was generally disposed of near the place where the murders were perpetrated when the travellers were from distant parts; but at villages off the main road or in advance of the place, and not at places where the travellers had rested or been seen. W. H. S.

† Colonel Colin Mackenzie, so well known for his successful researches into Indian history and antiquities, observes in a letter to me, "that it was the custom of many of the ancient heads of families, that have raised themselves by depredation to rank and power, to conciliate *Cali*; hence the sacrifices of human kind, of offerings of horses and ultimately of sheep by the Rajahs of Mysore,

an expedition is determined on, an entertainment is given, when the ceremony of sacrificing a sheep to *Jyu* is performed; and though perhaps not always, yet it would seem generally in the following manner. A silver or brazen image of the goddess, with certain paraphernalia pertaining to her; and sometimes also, one of *Ganesa;* and the images of a lizard and a snake, reptiles from which presages are drawn; together with the implements of Phansigari, as a noose, knife, and pick-axe, being placed together, flowers are scattered over them, and offerings of fruit, cakes, spirits, &c. are made; oderiferous powders are burned, and prayers are offered for success. The head of the sheep being cut off, it is placed, with a burning lamp upon it and the right forefoot in the mouth, before the image of *Jayi*, and the goddess is entreated to reveal to them, whether she approves of the expedition they are meditating. Her consent is supposed to be declared, should certain tremulous or convulsive movements be observed, during the invocation, in the mouth and nostrils, while some fluid is poured upon those parts. But the absence of those agitations is considered as indicating the disapprobation of the goddess, and the expedition is postponed.

and now the commutation of cocoanuts at the hill of Mysore, which derives its name from *Mahes Asura Mardana*, another name for *Cali*.

"At Chitteldroog also, the ancient Polygars worshipped and sacrificed to *Cali*, and even still at *Taljupur* on the western ghauts, 300 miles west of Hydrabed, on the road to Poonah. I was there in March 1797. It is a celebrated temple of *Cali*, where the poojah is performed by a low tribe, and not by bramins, who abhor these rites. It is even so much suspected that infamous rites and human victims were offered there, that my head bramin (the late valued *Boriar*,) horror-struck by the accounts he received, urged my departure from *Taljapur*, and was not easy till we got away.

About ten or twenty days afterwards, the ceremony is repeated; and if auspicious inferences be drawn from it, the Phansigars prepare to depart. But before they determine towards what quarter to proceed, some persons of the gang are sent on the high road, in the direction they wish to take, to observe the flight of crows and other birds, and to listen to the chirping of lizards. Should success be betokened, the same path is taken. If the signs be adverse, the sirdar sends some of the gang to make observations on another road, or at a place where two roads meet, and these votaries of superstition proceed in that direction, which promises, as they infer, the best success.

In the course of their progress, they observe the same scrupulous regard to omens. Emboldened by favourable ones, they are greatly discouraged by those of an opposite tendency. If they have not proceeded far from home, when unlucky signs are descried, they regard them as premonitions to return: under other circumstances they either perform certain ceremonies, or they halt for a few days, till the malignant influence, denoted by them, is supposed to be past, or else they bend their course in a different direction. To the intervention of bad omens, a traveller, over whom destruction was impending, is sometimes indebted for his safety.*

* It would be tedious to enumerate all the omens by which they allow themselves to be influenced in their proceedings. I shall briefly mention a few of both kinds, prosperous and adverse.

The following are favourable signs: A lizard chirping, and a crow making a noise on a living tree on the left side. A tiger appearing is deemed rather a good sign. The noise of a partridge on the right side, denotes that they will meet with good booty on the very spot, and they, therefore, are accustomed to make a halt.

These betoken misfortune. A hare or a snake crossing the

On returning also from a successful expedition, ceremonies are performed to *Jayi*.

The Phansigars keep the Hindu festivals of the *Dipivali* and the *Desserah*, which they celebrate in a manner similar to that observed among Hindus.

A tradition is current among Phansigars, that about the period of the commencement of the *Cali Yug*, *Mariatta* co-operated with them so far, as to relieve them of the trouble of interring the dead bodies, by devouring them herself. On one occasion, after destroying a traveller, the body was, as usual, left unburied; and a novice unguardedly looking behind him, saw the goddess in the act of feasting upon it, half of it hanging out of her mouth. She, upon this, declared that she would no longer devour those whom the Phansigars slaughtered; but she condescended to present them with one of her teeth for a pickaxe, a rib for a knife, and the hem of her lower garment for a noose, and ordered them, for the future, to cut and bury the bodies of those whom they destroyed.

White and yellow being considered the favourite colours of their patroness, and those in which she is arrayed; the cloths for strangling are of one or other of these, to the exclusion, I believe, of all other colours.

Ridiculous as their superstitions must appear, they are not devoid of effect. They serve the important purposes of cementing the union of the gang; of kindling courage and confidence; and, by an appeal to religious texts deemed infallible, of

road before them. A crow sitting and making a noise on a rock or a dead tree. An ass braying while sitting. An owl screeching. The noise of a single jackal. If a dog should carry off the head of a sheep which they have sacrificed, they consider it to betoken that they will get no booty for many years.

imparting to their atrocities the semblance of divine sanction.

To the ascendancy of the same superstitious feeling is also to be ascribed the curious circumstance that Phansigars are accustomed to refrain from murdering females, and persons of the Camala cast; which includes gold, iron, and brass-smiths, carpenters and stone-cutters, washermen, pot-makers, pariahs, chucklers, lepers; the blind and mutilated, a man driving a cow or a female goat, are also spared. These persons appear to be regarded either as the descendants or servants of *Jayi*, as her constant worshippers; or as having claims to the especial protection of the goddess, and are for these reasons exempted from slaughter.

The foregoing description of the Phansigars is meant to be more particularly applicable to those gangs that were settled in the northern parts of the Carnatic and in the ceded districts, antecedently to the year 1808. Since that time, they have become well known to the English Courts of Justice, and their habits have undergone some changes. Many have left the Company's territories, and fled to those of the Nizam and of the Mahrattas. But though the number of them is greatly diminished, Phansigars still infest the dominions of the Company. The gangs indeed, consist of fewer persons than formerly; their plans are less systematic;

two hundred murders; nor will this estimate appear extravagant, if it be remembered, that murder was their profession, frequently their only means of gaining a subsistence: every man of fifty years of age, has probably been actively engaged during twenty-five years of his life in murder, and on the most moderate computation, it may be reckoned, that he has made one excursion a year, and met each time with ten victims."

Yet Francis Bartolomeo says, in a note page 69—"During a residence of 13 or 14 years in India, I never heard of any traveller being robbed or murdered on the highway."—*Travels in India, translated by Forster.*

their range, is less ample; they roam the country more secretly; more frequently changing their names and places of abode; and adopting other precautionary measures to screen themselves from justice. Unfortunately few of the numerous Phansigars that have at different times been apprehended could be convicted in accordance with the evidence required by the Mohammedan criminal law; which admitting not the testimony of accomplices, and rarely the sufficiency of strong circumstantial evidence, unless confirmed by the confession of the culprits, their adherence to protestations of innocence has alone, but too frequently, exempted them from punishment. Those that have been tried and released becoming greater adepts in deceit, have, together with their old propensities, carried with them a knowledge of the form of trial, and of the nature of the evidence requisite to their conviction.

The habits and proceedings of the Phansigars, it is reasonable to conclude, have been modified and varied by different circumstances and events of a local or political nature in the several states infested by them, in some places approximating more than in others to the foregoing description. There is every reason to believe that in the Deccan, and more particularly in the territories of the Nizam, Phansigars are very numerous. They will be naturally encouraged to settle in greater numbers, and to carry on their practises with less caution and secresy, in a country a prey to anarchy or invasion, where the administration is feeble or corrupt, or where crimes are constantly committed with impunity. It is also not unreasonable to suppose, that they may occasionally act in concert with other classes of delinquents, and that their proceedings may sometimes be of a mixed nature, partaking of the peculiarities of those with whom they may be in league. In those countries, too, where Phansigari has been long practised, it may be presumed, that the ordinary artifices will at length become known, and as the success of those murderers must chiefly depend on the ignorance of travellers of their devices, they will perhaps find it necessary to resort to novel and unsuspected stratgems.*

I have heard of no instance in which a European was murdered by Phansigars. The manner in which they are accustomed to travel in India, is perhaps sufficient to exempt them from danger; added to which, apprehension of the consequences of strict inquiry and search, should an European be missing, may be supposed to intimidate the Phansigars, at least in the dominions of the company. Similar reasons influence them in sparing coolies and parties charged with the property of English gentlemen, combined with the consideration that while such articles would generally be useless to the Phansigars, they would find difficulty in disposing of them, and might incur imminent danger of detection in the attempt.

What constitutes the most odious feature in the character of these murderers is, that prodigal as they are of human life, they can rarely claim the benefit of even the palliating circumstance of strong pecuniary temptation. They are equally strangers to compassion and remorse—they are never re-

* There are a class of Byragee and Gosaen Thugs, who travel about the country as religious mendicants, and rob and murder occasionally. They pretend to alchemy, and getting the silver of the credulous under a promise of converting it into gold, they make off with it. They are well known to the Thugs, and often join them in their murders, when they meet on the roads.

W. H. S.

strained from the commission of crimes by commiseration for the unfortunate traveller—and they are exempted from the compunctive visitings of conscience, which usually follow, sooner or later, the steps of guilt. "Phansigari," they observe with cold indifference, blended with a degree of surprise, when questioned on this subject, "is their business," which, with reference to the tenets of fatalism, they conceive themselves to have been pre-ordained to follow. By an application of the same doctrine, they have compared themselves, not inaptly, to tigers, maintaining that as these ferocious beasts are impelled by irresistible necessity, and fulfil the designs of nature in preying on other animals, so the appropriate victims of the Phansigars are men, and that the destiny of those whom they kill "was written on their foreheads."*

This state of moral insensibility and debasement is calculated to give birth to pity, while it aggravates the horror with which we contemplate their atrocities. It ought not to be forgotten that, unlike many who adopt criminal courses, the Phansigars had not previously to divest themselves of upright principles, to oppose their practice to their feelings; but, that, on the contrary, having been trained up from their childhood to the profession, they acquired habits unfitting them for honest and industrious exertion: that a detestable superstition lent its sanctions to their enormities: and that they did but obey the instructions, and imitate the examples of their fathers.

* A Thug will never kill a tiger, and believes that no man who has violated this rule ever survived long. They believe that no tiger will ever kill a Thug, unless he has secreted some booty, or cheated some of the gang out of their just share. A mere tyro or understrapper, they think a tiger may kill, provided he be not of good Thug descent. W. H. S.

Our readers will almost deem it impossible that such organised gangs of murderers, amounting to several thousands, could carry on their villainy almost undiscovered so long; for two or three centuries at least. The difficulty, however, nearly vanishes when we reflect on the mode of travelling in India, just described, and on the peculiar system of the Thugs. In the first place they seldom murder near their own homes; but even this would be a point of little importance when we consider, secondly, that travellers, and generally from a distant part of the country, are their victims: thirdly, that they invariably murder before they rob.

Lastly, they avoid exciting suspicion by being careful to leave behind them no marks even of a crime having been committed. The travellers who became their victims were men seeking for service; or returning home with the savings of years; merchants going on business to a distant town; or others journeying either for business or pleasure. They might be murdered in the morning twilight within half a mile of the serai or village in which they had passed the night; while the Thugs who watched and had marked them for their prey were encamped at a short distance. No one missed them: the people of the serāi or village which they had left took it for granted that they had proceeded on their way; and those of the next halting-place in advance were ignorant of their approach. It is not till days, weeks, months, or even years had passed away that their relations, hearing nothing of their arrival at their intended destinations, make inquiries, and it is seldom that they can ascertain even the place about which the travellers were probably murdered. Unless the inquiry be made within a short time, and there may have been something in the appearance or equipage of the travellers to attract attention, the villagers and others who reside along the road would not recollect whether those inquired for had passed or not. But even supposing (as has occasionally occurred) that the relations succeed in tracing the travellers to a certain spot, beyond which all clue is lost; this gives a moral certainty that they have been murdered at no great distance, that is, within a few miles adjacent.—But how, within such a space, are they to pitch upon the spot where the bodies are interred?—and more,—where are the murderers? probably hundreds of miles away; and even should they by chance be again encamped on the very spot, what means are there of detection? In ordinary thefts, and by local thieves, the tracing and discovery of stolen property affords a very powerful means of bringing the matter home to the perpetrators; but this has but little effect against Thugs. They contrive to obtain full knowledge of the persons, residence, and destination of those they murder, and are careful not to dispose of any recognisable articles where they might by chance be perceived. Such as have any peculiar marks are destroyed.

Considering all these circumstances, it is not astonishing that so little has been done towards suppressing this association of miscreants. The fact is, that until these five or six years, no one had any correct notion of its extent: all that was known up to that period was, that travellers were occasionally enticed and murdered by people called Thugs, who assumed the garb of inoffensive wayfarers. By some extraordinary chance, such as one of the victims having made his escape, or some of the stolen property being unexpectedly recognised, or one of the gang having turned informer in consequence of a quarrel for the division of the spoil, a few of these miscreants were occasionally discovered and punished. Even had the various governments into which India is divided, been aware of the extent of the evil and anxious to destroy it, they would have been unable to do so: insulated efforts would have produced little or no benefit; the jealousies which existed would have prevented their combining for the purpose; and for a century and a half or more, there has not existed any paramount power which could devise a general plan of operations, and compel the rest to submit to it.

Other causes are not wanting which tended to prevent any attempts being made, even in detail, to arrest the proceedings of the different gangs of Thugs. Some of the native chiefs knowingly harboured and protected them as a source of revenue from which they derived considerable sums annually out of the profits of their plunder. The

Thugs lived in villages like other people, and generally cultivated small portions of ground to maintain appearances: so that the native chiefs, if questioned, pretended of course to know nothing of their real character; asserting that these people lived, cultivated, and paid their rent like others, and accounting for the absence of most of the male population during several months, by saying that they went for service and returned periodically with the amount of their earnings. In other cases, native chiefs who would have readily punished a gang of thieves when apprehended, were deterred from doing so by superstitious dread. The Thugs always endeavoured to impress the belief that they were acting according to the injunctions of their deity Bhowanee, and that all who opposed them would feel the vengeance of their goddess. The few instances in which Thugs were put to death by native chiefs were generally cases of personal vengeance, because these villains had murdered some relation or dependent of the chief, and were by good fortune apprehended immediately, "in the red-hand." It has unfortunately in several instances occurred that after punishing Thugs, the chief himself, his son, or some relation has died within a short time: whether some of the Thug fraternity took secret means to insure such an occurrence, cannot be ascertained; but they seized all such opportunities to substantiate the belief which they endeavoured to inculcate. In general, a native chief would merely extort a sum of money from the Thugs, or keep them in confinement for a short time, after which they were released; and not unfrequently they were discharged at once. Their own superstition however, as has just been explained, is now beginning to operate against them.

The following will show what extraordinary proceedings occur sometimes in India. A dispatch of dollars to the value of four thousand pounds sterling, made on account of a rich merchant of Indoor, Dhun Raj, was carried off by Thugs, who murdered the attendant guards, near a place called Burwaha Ghaut, on the Nerbudda. He contrived to ascertain who the Thugs were, and, being a man of considerable influence, to occasion their arrest and detention in gaol by the native chiefs in whose jurisdiction they lived: after some time an agreement was made with the Thugs to release them, if they would refund the money or its amount.

Some paid out of the fruits of former expeditions, others borrowed in anticipation of future success; and those who had neither money nor credit, pledged themselves to pay part of their future earnings.

The Thugs durst not break their engagements for fear of Dhun Raj, and after some time he realized the full sum of which he had been plundered. Finding, however, that he could turn his power and influence to so good an account, he began to assume the character of a patron of Thugs: he had always some of the principal leaders about his person, and yearly exacted large sums of money from the principal gangs in return for his protection, threatened those who refused with arrest and punishment: and such was his influence, that he could procure the release of a gang from almost any gaol in central India.

Though the British Indian government was free from the superstitions or the corruptions which prevented the native chiefs from punishing Thugs, it was not the less hampered by prejudices of its own, and by real difficulties which lay in the way of the object desired. Regarding the prejudices alluded to, it is necessary to explain a little of the secret springs that actuated the government. The members at the head of the administration have always had a tolerably correct idea of the oppressive nature of the British rule in India, and of the light in which it is held by the natives; but it has always been a primary object to prevent this knowledge from reaching the English public. To effect this, the reports forwarded to the Court of Directors, have always descanted on the admirable system of internal government which has been established in their territories; the blessings which the native subjects enjoy; and their consequent gratitude. The feeling descends through the various ranks of government servants, who generally take their cue accordingly. It may be observed too, that the majority of the officers of government, civil or military, are extremely ignorant of the natives of India, and of their real sentiments; and are therefore easily misled by a few designing favourites, who alone possess their ear, and have their own ends to serve.

To acknowledge, even had they been fully aware of it, the existence of such an evil as Thuggee over the whole of the British provinces, was by no means agreeable to the government, it would have contradicted their repeated assertions and representations. If an evil could be suppressed quietly and without incurring any additional expense, it would have been a source of deep satisfaction; but the proceedings of government have almost warranted a belief that they would prefer the existence of an evil, provided it were not generally known, even to the discovery of a remedy, if this should tend to produce a considerable sensation and excite inquiry. We could at least instance several public officers who have brought considerable annoyance upon themselves by too broadly bringing to notice the existence of evils, or the enormous extent to which crimes of the deepest dye, such as murders, gang robbery, and others, are perpetrated. Appearances are, however, kept up. The zeal and ability of the officer are praised, and his praiseworthy motives duly appreciated;—but then come certain remarks indicating an "apprehension of his being misinformed;" doubts that "the evil is not so bad as he has represented;" with a concluding observation that copies of the correspondence will be sent to the superintendent of police, judge of circuit, or some superior officer, who will be desired to report on the subject. This individual, if he have any tact, or any thing to hope or fear from the favour of government, frames his report according to what he sees is wished or expected from him; states the district to be not in worse order than others (which perhaps is true enough, owing to the vigorous measures of the magistrate in question, by which crime has been abated); and, by a careful adjustment of words and phrases, contrives to do away entirely with the impression which, in accordance with truth, ought to have been received. Occasionally, where the magistrate has persisted in his representations, the affair has actually ended by his removal, while his successor has reaped the full benefit of his exertions, and gained the entire credit of them.

A strong instance of the way in which the ends of justice may be defeated by a mistaken anxiety in public officers to gain a good name with the government by making it appear that crime does not exist, occurred in the district of Chupra in 1827. Two men were murdered by a gang of Thugs, who, almost immediately after, got drunk and quarrelled. Four of them in consequence gave information against the others, who were arrested with the property of the murdered men in their possession; these were committed for trial, and the four first allowed to turn King's evidence. The state of the case is as follows:—There was, first, the evidence of the approvers; second, the deposition of the wives of the men, who swore to the property found; and thirdly, the men accused of being Thugs could give no satisfactory account of themselves. The defence was merely a denial, and an assertion that the property claimed by the widows was their (the prisoners') own. The judgment given will scarce be credited by our readers. The prisoners were released; the approvers and the police were severely punished for perjury and for oppression; government was led to believe that no such crime as Thuggee existed in that part of the country; and the magistrate, Mr. Pringle, who had been active in apprehending many Thugs, and had reported the same, received a severe reprimand.

One fact yet remains to be mentioned, which will show the difficulties of the case. The judge, Mr. Elliot, ordered the property which was claimed by the widows to be retained in court, while all the rest of the property found on the prisoners was returned to them. Now, for whom was the above to be retained? It could not belong to any third person, but either to the prisoners or to the murdered men. If the judge disbelieved the whole story for the prosecution, and deemed the prisoners innocent, he should have restored to them this property along with the rest that was found upon them, and which they claimed as their own. If he believed the statement of the widows, that those things belonged to their husbands, then must the prisoners have been punished as the murderers, and the property would have been given to the widows. This little fact is one of those which either show a strange perversion of judgment, or denote a vacillation of mind indicating that the judge himself felt that all was not right in the orders he gave.* The truth of all that was stated on the part of the prosecution has since been fully proved by depositions of other Thug approvers; and not only so, but that Thuggee existed to a great extent in those districts, at the very time that Mr. Elliot was assuring government that no such crime occurred.

Many of the English magistrates were actuated by the same feelings. Some would not allow that Thuggee could exist in their districts, and even were excessively indignant at such statements being made by the officers employed in the suppression of this crime: they were perfectly astounded, when men dispatched by those officers proceeded to dig up the bodies of persons recently murdered in various places, sometimes within a short distance of the police functionary's residence. Others admitted that such a thing might occur occasionally; while a few boldly and openly stated what they had discovered, and gave much valuable information. Our limits do not permit us to add here, extracts from the official papers: we must,

* No mention of this order to retain that portion of the property is to be found in Capt. Sleeman's book. We derive it from a statement publicly made by Mr. Pringle.

therefore, refer our readers to various letters from Mr. Wright, a Madras magistrate.

But even if all the English magistrates in India had been aware of and cordially co-operated with each other, they would have effected little towards the suppression of Thuggee. The ordinary tribunals and modes of proceeding, which answered in some degree for the detection and punishment of ordinary offenders, were of little avail against Thugs. Except in the rare instance of a gang being apprehended with stolen property in possession, which the relations of the murdered persons were there to identify, the only witnesses who could ever be brought against them were some of their own fraternity; and the evidence of men whose preliminary step must be to confess themselves the most ruthless villains in existence, is naturally received with distrust, of which the case commemorated by Mr. Pringle is a memorable example, and doubtless may plead for the judge.

Such being the English mode of proceeding, it is no wonder that approvers and informers were slow to come forward; for no sooner did they lose the protection of the functionaries, than they were murdered by their accomplices. The dilatoriness and inefficiency of the courts; the great power which the subordinate police and court officers possess to disguise the real merits of a case; the influence which the Thugs contrived to obtain over these by means of bribes; the few instances in which stolen property or bodies were discovered; all conspired to increase the difficulty under which the ordinary magistrates laboured in detecting the perpetrators of this crime. But even where the bodies were found in wells, which was a common way of disposing of them when in a hurry or likely to be disturbed, in the Doab, Oude, and other parts, the owner of the ground and his neighbuors generally buried them as quickly as possible that the police officers might know nothing of the matter; and if these did become acquainted with the circumstance, a bribe would usually prevent their reporting it to the magistrate. The farmers and others had just grounds for what they did, owing to the strange mode in which the English government conducts its police affairs. In such cases as those now mentioned the common practice is to summon to court the owners of the neighbouring lands, and many of the neighbours;—at a distance, perhaps, from ten to eighty miles, and to fine them severely as a matter of course, if they could not produce the perpetrators of the murders.

But even when an insulated gang was actually brought to justice, it was but a drop in the ocean towards the suppression of Thuggee:—nor would, nor will any thing effect this, but a general system, which shall be in operation all over India. Different magistrates might receive information which, if it were combined and compared together, might prove of the greatest value, but which becomes useless when frittered away among separate officers, who have no communication with each other. The whole business too was so little understood, that few could bring themselves to credit the extent of such an organized system of murder. Although sufficient was known, so far back as 1810, to induce the commander-in-chief to issue a general order to the native soldiery who went on leave, urging them to take bills on the different treasuries for the amount of their savings, instead of carrying cash for fear of being robbed on the road, yet year after year passed, and men did not join their corps: but it was always supposed they had deserted, and little suspicion apparently was entertained of their being murdered, which however, was since discovered to have been the case in almost every instance. The scattered residences of the Thugs was another obstacle, and rendered them much more difficult to deal with than ordinary criminals, who inhabit the same locality. The members of a single gang often came from different parts of the country, some of which were hundreds of miles asunder. Numbers of them, perhaps the greater part, were residents of foreign states over which the magistrates had no control; and, although the British government might have requested the co-operation of the different princes, little or no good would have been effected. Even a system of Thug police, such as has now been established, if confined to the British provinces, could have been of no permanent use. The Thugs would have emigrated for the time to the native states, and although the crime might for a while cease in the British territories, as soon as the special Thug police was abolished, those miscreants would all have returned and prosecuted their trade as vigorously as ever.

Occasionally when a gang, residents of a foreign territory, were arrested, and moral proof against them was strong, but legal proof, according to the English system, failing; if the government made them over to their native chief in the hope that he would punish them, this usually ended in their being released by paying a sum of money—sometimes without. On the other hand, when British subjects were apprehended on a Thug expedition in a native state, they sometimes contrived, by flattering English prejudices, to obtain the protection of the functionaries. The established creed of the government is the superior excellence of their own administration, and the blessings enjoyed by their native subjects; and they descant largely on the tyranny and oppression in all native states. This is well known to the native dependents and officials, who play their part accordingly. With many of them the Thugs maintained a good understanding, and when any of those wretches, residents of British territories, were arrested by a native chief, a pitiable story was presented to some English functionary of "poor innocent British subjects on a trading expedition," or something of the sort, having been confined by a tyrannical chief, in order to extort money from them. Of course, a due proportion of compliments and flattery of the English was mixed up with the representation, and this would produce, often without the slightest inquiry, a strong letter from the English functionary to the native chief on the injustice of his proceedings, and generally insured the release of the Thugs.

9

IMPERIAL DOMESTICITY

The Complete Indian Housekeeper & Cook (hereafter *CIHC*) was a text in an established 19th-century genre—the household manual, of which the best-known example was *Mrs Beeton's Book of Household Management* (1861). Where *CIHC* departed from the genre was its setting: the British Empire and domesticity in the colony. Recipe and cookbooks for the white memsahib in India had appeared before *CIHC*, notably, the anonymous *The Indian Cookery Book* (1869) and *The Englishwoman in India* (1864). But *CIHC* was the complete guide, offering advice on the management of servants, wages, duties, care and finally recipes (the section on 'Native Dishes' was added in the 1898 edition).

This advice book was not meant as a guide for the memsahib to cook or dust the home. Rather, it was meant as a guide to controlling the domestic space without the messy business of cooking, cleaning, childcare and other domestic responsibilities. It advocated tight control over materials (from foodstuffs to furnishings), people (especially servants), events (mealtimes, social gatherings), processes (cooking, cleaning, childcare, travel) and products (food). Thus, as a sphere of imperial and imperious action, the English home in India represents a different modality of control, specifically in three areas: economy, hygiene and workflow management (Procida 2003, 135). The memsahib monitored, through instructions, physical inspection and often interrogation, of the servants and the account books, the food prepared, purchases made, and cleaning and clearing of the house.

Structure and Content

Organised into 43 chapters, the *CIHC* is a comprehensive text on domestic management. It defines itself in the 'Preface' as a 'practical guide'. Indeed, throughout the preface, it emphasises that everything in the book flows from the authors' 'practical experience' and insists that the advice and suggestions are all 'practical'.

The book opens with the 'Duties of the Mistress'. This 10-page chapter announces that 'housekeeping in India … is a far easier task in many ways than it is in England' (Steel and Gardiner 2010, 11). It exhorts the memsahib to 'give intelligible orders to her servants' and insists that 'she should learn to speak Hindustani' (12). This chapter insists on the enforceability of instructions and a firm 'hold' (their term) on the household. This firmness is necessitated, the chapter insists throughout, due to the childlike nature of the Indian servant. The pairing chapter to this will follow later, as number six, 'Duties of the Servants'.

After this extensive scene-setting, the chapters are organised around 'the storeroom' and financials ('accounts', 'Estimates of Expenditure') before turning to chapters on specific subjects like 'breakfasts, dinners, luncheons, etc'). Horses, cows and dairy, dogs, poultry and gardening are the subjects of subsequent chapters.

Noting the centrality of the 'camp' in British life in India, two chapters, 'Hints on Camp Life' and 'Hints to Missionaries and Others Living in Camp and Jungles' follow. Two connected topics, the management of children and health, constitute individual chapters, with home remedies and prescriptions for routine ailments.

The two principal geolocations—hills and plains—and British lives therein make up two chapters. More practical advice on clothing, wages (for servants), weights and measures bring up the rear in the original editions.

From Chapter 20, the *CIHC* is a recipe book, prefaced with chapters on 'advice to the cook', 'preliminary remarks on cooking' and 'advice on boiling, frying, roasting, stewing and baking'. Separate chapters on soups, fish, sauces, entrées (both plain and 'high class'), dressed vegetables, puddings, salads, game, pastes and pastries, confectionery, jams and preserves, sandwiches and supper dishes follow. The penultimate chapter is on 'Native dishes'. The concluding chapter, 'Miscellaneous', is an inventory of items such as vinegars, yeast, mango chips, etc.

Several tables and inventories dot the text. For example, a table showing the 'work assigned to each servant and the approximate wages demanded by good servants of each class at the present time in the various Presidencies' (Chapter 6), a table of 'wages, weights, etc.' (Chapter 18), a list of 'implements used by the sweeper', the 'bearer' (Chapter 6), etc.

The *CIHC* and the Raj

As one of the largest-selling advice books of its era—10 editions between 1888 and 1921 (Crane and Johnstone 2010, xxviii)—the *CIHC* is a significant text in colonial discourse about India. It is a text that helps us understand one specific aspect of imperial lives in the colony: domesticity.

Imperial domesticity—by which I mean the English household, home or camp in the colony—was complicated by the racial relations of white masters and brown servants. The dependency of the former on the latter clearly meant that the servant class had a major role in the efficient running of the household, the socialising organised in the houses, the bringing up of children and even the economics of the home. The book addresses all these aspects of the English home in the Indian subcontinent, the English camp and residence in the hill station and the plains.

Structured as an advice book, the *CIHC* encompasses 'practical' suggestions, all directed at the memsahib, on numerous 'domestic' subjects, from clothing to childcare. In the process, it also offers evidence of several ideologemes of Empire. It reiterates the stereotype of the lazy, corrupt, irrational native. It posits the English woman as a repository of English virtues, such as thrift. It constructs the English home in India as a social sphere, mediating between the personal and the public and over which the memsahib ought to have total control. It demonstrates not only interracial relations (home and social) inflected by colonialism in terms of the dynamics between the white householders and their native servants but also intra-racial dynamics between the servants. It foregrounds an English identity rooted in commodity culture. It pays considerable attention to the moral discourse of efficiency, thrift, appropriate childcare and the English 'appearance'.

Written in a chatty, often witty mode, the *CIHC* allows us a glimpse into that most veiled of spaces: the Englishman's home in India. It demonstrates the amount of control asserted, the hybridised and complicated nature of domestic arrangements, and the tensions and dynamics at work between the whites and the browns/blacks, and also among the servant classes.

Gender and Imperial Domesticity

There are two parts to the woman's role in imperial domesticity outlined in texts like the *CIHC*. First, as Nupur Chaudhuri has pointed out, the memsahibs functioned as 'agents of cultural exchange between colonizers and colonized' by bringing in dishes and recipes from the colony onto the *English* menu and table (1992, 232). In Susan Zlotnick's words, 'by virtue of their own domesticity, Victorian women could neutralize the threat of the Other by naturalizing the products of foreign land' (1996, 2–3). Second, the memsahib was expected to behave, as the custodian of imperial dignity, morality (including the moral economy of the household) and (racialised) English culture in the colony. The British home in India in which the *memsahib* asserted control over the space, the inhabitants, particularly native servants, generated an 'imperial discourse of domesticity' (Blunt 1999, 426). In this second role, there was little distinction between their role within the confines of the home and outside, since the personal/private and public spheres were blurred when it came to imperial femininity. As Rosemary George argues,

> Novel after novel suggests that it is the daily construction of the home country as the location of the colonizer's racial and moral identity and as the legitimization of the colonizer's national subjecthood that made possible the carrying out of the work of Empire. (1993–1994: 107)

The *CIHC* fits all the above descriptors. It is a work aimed at 'producing' the better quality of English wife, homemaker, mother and socialite. In the 'Preface' to the first edition, Steel and Gardiner write:

> the very possession of the book may be held to presuppose some desire on the part of the possessor to emulate the wife who does her husband good, and not evil, all the days of her life, by looking well to the ways of her household. (2010, 6)

The book, therefore, is an advice manual that would, from the moment of ownership by the woman reader, produces the kind of woman-wife-homemaker who does 'good' for and to the husband and the home. There is a larger implication of a well-run home, argue Steel and Gardiner:

> the end and object is not merely personal comfort, but the formation of a home—that unit of civilisation where father and children, master and servant, employer and employed, can learn their several duties. When all is said and done also, herein lies the natural outlet for most of the talent peculiar to women. It is the fashion nowadays to undervalue the art of making a home; to deem it simplicity and easiness itself. But this is a mistake, for the proper administration of even a small household needs both brain and heart … an Indian household can no more be governed peacefully, without dignity and prestige, than an Indian Empire. (16)

That is, the governance, care and administration of a household in the colony is a model, parable and metonym for the governance, care and administration of the Empire itself. The onus for this, they propose, lies on the women in the colony. As Fae Dussart puts it:

> Anglo-Indian mistresses privileged the domestic sphere as the place where the relations of power structuring racial and gender identities were learned by employers and servants alike. Mistresses (and, less often, masters) saw themselves as doing a service to imperial society by training their domestic employees in the duties of civilised life. (707)

A principal focus of the volume's management advice is the *control* of errant, lazy, indifferent and troublesome servants. Of equal importance, the *CIHC* suggests, is the material culture of the home.

Object Relations

The imperial home was the space, reason and site for displaying the residents' Englishness through the acquisition, use and display of material objects (an argument I have made before, Nayar 2020).

Steel and Gardiner's advice almost always foregrounds the use of specific brands of clothing, furniture, utensils, food products, decor, etc. Among the brands mentioned in the course of their advice are Snowflake American, Norwegian Anchovies, Acerboni and Co. (wine merchants in Calcutta), Maypole Soap, Bolton sheeting, Hall's sanitary paint, Mellin's, Benger's, Allenbury's milk powder and products. This focus on brands and certain specific items is, I suggest, integral to the British construction of their homes not only in the literal sense but also their identity. It is impossible to verify whether these recommendations of brands were indeed taken seriously and whether English households purchased and used them; but the point is that material goods of certain quality and brand value were central to the idea of the English home.

Steel and Gardiner propose nothing less than an objectification of Englishness in terms of a cosmopolitan taste and brand deployment. The English home, if it adopts the advice of Steel and Gardiner, would be a space where multiple products from multiple cultural origins may be found, and this defines Englishness itself. Thus, brands and objects are modes of *mediating* India.

In addition to this discourse of 'branding', the lives of the English in the home are intertwined with specific kinds of material culture. Even when they go to the hills—a journey many English families made at the beginning of the summer months—or on a camp, the appurtenances that make up English domesticity and splendour were to be taken along, as Steel and Gardiner suggest. Here is the advice on setting out for the hills:

> Preparations for the hills must be carefully thought out: what to take and what to leave behind for the master of the house. It is well when you have selected a house to make a rough plan of it, showing doors and windows and sizes of rooms: so do not forget paper, pencil, and measuring tape. Carpets for the sitting-rooms and all curtains must usually be taken, piano, small tables, comfortable chairs, nick-nacks, ornaments (many of these latter packed in among your dresses), chair-backs, tablecovers, something to cover the mantelpiece, and possibly a few pictures. You might also, without being accused of vanity, just see what your landlord provides in the way of looking-glasses: they are marvellous sometimes, and it is best to take one's own; unscrewed from its stand, it can be packed amongst the house linen, whilst stand and supports can be stowed away inside the bundle of carpets, blankets, and rugs. Lamps, some crockery, house linen, and plate must be taken, also kitchen and pantry gear. Books must not be forgotten, and it will be well to enquire from people with local experience whether any stores, wine, etc., should be taken up from the plains. The furniture provided in hill houses being of the scantiest, and wardrobes a luxury, a hanging wardrobe can be conveniently made out of a plank about three feet long, and nine inches wide, down the middle of which insert some six hooks in a row: bore two holes at each end, through which

pass strong cords, and fasten the ends of each to hooks in the roof. Tack cretonne round the board a little full, and cross the ends in front. Towel-rails can be extemporised by fastening bamboos by strings at either end to hooks in the wall. (192)

Clearly, there was to be no compromise in the residence when the family moved. Steel and Gardiner even provide a list of the camel loads that must accompany the family:

> The following is a list showing the way in which the property of a family, consisting of a lady, three or four children, and an English nurse, might be packed and loaded:—
>
> 1st camel load: Two large trunks and two smaller ones with clothing.
>
> 2nd camel load: One large trunk containing children's clothing, plate chest, three bags, and one bonnet-box.
>
> 3rd camel load: Three boxes of books, one box containing folding chairs, light tin box with clothing.
>
> 4th camel load: Four cases of stores, four cane chairs, saddle-stand, mackintosh sheets.
>
> 5th camel load: One chest of drawers, two iron cots, teatable, pans for washing up.
>
> 6th camel load: Second chest of drawers, screen, lamps,1 lanterns, hanging wardrobes.
>
> 7th camel load: Two boxes containing house linen, two casks containing ornaments, 1 ice-pails, angethis, door-mats.
>
> 8th camel load: Three casks of crockery, another cask containing ornaments, filter, pardah bamboos, tennis-poles. (193–194)

The houses in the hills are not always clean, they mournfully admit. This dirty residence, the authors say in a startling critique, may be blamed on the English residents. Steel and Gardiner write:

> Do not be alarmed at the dirty state of the house at the beginning of the season—it is English people's dirt, not entirely natives'—and arises simply from the fact that at the close of the previous season the fair occupier could not or would not take the trouble to leave the house in decent order before descending to the plains. (188–189)

Recipes for Domestic Comfort

Colonial culinary cultures were hybrid cuisine cultures, as exemplified in the *CIHC* with its recipes for English and native/Indian food.

The cookery advice chapters start with 'Advice to the Cook'. Here, Steel and Gardiner address the Indian cook:

> Most likely you belong to a family of *Khansamahs*, cooks, and *khitmutgars*; so, of course, it is likely you know a good deal about your business, but it is also certain that you do not know everything. Now it is no disgrace not to know what you have not been taught, but it is a disgrace not to try to learn. There are always new dishes being invented, and every year clever men are finding out the cause of this disease and that disease. Now as half the illness in the world comes from the stomach, for which it is your business to provide, it stands to reason that a cook ought to do his best to do everything in the best possible way. And it lends to the comfort of the whole house; for if the dinner is badly cooked, your mistress will be angry, the master will have an indigestion, and be cross; everything will go wrong, and whose fault will it be? Yours.
>
> All Indian people have a great respect for custom, and like to do as their fathers and grandfathers did. This is right enough, but it does not do to carry it to extremes. For instance, you all use matches. Did your fathers use them? No, because they had never seen them. Did they use kerosine oil? No, because even in England it had not been discovered. Therefore the first thing a cook should learn is not to be distrustful of new ways. Many of them save an immense deal of trouble. Supposing, therefore, you are really willing to be cleverer than your fathers were, the first thing you have to learn is to be a great deal cleaner than they thought it necessary to be.... Cleanliness, then, is no mere fanciful fad on the sahib-logues' part. It may be a matter of *life* or *death*. Never forget this. (223, emphasis in original)

They also urge the cooks, 'keep yourself clean'.

With this advice, Steel and Gardiner call upon the Indian cooks to (*i*) acquire the knowledge necessary for serving the English family, (*ii*) acquire a greater degree of cleanliness than they are traditionally used to, (*iii*) not adhere too closely to their (Indian) traditions and customs when it comes to cooking and working in the kitchen.

The English recipes and settings for meals that the *CIHC* describes are pieces of advice to ensure the *continuity* of English cultural identity from Britain to the colony, India. As perhaps compensation for the displacement, the distance from peers and communities back home, the advice manual reiterates the necessity of remaining *English* in food and taste. The *CIHC* instantiates this through its extended discussion and advice on English meat preparation, puddings and confectionery.

'Cookbooks and household guides could be seen as terms of reference for the job description of maintaining the colonial household.... Cookbooks for the colonial mistress gave her a sense of reliability and consistency in her efforts to maintain the colonial home', argues Cecilia Leong-Salobir (2014, 136). The recipes, place-setting protocols and purchase lists in the form of cookbooks and advice manuals were

> important manuals for the colonial mistress to refer to each day, in pointing out to the household cook which meals were to be ordered ... these publications also served as a tool of empire as they helped to strengthen the colonial community. (149)

Texts like the *CIHC* offered advice on how the memsahib could assert control of the home *without* having to do the work herself, thus retaining her authority and identity as the *English* mistress of the house and at least partially and metonymically reflecting the organisation and conduct of the Empire itself. As Mary Procida summarises it:

> Anglo-Indian cookbooks contributed to the construction of a cultural identity that welcomed, indeed required, the active participation of the colonized peoples in shaping the daily lives of the imperialists. However, ceding control over the intricacies of culinary preparation did not mean that Anglo-Indians were similarly relinquishing their position of imperial dominance. Anglo-Indian cookbooks provided their readers with a recipe for imperial control that allowed them to retain their sway over the colonized peoples without becoming bogged down in the burdensome activities of daily life. (2003, 124)

Indeed, almost no memsahib knew any cooking, notes Procida (127–128). The memsahib was the manager and not the worker when it came to imperial domesticity.

Then the authors turn to 'native dishes'.

In the chapter 'Native Dishes', Steel and Gardiner describe *burtas, chitchkee curry, dal, dal pooree, dumpoke, kulleah dekhanee, kedgeree* and *pilau*. They preface the accounts with this statement:

> It may be mentioned incidentally that most native recipes are inordinately greasy and sweet, and that your native cooks invariably know how to make them fairly well. (305)

The inclusion of Indian dishes in the text suggests an increasing interest in and fondness for them among the English in India, and this overall suggests the hybrid cuisine culture of the colony.

Race in/and the Imperial Home

The aim of segregating the white inhabitants from their dark-skinned servants was not quite achieved in the English home, as Swati Chattopadhyay's work on colonial Calcutta has demonstrated (2000, 2002). This meant negotiations with the bodies, personalities, attitudes and the very presence of the native/colonised people within the confines of the home was an everyday affair. Regulating these negotiations and interactions was therefore of considerable concern and interest to the authors of the *CIHC*, and their advice and suggestions on the subject are fascinating instances of colonial discourse.

The first move in describing the 'race' of Indian servants in *CIHC* is to infantilise them. Steel and Gardiner write:

> Certainly, there is at present very little to which we can appeal in the average Indian servant, but then, until it is implanted by training, there is very little sense of duty in a child; yet in some well-regulated nurseries obedience is a foregone conclusion. The secret lies in making rules, and keeping to them. The Indian servant is a child in everything save age, and should be treated as a child; that is to say, kindly, but with the greatest firmness. (12)

And later:

> To show what absolute children Indian servants are, the same author has for years adopted castor oil as an ultimatum in all obstinate cases, on the ground that there must be some physical cause for inability to learn or to remember. (13)

As a part of this infantilising, the authors also portray the natives as irrational, superstition-ridden and even silly:

> He [the *khitmutgar*] should not make a separate journey to the pantry for each separate article, but use a tray, like a *reasonable* human being. (83, emphasis added)

The gardener, they write, prefers to entrust everything to Providence:

> Do not trust the *mali* to ask for manure when wanted. His belief in Providence is too strong for him to be a safe guide… (133)

The chapter on servants (Six) opens with a warning that a household does not require too many servants:

> As a rule, the fewer domestics you have the better they will perform their duties. Nothing, in fact, upsets the smooth working of a household like too much leisure or a too minute division of responsibility. (48)

However, if there are servants, they need to be kept busy and gainfully employed:

> With the number of servants in Indian houses, there is no reason why the table should not be laid, and the dinner routine gone through with the same details when you are alone, as when there are guests in the house. In addition, it is fatal to a cook to let him get slack under any

> circumstances, while there is really no more reason why your husband should be treated to an ill-considered meal than your guest; perhaps less, since the guest will not complain, and the husband most certainly will. (60)

Cautioning against taking on the work themselves and thereby pandering to the laziness of the servants, they write:

> A good mistress in India will try to set a good example to her servants in routine, method, and tidiness. Half an hour after breakfast should be sufficient for the whole arrangements for the day; but that half hour should be given as punctually as possible. An untidy mistress invariably has *untidy*, a weak one, *idle* servants.... Anxious housewives are too apt to accept defeat in this way; the result being that the lives of educated women are wasted in doing the work of lazy servants. (15, emphasis in original)

The stereotype of the lazy native—a long-standing one in English colonial discourse—enables the language of surveillance and control. The Preface to the first edition launches the discourse of native indolence when it describes the 'the crowd of idle, unintelligible servants' (6). As an example, Steel and Gardiner write that if a detailed menu card is not drawn up by the memsahib, the cook will do no work:

> It [the menu] is also a means by which she can check the idle cook's constant excuse, 'Kuchch hukm nahin milla' ('I had no order'). (62)

If there is no supervision, the native servants lapse into their typical laziness:

> a few days of absence or neglect on the part of the mistress, results in the servants falling into their old habits with the inherited conservatism of dirt. (12)

The effort at control of such lazy domestics ought to begin with, first, a demonstration on the part of the memsahib herself, and then a clear understanding of the system and hierarchy of servant classes.

The *CIHC* then offers a taxonomy of the servants:

> In the following chapter the authors have adopted the division of labour which obtains in Bengal and Northern India. In Bombay, Madras, Ceylon, and Burmah the manner of life is so different, that residents in these Presidencies will find it necessary to piece the duties of the various servants together into a new classification. Nevertheless, it is none the less certain that the work has to be performed, whether the worker be called by one name or another; also, that the majority of servants, from Himalaya to Cape Comorin, are absolutely ignorant of the first principles of their various duties. The *masaul* doing the lamps in Bombay is quite as likely to do them badly as his congener,

> the Bengali bearer, while the Madras butler's besetting sins are not far removed from those of the Oude khidmutgar. The authors, therefore, believe that, given this slight difference in classification, the following brief outline of household duties will be found useful all over India. To facilitate this alteration, they give a comparative table showing the work assigned to each servant and the approximate wages demanded by good servants of each class at the present time in the various Presidencies. (64)

The taxonomy of servants, however, aligns them on a continuum of inefficiency and vice, and the cautionary tales and examples are aplenty:

> [khidmutgars] should be generally discouraged from making it [butter] the medium for a display of his powers in plastic art; it is doubtless gratifying to observe such yearning after beauty, even in butter, but it is suggestive of too much handling to be pleasant.
>
> Servants in India are particularly careless in serving up cold viands. (56–57)

Everyone, they imply, adopts shortcuts and works only under great pressure. Take, for instance, the comments on the gardener:

> Here is the crucial test of a gardener. Mali believes his thumb to be all-sufficient for planting, whilst the addition of a forefinger provides him with the best of trowels. With his marvellous trust in Providence, he will sit down contentedly in the sun with a basket of young lettuce plants (plucked up by the roots decisively by the aforesaid finger and thumb), and proceed to slide along in a sitting posture, leaving a curious plantigrade trail behind him, bordered on either side by dejected little plants thrust into the ground by one swift action of his thumb. That is his notion of transplanting… (137)

The lack of discipline among the servants should worry the memsahib, particularly in the case of ayahs, argue Steel and Gardiner:

> With very few exceptions, the Indian ayahs are singularly kind, injudicious, patient, and thoughtless in their care of children… (92)
>
> This more frequent employment of English nurses is no doubt improving the regime of Indian nurseries; but even now it is no unusual thing to see an English child eating his dinner off the floor, with his hands full of toys, while a posse of devoted attendants distract his attention, and the ayah feeds him with spoonfuls of *pish-pash*. Appetite is no doubt variable in Anglo-Indian children, but it is possible that a little more pomp and circumstance, and a wholesome conviction that food is not forthcoming except at meal-times, would induce Sonny or Missy Baba to treat dinner with graver circumspection. Where, save

> in India, do we find sturdy little tots of four and five still taking their bottles and refusing to go to sleep without a lullaby? (94–95)

Wet nurses, a controversial feature of the English home in India (Hassan 2016; Buettner 2004), are treated as necessary and yet troublesome by Steel and Gardiner:

> The horror of native wet nurses universally expressed, even by missionary ladies, in the answers received from their correspondents, have impressed the authors so deeply that they feel bound to call special attention to it.... The milk from all these it is true—to the shame of humanity be it said—is free from a certain specific contagion; but it is a contagion from which, alas! the West is no more immune than the East. Therefore the objection cannot be on this ground. What remains, therefore, but race prejudice to account for the fatuity of fearing lest the milk of a native woman should contaminate an English child's character, when that of beasts which perish is held to have no such power? The position is frankly untenable. Therefore if the Western woman is unable to fulfil her first duty to her child, let her thank heaven for the gift of any one able to do that duty for her. (2010, 176)

In addition to this 'problem' of native incompetence, the *CIHC* also emphasises, as yet another instance of imperial categorisation, the types, castes and communities of servants:

> Unless you can get a woman from a regular ayah's family, the Mahomedan ones are apt to be a nuisance; and the reason which leads many ladies to employ them, viz., the dislike to a sweeper or low-caste woman, is in itself foolish. For no one who has lived long in India can fail to see that the sweeper is very often cleaner in his ways, and certainly in his house, than the Mahomedans. Nor does it follow that because a woman belongs to the sweeper caste she should necessarily do all the dirty work of the establishment. But to whatever class she belongs, the ayah's household duties are virtually the same, except that she will not condescend to the broom if she is a Mahomedan. (2010, 92–93)

The slovenliness of all classes of servants, which compounds their incompetence and their laziness, is a byword among the memsahibs, as Steel and Gardiner seem to indicate. Through the narrative, they bring together dirt and servant behaviour. They write:

> Dirt, illimitable, inconceivable dirt must be expected, until a generation of mistresses has rooted out the habits of immemorial years. Till then look at both sides of your plates, and turn up the spare cups ranged so neatly in order in the pantry… (86)

Steel and Gardiner implicitly signal and invoke the European civilisational mission when they suggest that it takes years of training by English memsahibs to dislodge the culture of dirt and dirtiness. It would take a lot, as they suggest, to root out the conservatism of dirt in the servants. About the *khitmutgar*, they have this to say:

> This servant is a curious mixture of virtues and vices. As a rule, he is a quick, quiet waiter, and well up in all dining-room duties; but in the pantry and scullery his dirt and slovenliness are simply inconceivable to the new comer in India. (82)

As for the cook, the experience is worse, suggest Steel and Gardiner:

> Even supposing the kitchen is kept in a cleanly state, it by no means follows that the food will be cooked cleanly, and the mistress must always be on her guard against the dirty habits which are ingrained in the native cook. The strictest morning parade will not prevent him stirring the eggs into a rice pudding with his finger… (78–79)

The figure of the dirty home, dirty vessels and dirty native persons occurs over 50 times in the text. Weekly inspections of cooking and eating utensils are recommended because otherwise, India's persistent dirt permeates everything enough to induce sickness:

> No more fruitful source of danger and disease can be imagined than a dirty copper saucepan; and unless proper supervision is given, we advise every mistress who has any desire to avoid serious risk, both to her own family and her guest, to use nothing but steel or enamelled utensils. (19)

The memsahib also needs to monitor the servants for another reason: immorality amongst them. Steel and Gardiner write: 'Few mistresses have been long in India without having had the trouble of scandals between the ayah and other servants' (95).

But such control should not lapse into oppression, they caution. When writing about camp life, Steel and Gardiner have this to say: 'one of the chief duties of the mistress in camp is to see, as far as in her lies, that no oppression is committed in her name'.

Home and Political Domesticity

The home was not simply a 'family-space', since the memsahib was also expected to have guests, host parties and other social events, all of which constituted the home as an instance of the social sphere, signalling a political domesticity. As I have argued elsewhere,

> the social sphere assimilates into itself the features of both the public and the domestic, thus converting the hitherto private space of

> domesticity.... Political domesticity is the transplantation of mundane Anglo-Indian domesticity into the social sphere, thereby investing it with greater official and political—imperial—weight. Political domesticity is the domesticity characterized by the participation of the colonial social sphere in the household, and the extension of the household into the social. (2012, 125–126)

The true memsahib moves smoothly between the domestic and the social sphere, and *CIHC* is conscious of this requirement and works as an advice manual for this move as well.

The memsahib had to fit in in this *English* social sphere. Her clothes, dancing skills, social etiquette, ability to get proper meals, organise festivities for children, and behave with a consciousness of rank and hierarchy were all under scrutiny in the social sphere. Whether she would be a good, true memsahib was determined in the social sphere.

First, a moral and thrift economy of the household needs to be practised by the memsahib, say Steel and Gardiner.

> The bazaar account varies enormously according to the house-keeping. For years and years one of the authors, for a household of two, entertaining moderately, kept hers to Rs. 30. (48)

They offer suggestions as to the kinds of social activities possible:

> Afternoon teas are, as it were, outclassed by tennis parties, and as these latter are a form of entertainment suitable to the limited purses of most people, a few hints may be given as to the refreshments required, etc. (57)

The fare should be moderate so that the guests do not overeat, argue the authors:

> Even when guests are invited to tiffin, there is no reason why they should be tempted to over-eat themselves, as they too often are, by the ludicrously heavy style of the ordinary luncheon party in India. (57)

Secondly, the social scene is an imperial spectacle, even with a limited budget and menu, given that the household has plenty of native servants.

> Everyday dinners, then, are the test of capacity for entertaining; the effort at success should be made there, and not intermittently, when, with a sigh, you accept the inevitable necessity of asking the Browns, Joneses, and Robinsons to a fearful' feast. With the number of servants in Indian houses, there is no reason why the table should not be laid, and the dinner routine gone through with the same details when you are alone, as when there are guests in the house. (60)

Such a spectacle requires the servants and necessary viands to be at hand, for quick and easy distribution. Hence, the protocols of the table, the dining room and the verandah are emphasised, making it clear that these are now social spaces where the guests gather and spend time.

> In India it is customary to speed the parting guests with cigars, etc. The best plan is to have a table in the verandah, and servant in attendance with soda water, whiskey, cigars, etc. More guests avail themselves of the privilege when served in this way. (63)

And:

> If the *abdar* has to serve a large number of people, especially in the hot weather, when guests are naturally in a hurry for something cool to drink, it requires method and preparation to be successful.... The *abdar* should not dodge round the table in serving the guests, but go round methodically, beginning with the lady at the host's right hand. (69)

The imperial spectacle is put in place through effective political and social communication wherein the native bearer, cook and attendant are made to understand the cultural practices of the ruling race, as the above bits of advice suggest.

But the memsahib also adapts in another way—in her own persona:

> There can be no doubt, however, that where the climate ranges between such extremes of cold and heat, as it does in many parts of India, it becomes necessary to yield to it in the matter of dress, unless fashion is to be set before health and comfort. And there is really no reason why the Englishwoman in India should burden herself with the same number of petticoats, shifts, bodices, and what not, that her great-grandmother wore in temperate climes. We do not advocate any sloppiness in dress; on the contrary, we would inveigh against any yielding to the lassitude and indifference which comes over the most energetic in tropical heat, but we would have people as comfortable as they can be under the circumstances. (209)

Seeking to balance comfort with the demands of imperial accoutrements, Steel and Gardiner offer the above. Slovenliness is unacceptable, they make clear, in the memsahib, and hence practical suggestions regarding costumes that balance costs, maintenance and fashion are offered:

> A few, and for small stations, very few, good evening dresses should be brought out, if only for the reason that on the occasions on which they have to be worn you naturally want to appear well and fashionably dressed. This you cannot hope to do, unless you are a millionaire, if you get more than one good dress at a time, since they will go hopelessly out of fashion before you have a chance of wearing them. On the other hand, there is a vast amount of friendly entertainment in India, where pretty demi-toilette is required. For this the married lady will find tea-

> gowns very suitable, while girls are the better for at least two simple but nicely-made dresses of nuns-veiling or pongee silk. Ball dresses are a necessity, and one should always be ready for an occasion. (211)

***

The Complete Indian Housekeeper and Cook is one of those texts that captures the complexity of the Empire in that most unusual of spaces: the home. It demonstrates the operations of racial dynamics, assertions of imperial control, the employment of managerial discourses/practice directed at this control, and the insistence on and defence of *English* identity in the colony.

CHAPTER VI

THE DUTIES OF THE SERVANTS

In the following chapter the authors have adopted the division of labour which obtains in Bengal and Northern India. In Bombay, Madras, Ceylon, and Burmah the manner of life is so different, that residents in these Presidencies will find it necessary to piece the duties of the various servants together into a new classification. Nevertheless, it is none the less certain that the work has to be performed, whether the worker be called by one name or another; also, that the majority of servants, from Himalaya to Cape Comorin, are absolutely ignorant of the first principles of their various duties. The *masaul* doing the lamps in Bombay is quite as likely to do them badly as his congener, the Bengali bearer, while the Madras butler's besetting sins are not far removed from those of the Oude *khitmutgâr*. The authors, therefore, believe that, given this slight difference in classification, the following brief outline of household duties will be found useful all over India. To facilitate this alteration, they give a comparative table showing the work assigned to each servant and the approximate wages demanded by good servants of each class at the present time in the various Presidencies.

BENGAL.	BOMBAY.	MADRAS.	CEYLON.	BURMAH.
1. Bearer, 10 rs. to 16 rs. Head of house, valet, housemaid.	1. Butler, 15 rs. to 30 rs. Head of house, valet, wait; does marketing.	1. Butler, 15 rs. to 30 rs. Head of house. As Bombay.	1. *Appu*, 20 rs. to 35 rs. Head of house. As Bombay.	1. Boy, or butler. Same as Madras. Double wage.
2. Cook, 14 rs. to 40 rs. As a rule caters also.	2. Cook, 20 rs. to 30 rs. Cooks.	2. Cook, 10 rs. to 25 rs. Cooks.	2. Cook, 25 rs. Cooks.	2. Cook. As Madras.

BENGAL.	BOMBAY.	MADRAS.	CEYLON.	BURMAH.
3. *Khitmutgâr*, 10 rs. to 18 rs. Waits at table.	3. *Masauls*, 15 rs to 20 rs. Waits at table.	3. Mateys, 10 rs. to 15 rs. Waits at table.	3. Boys, 12 rs. to 15 rs. Waits at table.	3. Mateys, 20 rs. Waits at table.
4. *Khansamah*, 10 rs. to 20 rs. Housekeeper and head waiter. Head, as it were, of the commissariat department. A useless servant.	4. None.	4. None.	4. None.	4. None.
5. *Musolchi*, 6 rs. to 10 rs. Scullery man.	5. Cook's Boy, 7 rs. Do.	5. *Tunny ketch*, 6 rs. Cook's help; a woman generally.	5. Kitchen coolie, 5 rs. to 10 rs. Scullery man.	5. Cook's coolie, 12 rs. Kitchen help.
6. *Mehtar*, 6 rs. to 8 rs. Sweeps, under-housemaid.	6. *Humal*, 10 rs. to 15 rs. Does bearers's and superior sweeper's work.	6. *Musolchi*, 8 rs. to 10 rs. As Bombay.	6. House coolie, 10 rs. to 12 rs. Superior sweeper and inferior bearer's work.	6. *Humal*, or house coolie. As Madras, 16 rs.
7. *Bhisti*, 8 rs. Carries water.	7. Waterman, 8 rs. Carries water.	7. Waterman, 6 rs. Carries water.	7. None, except in country.	7. Waterman, 14 rs.
8. *Ayah*, 10 rs. to 20 rs. Lady's maid, nurse.	8. *Ayah*, 12 rs. to 20 rs. Do. do.	8. *Ayah*, 12 rs. to 18 rs. Do. do. Does needle-work.	8. *Ayah*, 20 rs. Do. do. Does needle-work.	8. *Ayah*, 12 to 18 rs.
9. *Dirzi*, tailor, 15 rs. Not kept in Calcutta.	9. *Dirzi*, 15 rs.	9. *Dirzi*, 10 rs.	9. *Dirzi*. Seldom kept.	9. *Dirzi*. Seldom kept.
10. *Dhobi*, washerman, 10 rs. for two persons, 16 rs. for a family.	10. *Dhobi*, 8 rs. each person.	10. *Dhobi*, 6 rs. each person.	10. *Dhobi*, 5 rs. each person.	10. *Dhobi*, 8 rs. each person.
11. *Syce*, or grooms, 8 rs. Does groom's work.	11. *Ghora wallahs*, 15 rs. Do.	11. Horsekeepers, 10 rs. Do.	11. Horsekeepers, 12 rs. Do.	11. *Syce*, 12 rs. Do.
12. Grasscutters, 6 rs. Seldom kept.	12. Grasscutters, 6 rs. Seldom kept.	12. Grasscutters, 6 rs. Seldom kept.	12. None kept. Women bring grass.	12. Grass generally bought.
13. Gardener, *Málee*, 6 rs. to 30 rs.	13. *Málee*, 6 rs. to 30 rs.	13. *Málee*, 6 rs. to 6 rs.	13. Gardener, 10 rs. to 12 rs.	13. Seldom kept.
14. *Gow wallah*, cow man, 6 rs. to 8 rs.	14. Seldom kept.	14. Cow man, 6 rs. to 8 rs.	14. Not kept.	14. Not kept.

It will be seen that the chief difference in the distribution of household work lies in the head man in Bengal being the bearer; and in Madras, Bombay, &c., the butler. The difference is greater than it seems on paper; for while the bearer is invariably a Hindu, the butlers are Christians or Mahomedans. In the former case the whole of the household goods, barring those connected with food, are placed in charge of one man; in the latter, everything, without any exception. In Bombay the various duties of the servants are not so marked as in Bengal; but most of the house-servants dust, sweep, wait at table, and cook, if required to do so. Roughly speaking, butler and *hamal* divide the bearer's duty in Bombay, while in Madras they are performed by the butler and *musolchi*. Both in Madras and Bombay an inferior sweeper, either male or female, is kept. Details regarding the duties of the Bengal servants will be found below, with a few recipes for things required in their work.

Duties of the Bearer.

The implements required by the bearer are—

12 Soft dusters per week.
1 Feather broom.
1 Bottle home-made furniture polish.
1 Clothes brush.
1 Corkscrew.
1 Pair scissors.
1 Chimney brush.
1 Tin Putz Pomade.
2 Funnels.
1 Bottle brush.
1 Ice breaker.
1 Salver for cards.
1 Bottle benzine.
Hammer, tacks, glue, string, &c.

The bearer should be the head servant, and the greatest care should be exercised in engaging one who is honest and respectable. Being his master's valet, the other servants give weight to his opinion, and follow his lead, knowing that he has opportunities for private communication with the authorities. Ear-wigging, it must be remembered, is supposed by the Oriental to be all-powerful. The discipline and respectability of the servants' quarters depend to a great extent on the character of the bearer, who should be held responsible.

The bearer must be an early riser. He has charge of every single thing in the house, save those in the dining-room and pantry, and any loss or breakage has to be accounted for by him; therefore it is to his own advantage that he should keep an eye on the under-servants. In addition, one of the greatest alleviations of Indian discomfort lies in his hands; that is, keeping the house free of mosquitoes. To do this he must in the hot weather shut every window before dawn. They may be opened afterwards; but if they are not shut between four o'clock and six o'clock mosquitoes will come in.

His next duty is to remove the lamps used the night before to the lamp-room, taking those used in the bedrooms from the *ayah* or *khitmutgâr*, as the case may be, whose duty it is to bring them out to the bearer. This should be done at the opportunity afforded by the taking in to the bedroom of the early cup of tea. He should also call upon the *khitmutgâr* to remove coffee cups, tumblers, &c., that may have escaped notice. He should not remove them himself.

When the sweeper has swept the outer verandahs, the upper and lower windows should be thrown open, but not till then, or the dust will come in.

One day a week the drawing-room should receive a thorough cleaning, summer and winter; and after a dust-storm a complete turning out is also necessary; but on other days the sweeper should, with a soft brush and dustpan, sweep over the whole room, shaking mats, &c., outside, as they are apt to harbour vermin. The bearer meanwhile should remove the flower-vases and place them on a table in the verandah, fold up newspapers and put them in a certain fixed receptacle, replace books in the bookshelf, restore chairs to their proper place, and sort everything up as far as possible. It is a good plan to have a separate basket for all papers, envelopes, &c., found on the floor anywhere about the house, as it is then a sure find for lost letters or memoranda. Punkahs and thermantidotes often blow scraps of paper off tables.

When this is done the whole room should be carefully dusted.

The weekly turn-out should include a polish to all articles of furniture, a smart beating of the backs of the carpets, and a cleaning of windows. Dirty windows are the sign of a bad bearer. If the bearer is valet also, he should now attend to his master's room, brushing and folding the clothes used the day before, tidying the dressing-table, and not forgetting to dust the mirror.

As a rule, the gardener or the mistress arranges the flower vases, but it is the bearer's duty to take them back into the drawing-room when they are ready. He should remember that as he is responsible for all the ornaments and the many valuable things left lying about a drawing-room, it is to his interest *not* to let strangers in. On the weekly cleaning day the flower vases should be thoroughly washed out with soap and water, taking care to remove all sediment with a bottle brush. If soap and water fails to restore the polish of the glass, a few drops of sulphuric acid in the water is infallible.

After breakfast the bearer should be in attendance on his mistress at the godown, and report *openly* to her anything which has occurred in the compound during the last twenty-four hours which she ought to know. He need fear no enmity from other servants if he does this fearlessly, openly, and honestly.

If he has charge of the wine, he should ask for what is needed, and keep his mistress informed as to the supplies in his charge. He should see the grain weighed out for the horses, cows, and poultry, and should never fail to report anything unsatisfactory in their management.

The bearer should be ready to receive callers from twelve o'clock till two. Unless his mistress has told him to say "*durwâza bund*" (the Indian equivalent for not at home), he should *at once* usher the visitors into the drawing-room and present their cards to his mistress, wherever she may be. He must never do this with his fingers, and a small tray for receiving the cards should always lie on the verandah, or hall table.

One of the most important parts of a bearer's work is the charge of the lamps, and yet not one man in a thousand knows anything about it. Most lamps in India burn kerosene oil, and the great secret of making them give a good clear light is cleanliness. When a tin of kerosene has to be opened, it is only necessary to make a hole in two opposite corners of the top, about the size of a pea. This can be done with a round nail and hammer. As a full tin of oil generally runs twenty-five bottles, the bearer should have that number ready. He should then decant the whole tin into the bottles, and at once report any deficiency to his mistress. By this means fraud on the part of the supplier will be detected at once, and also the very common adulteration of the oil, as the bearer will be able to see if it runs clear and uniform in tint to the very bottom. To fill the lamps the reservoirs should be removed from their stands to a separate table and most carefully filled by means of a proper can or an old teapot. If any kerosene is spilt on the reservoir, it should be thoroughly removed. If it is necessary to remove the burners, before replacing them the loose ends of wick should be squeezed dry by drawing them downwards through the fingers over a basin or empty tin kept for the purpose. The burner should then be held to the light, to see that all air-holes are free from dust or dirt. Any clogging is fatal. When the burner is replaced, the wick should be very slightly turned up and *cleaned,* not cut, by gentle rubbing with a duster and a final squeeze between finger and thumb. If any threads or unevenness appear, they may be carefully removed with the scissors, but as a rule scissors should never *touch* the wick. If due care in filling the reservoirs at a different table is observed, and the chimneys and globes are never touched with greasy fingers, it is hardly ever necessary to use water in cleaning them, a chimney brush and dry duster being quite sufficient. The overpowering smell of most Indian lamp-rooms is simply due to wasteful carelessness in filling.

The wick of a lamp should *never* coil round in the reservoir. Even the best oil has a sediment, and when the wick lies in it for weeks and weeks, the fibres get clogged, and so the oil is prevented from rising through them. Therefore, when a new wick is put in, it should only just reach to the bottom of the reservoir; if the lamp is kept well filled, as it should be, it is surprising how long even this little bit of wick will burn brilliantly; and though this plan involves more frequent change of wick, and a slight excess in the amount used, this is more than compensated for by the satisfaction of clear white light. Once a week every reservoir should be completely emptied and wiped out with a rag. The oil from them should be put with that squeezed from the wicks, and filtered before it is used again.

Candlesticks must be cleaned every day, and every trace of grease removed with hot water.

In the evening, when the bearer lights the lamps, he should also see that each bedroom has its candle and box of matches; at the same time, he should satisfy himself that the sweeper, *bheesti,* and other servants have done their work. On bringing the lamps into the drawing-room he should tidy it up, remove bits of thread, torn papers, &c., from the floor, draw the curtains, and if there is a fire, see that the wood-box is full. If the bearer is also *âbdâr, i.e.,* serves the wine at table, it is his duty to inform the *khitmutgâr* what wine-glasses will be required, and satisfy himself that they are duly placed on the table. If the *âbdâr* has to serve a large number of people, especially in the hot weather, when guests are naturally in a hurry for something cool to drink, it requires method and preparation to be successful. The ice should be broken into pieces before dinner is announced, and wrapped in a napkin. The best way of breaking up ice is to use a short sharp steel skewer; a large darning-needle fixed in a handle answers well. No hammer is required, as the lightest pressure with the sharp point will split the ice. The soda-water should be ready to hand, champagne wire removed, claret uncorked, and the wines for dessert decanted in scrupulously clean decanters. The *âbdâr* should not dodge round the table in serving the guests, but go round methodically, beginning with the lady at the host's right hand.

The bearer should always be on guard against the ravages of white ants, fish insects, and other vermin; and in the rainy season he must not forget the periodical airing of all woollen clothes, blankets, rugs, &c.

Another important work of the bearer is making the beds, excepting, of course, those in the ayah's charge. It may generally be asserted that no native servant has the faintest idea how to make a bed, and therefore those mistresses who desire to make their guests comfortable will do well to give at least one practical lesson on this subject, insisting on the mattress being turned, the sheets evenly spread and separately tucked in, and the pillows well shaken up. An Indian bed too often consists of a hard felted surface, with more than a suspicion of crumbs, and covered by frantically crooked sheets and blankets, which the slightest movement reduces to chaos, while a sudden turn lets them loose in disastrous avalanche on the floor.

Recipes for the Bearer.

1. **Armenian Cement.**—Half oz. isinglass soaked in water till soft. Strain, add 2 oz. spirits of wine, and dissolve with gentle heat. Dissolve ¼ oz. selected mastic pearls in 2 oz. spirits of wine. Mix both solutions whilst warm. Powder 1 drachm gum-ammoniac, and mix on a slab with enough solution to damp it through. It will then incorporate with the rest of the solution if stirred over gentle heat. Strongest cement known. It will join polished steel.

2. **Ants, to keep from Tables, &c.**—Tie a rag dipped in castor oil round the legs of the table or cupboard.

3. **Ants, White, to keep away.**—Tar the floor with thin tar. Infallible, and cleanly. Indigo in the concrete is said to be efficacious.

4. **Brass Work, to clean.**—Cut a lime in half, rub over the brass, wash the article thoroughly in soap and water, dry and polish. One teaspoon of sulphuric acid mixed in quarter of a pint of water, and used instead of the lime, is still better. Sapolio and Brookes' soap also do well, but Putz pomade is the best.

5. **Brass Work, Benares, to restore the Gold Colour.**—Coat the ornament with a paste of powdered sal-ammoniac and water. Heat over, or rather in, a slow charcoal ash fire, rub dry, and polish with bran.

6. **Brass Work, to preserve untarnished.**—Coat lightly with pale paper varnish.

7. **Bottle Wax.**—One lb. resin melted with ¼ lb. suet and ¼ lb. shellac.

8. **Bottle Paste or Dextrine.**—Wet 2 oz. arrowroot with 2 oz. cold water. Soak 80 grains gelatine in 14 oz. water for one hour. Bring to the boil. When the gelatine is quite dissolved, add the arrow-root, and boil for four minutes. Pour into a bowl to cool. When nearly cold, add 1 oz. spirits of wine, in which 6 drops of pure glacial carbolic acid have been mixed. Stir well, bottle, and cork. It will keep for months.

9. **Carpets, to remove Ink Stains.**—Wash, if possible, while still wet, with fresh, hot boiled milk. Sponge again and again with hot water. Time and patience must be plentifully used. A weak

solution of oxalic acid may be tried if the stain is very dark, but the risk of injuring the colour is very great. It is, however, possible to re-dye the injured portion, with a result certainly preferable to a black spot.

10. **Chairs, to prevent the Leather from Cracking.**—Rub with white of egg beaten thin with water.

11. **Chimneys, to prevent Cracking.**—Set in a pan of cold water, and gradually heat to boiling point. Let the chimneys remain in the water till cold.

12. **Cloth or Velvet Embroidery, to clean.**—Bake a very thick *chapâtti* (unleavened cake) of coarse *atta* and water. When barely cooked through, take the inside doughy part, form into a roller, and with the palm of the hand roll in over the embroidery. The fluffs and hairs stick to and come away on the dough, which also acts, like bread, as a cleanser. Excellent for velvet.

13. **Dubbin for Boots.**—Melt 2 oz. mutton suet, 4 oz. black resin, and 1 pint fish oil. One of the best dressings for boots is plain castor oil. Vaseline is also good.

14. **Glue, Strong.**—Digest by gentle heat in a corked bottle 3 oz. rectified spirits of wine with 4 oz. of fine pale shellac. The Chinese use nothing else for all their wood-work. Excellent for pianos.

15. **Furniture Polish.**—Mix in a bottle equal parts of linseed oil, turpentine, vinegar, and spirits of wine; or half a teacup shredded beeswax dissolved in 1 teacup turpentine. The sanitary polish called Ronuk is very good.

16. **French Polish.** — Put into a bottle enough pale shellac slightly broken to fill it one-third, fill up with spirits of wine. Digest in the sun.

17. **Grease Spots, to remove.**—Rub with oil of turpentine and air in the sun; or place a double fold of blotting-paper over the spot, and rub with a moderately hot poker.

18. **Patent Leather, to preserve.**—Use plain boiled linseed oil. The easiest plan to make a good drying oil is to powder 2 oz. of litharge and 1 oz. oxide or sulphate of lead. Put into a pint bottle of linseed oil, agitate occasionally for ten days. Set in the hot sun for two more, then decant the clear portion.

19. **Scouring Drops.**—Mix 2 oz. rectified spirits of turpentine with 2 drachms essential oil of lemon or cloves. Rub on with a clean rag till the stain disappears.

Duties of the Sweeper.

The implements required by the sweeper are—

1 Native broom for verandahs.
1 Dust-pan and brush.
1 Carpet-switch.
1 Hearth brush.
1 Ash-pan.
1 Dust cloth.
1 Slop pail and cloth.
1 Bath-room basket.
1 House flannel.
1 Scrubbing brush.
Soap.
12 Dusters of all sorts.
Set boot brushes.
1 Turk's head for cleaning walls.
1 Carbolic or Phenyle bottle.
1 Wooden spud.
1 Tin whitewash and brush.
1 Comb and brush for dog.

In most houses the sweeper is engaged simply because he is the husband of the *ayah*. This is an immense mistake, as the whole cleanliness of the house depends upon him. Again, his duties give him the *entrée* to every room, therefore the trust reposed in him must necessarily be great. He is, in fact, the under-housemaid, and should never be allowed to degenerate into the dirty, unkempt drudge, whose sole notion of work is to raise a dust-storm with a broom, and try experiments on the relative fragility of your pet ornaments by flicking them with a greasy duster. Housekeepers will find a rupee or two more well expended in securing the services of a man who is presentable, and who is both fit to, and capable of, receiving orders direct. Care should also be taken that the sweeper is not imposed upon by every other servant; as a rule, he is simply hunted from pillar to post, and made to do odd jobs for everybody; the *khitmutgârs* being special offenders in this way, calling on the sweeper at all hours to clear up their messes, and generally to be the scapegoat for their dirty habits.

When a large number of servants are kept, making a full compound, and there are also dogs and poultry to be looked after, we *strongly* recommend the employment of an under or mate sweeper, who should do the outdoor work. So much of the cleanliness and consequent healthiness of a house and compound depends upon the sweeper, that it is *worth while* to make sure the work is not scamped; and the plan here advocated, of having two sweepers, will be found to be far more satisfactory in large establishments than the employment of an upper and under bearer, neither of whom will do any real eleaning. The under-sweeper (who will seldom require more than six rupees a month) should have the charge of the servants' houses, eompound, and stableyard, look after the dogs and poultry, sweep the verandahs, remove the refuse from the cook-house, and be generally responsible for outside cleanliness. The upper sweeper should be virtually the under-bearer, leaving the head man available as butler and valet.

The sweeper's first duty in the morning is to see to the bath-rooms and empty the slops, taking eare to observe all regulations as to the disposal of refuse, and to keep everything sweet and clean. His next is to sweep the verandahs, then the dining-room and hall, and lastly, the drawing-room. A damped brush or duster is best for Persian carpets. If there has been a fire, he should, after placing the dust-cloth over the rug, proeeed to remove the ashes, and thoroughly elean the hearth. It will be found a good plan to make the sweeper keep a pot full of colour-wash to take the place of hearthstone. With this he should wash over the inside of the arehed reeess which in most Indian houses does duty as a fireplaee; by thus removing the smoke and dust marks, the hearth has a much tidier appearance. Once a week, every room in the house should have a complete cleaning out, beginning with the upper windows and walls, and finishing with a rub down to all the doors and frames. Such of the boots and shoes as have not been cleaned over-night should now be attended to: in some houses the bearer cleans the boots, and he always remains responsible for their being ready when wanted, and should always keep clean the patent leather, and the finer kinds of shoes; but in many respects it is better to make the sweeper do the dirty work.

After each meal it is the sweeper's duty to go into the scullery, and, under the *khitmutgâr's* orders, remove all refuse to *its proper place*. In large stations there is generally a reeognised place for the refuse heap, whieh is periodically eleared away by conservancy earts; but in other cases the best plan is to dig a long trench, three feet deep by two broad, in some eonvenient corner of the garden, piling up the earth on one side only. As the sweeper throws in the refuse he should cover it with dry earth from above, taking care not to use the treneh in various parts, but work steadily from one end, and to fill it up only to about two feet, and after that to make it level with pure earth. When one trench is filled, another may be dug alongside. In this way all refuse becomes valuable manure for the garden.

The sweeper's last duty at night is to see that everything in his charge is clean, and to give both scullery and kitchen a final sweep-out. On this depends much of the health of the household. The sweeper should always have on hand a supply of some disinfectant, and should be instructed how to use it, or whitewash if that is preferred. His duties in regard to dogs and fowls will be found under those headings. The following recipes will be found useful for the sweeper :—

1. **Boots, to black.**—Remove every atom of dust or mud with the brush, or, if necessary, a damp cloth. Put on the smallest possible amount of blacking, and leave it to dry thoroughly, then polish as hard as you can. Do not forget to take the laces out before blacking laced boots or shoes. If the leather feels sticky, too much blacking has been used. For brown shoes, use one tea-cup shredded beeswax dissolved in one tea-cup turpentine, or the usual brown boot polish. Polish with a silk cloth.

2. **Chitai Matting, to clean.**—Wash with strong salt and water Dry at once with a soft cloth.

3. **Grey Wash for Fireplace.**—Make a *gharra* full of rather thick whitewash, colour with powdered charcoal, and add a little rice-water or glue.

4. **Iron, to clean.**—Use powdered bathbrick and oil, with plenty of elbow-grease.

5. **Red Wash for Fireplace.**—Mix one pice worth of *hirmchi* with one pice worth of *géru* in sufficient rice-water to make the whole to the consistency of whitewash.

6. **Rust, to remove.**—Take powdered polisher's putty (or crude peroxide of tin) mixed with a little oxalic acid and water. Apply on the rust spot as a paste for a few minutes. Wash off carefully, dry and polish. Both Brooke's soap and Putz pomade are excellent for metal work.

7. **Whitewash Marks on Wood, to remove.**—Mix 1 oz. salt with 1 oz. linseed oil and 4 oz. of water. Rub on with a damp duster till the spot disappears.

8. **Windows, to clean.**—Remove varnish or putty marks with spirits of wine. Wash with soap and clean water on both sides of

the pane. Polish with a dry rag. If the polish has gone, it may be restored by dry, powdered tripoli, and a very fine polish may be given by dusting powdered chalk, tied up in a piece of muslin, on to the glass, and then rubbing it off with a dry, clean rag. Greasy cloths will never clean glass.

9. **Windows, to preserve Glass from Paint.**—Make the painter or varnisher use a thin slip of glass as a guard. Put this close to the woodwork, when all surplus stuff will be smeared on it, not on the real window glass below.

Duties of the Cook.

The implements required are mentioned hereafter.

The first duty of the cook is to have a tidy cook-room, and for this his mistress is mainly responsible in the first place. We cannot insist too often on the folly of expecting cleanliness when there are no appliances rendering it possible to be clean.

The cook-house, then, must be airy and wholesome. The floor should be of broad, flat bricks, such as are used for mosques and public buildings, set close in really good mortar. There will then be no difficulty in getting it swept and *washed* out every day.

No better mode of open fire cooking exists than the *chûla* arrangement for charcoal, at present in use in most parts of India, and which closely resembles that seen on the Continent. It is convenient, economical, safe, and suitable in every way to the requirements of the climate. But it is *not* necessary that the whole erection should be made of mud and loose bricks, as is very generally the case. Good bricks, well set and surmounted by a strong sheet of iron clamped to the bricks, with holes cut to correspond to the round brick *chûlas* below, will make as good and as cleanly a kitchen range as any cook need desire. A hot case with an oven beneath it can be built on one side. Such an oven is very simply made; it is merely a framework of sheet iron with a door in front, let into the bricks with a place for charcoal below and above, and a space of about one inch left between the iron and bricks at the back to act as a flue.

The expense of such simple arrangements is trifling in the extreme, and no practical cook who has ever personally superintended the working of that diabolical invention, a native *tizâl* or oven, will ever allow one in her kitchen. The mischief it can do to the best made cakes is simply incredible; and it is impossible to say which is more difficult, to get the lid *on*, or, having succeeded in that, to get it *off* again. The mere sight of a *tizâl* with two crooked legs, the missing third supplied by a tottering pile of bricks, and three inches of dust and ashes inside to prevent the utter cremation of the wretched cake, is enough to dishearten any one. No one need be astonished if, in the frantic effort to get the lid full of burning coals off or on, the whole frail structure collapses, and *khitmutgâr*, charcoal, ashes, cake, and tins are mingled in hopeless confusion. If the initial expense is not a bar, we strongly recommend every housekeeper to have a kerosene oil stove with an oven on a table in a verandah, where she can use it for dainty cooking. We also strongly advise, where possible, the introduction of American stoves, simply for the sake of their ovens. No one who has not tried the effect of making stock, boiling vegetables, preparing stews, &c., in an oven has any idea of the saving of trouble and the vast superiority of the food so prepared. It is more nourishing and infinitely more palatable. In addition, it is more hygienic, the very high temperature of the air in the oven effectually sterilising it, and preventing the entrance of flies, &c. Such stoves as the Constantine, Empress, Victoress require no fixing, and burn wood or charcoal.

A point which must be insisted on in a cook-room is the raising of the washing-up place or sink so far from the ground that the refuse water will fall into a proper and movable receptacle outside, and *not* filter into the ground. It cannot be right that food should be cooked in a house whose very foundations are saturated with sewage. The sink, then, should be at least two feet from the ground, with a high ledge round, and a stand for water vessels on one side. These are best made of old kerosene tins with iron handles, and in each should be a tin-dipper—any empty tin will serve the purpose. Every kitchen should contain two tables—a dishing-up table, which is best close beside the range, if not part of it, and a working table. Beside the latter there should be another stand for two water vessels, as it is by no means advisable that water which has been standing, so to speak, in the *sink* should be used for cooking.

The cook should be provided with a cupboard which locks for his stores, and an open bunker for his charcoal. Shelves for saucepans, and a row of hooks for different utensils, are of course necessary.

With regard to the utensils themselves, the best and safest are the aluminium saucepans now so much used at home. Copper is a constant source of anxiety, any slight fit of indigestion rousing suspicions of the *dêgchies ;* so that, if possible, it is best to use nothing but aluminium [1] and steel, especially when cooking for children. The number of utensils must, of course, vary with the style of establishment, but a small household, no less than a large one, requires the little conveniences and requirements which are so often conspicuous by their absence in Indian cook-rooms. The following list only gives absolute necessaries, if clean and wholesome cooking is expected. The Urdu name is given against each.

6 Stewpans or saucepans, of sizes, with covers	*Dêgchi*
2 Frying-pans	*Fry-pân*
1 Omelet-pan, enamelled	*Momlet-pân*
1 Large kettle with cock	*Kitthi*
1 Colander	*Turkâri ke chulni*
1 Wire frying basket	*Tôkri*
1 Egg poacher	*Unda poach-dân*
1 Large boiler	*Dêgchâ*
2 Small tin saucepans	*Sârse-pân*
1 Mortar and pestle	*Imâmdusta*
1 Curry stone	*Sil*
1 Gridiron	*Gridârni*
2 Iron charcoal stoves	*Ungêthi*
1 Roaster	*Kubâb-dân*
1 Chopper	*Châppa*
1 Saw	*Âri*
6 Kitchen knives	*Chûri*
6 Forks	*Kârnta*
6 Metal spoons	*Chumchâ*
1 Gravy strainer	*Gravy ke chulni*
1 Potato muller	*Âlu mulne ke lukri*
2 Graters	*Grâte-dân*
3 Dredgers	*Mirich, âtta,* and *nimuk dâns*
2 Ladles	*Chumchâs*
1 Whisk	*Kûchi*
12 Bowls, of sizes	*Piyâle*
1 Coffee mill	*Câffë ke chukki*
1 Coffee roaster	*Câffë senk-dân*
1 Set scales and weights	*Turâzu*

[1] Aluminium saucepans are to be had in Madras and also in Cawnpore.

1 Meat safe . .	. *Dûli*
1 Hair sieve .	. *Chulni*
2 Wire sieves . .	. *Chulna*
1 Jelly-bag . .	. *Jeli ki thaili*
1 Mincing board . .	. *Mêz*
1 Paste board .	. *Crâs ke mêz*
1 Rolling-pin .	. *Bêlun*
24 Dusters and cloths	. *Jâhrun*
Moulds *à discrétion*	*Sâncha*
Pie dishes .	. *Pi-deesh*

If high-class cooking is attempted, a *bain marie* becomes absolutely necessary for the sauces; but this can easily be made in any bazaar out of an old kerosene tin cut down to six inches, the edge turned over an iron wire, and handles put at each side. This, half filled with water, in which four small bazaar-made tin saucepans can be plunged, is all that is necessary, and the whole arrangement need not cost more than two rupees. In fact, a very little supervision and ingenuity suffices to fit up a cook-room properly at a small cost. Small enamel pans are now to be bought in most shops, and there are an infinity of labour-saving trifles which repay their cost in kitchen work, such as egg-beaters, bread crumb mills, vegetable slicers, &c., which it is well worth while to add to the above list.

Having thus placed the cook in a decent kitchen, with decent appliances, the harder task remains of getting him to keep it in a decent state. This will never be accomplished unless the mistress takes the trouble of seeing that her orders are obeyed. The sweeper should go into the cook-room twice a day—once before breakfast, and once after dinner—at both of which times every particle of refuse should be removed, and the sink swept and washed clean. The ashes must also be removed, and the whole place put into thorough order, saucepans hung up, waterpots re-filled, tables washed down. A little method is all that is required, for once the sweeper and the *bheesti* are on the spot, it is no trouble to the cook to insist on their doing their duty thoroughly.

Even supposing the kitchen is kept in a cleanly state, it by no means follows that the food will be cooked cleanly, and the mistress must always be on her guard against the dirty habits which are ingrained in the native cook. The strictest morning parade will not prevent him stirring the eggs into a rice pudding with his finger, but a practical illustration that the method is both troublesome and ineffectual may do some good. In the same way, once the saving of time resulting from proper appliances is brought home to the cook, you may trust him to use them; but not till then.

It would take page on page, chapter on chapter, to tell the many evil habits in which Indian cooks have been grounded and taught; but in the Cookery Book published as a companion to this volume, most of them are mentioned in the various recipes as things not to be done. There is therefore no need to detail them here.

In regard to catering, the authors much prefer the less common system of allowing the cook to do the marketings, without the intervention of the *khansâmâh.* If one man is responsible for the quality of the provisions, and another for the preparation of them, it is impossible to get a firm grip of blame on either, in the event of unpalatable food. One throws the fault on the other, and even if the *khansâmâh* is held responsible, it must always be with a mental reservation, if the mistress be herself a practical cook; for the best food will not stand bad cooking, any more than good cooking will take the place of good food. It is certainly a great satisfaction to be able to award praise or blame with a free hand, and for this reason alone divided responsibility is objectionable. Again, the man who is to do the cooking alone knows *what* he intends to make, and what sort, size, and quality of ingredients he requires. The bazaar is seldom so far away but that the cook can get to it before breakfast if he arranges his work methodically, while the commission he of course makes on every article is so much inducement for him to work well. As half the comfort of life depends on the actual cooker of food, it is as well to keep him pleased with himself and with his service. Yet for one mistress who makes a point of commending a well-cooked dish, how many are there who never dream of praise, and whose only criticism is unmeasured and often unreasonable blame?

There are certain delusions current in cook-houses in India, such as the belief that it is the *yolk* of the egg which clears soup, against which it is useless to argue. Autocratic high-handedness is the only weapon of any avail. As an instance in point, one of the authors ordered potted sheep's head several times, and in spite of minute instructions the result was failure. At last the head was ordered for inspection, and it was *skinned*. The reply to an indignant query as to why strict orders had been disobeyed, was that sheep's heads were always skinned—it was *dustoor, i.e.* custom; together with the remark that skinning or not skinning had nothing to do with the non-setting of the jelly, which every one knew came from *bones* and not skin. The offender was told to boil an unskinned head for twelve hours. He came next day with a new light on his face. "*Mem Sahib,*" he said, "*do they by any chance make gelatine of skins, for, as the Lord sees me, I can hardly cut that jelly with a knife!*" Here was a case of sheer ignorance of facts well known to an English child; and it must never be forgotten that this is not the exception, but the rule. An Indian cook does not understand why eggs will not rise if whipped slowly, or why syrup will never crystallise unless stirred. He often stands confounded before his own failures, unable to tell *where* he has gone wrong, or how; and if his mistress is a practical cook, he will give a smile of wonder and relief when she points out what he must have done to have caused that specific result. The consequent testimony, "*Béshukk—âp such furmâta hai—aisa hua*" ("Without doubt, your honour speaks truth—it was so"), will go further to raise a mistress in his estimation than any amount of theoretical knowledge she may display. It must not be forgotten either that the best cooks are liable to failures. The fire may be too slack, and yet the delay of increasing it may be *worse* than making the best of what you have. Attention may be distracted for half a second, and lo! the custard curdles, the caramel burns. In cooking, as in other things, the charity born of sympathy covers a multitude of sins.

In regard to the actual duties of a cook in India, they are confined entirely to cooking. He has nothing whatever to do with the morning tea, boiling the kettle, making the toast, &c. That is the *khitmutgâr's* work, and even when poached eggs are taken it is best not to make the cook responsible, for the early morning is his marketing time. In the same way he is in no way responsible for the proper serving of breakfast, only with the dressing and dishing up of the hot dishes, whatever they may be. Tea, coffee, eggs, milk, toast, butter, &c., are in charge of the *khitmutgâr;* and so is the afternoon tea. Beyond this, everything which comes to table is in the cook's care, and he must arrange with the table servants how the various dishes and sauces are to be served.

A considerate mistress will always look a day or two ahead in her orderings, but the cook should be encouraged to act on his own responsibility in minor details, and be praised when he has contrived some fresh pudding or side-dish. This is an immense relief, especially in the hot weather, when one racks one's brains in vain to think of something new, and everything that comes to mind seems a Dead Sea apple of dust and ashes.

Never let a cook *run down* in his cooking, even when he is in camp; for it is a dead certainty that once the niceties of dishing up and dressing are disregarded, a general slackness will set in. *"I can't cook well'm,"* said an English servant to one of the authors; *"there ain't really enough cookin' to do; my 'and gets h'out."* This is still more true with an Indian servant. So insist on everything being done every day in the same style. Then, if a friend comes into dinner unexpectedly, you need have no anxieties. The dinner may be plain, even frugal, but it will be correct, even to the most minute details.

Between the Scylla of sheer pitchforking of viands on to the dish, and the Charybdis of what cooks call *"sujāwul,"* or decoration, *simply as decoration,* the mistress will find it a little hard to steer a middle course; but the one fault is as bad as the other, and cutlets coloured pink with cochineal, and green with spinach, may in the opinion of some be as unappetising to the look as a heterogeneous mass of chops and garnishing swimming in a loose gravy, which shows by a high-water mark on the dish that it underwent a tide on its way from the cook-room. A good cook is not made, he is born; so if you are lucky enough to find one, do anything to keep him—short of letting him know that you are anxious to do so!

Finally, if in the hot weather the results of his hands are poorer than usual, and he shows a captious dislike to criticism, give him a blue pill, or present him with a bottle of Eno's Fruit Salt. It is very bilious work stooping over a hot fire with the thermometer above 100°. The use of English cooking stoves is gradually growing. If the cook has one he is to be encouraged to use the oven for every possible process of cookery. Soups, stews, vegetables, are all better done in the oven than on the top of the fire.

Duties of the Khitmutgâr.

The implements required by the *khitmutgâr* are numerous—

1 Set of plate brushes.
2 Chamois leathers.
1 Box plate powder.
1 Box polishing paste.
1 Brazier or *angithi*.
1 Earthen butter cooler.
2 Galvanised iron pails.
1 Decanter drainer.
3 Wooden or tin tubs.
1 Plate rack.
1 Scrubbing brush.
1 Hot case.
1 Knife board.
1 Tin for washing knives.
1 Jug mop.
1 Wooden butler's-tray.
1 Toasting fork.
Kitchen paper for wrapping spare plate.
1 Bread pan.
Wire covers for jam, &c.
1 Silver basket.
Endless dusters and tea cloths.
1 Pair butter spats.

This servant is a curious mixture of virtues and vices. As a rule, he is a quick, quiet waiter, and well up in all dining-room duties; but in the pantry and scullery his dirt and slovenliness are simply inconceivable to the new-comer in India.

The best of them will, if put to it, give a final polish to your teacup with some portion of his own clothing; or place fresh-made mustard on the top of the old to save the trouble of cleaning out the pot. Much of this is, of course, due to heredity, all Mahomedans of the lower classes being apparently blind to dirt; but more is the result of almost every table-servant beginning work as what is called a *musolchi*—a nameless, abject, adjunct of the scullery, who washes up by the light of Nature. Dirty habits thus grow unchecked by the mistress's eye, and cling to the learner long after he has risen to higher things; whereas, if the sensible plan, advocated elsewhere, is adopted, of having no *musolchi*, the *khitmutgâr* would have to learn his work thoroughly from the beginning. But whatever may have been his training in the past, the mistress should insist on her *khitmutgâr* washing up, in the present, with his own hands. Plate, glass, teacups and breakfast cups, &c., should be washed in the pantry. Dinner plates and dishes should be washed either in another scullery, if available, or in the verandah; for if the pantry and scullery work are done together, there is no possibility of keeping the pantry as it should be—sweet, clean, and free from flies. In addition, there is a certainty that the same greasy water will be used for plates and cups alike.

The pantry should be provided with a washing-up table—King's patent washing-up table, price 16s., is a great boon—and at least three wooden or tin tubs. A supply of cold water can easily be secured by placing a cask against one of the outside walls with a few inches of leaden pipe, and a tap inside, while a sink below the tap is also easily made to connect with a removable zinc tub outside: cask to be filled and tub emptied every day. Even if this be not done, the usual habit of emptying the dirty water on the floor, to trickle away through a hole, should be sternly repressed. The scullery or verandah should also have a washing-up table, a plate-rack, and at least two wooden tubs, and a pail for scraps.

In regard to dusters, tea-cloths, &c., the supply must be much larger than is necessary for an English household. The best plan is to give out the week's supply to the bearer, and make him responsible for issuing the fixed daily number of clean cloths, and taking back the same number of soiled ones. Otherwise your fine glass cloths will be used for scrubbing the kettle, and being black with grease and dirt, will fall to pieces in a few washings from the manipulation necessary to remove the filth.

One thing must be fought against root and branch, and that is the extraordinary want of forethought, and desire to save themselves much washing-up, which leads every *khitmutgâr* to vary his waiting at table by constant dives into the pantry, whence he returns breathless with a hastily-wiped spoon or a forgotten butter-knife. Everything required for each meal should be in the dining-room before that meal is announced, and a running accompaniment of washing should be ruthlessly repressed. If milder measures fail, lock the pantry door before sitting down to meals for a few days, and fine one *pice* for every missing article. Good habits are quickly learned when there is no possibility of continuing bad ones. In regard to details of the *khitmutgâr's* duties, it will, perhaps, be as well to begin with the things he is to leave undone, since his offences are by no means of the negative order.

Therefore he should not lay the table for any meal more than one hour before that meal is to be served. He should not devise ingenious patterns with the spare silver. He should not attempt to fold up the cloth unaided, and so reduce it to creases. He should not make a separate journey to the pantry for each separate article, but use a tray, like a reasonable human being. He should not wash up glass, china, plates, and silver in one small *dêgchi* with a rag tied to a stick. He should not clear away the table and lay it for the next meal whilst the family are still at table. He should not use the table napkins as kitchen cloths. He should not conceal, or attempt to conceal, a dirty duster about his person when waiting at table. He should not leave things to be washed up till they are wanted. Finally, he should not say the kettle is boiling when it is not. This is an inexcusable offence, but universal.

The *khitmutgâr's* first duty is to send in the *chôta hâzri* to the bedrooms at the appointed hour. The tray should be covered with a tray cloth, and a cosy be invariably provided for the teapot. This done, the sweeper should be called to sweep the dining-room, and the *under-khit* should then throw open the windows, shake out the curtains, dust and polish chairs and tables, whilst the head *khit* turns his attention to the sideboards, burnishing up the set silver, if any, and putting everything in order. He should also remove the flower vases, see that they are clean, and place them ready for re-filling on the gardener's table on the verandah.

Before laying the table for breakfast or any meal, the *khit* must first inquire of the cook what dishes are to be served, otherwise he cannot know what articles will be required. This is rarely done, and is at the bottom of half the frantic dives into the pantry of which we have complained above.

The *khit* should then lay the table carefully, placing on the sideboard every extra which may be wanted, and he should satisfy himself that the *under-khit* has put a sufficiency of plates and dishes into the hot ease. This ean easily be made in the bazaar out of an old tin-lined packing-case. A few wire shelves and a pan of charcoal will turn it into a very efficient plate-warmer. These rules are to be observed at every meal. In regard to breakfast, specially, it may be notieed that every dish should be brought in at once on the butler's-tray and plaeed either on the sideboard or table, aceording to the eustom of the house. If a person refuses one dish, another should be handed at once, as there are no set eourses at breakfast. Nothing save meat dishes and plates should be removed from the table until the guests have risen, and butter, &c., taken from their places to be handed round, should be returned to the same spot. Washing up must never be commenced till the family have left the dining-room, as the pantry is generally close by, and the clatter is annoying. Everything should be cleared away at once; the cups put ready to wash in the pantry, the greasy plates outside; the jam, sugar, butter, bread, eruets, &e., returned to their places; the cloth brushed, folded, and plaeed in the press.

When all this is done eomes the time for washing up.

Then the knives should be put to stand in an upright tin made for the purpose, and sufficient hot water poured in to cover the blades only. The silver should next be placed in one of the tubs in very hot water. The *under-khit* should meanwhile be seraping off the remains from the plates outside, and plaeing everything to be washed in a large tub of hot water. Cups, plates, dishes—every bit of china—should first be washed in clean hot water and then rinsed and well rubbed with *the hands* in clean eold water, and set to drain on the table or rack. When all are washed the tubs should be emptied and put aside, and then, and not till then, should drying be eommeneed. In this way one tea-eloth will do the work of six, whieh are used a little, then thrown on the floor, then taken to soak up greasy water, then perhaps used to rub down the table. Everything, as it is dried, should be put in its proper place.

The *under-khit* should follow the same rules with the meat plates, &c., except that they should be set to drain in the rack, and not wiped at all. He should then take the knives in hand and clean them, not forgetting to wipe the handles with a damp cloth. The *khit* meanwhile should be busy on the silver, putting each article as he washes it into a pan of clear, cold water, whence it should be taken piece by piece, wiped dry with a soft cloth, polished with another, finally rubbed with a chamois leather, and put, as it is done, into the plate basket. These rules for washing up apply to every meal. After breakfast the *khit* should attend his mistress to the storeroom and ask for everything he may want for the table.

Lunch should not be laid till half-an-hour before the time for serving it. If due method is observed in washing up, a good two hours' recess will have clapsed between the end of breakfast work and the laying of lunch. This is quite sufficient leisure for any but the idle. As at breakfast, the *khit* should inquire what dishes are to be served, and make arrangements accordingly. Washing up follows the same lines, the upper *khit* taking glass and silver. Between lunch and afternoon tea-time (which is often irregular in time) the *khit* should not leave the house, but should occupy himself with the spare silver, which cannot have too much elbow-grease. The *khit* will thus be at hand to bring tea at any time, should the advent of visitors require it to be brought, either earlier or later than usual; if the kettle is boiling, which it should be, on a charcoal brazier in the verandah, a sharp servant will appear with the tray, toast, cakes, &c., less than five minutes after it has been ordered. Yet how often has not every Indian visitor been kept wearisomely waiting for the tea, the offer of which he was unwise enough to accept.

When his mistress goes out, the *khit* is once more at leisure, if he has been wise enough to see to his preparations for dinner between lunch and tea-time. Dessert should then be arranged, and creased tablecloths or napkins taken to the *dhôbi* (washerman) for an iron. A *khit* should always be reminded that an untidy table, dull glass, and tarnished silver tell his character far more truthfully than his *chits* (certificates) tell it; and that even should he lose the latter, as *chits* through some fatality are always being lost, he need fear no difficulty in finding, and keeping, a good place if his glass, china, and silver attest his industry.

The procedure at dinner is much the same as at lunch; but special care should be taken to avoid delay between the courses. Vegetables, especially potatoes, should be handed with the joint,, and not ten minutes after, when people have finished their meat. To facilitate carving at the side-table, the cook should never put sauce or gravy in the dish, but in a separate bowl. A servant should never put anything down, even for an instant, on the dinner-table, and he should never dodge round the table, but serve steadily from right to left.

Silver should receive a special cleaning twice a week, and once a week the pantry should be cleared out, and everything in it receive an extra wash. Water carafes must be emptied every night and set to drain in the decanter drainer. Silver should be counted over every night, and glass and china once a week. If a breakage is not reported, and the mistress discovers it, cut the *buksheesh* money remorselessly; not so if it is reported, since accidents will occur.

Dirt, illimitable, inconceivable dirt must be expected, until a generation of mistresses has rooted out the habits of immemorial years. Till then look at both sides of your plates, and turn up the spare cups ranged so neatly in order in the pantry. Probably one-half of them are dirty.

The following recipes will be found useful by the *khitmutgâr* :—

1. **Brass, to clean.**—Use Putz pomade, or rub with finely pounded bathbrick mixed to a paste with sweet oil, or powdered sal-ammoniac mixed in the same way with water. Polish with equal parts of bran and whiting.

2. **Bread, to freshen.**—Soak the loaf for oue minute in boiling water, then bake till dry in a hot oven.

3. **Butter, to keep sweet.**—Press the butter into the bottom of an empty jam jar, then invert the latter in a soup plate of water. This keeps out the air effectually. If the butter is kept actually in the water, the latter should always have salt or boracic acid in it, and be changed every day.

4. **Coffee, to make Essence of.**—For every two tablespoons of ground coffee take one breakfast cup of cold water. Place in a wide-mouthed jar and stand all night. Place the jar in a *dêgchi* of water, and let the whole come to boiling point. Strain and bottle. It will keep for a week, the addition of an equal quantity

of *boiling* water making it hot enough to use. Similar essence may be made in any machine by adhering to the same proportions of coffee and water.

5. **Glass, to clean.**—Wash in warm water with *bâsun* (parched gram flour) mixed to a paste with water, and use like soap. Rinse well, and polish. The stains or rims in neglected water carafes, decanters, &c., are best removed by a few drops of strong hydrochloric, or, at a pinch, sulphuric acid in a tumbler of water. This should be poured into the carafe and well shaken. Rinse thoroughly in clean water, as the acid bites into the glass.

6. **Plate, to clean.**—Powder, mix, and bottle four ounces each of common salt, alum, and cream of tartar. Add a teaspoon of this mixture to every quart of water. Boil the plate in the water for five minutes. Remove and plunge in cold water. Dry and polish, using a little powdered chalk tied in a muslin bag, and dusted over the silver during the final polish. Elbow-grease is the only secret of bright plate. Every now and again wash with Sapolio.

7. **Table Linen, to remove Wine Stains from.**—Put a soup plate under the stain while wet and squeeze a lemon or pour boiled milk over it. After five minutes wash out with water. A careful servant will remove all small grease stains from table linen as they appear by rubbing bread on them, and see all creases ironed out.

8. **Tea, to make.**—Use boiling water, and warm both tea and teapot before the fire. Fill the pot at once with the amount of water required. Infuse for five minutes, and decant into another well-warmed teapot.

9. **Toast, to make.**—Cut *stale* bread into thin, even slices. Hold at some distance from the fire at first in order to dry it (or if there is an oven, place in that); then closer to give it a golden brown tinge. Toast should be crisp and yellow brown, not tough and dirty white, streaked with burnt black. Place the toast when made in the toast-rack at once. The Christy bread-knife enables any one to cut thin toast even out of new bread.

The Duties of the Musolchi or Scullion.

The implements required by the scullion are, as a rule, confined to a pail of greasy water and a rag swab. The wisdom of having such a servant at all is doubtful; but if the most prominent duty of a table attendant—cleanliness—is delegated to a nameless drudge on six rupees a month, a very great deal of supervision must be exercised by the mistress to ensure obedience to orders. In most houses the scullion is an unknown quantity, a gruesome ghoul of spurious cleanliness, bearing, as his badge of office, a greasy swab of rag tied to a bit of bamboo.

It is said that good *khits* will not work unless a *musolchi* is kept; but this is not the authors' experience, and one of them has never allowed such a servant in the house; though in the cook-room she acknowledges a drudge may be necessary in a large family. Indeed, it seems absurd that *khitmutgârs* should be above the washing of valuable glass and china; for it must be remembered that if *once* a *musolchi* is admitted to the pantry, he will be used for everything and anything. There is no objection whatever to his doing the preliminary clearing of the dinner-plates in the verandah, as elsewhere advised. Indeed, this *is* the scullery-maid's duty, and the *musolchi* should be a scullion, and nothing else; the pantry is a step above him, and on no pretence should he be allowed to flourish his swab there. Under the system, or no system, which obtains in most houses, the *musolchi* and the sweeper are the only two servants who ever condescend to clean anything. Curiously enough, in these cases they acquire a strange similarity in dress and demeanour; possibly because, being everybody's slave, they lose all spirit and self-respect. Both slink from sight, and become furtive even in *their* methods of work, and both contrive to assimilate an incredible amount of pure griminess around their own persons.

In many so-called good houses the *musolchi* is the motive-power underlying the simulated activity of the Mahomedan servants. He lights the early fire, makes the tea and toast, and prepares everything for the *khitmutgâr*, who is generally a lordly relative. It is he who washes up the early breakfast cups and saucers, and makes it possible for his real master, the *khitmutgâr*, to lay the table leisurely.

Breakfast over, the lordly one retires for recess, while the *musolchi*, left in sole possession of the pantry, proceeds to wash up everything in one poor pennyworth of water, with an intolerable amount of greasy cloth. *Jharans* (cloths) here, there, everywhere; all more or less filthy, all more or less capable of leaving a fine bold smear on your plates and dishes

The process, as patented by the unchangeable law of *musolchi*-dom, is simple :—

1. Plates are plates, and include cups and saucers, teapots, side-dishes, and milk-jugs.
2. Spoons are spoons, and include knives, forks, toast-racks, &c.
3. Water is water, so long as it is fluid.
4. Cloths are cloths, so long as they hold together. After that they are used as swabs.
5. The floor is a floor, and nature made it as a table.
6. Variety is pleasing ; therefore always intersperse your stoneware plates with china teacups.
7. At the same time, union is strength ; so pile everything together, use one water and one cloth, and do not move from your station till everything is dried and spread carefully in the dust.
8. Only one side of a plate is used by the *sahib logue ;* it is therefore purely unreasonable for them to cavil at the other side being dirty.

The cleaning of knives follows, and *musolchi*-dom has long ago reduced this to a science in the way of destruction. Given a little of his own productions in the way of broken china, and a slanting wooden board destitute of leather, and the *musolchi* will produce an Indian knife, *i.e.* a two-edged pliable spatula, out of the best shear steel, in an incredibly short space of time. In extreme cases he has been known to clean your silver with bathbrick ; and being invariably a slave to his work, he may be seen all day wiping and smearing, smearing and wiping, whilst the *khitmutgârs* lounge on their beds or smoke pipes in the kitchen. Such a state of affairs will, however, never be allowed by a good mistress. Even if a *musolchi* be kept, which is by no means advisable, he should be a responsible servant on good wages ; indeed, it is an admirable plan, if *khitmutgârs* object to washing up, to keep one *khit* and put on a *musolchi* on higher wages ; it generally settles the matter.

Where a *musolchi* is really needed is in the cook-room. There, just when clean hands are necessary, the scouring of a saucepan may become imperative ; and some one to stand between the cook busy at his pastry board and the fire which requires fresh fuel, is a vast aid in preventing the thousand and one trivial accidents and dangers that beset the culinary art. Only those who have actually cooked a whole dinner know the immense relief it is to have some one at hand to prevent those sudden interruptions, which seem invariably to come at the most critical moment.

The *musolchi*, then, finds his proper place amongst the pots and pans, and the utmost he should have to do with plates and dishes should be the clearing away of bones and fragments from the dinner-plates, and, perhaps, a preliminary washing of the same,—the *khitmutgâr*, however, being held entirely responsible for the cleanliness of every dish, plate, cup, saucer, or article of any kind or sort which he puts on his master's table. By keeping the *musolchi* in the kitchen, and at the same time recognising him as your servant and *not* a general drudge, another advantage is secured. He can be trained as a regular cook, and should be taught to look forward to promotion during the time his superior may be on leave, or sick. It is an immense comfort to know that a sudden attack of ague in the kitchen need not result in starvation to the dining-room. Before leaving the subject of cook room and table servants, it is bare justice to say that a lengthier experience of England has made the authors admit that their blame of the East applies to the West also. They have seen an experienced parlour-maid use a whale-bone scrubbing brush to a silver tray, a cook boil her under-clothing in the stock pot, and a housemaid empty slops into the bath! In fact, Indian servants are no dirtier than, if as dirty, as those of other countries.

The Duties of the Bheesti.

With the implements required by the *bheesti* the mistress has little to do beyond providing him with a few clean dusters and seeing that he has a sufficiency of hot and cold water cans, and at least one filter.

Bheesties are, as a rule, the cleanest servants in an Indian household, and are, as a class, more ready to turn their hands to an odd job than any of the others. The duties, however, in which he comes absolutely under the mistress's eye are few.

The first is to bring daily a supply of drinking water from

some approved source, see it boiled in the vessel set apart for the purpose, and put it to cool in earthen pots beside the filter. These earthen pots should be emptied out every day, as also the filter and every receptacle of filtered water. As often as not, if this rule be not strictly enforced, filtered water is quite, if not more unsafe, than that drawn fresh from the well.

The *bheesti's* next duty is to keep a supply of fresh water in the bathrooms, and to heat the water required for the morning baths. It will be found a good plan to give out, or allow, the wood or charcoal for this purpose quite separately from the kitchen fuel; for complaints of stinting on the one side, or extravagance on the other, are sure to arise as an excuse for tepid baths, or large consumption. The water-jugs, carafe, sponge, and soap dishes are in the *bheesti's* charge, and it is his duty to keep them clean and duly filled with fresh water. We strongly advise the placing of an ordinary three-*gurrah* filter close to the servants' houses, so that those who desire it can always have a supply of fresh water. Such little evidences of care for their health are duly appreciated by the servants; and, in addition, the removal of one of the chief causes of epidemic disease—impure drinking-water—is a source of safety to the entire household.

In regard to the supply of water in bathrooms, the *bheesti* must be made to scrub out the earthen vessels at least once a week, and boiled water should be put in the carafes.

What is generally called a "Punjâb tub" will be found a great convenience for heating bath-water. It consists of an ordinary wooden cask, with a small iron cylinder fixed upright through it like a chimney. This has a grating slightly above its joint with the cask bottom. The cask, which is open at the top and raised on bricks, is then filled with water, and charcoal burned in the cylinder This is an inexpensive and rapid method of heating water. If the Punjâb tub be placed in the verandah near the pantry, it will be found an exceedingly useful aid to the *khitmutgârs* in heating water for washing up, and thus taking the place of the English boiler.

Filters are often a source of great trouble, and the following, recommended publicly by an authority, will be found excellent.

Cut the bottom neatly off a quart bottle. This may be done with an ordinary steel file well moistened by oil of turpentine, or by tying a hank of cotton thread dipped in turpentine round the bottle, setting light to it, and immediately dipping the bottle into cold water. Get a new cork, and through the centre put the glass tube of a Maw's feeding-bottle (to be had in any bazaar), pushing it well through and letting the indiarubber tube remain as in the feeding-bottle. Cork the bottle tight, place a bit of sponge in the neck to prevent the tube getting clogged, and fill the bottle with, if possible, animal charcoal finely pounded—but free from dust —and silver sand, in equal parts. Place another sponge at the open end of the bottle, and either close by tying a piece of muslin over, or get a tight fitting tin cover made in the bazaar; it must, of course, be perforated with small holes. If this filter be placed in an ordinary *gurrah* of water, and the indiarubber tube attached to the glass tube be allowed to hang over the side into a proper vessel, such as a *surâhi*, water will filter over rapidly when once it has started. This must be effected as with a baby's bottle, by squeezing the nipple or by sucking it. In this case, the nipple should be removed afterwards. The advantage of this filter is the ease with which it can be cleaned and renewed. The Berkefield Filter Co., Oxford Street, London, supply excellent filters. And the Gem Still provides a convenient method of obtaining absolutely pure water.

It has lately been discovered that the addition of even a few grains of alum to a gallon of water is almost the best filter there is. In fact, if the water is first boiled, then put to cool in a small-mouthed vessel in a clean place, with two grains of powdered alum to every gallon, it will, after an hour's settling, and carefully decanting to another vessel, be practically as pure as it is possible to get water undistilled.

Permanganate of potash added till the water is faintly pink is supposed to destroy most bacilli. It is also put into wells nowadays, about 2 oz. every week or so for a well in constant use.

The Duties of the Ayah.

Many ladies keep no *ayah;* the implements one requires are few, and consist chiefly of dusters, brushes, &c.

The *ayah's* duties naturally vary immensely with her situation. If there are no children, she is virtually a lady's maid, while if an English nurse is kept, her responsibilities are almost *nil*. On the other hand, when she is really head nurse, she is of all the servants the most important.

In the latter case, again, her duties would vary very much

according to the part taken by her mistress; so that it is hardly worth while treating of the *ayah* simply as a nurse. We may only remark that with very few exceptions, the Indian *ayahs* are singularly kind, injudicious, patient, and thoughtless in their care of children; but to expect anything like *common sense* from them is to lay yourself open to eertain disappointment.

Unless you can get a woman from a regular *ayah's* family, the Mahomedan ones are apt to be a nuisance; and the reason which leads many ladies to employ them, viz., the dislike to a sweeper or low-caste woman, is in itself foolish. For no one who has lived long in India can fail to see that the sweeper is very often cleaner in his ways, and certainly in his house, than the Mahomedans. Nor does it follow that because a woman belongs to the sweeper caste she should necessarily do all the dirty work of the establishment. But to whatever class she belongs, the *ayah's* household duties are virtually the same, except that she will not condescend to the broom if she is a Mahomedan. In this conneetion it may be remarked that the degradation which attaches to the mere act of cleansing anything in India is mainly responsible for the inconceivably filthy ways of its inhabitants. Most of them cannot afford to pay for a cleanser, and so learn to live on contentedly in dirt.

We will begin with the duties of an *ayah* as housemaid and lady's maid. At the time specified by her mistress, she should knock at the door of the bedroom and bring in the early tea, placing the tray on the table, or wherever her mistress directs. She should never forget to *salaam* to her mistress, and ask if anything is wanted, and what time her mistress desires to rise. She should then draw back the curtains and leave the room, remembering to take away the lamp, dirty boots, &c. Having unbolted the bathroom door whilst inside, she should now go round to the outside, and put everything in order, taking special care that the water is fresh, and the jugs, basins, &c., scrupulously clean.

At the appointed time she should bring in the hot water, carefully close the outer door, and after putting towels, soap, &c., in order, go into the bedroom and collect such clothes as her mistress may want. She should never place these in the bathroom till the water has been brought in by the *bheesti*, and the outer door closed. When all is ready, she should take her mistress's dressing-gown and slippers to her. During the bathing time the *ayah* should be arranging and dusting the dressing-table, and carefully putting away everything that is lying about. The bed should also be turned down, and the dress which her mistress is to wear carefully looked over, and hung ready on the back of a chair. Whether the *ayah* does her mistress's hair or not depends upon individual capacity and custom ; but most *ayahs* have to do the brushing of the hair, and they generally do it very gently and well.

As soon as her mistress has left the room, the *ayah* should open the windows and put everything in thorough order, making the bed last of all. Not till everything save dusting is finished should the room be swept, especially if she has to call in another servant with a broom. Once a week a more elaborate cleaning should take place, boxes, &c., be moved, lest vermin of any sort should lurk behind them, and both windows and doors receive a polish. Her mistress's room done, the *ayah* will see that the bathroom is set in order, squeeze out the sponge, dry and fold the towels, &c.

If there are no children, she has little else to do during the day, except to lay out walking things, boots, parasols, &c., as may be required. To ensure these being ready, she should come with the other servants after breakfast to take her orders ; and if she desires to please, will take her recess between breakfast and twelve o'clock, so as to be on the spot when her mistress is most likely to require her. When the order is given for luncheon, she will take hot water to her mistress's room, and at the same time ask what dress she proposes wearing in the afternoon and evening. At dusk she will go to the bearer for candle and lamp, draw the curtains, if necessary light the fire, and be ready on her mistress's return from her evening drive to take her wraps. While her mistress is dressing for dinner, the *ayah* should arrange everything for the night ; turn down the bed, &c., see that fresh water is in the carafe, and lay dressing-gown and slippers ready for use. She must not forget to see that there are matches at hand, and that anything likely to be required is in its place. If a lady guest comes to the house without a servant, the *ayah* of the house should attend to her wants exactly as if she were a mistress, and any neglect in this point should be punished at once.

Where there are no children, an *ayah* should always have time to hem dusters, give out the *khitmutgár's* cloths, and do many little odd jobs about the house. Indeed, a really good woman will be an immense help, and put her hand to anything, from arranging flowers to sewing on buttons. Being the only woman-servant in the house, the *ayah* should be treated with consideration and respect. Whether she be a sweeper or not, it should be generally understood that you hold her to be the equal of any other servant in the house. If she has charge of children, this point must be still more insisted upon, and you should endeavour to instil into her a sense of her great responsibility, and the confidence you have in her. To treat, however, of the *ayah* as a nurse would involve a chapter on the management of children, and lead us into controversial waters; besides, the employment of English nurses is now becoming so general that ere long such a thing as a child's *ayah* will be unknown.

One thing is certain: Indian children are proverbially captious, disobedient, and easily thrown out of gear. Whether this be the fault of the mother, the *ayah*, or the climate is a moot point; perhaps the safest plan is to attribute it to all three. This more frequent employment of English nurses is no doubt improving the régime of Indian nurseries; but even now it is no unusual thing to see an English child eating his dinner off the floor, with his hands full of toys, while a posse of devoted attendants distract his attention, and the *ayah* feeds him with spoonfuls of *pish-pash*. Appetite is no doubt variable in Anglo-Indian children, but it is possible that a little more pomp and circumstance, and a wholesome conviction that food is not forthcoming except *at* meal-times, would induce Sonny or Missy Baba to treat dinner with graver circumspection. Where, save in India, do we find sturdy little tots of four and five still taking their bottles and refusing to go to sleep without a lullaby? Without going further into the subject, we can only assure every young mother that there is no climatic reason whatever why discipline should be set aside in an Indian nursery, and that it is as possible to insist on cleanliness, decency, and order there as in an Indian pantry or cook-room. The whole secret lies in refusing to listen to the word *dustoor*, or custom.

Few mistresses have been long in India without having had the trouble of scandals between the *ayah* and other servants. In this connection, one word of warning. A steady, well-doing woman may lay herself open to deliberate slanders by her very virtues; and in sifting a story of this kind, it must not be forgotten that the Mahomedan men-servants as a rule have no shame, and will say anything.

The following recipes will be found useful to the *ayah* :—

1. **Brushes, to wash.**—Dissolve one teaspoonful of carbonate of soda or brush powder in a basin of hot water, and whisk the brush on it till clean, taking care not to wet the back lest the ivory or wood should split. Dry in the shade, with handles upwards.

2. **Dentifrice.**—One oz. betel-nuts roasted to charcoal and ground fine, 1 oz. lump sugar, cream of tartar and Peruvian bark, of each ½ oz., powdered cinnamon, 1 drachm. Pulverise. Or equal parts of betel-nut charcoal and common salt. Both these whiten the teeth.

3. **Grease Spots, to remove.**—Use a hot iron and blotting-paper. A piece of cardboard split to a rough edge, and rubbed gently on the spot, will often remove grease from silk. But no house should be without benzine.

4. **Hair, to wash.**—Bruise one dozen soap-nuts (*rēta*), and steep for an hour in a pint of hot water. Pound one tablespoonful of poppy seeds (*kish-kâsh*) on a curry stone, and steep in half a pint of hot water. When wanted for use, strain the water from the soap-nuts into a basin, using pressure to extract all the juice. Into a separate basin strain the liquor from the poppy seeds, which should look like milk. Wash the hair thoroughly with the *rēta* water, rinsing it well out before using the poppy-seed milk. The latter should only be lightly rubbed on to the hair, and just rinsed out. It gives the hair a beautiful softness and gloss, without being greasy. It is also a specific against scurf.

5. **Hair Wash.**—Dissolve in two quarts of boiling water 1 oz. of borax and 2 oz. of camphor; use to wash the hair, rinsing it well.

The Duties of the "Syce" or Groom.

The implements required by the *syce* are :—

2 Dusters.	1 Burnisher.	1 Set blacking and harness brushes.
1 Chamois leather.	1 Body brush.	
1 Sponge.	1 Mane comb.	1 Clippers (?).

The stable may seem outside the domain of the mistress, but as a matter of fact, so many Englishmen in India are over-busy, that, unless the mistress keeps an eye on the horses, the animals are apt to be neglected. Now, if the good house-mother's proudest boast is that not even "the cattle within her gate" fail to feel her kindly care, she will often find it necessary to take an active part in teaching the *syce* his duty, and seeing that the horses receive proper attention. It will, in the authors' opinion, be invariably found a good plan to *limit* the number of servants employed in the stable as much as possible. The old plan of a *syce* and a grass-cutter to each horse is a thing of the past in almost every part of India. Grass is generally bought; but as this costs quite as much as the wages of a man who is available for other stable work, the authors fail to see the advantage. The number of *syces* or grooms should have reference merely to the amount of harnessing and out-work necessary during the day.

If one grass-cutter were given to each horse, one *syce* to every three horses would, as a rule, be found sufficient. The *syce* should be made responsible for the horses under him, and any complaints he may make about the grass-cutters should be attended to at once. He is thus placed in a position of responsibility, and for the extra work involved may be given a small increase of wage. His duties also become those of an English groom. Every morning after breakfast he will come for orders, and again after dinner at night; since, if a horse is to be taken out early in the morning, a good *syce* will wish to know it, in order that he may arrange that the animal gets its food in good time. Without grass-cutters two *syces* should be enough for three horses.

The routine of an ordinary Indian stable should be as follows: At daybreak the horses should receive quarter of their daily allowance of corn, and in hot weather this may be preceded by a limited drink of water. In cold weather this is not necessary; a light grooming should then be given, night clothing removed, the bedding gathered to one corner, and the stall cleaned. After this the grass-cutters should go out for their daily bundle of grass, under orders to return by twelve. It is not by any means necessary for grass-cutters to go out every day for grass, as they can quite well cut a double quantity in the time allowed. In fact, in large stations they invariably do so, and sell one bundle before returning home. Supposing, then, six horses are kept, it will only be necessary for at most four grass-cutters to go out, so that two can remain to help the two *syces*.

The *syce* must be ready at the door to take over the horses which have been ridden, and he should invariably have a light saddle-cloth with him to throw over the horse before leading him away. It is not, of course, necessary, but it will be found a good plan, after district or cross-country work, to put on bandages for the first hour after the horse comes in. The *syce* should have orders first to loosen the girths, then to bandage the legs, then remove the saddle and set to work at once, first with a wisp, then with a pad or cloth, and finally with hand and arm-rubbing. Remarks have been made on the omission of a curry-comb in the list of implements for the *syce*. This is no oversight. A curry-comb is an abomination, and quite unnecessary. Except under unusual circumstances, there will always be two men at leisure to attend to one horse; and as freedom from chill and its many consequent evils depends in a great measure on quickness of grooming after work, it should be a recognised rule in the stable that the grass-cutters are not on *one* particular horse, but on all.

As soon as the horse is groomed, he should be watered and given a small supply of grass. Meanwhile the horses which have not been out will have been exercised, and when all have been looked after and watered, the whole stable should get the mid-day meal of corn. At three the horses may again be watered, at four they get the next feed of corn and should be thoroughly well groomed, so as to be ready for the evening exercise. On their return from this, they should get their last feed and be made up for the night. With regard to the *times* of feeding, people will, of course, consult their own convenience; but it should never be less than three times a day: the gram should be given dry or merely sprinkled with water, and should be mixed with, at least, an equal quantity of chaff or chopped hay, to ensure thorough mastication and digestion. The horses should invariably be given water not less than half-an-hour before, and *never* immediately after, his gram. It is a mistake to feed horses out of their stalls.

In regard to the food, variety is a thing to be looked to, and horses kept from year's end to year's end on nothing but gram are seldom in such good health as those whose food is judiciously changed. Almost every grain may be given, mixed with either bruised barley, gram, or oats. A small corn-crusher will be found both economical and convenient where many horses are kept; you are then certain of getting the food unadulterated, and the horses prefer freshly-crushed grain. Each grass-cutter in turn grinds the corn for the day, and, roughly speaking, it takes five minutes to crush one horse's rations.

The quantity of food must vary immensely with the work given, but it may be remarked that, considering the small amount of work horses do in India, they generally get too much corn. The recognised scale of forage for the largest carriage horses in full work in England is per diem—

Hay . . .	12 lbs.
Corn	12 lbs.
Chaff	2 gallon measures.
Bran	2 quart measures.

For ponies of 14 hands in full work the English allowance is—

Hay	10 lbs.
Oats	8 lbs.
Chaff . .	2 gallon measures.
Bran	2 quart measures.

In the country in England, a ten miles' drive to the county town and back is supposed to be nothing out of the way; but in India, if any distance over ten miles has to be *ridden,* an extra horse is laid out. Much, of course, depends on the grass, and for this reason it is always advisable to make the grass-cutters bring their bundles into the verandah for inspection at twelve o'clock. If the gram, oats, &c., be kept in lockers in the same verandah, the mistress can then see the grain taken out, and so, at very little trouble, avoid the *buniya's* bill. It is not necessary to weigh out the grain; and if a week's supply is put into the lockers every Monday morning, and the feeds measured with a wooden corn-measure, you will scarcely ever be out more than half a *seer*. Under the ordinary system of a *buniya's* account, you are never certain what kind of stuff the horses are getting, while any change in quantity or kind in the food leads to trouble-some complication, and gives cover to cheating. Once, if not twice a week, horses should have a bran mash, a recipe for making which will be found at the end. It also tends to keep horses in health to give them some green food—a *seer* or two of earrots, green wheat, lueerne, grass, or even sugar-cane—and if the mistress takes a pride in her horses, which it is to be hoped she will always do, this little treat will be given during her daily visit to the stable. It will be a distinct pleasure to most women to hear the whinnyings and neighings whieh will then follow at the first glimpse of the *Mem Sahib.*

Always eneourage your *syce* to speak to you at once if anything ails the horses, and never negleet sueh information. If a horse is reported lame, it does not take much trouble to put on your hat and go out to see. Even if you know little what to do, it impresses the *syces* with your anxiety, and they themselves will look on the matter more seriously.

In cold weather always give out blankets to all the stable-servants, to prevent them from stealing the coverings of their horses. These blankets should be of good quality, marked with your initials, and should be attached to the *service,* and not given to the individual. At the commeneement of the hot weather they should be washed and put back into store. The same proeedure should be adopted with regard to the horse-elothing, otherwise it will be used to wrap up bundles, &c. &c. Do not grudge warm clothing to your horse ; if he is deeently groomed, his skin will be very suseeptible to the ehanges of temperature ; and with good elothing, he will keep in condition on less food. It is false economy to deny him what is equivalent to an extra feed of corn.

It is not always possible to have *good* stables, but it is in every one's reaeh to have clean, wholesome ones, by knocking ventilators through the walls near the roof, and converting stalls into loose-boxes by movable bamboos. Heel-ropes should never be seen in a private stable, and the mere sight of them eondemns the management. It is said that some Waler horses require heel-ropes, owing to a bad habit of rubbing mane and tail, espeeially during hot weather ; but there can be no doubt that such symptoms point to disease, and these eases may therefore be treated as abnormal. The floor of the stable is nearly always of mud, but it should be quite level ; and onee a week at least it should be *leped* or plastered with a thin paste of cowdung, sand, and water, as should be the walls to a height of four feet. Stables should always have a verandah in front, and it is wonderful how greatly a cheap bamboo or grass chick to the arches will reduce the temperature in the hot months. The *syces* should not be allowed to sleep *en masse* with wives and families in the spare stalls or verandahs, as they disturb the horses, but *one* man must always do so in case of sudden illness.

If horses are picketed out at night, as they often are during the summer, the safest and most comfortable plan is to have a wooden post about four feet high permanently let into the ground. The horse should have a light iron chain to his headstall, with a ring at the end large enough to slip over the post. If the bedding be arranged round the post in a circle, the horse can always shift his quarters without fear of entanglement or breaking loose. The best bedding in India is rice straw; but where grass is plentiful, many people use *drubh*[1] grass, which a horse will seldom eat.

The best manger for a horse is a square of hemp matting or *tât* on which the gram can be spread on the ground. This enables the horse to eat in a natural position, and prevents bolting; nose-bags are an abomination in a private stable. Watering buckets of galvanised iron are the best; and though it is more reasonable to allow a horse an unlimited supply of water all day long, by means of a suitable receptacle in his stall, yet without constant supervision it is hard, on this plan, to ensure the water being fresh. Therefore, unless unusual care can be given, it is best to keep to the bucket. Hay should never be in a rack. The seeds and spikes are apt to fall into the horse's eyes, and it also conduces to greediness.

In regard to grooming, body brushes, &c., the real secret of a good coat lies in sheer, honest, hard work. As the *khitmutgâr* when pulled up about the dulness of the plate cries loudly for *pureah* (plate powder), so the *syce* will clamour for brushes and curry-combs when brought up for neglect. Elbow-grease is more effectual on a horse's coat than anywhere else—which is saying a good deal—and, while it is quite possible to get on without a brush, it is impossible to dispense with the hand and arm. In fact, a *syce* who does not take off his coat and turn up his sleeves before beginning to groom his horse, knows nothing of his work. There is a great art in making a horse look smart, which is seldom

[1] A kind of coarse rye grass.

thought of in India; but if the *syce* sees that his employers expect it and notice it, he will soon learn, like an English groom, to take a pride in the appearance of his horse. The following rules should be impressed on all the stable helpers:—

1. Give water before and never after food.
2. Do not soak the corn. It may be damped for ten minutes.
3. Report the least injury or symptom of illness.
4. Beat the grass well, and let it dry a day before using it.
5. Always have two men to groom a horse.
6. Never wash a horse's legs except on rare occasions, and then dry carefully at once.
7. If you must steal, steal from men, and not from dumb animals.

The *syce*, however, has other duties besides keeping his horses. He must look after the saddlery and harness, also the dog-cart or carriage, unless a coachman is kept. For saddlery there is nothing like good English soft-soap. If washed with this once a week and carefully dried, scarcely anything else will be required. A recipe for dubbin is, however, given at the end; though we doubt if anything home-made can be cheaper or better than the soaps and *mom roghan* sold by the N. W. Soap Company at Cawnpore.

Bits and stirrup-irons should be cleaned with dry sand or pounded brick and burnished with a regular steel burnisher. If washed in water, they must be dried at once. In hot weather constant care is necessary to prevent insects getting to the saddle stuffing; and it is a good plan to have bags of camphor and *nim* leaves tacked along the top of the saddle-horse or stand. Girths, if white, should be sponged and pipe-clayed, then dusted out; *numdahs* or saddle-cloths dried in the sun and brushed, instead of being utterly neglected.

Carriages, when it is necessary to wash them, require plenty of water, and not half a bucketful, as the *syce* seems to think. But in India the roads are seldom so muddy as to make daily washing necessary. A dry duster is generally sufficient for the most part, and splashes can be removed from the wheels gently with a sponge. A spoke brush or carriage mop is rather a dangerous implement in a native's hands, and we prefer to give him nothing but soft dusters, a sponge, wash-leather, and carriage brush. It is always necessary to have a large dust cloth which will completely cover the carriage almost to the ground. Without this, the most careful *syce* will not be able to send his carriage out as neat as it should be. If the hood is movable, the best plan is to have a hook and pulley to the roof of the coach-house, and so keep the hood out of harm's way when it is not in use.

Harness requires care to keep it strong, and it is usual to put a little lamp-black in the composition used for it. A good recipe for harness paste is given at the end. The mountings should be kept bright with powdered whiting, and the patent leather portions carefully polished with drying oil. Whips should be hung up by the lash, otherwise they will warp.

The following recipes will be found useful to the *syce* :—

1. **Waterproof Harness Dressing.**—Melt 2 oz. mutton suet with 6 oz. beeswax (*kuchcha môm*). Add 6 oz. powdered sugar-candy, 2 oz. soft-soap, 2 oz. lampblack, 1 oz. powdered indigo, and 1 teacupful of turpentine. Use like boot blacking.

2. **Wheel Grease.**—Melt and strain into a tin 2 lbs. fat and 1 bottle common mustard oil.

3. **Waterproof Brown Harness Dressing.**—Melt 1 lb. mutton fat, 5 oz. beeswax; boil and skim. Then add 1 pint turpentine.

4. **Saddlery, to clean.**—Wash with soft-soap. Then apply with a sponge the following recipe: Warm 1 *seer* milk, add ½ *chittâck* dilute sulphuric acid, and when cold 2 *chittâcks* hydrochloric acid. Strain and bottle.

The Duties of the "Dirzie" or Tailor.

These are almost too well known to require description; indeed, they are only referred to here in deference to request. The tailor's duties, briefly, are to give his mistress eight hours *at least* of steady sewing work. If, as is usual, he gets a Sunday holiday, his hours should be longer, but in daily work the tailor should be in his place by eight o'clock A.M., and work till five o'clock, with a break of one hour for food in the middle of the day. In the hot weather it is better to make him work from seven o'clock till eleven, and again from three till seven P.M.

Few *dirzies* can be trusted to cut out without any supervision, and it is far better for the mistress either to do it herself, or to order the tailor to show her the patterns tacked on to the stuff before the fateful scissors are brought into use. In most large towns, however, *dirzies* are to be found who are to all intents and purposes dressmakers, and excellent ones into the bargain. They have not, of course, much taste, and their original draperies are almost always wooden-y; but small dressmakers at home have the same faults. The price charged by such *dirzies* for making a dress varies from five to ten rupees, and as a rule they finish their dresses very neatly indeed. To ladies in out-stations, Butterick's, Schild's, or Weldon's paper patterns will be found invaluable; and by giving the bust and waist measurement when ordering the pattern, there is seldom any radical alteration necessary. If, in addition, the lady is wise enough to have an accurately modelled dress form on which to fit the bodice, the *dirzie* is quite as likely to produce a good fit as the most expensive dressmaker. The difficulty about dress forms is their unwieldiness. Several kinds, however, pack into a fairly small space, while the bazaar dress form, to be had from Butterick's for about fourteen shillings, folds up like an umbrella, and can be altered to any size. All that is necessary to make the bodice part of this form efficient is a wadded bodice made to button over the wire frame. It then answers quite as well as many more expensive kinds, whilst it is nearly as portable as an umbrella. It is an excellent plan to pay five shillings at Redmayne's, or any other good dressmaker, for a scientifically-cut bodice pattern, made to actual measurements.

The *dirzie* should always be supplied with a locking box for his work, a sheet for spreading on the ground, an iron and an ironing board. He is supposed to supply his own scissors and thimble. Where a permanent *dirzie* is not kept, it is an admirable plan to have a man in regularly once a week or fortnight to do general repairs. It must not be forgotten, however, that there is an appreciable chance of infection in giving work ont to be done in the bazaars, as the natives are almost criminally lax in all kinds of infectious disease. A permanent tailor almost always saves his own wages, especially if in spare time he is set to do embroidery. Many of them are excellent hands at many kinds of silkwork. Indeed, one of the authors had a complete set of curtains embroidered by her tailor when regular work was slack.

The Duties of the "Dhobi" or Washerman.

The *dhobi's* duties do not bring him much under the eye of the mistress, but there are a few points about his work which require notice. To begin with, it is necessary to fix the place where he is to wash, and insist on his keeping to it. Those who have children, and indeed all who regard their own safety, will arrange for all the washing to be done at their own well. It is both disagreeable and dangerous to have one's wearing apparel steeped in water in which the clothes of smallpox and cholera patients have been cleansed. Yet, if the *dhobi* be allowed to wash at the *ghât,* there can be no certainty that such may not be the case. The *dhobi* should also be carefully watched to see that he does not wash other people's clothes at the same time as those of his ostensible master. It will be found almost impossible, especially in large stations, to prevent the *dhobi* from doing extra washing, but there is no reason why he should wash it in your compound. For this reason it is advisahle, every now and again, to make a raid on your *dhobi's* house, and ruthlessly confiscate any clothes in process of being washed or ironed, which do not belong to you. This generally leads to an *éclaircissement,* in which you, being in possession, have a strong position. As a rule, where there are ladies and children, the *dhobi's* wife comes to count over the dirty clothes, and in many houses this is done twice a week—the clothes given out on Monday coming back on Thursday, and those given on Thursday on Monday. As there is no difficulty—except during the rainy season—in drying the clothes, there is no hardship in giving out the dirty linen even three times a week; in fact, on an emergency, twenty-four hours is sufficient for a small wash.

In regard to the method of cleansing adopted in India, nothing can be more primitive or ineffectual. Cold water, bad soap, and much beating on stones remove the dirt with less certainty than the buttons, and in the effort to bring a presentable *jâogân* (wash) to his mistress, with the least possible labour to himself, the *dhobi* is apt to forget that lace and embroidery is an integral part of underclothing. There is, however, no reason whatever why the recent improvements in cleansing clothes which have revolutionised laundries at home should not be adopted in India. "Sunlight," "Paraffin," "Scotsman," and other soaps make almost all handling needless, the only necessity being warm water and thorough soaping. These, however, owe almost all their efficacy to the paraffin they contain, and this may be used in its pure state with equal advantage. The procedure adopted in most home laundries in England is as follows: A boiler is filled with water, to which one tablespoon of paraffin or kerosene oil has been added to each gallon of water, with a sufficiency of soap to make it blend. The clothes are dipped in this, well rubbed with soap, rolled tight, and set to soak for three hours. The fire is then lit, and the whole boiled for one hour, after which the clothes are removed, well rinsed in two waters, and hung out to dry. No rubbing of any kind being required, the saving in wear and tear is enormous.

Flannels only require steeping for a quarter of an hour, and should *not be boiled;* or if they are simply well rinsed out in warm water in which soap and paraffin have been mixed, they will be found quite clean. They should be at once wrung out and set to dry in the shade. When half dry, pull out carefully and iron. Shrinking is nearly always caused by not having all the waters used of the same temperature, by ineffectual wringing, and slow drying.

Table linen should always be ironed whilst still wet, or it will not glaze. Borax should also be put with the blue.

Coloured clothes are the better of a little alum in the water, and coloured woollen stuffs and embroideries should be washed in water in which bran has been boiled.

It is a good plan to order all flannel things, socks, &c., to be returned the day after they are taken, as this ensures rapidity in washing and drying.

The *dhobi* requires a table, a box for the clothes, an ironing blanket, and a heavy sheet for carrying the dirty clothes.

He will also be the better for a polishing iron—that is to say, one with a convex copper surface. Without some such thing the shirts will never look glazy. It is made moderately hot and rubbed up and down till the polish appears.

It will be found useful to have a supply of "Maypole Soap" of different tints for renovating blouses which fade. The directions are given on each packet.

Scrubb's Ammonia is also useful for woollen tennis dresses.

10

IMPERIAL ETHNOGRAPHY

The People of India (1908, hereafter *TPI*) was an attempt to provide a compendium of ethnographic details about the subcontinent's inhabitants. It is in the same lineage as two other, equally massive, projects designed and executed by East India Company personnel and experts. The first was the geographical effort of just a century earlier—the Great Trigonometrical Survey of India—and, just before *TPI*, the first census (1901). Indeed, *TPI* could well be spoken of as the Census of India's companion volume.

Sir Herbert Risley was deemed an expert at anthropometry, having published numerous scholarly essays in the *Journal of the Asiatic Society of Bengal* and the *Journal of the Royal Anthropological Institute*, among others, besides manuals on the subject and delivering lectures on it at various venues. His handbook, *The Tribes and Castes of Bengal* appeared in 1891–1892 and was a forerunner to *TPI*.

Risley was one of a group of colonial anthropologists and demographers who sought to systematise their understanding of the people of the subcontinent in the form of ethnographic documentation, the census and folklore studies: William Crooke, Denzil Ibbetson, Edward Gait, R.A. Burn. Risley and Crooke published the first handbooks of the subcontinent's tribes and castes: Crooke's are *An Ethnographical Hand-Book for the North-Western Provinces and Oudh* (1896), *The Tribes and Castes of the North-Western Provinces and Oudh* (4 volumes, 1896) and Risley's works are *The Tribes and Castes of Bengal: Anthropometric Data* (1891) and *The Tribes and Castes of Bengal: Ethnographic Glossary* (1891).

Risley sought to harness the 'science' of anthropometry to colonial knowledge production and, proceeding from this, a reliable classification of the peoples. From the shape and size of the head to the width of the nose (the 'nasal index' as he called it), Risley sought to put the interpretation of the caste system and Indian society in general into a 'scientific' frame. Risley declared:

> the caste with the finest nose shall be at the top, and that with the coarsest at the bottom of the list, it will be found that this order substantially corresponds with the accepted order of social precedence … the social status of the members of a particular group varies in inverse ratio to the mean relative width of their noses. (*The People of India*, 29)

Having developed scales of evolution of people and cultures, Risley also made extensive comments on matters of native religions and faith and the necessity of science, Christianity and modernity, which are sprinkled throughout the volume.

In the process of examining the various communities and categories of people that were grouped under 'castes', Risley produced an imperial *systematisation* (but *not* invention) of social identities, community and belonging. As commentators have noted, by focusing on the divided nature of Indian society, Risley also proposed that the organisation into castes

> is a machinery admirably fitted for the diffusion of new ideas; that castes may in course of time group themselves into classes representing the different strata of society; and that India may thus attain, by the agency of these indigenous corporations, the results which have been arrived at elsewhere through the fusion of individual types. (293)

But Risley, for the same reasons, also ruled out Indian society being ever capable of self-rule. In the words of Nicholas Dirks, 'the caste system … worked both to explain how Indian society could be orderly in the absence of either political authority or tradition, and why it was that Indian society would never become mobilized around the political aims of national self-determination' (2001, 194).

Structure and Content

The People of India is divided into seven chapters: the physical types, social types, caste in proverbs and popular sayings, caste and marriage, caste and religion, the origin of caste, caste and nationality. Seven appendices offer multiple kinds of data: caste-related proverbs, maps of castes, anthropometric data of various communities, infant marriage laws, modern theories of caste, polygamy and the Santhal and Munda tribes. About 30 photographs and plates constitute the final pages.

The chapter on 'Physical Types' foregrounds the method (anthropometry), introduces the 'general classification of mankind', compares human 'stature' in Europeans and Indians and moves on to discuss the various types of people: Turko-Iranian, Scytho-Dravidian, Mongoloid, Indo-Aryan, and so on, and makes a case for the 'non-Indian origin' of the Aryans. In the chapter on 'Social Types', Risley discusses the castes of India and the crossing of castes before turning to totemism practised in various parts of the subcontinent. He concludes this with chapters on social precedence among Hindus and Muslims. The third chapter puts together proverbs around castes and provides a 'gallery of popular portraits' (Risley's term, 131) of various types: the potter, the weaver, the carpenter, the Parsi, the Bhil and others. Risley then turns to the question of marriage and the prohibitions founded on caste. Including subjects like female infanticide, polyandry, child marriage and others, Risley also contrasts marriage practices between India and Europe.

In the chapter 'Caste and Religion', Risley compares Hinduism and Islam, provides short introductions to animism, pantheism, paganism and concludes with sections on conversion, the influence of Islam and Christianity, and the rise of movements like the Arya Samaj. 'The Origin of Caste' elaborates theories on the origin of caste in India, through summaries of Ibbetson, John Nesfield and others. In the chapter on 'Caste and Nationality', Risley explores European notions about caste in India, the linkage between caste and monarchy and caste and nationality before concluding with the possible futures for Indian nationality.

Epistemic Violence

Risley's underlying assumption that anthropometry would enable the proper classification of the people of the subcontinent embodies what Gayatri Spivak (following Foucault) and later thinkers like Castro-Gómez (2002), Claudia Brunner (2021) have termed 'epistemic violence'. Risley's account is an excellent instance of such an epistemic violence defined as 'violence against the subject of knowledge, the object of knowledge, the beneficiary of knowledge, and against knowledge itself' (Shiva 1990, 233–234).

Linking knowledge with power and violence, Gayatri Chakravarty Spivak (1992) proposes that entire communities are silenced so that not only their voices but also the different types of knowledge they carry is censored, disappeared or lost. Epistemic violence was a characteristic of colonial rule and dynamics, and structured the social relations between rulers and the ruled. In the process, the colonial ruler 'worlds' the world of the ruled, that is, constructs the world of the colonised subject. Epistemic violence has both, a discursive and a material component. The discursive component has to do with the representations of the colonised people, where they have no say in how they are represented and the colonial's representations of them in history textbooks (such as James Mill's for British India), literature (the vast corpus of English literature *about* India) and tracts (the law, social reform literature, etc.) then become the standard, 'authentic' accounts of the colonised. The material component includes imperial military action, capitalism and forms of exploitation that consign the colonised to the lower orders of humanity.

Risley presents his work as grounded in scientific rationality and reason. Of the book's focus—caste and social hierarchy—Risley would claim that it is based on 'a foundation of facts which can be verified by scientific methods' (5). The Englishman is the observer, the colonised, the observed, and it is the observer who constructs the colonised's past. But in the process, the European ethnologist runs into trouble for, as Risley says, 'India in particular is conspicuous for the absence of the pre-historic evidence of which ethnologists in Europe have made such admirable use' (4). That is, instead of being worried that the European method of ethnological enquiry may be flawed when tackling the subcontinent, Risley dismisses the land as offering *no* evidence of its prehistoric past. Instantiating the epistemic violence at the heart of colonialism, Risley points to the so-called silence in the Indian historical or evidentiary narrative. This is *TPI's* 'socio-epistemic circumstances of the silencing' (Dotson, cited in Brunner, 202).

In short, Risley dismisses what counts as ethnological evidence in India *for* Indians, and allows only that which the European determines *as* fact. The scientific present of the European interprets the native past within its frames, presents the interpretation as authentic and arrived at scientifically—all in the face of inadequate native 'facts' and 'evidence'. Epistemic violence here is the construction of what counts as facts and as evidence in the matter of interpretation.

A related mode of epistemic violence is the construction of a timeline for Indian cultural and social developments. When Risley argues that 'the most modern developments of the [caste] system has … tended to preserve in comparative purity the types which it favours' (5), he has located India's social hierarchy as unchanging and frozen in time. Indigenous knowledge, social ordering and cultural forms are all stuck in the past, while the 'West' has moved on. Even in religion, says Risley, we can see 'survivals of ideas which have every appearance of going back to a far older phase of the religious instinct' (230). While he admits that 'a religion which has succeeded in swallowing Animism is not likely to strain at swallowing Science' (255), he remains committed to the view that Indian 'science' is primitive. The Indian present, in science, society and culture, is, in other words, what the West *used* to be, and while the West's historical progression has been evident, India remains embedded in antiquity.

Then, Risley constantly highlights, as a contrast to the European/British 'rational' mind and culture of reason, the barbaric, primitive people of the subcontinent. He would mock the Arya Samaj's efforts at 'discover[ing] in the *Rig Veda* an anticipation of the discoveries of modern science, and to interpret the horse sacrifice … as an allegorical exposition of the properties of heat or electricity' (262). The colonised's knowledge systems, whether science or history, is dismissed as being non-scientific and founded on myth. Western thinking is 'knowledge' and that of the colonised is 'myth'. For instance, Risley argues about one community:

> In a country where history masquerades in the garb of legend there is nothing *prima facie* improbable in the conjecture that the story of … may be really a mythological version of the true origin story… (75)

The epistemic violence of the imperial archive, of which *TPI* is a significant member, meant that the colonial subject was always only pre-modern, primitive and never reaching the state of modernity that the West had acquired. The violence of rejecting all native knowledge creates a frozen-in-time India. As Risley puts it:

> Here we have before our eyes a society in many respects still primitive, which preserves, like a palimpsest manuscript, survivals of Immemorial, antiquity. (4)

Ethnology as a discipline incorporated epistemic violence into its very structure; administrators drew upon 'scientific' evidence for hereditary 'criminal' communities well before Risley's efforts so that by the mid-19th century, specific communities had been identified as 'criminal'. Mark Brown writes:

> Central to such statements was a crucial meshing of quasi-scientific ideas about hereditary behaviour (phrased in the bill as an 'addiction to non-bailable offences') with a logical linking of conduct, 'profession' and caste. Since Sleeman's dealings with the thugs the idea of hereditary criminal conduct had found a place in official discourse on crime. But by the late 1860s, with the development of more elaborate 'scientific' taxonomies of criminal behaviour, the presumption that Indian society harboured hereditary criminal communities was widespread. (2003, 212)

Numerous communities across India, as a result, were listed under this category, and in 1911, between the first and second editions of Risley's book, V.T.P. Vivian published *A Handbook of the Criminal Tribes of the Punjab*. Like Risley but directed at a single purpose—identifying 'troublesome' tribes and communities—Vivian's work was also founded on historical surveys, data and 'science'. Examining the origin stories of such communities, their appearance and modes of dress, language and 'criminality', Vivian prepared a categorisation of such tribes. Employing the language of science, especially the science of heredity (in the wake of Darwin), Vivian writes:

> They have of necessity adopted less violent forms of crime, and with them methods that render the discovery of their offences a matter of far greater difficulty. They have spread over the face of India in every direction, wanderers and unsettled; yet they keep intact their distinctive language, their customs, and their connection with the different – even distant – branches of the tribe.... [Records] show that their inherent criminal propensities are very far from eliminated from their character in the present day. Customs die hard, and it cannot be supposed that the hereditary thief will in a short generation or two abandon the calls of his blood and settle to a quiet life of cultivation or cattle-breeding, because a paternal Government has ordered that he is to do so. Trade of any kind he will not learn; the influences of heredity, equally with the caste-system, are against it; he learns his own

> ancestral and (to him) honourable profession from his earliest days and would think it beneath him to adopt any meaner craft. (cited in Brown 2003, 216)

Thus, science was made to speak the language of the law, as well as the language of cultural analysis when arguing a case for the inherent, embedded and 'natural' propensity of some classes of people for crime.

If ethnography and ethnology arose with the European encounter with non-white races, so did the discipline of anthropology. In an early essay, Diane Lewis writes:

> Since anthropology emerged along with the expansion of Europe and the colonization of the non-Western world, anthropologists found themselves participants in the colonial system which organized relationships between Westerners and non-Westerners. It is, perhaps, more than a coincidence that a methodological stance, that of the outsider, and a methodological approach, "objectivity," developed which in retrospect seem to have been influenced by, and in turn to have supported, the colonial system… (1973; also Asad 1973)

Lewis demonstrates how the study of human variety and characteristics was a part of both academic/research work and colonial/imperial processes, and texts such as Risley's clearly demonstrate Lewis's argument and resonate with the arguments about epistemic violence. He set out to prove that a caste or community's 'status and its racial composition, as measured anthropometrically, were correlated' (Fuller 2017).

The 'Ethnographic State' after 1857

Risley, early in his text, admits to the difficulty of knowing India:

> I have always been much impressed by the difficulty of conveying to European readers who have no experience of India even an approximate idea of the extraordinary complexity of the social system which is involved in the word caste. (69)

The variation and variety among the Indians, whether one takes skin colour or the shape of the head, Risley mourns, was far too much for anyone to comprehend. Very early in *TPI*, he would write:

> The difficulty which besets all attempts to classify colour is enhanced in India by the fact that, for the bulk of the population, the range of variation, especially in the case of the eyes and hair, is exceedingly small. The skin, no doubt, exhibits extreme divergencies of colouring which any one can detect at a glance. At one end of the scale we have the dead black of the Andamanese, the colour of a blackleaded stove before it has been polished, and the somewhat brighter black of the

> Dravidians of Southern India, which has been aptly compared to the colour of strong coffee unmixed with milk. Of the Irulas of the Nilgiri jungles, some South Indian humourist is reported to have said that charcoal leaves a white mark upon them. At the other end one may place the flushed ivory skin of the typical Kashmiri beauty and the very light transparent brown—"wheat-coloured" is the common vernacular description—of the higher castes of Upper India, which Emil Schmidt compares to milk just tinged with coffee and describes as hardly darker than is found in members of the swarthier races of Southern Europe. Between these extremes we find countless shades of brown, darker or lighter, transparent or opaque, frequently tending towards yellow, more rarely approaching a reddish tint, and occasionally degenerating into a sort of greyish black which seems to depend on the character of the surface of the skin. (14)

Then later he speaks of the 'disordered kaleidoscope' that was India (281).

It is this 'extraordinary complexity of the social system', the 'disordered kaleidoscope' and the 'range of variation', as Risley puts it, that the English ethnographer and anthropologist undertakes to transform into not only manageable data but also a device of the state, in the process producing a particular kind of state.

Nicholas Dirks in his influential—and controversial—book, *Castes of Mind*, argued that after 1857, the British Empire took on the form and modality of an 'ethnographic state' made possible by 'the enumerative technology of the census and the ethnographic survey' (16–17). Dirks writes:

> The ethnographic state was driven by the belief that India could be ruled using anthropological knowledge to understand and control its subjects, and to represent and legitimate its own mission ... the collection of material about castes and tribes and their customs, and the specification of what kinds of customs, kinship behaviors, ritual forms, and so on, were appropriate and necessary for ethnographic description, became increasingly formalized and canonic. (44–45)

The counting of castes, as Dirks and commentators like C.J. Fuller have argued, was meant to generate a better understanding the Indian social system. In the process of counting and classification of castes, tribes and communities (and counting and classification are not 'neutral', Fuller 2017), they created, disseminated and debated different theories—occupational versus status—of caste. It normalised caste as well. In the ethnographic state, the caste system was treated as normal to Indian society, almost equivalent to the class hierarchies of England (Fuller 2016; see also Gottschalk 2013).

What is significant here is also that the counting-and-classifying framework associated particular castes with inherited cultural traits

(Leonard 2016). Thus, the identification of certain communities as 'criminal tribes' was also the result of such ethnographic and enumerative processes.

Risley, argues Zak Leonard, conceived of each caste as a racially homogeneous, endogamous unit and concluded that caste functioned essentially as a sociological group based on occupation and linked physiological differences amongst the population to environmental factors (177). Risley does spend considerable time on endogamy among the native peoples. He defines caste as

> a collection of families or groups … claiming common descent from a mythical ancestor, human or divine; professing to follow the same hereditary calling … a single homogeneous community … invariably endogamous. (68)

Then, Risley also describes the caste system as thriving and a bulwark of the Indian social order. Speaking of the Census of India (1901), Risley narrates how he proposed social precedence as a basis for classification (111). As a result of employing this principle, he says, the feedback from the people demonstrated something:

> The best evidence of the general success of the experiment, and incidentally of the remarkable vitality of caste at the present day, is to be found in the great number of petitions and memorials to which it gave rise, the bulk of which were submitted in English and emanated from the educated classes who are sometimes alleged to be anxious to free themselves from the trammels of the caste system. If the principle on which the classification was based had not appealed 'to the usages and traditions of the great mass of Hindus, it is inconceivable that so many people should have taken much trouble and incurred substantial expenditure with the object of securing its application in a particular way'. (112)

The 'vitality of caste', for the ethnographic state, was primarily manifest in the rigid cultural practices.

> At this stage of the grouping a sharp distinction may be noticed between Upper India and Bombay and Madras. In Rajputana, the Punjab, the United Provinces, the Central Provinces, Bengal, and Assam the grade next below twice born rank is occupied by a number of castes from whose hands Brahmans and members of the higher castes will take water and certain kinds of sweetmeats. Below these again is a rather indeterminate group from whom water is taken by some of the higher castes but not by others. Further down, where the test of water no longer applies, the status of a caste depends on the nature of its occupation and its habits in respect of diet … in the social system of Upper India, are people … who eat beef and various sorts

> of miscellaneous vermin.... Where these fantastic notions prevail and the authority of the Brahman is unquestioned, it follows as a necessary consequence that the unhappy people who diffuse an atmosphere of impurity wherever they go are forbidden to enter the high caste quarter of the village, and are compelled either to leave the road when they see a Brahman coming ... such is the logic of intolerance in parts of Southern India. (113–115)

Risley is referring here to petitions submitted by various communities about their location in the Census, in terms of their caste identities. The census, an important contributor to the ethnographic state, was seen as the final *official* statement on social hierarchy. The petitions, as Dirks argues, demonstrate how 'caste became politicized all over again. Caste associations sprung up to contest their assigned position in the official hierarchy, holding meetings, writing petitions, and organizing protests' (49).

But this state was not formed solely through the English ethnographer's efforts, wandering solitarily through villages and communities to document them. A certain co-opting of local expertise was a part of the making of the ethnographic state. As early as 1886, Risley circulated a list of the main Bengali castes to numerous British and Indian officials in the region. He asked correspondents to respond to the list, 'particularly noting castes from which Brahmans could take water, which were entitled to village barbers' services, and which could enter the courtyards of great temples' (Fuller 2017). Committees of 'native gentlemen' were also consulted by Risley to verify the accuracy of lists of ranked castes, notes Fuller (2017). Such a co-optation of local experts in the process of knowledge formation was integral to the ethnographic state.

National Identity and Nationalism

Risley (and other ethnographers) saw in the caste system both a cohesive force that ordered Indian society *and* simultaneously prevented it from being infused with a sense of national identity, belonging and destiny (Dirks 194). Risley was so interested in the link between caste and national identity that he devotes an entire chapter to the subject. He argues:

> So long as a regime of caste persists, it is difficult to see how the sentiment of unity and solidarity can penetrate and inspire all classes of the community, from the highest to the lowest. (293)

But he does hold out some possibilities though:

> The factors which in other countries are regarded as essential to the growth of national sentiment either do not exist at all in India, or tend to produce separation rather than cohesion. We have also observed that the influence of caste seems at first sight to favour particularist

> rather than nationalist tendencies. Are we then to conclude that the conception of an Indian nationality rests upon no substantial or even intelligible basis, and may be brushed aside as a figment of the prolific oriental imagination stimulated by its recent contact with Western thought? Such a conclusion would, I think, be premature.

And here Risley points to two factors that may help India achieve these 'nationalist tendencies':

> (1) The consciousness of a certain community of intellectual pursuits and aspirations, derived from the common study of the history and literature of England, and from the common use, for certain special purposes, of the English language in addition to a provincial vernacular.
>
> (2) The consciousness of being united and drawn together by living under a single government, by taking part in the administration of a common system of laws, and by sharing in the material benefits of a common civilisation. (294)

He also proposes that the English language may be a unifying factor:

> It is possible indeed—distant as the prospect now appears—that English may after all stand the best chance of becoming the national language of India. Its adoption would at any rate avoid the antipathies and antagonisms with which any Indian vernacular would have to contend. English is already the medium of communication for the upper classes, at any rate on certain subjects, all over India. (290)

Risley's view of English as a unifying force—something Macaulay and Ram Mohan Roy hinted at in their writings on the need for Western education in India—was a surprise element in this ethnographic account of the largely hopeless scenario (from his point of view) of Indian nationalism.

***

The People of India is a text that shows us how science and the Empire worked together to gather, order and interpret the subject peoples. The science-constructed models of subject behaviour drew up characteristics and thereby constructed objects that were then interpreted as pre-modern, primitive and barbaric. These scientifically *proven* details and accounts then became the foundation for policy—such as the notifications on 'criminal tribes'—and political decisions.

THE PEOPLE OF INDIA

BY

SIR HERBERT RISLEY, K.C.I.E., C.S.I.

DIRECTOR OF ETHNOGRAPHY FOR INDIA, OFFICIER D'ACADEMIE, FRANCE, CORRESPONDING MEMBER OF THE ANTHROPOLOGICAL SOCIETIES OF ROME AND BERLIN, AND OF THE ANTHROPOLOGICAL INSTITUTE OF GREAT BRITAIN AND IRELAND.

"In good sooth, my masters, this is no door. Yet is it a little window, that looketh upon a great world."

WITH TWENTY-FIVE ILLUSTRATIONS.

CALCUTTA:
THACKER, SPINK & CO.
LONDON: W. THACKER & CO., 2, CREED LANE, E.C.
1908.

CHAPTER VII.

CASTE AND NATIONALITY.

Rien n' est bête que de bouder l'avenir.

Anatole France.

So sind sie Particularisten von Natur: das nationale Bewusstsein erscheint bei ihnen erst als Erzeugniss der fortschreitenden Bildung.

Von Sybel, 1890.

It will be seen from the picture imperfectly outlined in the preceding chapters that caste in India is something more than what is called a social system, something beyond a mere mode of grouping the loose atoms of humanity which the wheel of circumstance has created and a turn of the same wheel may destroy or transform. We should rather conceive of it as a congenital instinct, an all-pervading principle of attraction and repulsion entering into and shaping every relation of life. For Hindus caste is bound up with their religion, and its observance is enforced by the authority of the priests; its influence is conspicuous in the social usages of most Indian Muhammadans; and it extends even to the relatively small communities of Christians. Thus it forms the cement that holds together the myriad units of Indian society. In the words of Sir K. Sheshadri Iyer, the great Dewan of Mysore, 'the whole social fabric of India rests upon caste.' Were its cohesive power withdrawn or its essential ties relaxed, it is difficult to form any idea of the probable consequences. Such a change would be more than a revolution; it would resemble the withdrawal of some elemental force like gravitation or molecular attraction. Order would vanish and chaos would supervene. Yet we are told from time to time, in tones of settled conviction, that the bonds of caste are being burst asunder by the disruptive force of modern ideas and that the Indian spirit is now about to be liberated from this prison-house of the past. Such facile assurances proceed for the most part from philanthropic Englishmen who have seen little of India beyond

European idea that caste is breaking up.

the Presidency towns, who know none of the vernacular languages, and who derive their impressions from the small body of Anglicised Indians whom Sir Henry Cotton describes, with rather needless acidity, in one place as 'a disorganised class within the community,' and in another as 'an artificial and exotic product.'*

Let it be admitted, however, that there is some excuse for those who, in their just and natural admiration for the educated Indian, leave out of view the people of India and the governing principle of Indian society—caste. Anyone who has the curiosity to glance at the second chapter of this book will see that from the sixteenth century onwards almost all observers have been struck by the prohibitions on food and drink, and the rules about personal contact which caste entails, and have hardly noticed its restrictions upon marriage. Both sets of rules are, of course, inherent in the system. But they do not stand upon the same footing, and the penalties attached to their violation differ widely. A marriage, or even a *liaison*, with a member of another caste *ipso facto* involves final and irremediable excommunication. A slip in the matter of food can within limits be expiated by penance. Moreover, the rules about diet and contact with other castes rest upon a metaphysical theory of ceremonial pollution which admits of many exceptions. Ever since the time of Manu it has been recognized that the devout traveller, when in danger of starvation, must pocket his caste scruples and satisfy his hunger as best he can. In modern times, and especially since the introduction of railways, this comfortable doctrine has been developed and elaborated by Brāhmanical casuistry. It has long been held, for example, that sweetmeats, a generic and elastic term which includes all the promiscuous messes sold on the railway platforms, may be taken from almost anybody. Nice enquiries about the caste of itinerant vendors of sweet-stuff cannot be prosecuted from the window of a third-class carriage during a short stoppage, and a modern proverb sums up the position in the practical query—'You have eaten the food he gave you, why ask about his caste?' On the same principle the wise man finds it convenient to forget that ice was once water, that soda water, before it found its way into a cunningly contrived bottle, owned the same humble origin and did not necessarily come straight from the Ganges; that certain essences and extracts used for medical purposes

Founded on misconceptions of fact.

* *New India*, p. 260.

bear an ascertainable relation to beef, and that imported biscuits must have passed in their making through the hands of all sorts of casteless folk. Nor is he so indiscreet as to enquire at how many paces' distance his neighbour can convey pollution, when he must in any case rub shoulders with him in a railway carriage for twelve hours on end.

The every-day occurrences which an observant tourist may notice in the course of his cold-weather progress through India manifestly conflict with his preconceived notion of caste as a rigid system of unalterable prohibitions. To people who do not understand all that is implied in the cry of *Pāni Pānre,* which one hears at each halt of a train in Northern India, the apparent difference between the theory of the guide-book and the practice of the people may well seem marked enough to warrant the belief that English education, modern civilization, the growth of industries, the march of progress, and all the rest of it are making short work of an ancient and famous institution for which the Indian world has no longer any use. Yet what the tourist sees from his railway carriage comprises only the accidents of caste, which may change from year to year as convenience or fashion may dictate. The substance of the system lies hidden from the eye of the globe-trotter (and scarcely perceptible even to those who are not globe-trotters) in the hard and fast rules which regulate marriage. In this department of life, where the fact or fiction of community of blood has continually to be reckoned with, there are no signs of compromise or concession. People must marry within the caste or sub-caste in which they were born, or must take the consequences. Even the most advanced of modern Indians have had occasion to discover that exclusive dealing in husbands is a formidable weapon to use against a family man, and that the frivolous foreigner who defined caste as 'a turnpike to matrimony' had, at any rate, hit off an aspect of it which comes home to the father of marriageable daughters. As for the mass of the people, all that they know or care to know is that whoever kicks over the connubial traces is promptly turned out of his caste, and must either become a Muhammadan or must join some dubious sect which offers a sympathetic welcome to persons caught out in sexual delinquencies. The idea that any properly constituted Hindu should *wish* to marry outside his caste would seem to them too preposterous to be worth discussing. As long as the people think thus, so long will caste endure, whatever philanthropists may say.

Quite apart, moreover, from caste developments many things are happening in the India of to-day which tend to bewilder an observer recently arrived from Europe, and unable to command a wider outlook than is afforded by his own immediate surroundings. It is hardly possible to imagine a more startling series of contrasts than is disclosed directly one penetrates below the mere surface of Indian society. One sees there a sort of disordered kaleidoscope in which the oldest and the newest ideas of the human spirit whirl round together in the most bewildering fashion. Science and religion, expediency and prescription, contract and status, the Western enthusiasm of humanity, the Eastern carelessness of human life—all these mighty opposites are mixed and jumbled up together in a fantastic medley out of which a benevolent despotism, controlled in the last resort by a distant but not unwise democracy, is constantly attempting to evolve an order of things which, while satisfying the comparatively simple wants of oriental life, shall not fall too conspicuously short of European ideals of progress and prosperity. An illustration or two will show at a glance how great a gulf is fixed between the educated minority and the great body of the Indian people, and what savage impulses throb behind the deceptive veil of apparent culture. Not very long ago, while a talented Bengali professor, well known to the scientific world of London, was lecturing to crowded audiences on the transcendental properties of metals under the influence of electricity, widows were being burnt alive in Bihar, incidents curiously suggestive of human sacrifice were occurring in Orissa, and in Calcutta, the *soi-disant* centre of light and leading, a large section of the population, shrewd enough in the business of daily life, were deterred from going out after dark by their dread of a mysterious personage who was believed to be hunting for heads to cement the foundations of the Victoria Memorial Hall. In the face of such vigorous survivals of ideas far more primitive than caste itself, we may be excused for receiving with some scepticism the argument that because a few archaic taboos on food, drink, and personal contact have been relaxed, therefore the entire fabric of caste, undermined by European science, must be tottering to its fall.

Sir Henry Cotton takes a more just view of the general situation when he writes :—

'The country recoils from such a social revolution as our Western civilisation has thrust upon it. It still needs the hierarchical leadership of caste. The tendency to reduce the power of the dominant classes and to destroy, if possible, all distinction between the different strata of society is much in vogue among headstrong administrators, who are too apt to transplant the radical associations of our democracy into a country altogether unsuited to their growth. But there is no more patrician *milieu* in the world than that which has for centuries flourished in India and is still vigorous, in spite of attacks upon it.'

Not shared by Sir Henry Cotton.

'Those reformers who are in the habit of describing caste as the root of all evils in Hindu society overlook the impossibility of uprooting an institution which has taken such a firm hold on the popular mind. They forget that the attempt to abolish caste, if successful, would be attended with the most dangerous consequences, unless some powerful religious influence were brought to bear upon the people in its place. They forget also that caste is still stronger as a social than as a religious institution, and that many a man who has entirely lost his belief in his religion, is zealous and tenacious of his position as a high-caste man, and scrupulously performs all customary rites and ceremonies. Caste is now the framework which knits together Hindu society; it is the link which maintains the existing religious system of Hinduism in its present order. The problem of the future is not to destroy caste, but to modify it, to preserve its distinctive conceptions, and to gradually place them upon a social instead of a supernatural basis.'*

The late Babu Guru Prasād Sen, a native of Eastern Bengal, who practised as a pleader in Patna, and wrote an instructive little book on Hindu social life, lays equal stress on the necessity of retaining caste unless Indian society is to fall utterly to pieces. He dwells upon its value as the guardian of a proper *esprit de corps* among the groups to which it gives rise, and notices the wholesome influence which it exercises by maintaining unbroken the traditions of remote ancestry; by preserving the distinct existence of the Hindu people; and by enforcing the due subordination of the various parts of society to the whole.

The opinion held by Sir Henry Cotton and Babu Guru Prasād Sen that caste, so far from being moribund, still maintains its ancient place in the Indian social system, receives striking confirmation from the returns of the last Census. It may be said with confidence that the tendency to rebel against the prescriptions of caste has not spread beyond the relatively small circle of those who, in Mr. Gokhale's words, 'have come under the influence of some kind of English education.'† Outside those limits caste, with all its restrictions, is regarded as the natural law governing human society. Now the male adults who described themselves in the Census of 1901 as being able to read and write English—a test not necessarily representing a high standard of English education—numbered in the whole

---

* *New India*, pp. 225 and 252.

† Presidential address to National Indian Congress, 1905.

of India just 707,000, or less than one per cent. of the male adult population. Even if the whole of this company of *literati*, scattered over all the provinces and states of India, were banded together to beleaguer the citadel of caste, many generations must pass before their attack could effect a practicable breach. The walls of immemorial usage will not crumble at the first blast of the trumpet of reform. But how many even of the advanced members of the literate class seriously contemplate the disruption of the social regime under which they live? So far as can be gathered from the various sources of information available, the number of such iconoclasts is extremely small, while their ranks are mainly recruited from among those who, for one reason or another, have become alienated from their own people and have lost touch with Indian society. Nor does English education of itself, at any rate in its present stage of development, necessarily incline an Indian patriot to enter upon the uncongenial task of demolishing indigenous institutions and reconstructing them on a foreign model. On the contrary, with the growth of national or provincial self-consciousness which has manifested itself within the last few years, the opposite tendency may be observed, and Indian religion, philosophy, usage, and family life are extolled as intrinsically superior to anything that the Western world has succeeded in producing.

Whose views are confirmed by statistics and by the best Indian opinion.

If then the regime of caste, with all that it implies, is likely to survive for an indefinite period in India, what influence may it be expected to have over the growth of the modern idea of an Indian nationality? At first sight the two things appear to be antagonistic and incompatible: the principle of separation conflicts with the principle of consolidation. This indeed seems to be the deliberate opinion of two competent Indian critics. The disordered state of things arising from particularism in India was vividly described a few months ago by an advanced Bengali politician in a letter to a Calcutta newspaper: 'We must not forget that India is not yet a nation; we must not forget that it is a congeries of races, which are not always friendly to each other: we must not forget the ancient hate, the ancient prejudice, the ancient clashing of castes and creeds which still hold India under their vice-like grip.'* A serious student of social problems in India, who stands aloof from politics,

* Hon. Babu Bhupendra Nath Basu of the Bengal Legislative Council.—*Statesman*, 28th May 1907.

and approaches the subject of reform from the firmer ground of religion and philosophy, writes in an equally despondent tone. After referring to the high ideals of public and private life that prevailed in ancient India, he goes on to say:—'Truth (satya) and duty (dharma), the good old rule of not doing to others what was disagreeable to one's own self, was held up as the ideal by the sages of those times, and many tried to live it. And it is because we have lost that ideal, that we present the spectacle of a people rent asunder by mutual dissensions, divided into thousands of castes and sub-castes, sects and sub-sects, with all spirit of nationality crushed out, weak in body and mind and slaves of circumstances.'* Yet clearly Sir Henry Cotton and Babu Guru Prasād Sen do not regard the matter in the same light as the most recent observers on the spot. For both of them look forward with enthusiasm to the birth of an Indian nation; and the latter, while asserting with some emphasis that 'there was no Indian nation at the date of Vikramāditya, or at any period of past Indian history,' goes on to quote with approval Comte's reference to caste as 'a necessary preparation' for the wider sentiment of patriotism. Sir Henry Cotton † dips even further into the future, and does not hesitate to sketch, in terms which recall the seventh book of the Mahābhārata, the main outlines of the political organization in which the national spirit will find its appropriate embodiment and expression. 'What is required,' he says, 'in the absence of an emasculating foreign army, is an organization of small States, each with a prince at its head, and a small body of patrician aristocracy interposing between him and the lower orders of working-men. For such an arrangement the country appears to be eminently adapted; the United States of India should be bound together by means of some political organization other than the colonial supremacy of England. The basis of internal order is to be found in the recognition of a patriciate accustomed by hereditary associations to control and lead,'—in other words a Council of Nobles.

Apparent antagonism of Caste and Nationality.

In an interesting essay in the *Empire Review* for September, 1907, Mr. A. M. T. Jackson has shown how the theory of the traditional Hindu Kingship—the political ideal which the genius of the warrior

* *Hinduism: Ancient and Modern*, by Rai Bahadur Lala Baij Nath, B.A., District and Sessions Judge, Ghazipur. New edition, 1905, p. 104.

† *New India*, p. 227.

Sivaji sought to revive and which the intriguing spirit of the Brahman Peshwas effectually shattered—was rooted in caste. At the head of it stands the King, the one absolute and responsible ruler, uniting in his own person all legislative, judicial, and executive functions, but assisted in their exercise by a purely advisory Council consisting of members appointed by himself in certain proportions from among the leading castes. Subject to the orders of the King, whose duty it is to enforce the rules of the various castes, 'each of the functions required in a civilised community is discharged by a separate section of the people. The worship of the gods is the business of one caste, banking of another, shoe-making of another, and so on. By analogy the business of government is also assigned to one particular section, instead of being the common business of all as it is usually held to be in Europe. In India, this arrangement reacted upon the body politic in two ways. Firstly, the exclusion of most of the castes from politics left little room for the growth of feelings of common interest and public spirit; secondly, the efficiency of the governing section became of immense importance. Only if this section were strong could it perform its function of keeping each caste to its proper duties, and thereby combine the parts into an organic whole; while if it were weak, society would fall apart into disconnected atoms. Anarchy is the peculiar peril of a society that is organized on the basis of caste, and the dread of anarchy leads to monarchy as the strongest defence against it. Indian thinkers were well aware of the weakness of divided counsels, holding that one person should be appointed to one task, and not two or three. "It is always seen that several persons, if set to one task, disagree with one another." '*

Caste and Monarchy

Under the rule of the model King depicted in the Mahābhārata, of whom it is written that 'he should always have the rod of chastisement uplifted in his hands,' the forces of caste were kept under proper control, and the system was prevented from degenerating into an organized tyranny. Monarchy seems to have guarded against this danger; would a democracy of the modern type be able to do the same? In considering how such a democracy would work in India, it must not be forgotten that caste would provide the party in power, the party

Caste and democracy.

* *Mahābhārata* VII., p. 258.

that had spoils to divide, with what Americans call a 'machine' surpassing in efficiency the wildest dream of the most ingenious wire-puller It already possesses a ready-made system of standing caucuses each under the control of a 'boss' or a committee of 'bosses.' Once organized for political purposes, it could whip up voters *en masse* and could secure the adoption of any conceivable ticket. Men would be compelled to vote solid by penalties compared with which the Papal interdict that drove an Emperor barefoot to Canossa was a clumsy and ineffectual instrument. In a society where every one is peculiarly dependent on his neighbours, the recalcitrant voter would speedily find himself cut off not merely from the amenities, but also from the barest necessaries of life. No one would eat with him, drink with him, smoke with him, or sell him food; the barber would not shave him; the washerman would decline to wash his clothes; the Brahman would deny him the offices of religion; no man would marry his daughter; and the attendants of the dead would refuse him the accustomed funeral rites. These are some of the blessings which popular government, controlled and directed by caste organization, would confer upon the subjects committed to its charge. Whatever future centuries may have in store for the people of India it may be hoped that they will be spared the misfortune of government by social ostracism.

Caste and nationality.

The discussion of speculative constitutions is a futile pursuit. But the relation between caste and nationality, between the idea of a rigidly exclusive matrimonial group and the idea, whether realized or not, of a wider community embracing many such groups—has taken rudimentary shape in India before now and may yet make itself felt on a larger scale. If what might have been the germ of a nation can shrink into a caste, as we have seen in the case of the Marāthas and the Newārs, may not the converse process be possible and a number of castes, without sacrificing their individual characteristics, draw together into that larger aggregate which we call a nationality? For the answer to this question no antecedent experience can be appealed to, since the institution of caste is peculiar to India, and the historical causes by which certain Teutonic tribes (which under different conditions might have hardened into castes) were converted into nations can hardly be expected to repeat themselves here at the present day. It seems of interest however to attempt to determine to what extent the continuance of caste is in itself favourable or adverse to the growth of a consciousness of common nationality among the people of India.

In the first place, let us endeavour to make clear what is meant by *nationality*. This abstract term, originally denoting the fact of belonging to a particular nation (as we speak of the 'nationality' of a ship), has within the last fifty years acquired a concrete meaning implied rather than expressed in such phrases as 'oppressed nationalities.' The standard literature of the subject approaches the question from the European standpoint, and the development of the idea of nationality in Asia has as yet received no exhaustive treatment. As the word is ordinarily used, it seems to imply that the persons composing a nationality are keenly conscious, and may even be passionately convinced, that they are closely bound together by the tie of common interests and ideals, that in a special and intimate way they belong to one another, and that the moral force and enthusiasm by which their sentiment of unity is inspired render it independent of the government or governments under which they may happen to live. This feeling of self-consciousness gives to a body of men a sort of personality, so that they become 'a moral unity with a common thought.' The idea is not necessarily associated with democratic tendencies; it may equally arise from loyalty to a dynasty. Nor is it invariably directed towards consolidation; it can be seen at work as a disintegrating force which fastens upon a particular racial, linguistic or geographical group and seeks to detach it from the political system of which it forms part. When a homogeneous multitude of men, animated by this complex sentiment, are united under a single government expressing their common aspirations and carried on by themselves, they are no longer described as a nationality, but are recognized as a nation. Thus we speak of the Polish, Finnish and Bohemian nationalities, and of the Greek, German, and Italian nations. The factors which go to the making of a national consciousness are of somewhat indefinite character and have been variously described. The most precise enumeration of them is perhaps that given by Sidgwick in *The Elements of Politics*. He notices the following:—The belief in a common origin; the possession of a common language and literature; the pride that is felt in common historic traditions, in the memories of a common political history, and of common struggles against foreign foes; community of religion; community of social customs. The last

The factors of nationality.

factor is in India so closely associated with religion that it need not be specially considered.

Belief in a common origin, frequently traced back to a mythical ancestry, figures largely in the inherited traditions of most European nations. Into the foundations of such beliefs it would be unkind to enquire too narrowly : in the nebulous domain of national sentiment a picturesque legend carries higher value than the most authentic historical documents. If people can succeed in persuading themselves that they come of the same stock, they will not thank any one for showing that their descent is extremely mixed, and that pure races exist only in theory. It may perhaps be argued that in these respects the general position in India is not altogether dissimilar to that in Europe, and that the diffusion of patriotic fiction may in either case be expected to bring about much the same result. But in India we have to reckon with the existence of a number of distinct physical types, the contrasts between which strike the most superficial observer; and these types not only occupy widely different stages of intellectual advancement and general culture, but are organized in a social system which tends to stereotype and perpetuate their hereditary or acquired characteristics. Can we look forward to a time when these antagonistic masses will be animated by the conviction of their common origin, and will sink their natural antipathies in the idea of a united nationality? Can we suppose, for example, that the Muhammadans will readily surrender their cherished tradition of descent from Arab and Moghul conquerors, that the Rajputs will claim kinship with the Bengalis, or that the millions of Dravidian and Mongoloid people will be recognized as owning the same parentage as the Brahmans of Benares and Ajodhya? No student of ethnology will ignore the influence that has been exercised by fiction in forging imaginary affinities between people of very different origin, but in India this influence has hitherto been directed towards separation rather than consolidation, and even when that tendency has been reversed, an immense amount of leeway will still have to be made up.

Community of origin.

There are at present no indications that the factor of language, which has done so much to promote national movements in Europe, is likely to play the same part in India. At the last Census of the Empire no less than 147 distinct languages were recorded, 22 of which were spoken by more than a million people. The situation, therefore, so far as

Language.

language is concerned, is even more complex and chaotic than it is in the Austrian dominions, where the Parliamentary oath may have to be administered in eight different languages. It is perhaps conceivable that one of the many dialects of Hindustani might in course of time become established as the vernacular of the whole of Northern India, though the linguistic jealousies of Hindus and Muhammadans as to the script and vocabulary of the language will not readily be appeased. But to suppose that the Dravidians of Southern India will ever abandon Tamil and Telugu in favour of some form of Indo-Aryan speech, or that the peasantry of Bengal and Orissa, Mahārāshtra and Gujarāt will change their characteristic languages and alphabets, requires almost as large an effort of the imagination as the dream that English itself may in the remote future become the *lingua franca* of the three hundred millions who inhabit the Indian Empire. Speculations of this kind pay but a sorry tribute to the vitality of the Indian vernaculars and the attractions of the valuable literature which they possess—a literature which appeals to the most intimate feelings of the people and is closely bound up with their religious beliefs and their social obligations. The day is far distant when the Rāmāyana of Tulsi Dās will lose its hold over the peasantry of Upper India ; and when the hymns of Tukārām will cease to be household words in the Marātha country. Nor do the classical languages of India supply a bond of union which may form the basis of a common nationality. The tendencies of Sanskrit writings are hierarchical rather than national, while their contemplative and metaphysical tendencies are absolutely at variance with the actively militant spirit of the Arabic and Persian classics on which Indian Muhammadans are brought up. It is difficult to imagine any form of symbolical interpretation or intellectual compromise by which the quietist philosophy characteristic of the Hindu scriptures could be reconciled with the fiery dogmatism of the Koran, or to conceive how two races looking back to such widely different literatures could be brought to regard them as the common heritage of one united nationality. We can only conclude therefore that in India, so far as can be at present foreseen, the development of the national idea is not likely to derive much support from popular speech or learned tradition.

It is possible indeed—distant as the prospect now appears—that English may after all stand the best chance of becoming the national language of India. Its adoption would at any rate avoid the antipathies and antagonisms with which any Indian vernacular would have to contend. English is already the medium of communication for the upper classes, at any rate on certain subjects, all over India. As the men of the elder generation, who prefer the vernacular, die off, and English comes to be the language of the family as well as the language of public life, it may spread in Northern India as it has spread in the south and may extend to classes which are not now touched by it. This process would be greatly expedited, and at the same time the development of nationality promoted, if the modern 'direct' method of teaching were introduced and colloquial English were taught to British Indian children as thoroughly as colloquial French is taught in Pondicherry and Chandernagore. There would then be less temptation to mix the two languages, taking the structure of the sentence from one and the vocabulary from the other. This, I believe, is more common in Upper India than in Madras. When such expressions as '*āpnār* theatricals *bŏrŏ* tedious *hŏbe*' can be heard in the best Indian society, one feels that those who use them are hardly on the right road to a real command of either language.

Political history.

We may look back in vain through India's stormy past for memories of a common political history and common struggles against foreign foes. Wave after wave of conquest or armed occupation has swept over the face of the country, but at no time were the invaders confronted with resistance organized on a national basis or inspired by patriotic enthusiasm. If here and there a local chieftain fought for independence, as Porus opposed Alexander and Prithiraj resisted Muhammad Ghori, his nearest rivals hastened to offer their swords to the foreign enemy. Tribal jealousies, dynastic intrigues, internal disunion combined to create a political vacuum which the first comer who knew his own mind was irresistibly impelled to fill. Even the Marātha confederacy, which to some may have seemed stable enough to form the nucleus of a national dominion, was broken up by the personal disputes which arose among its leaders. The Sikh league, held together for a time by the masterful personality of Ranjit Singh, began to fall to pieces at his death. Illustrations might be multiplied without limit, but it is an unwelcome task to dwell upon a picture of general discord and confusion. The facts are beyond dispute, and they point to the inevitable conclusion that national sentiment in India can derive no encouragement from the study of Indian history.

In the series of lectures published under the title '*The Expansion of England*' the late Sir John Seeley speaks of religion as 'the strongest and most important of the elements which go to constitute nationality', and throws out the idea that Hinduism may prove to be the germ from which that sentiment may be developed in India. He then draws attention to the failure of the Hindus to organize a national resistance to the advance of the Muhammadan invaders, and of the Marātha confederacy, which he describes as 'an organization of plunder,' to inspire Hinduism with the spirit of active patriotism. There he leaves the subject, after a passing glance at the 'facile comprehensiveness of Hinduism' which in his judgment 'has enfeebled it as a uniting principle' and rendered it incapable of generating true national feeling. It may be admitted that the flame of patriotic enthusiasm will not readily arise from the cold grey ashes of philosophic compromise, and that before Hinduism can inspire an active sentiment of nationality, it will have to undergo a good deal of stiffening and consolidation. The Arya Samaj seems to be striking out a path which may lead in this direction, but the tangled jungle of Hinduism bristles with obstacles, and the way is long. Meanwhile, it is curious to observe that Sir John Seeley's forecast leaves Islam entirely out of account, though in an earlier lecture he dwells on the fact that the population of India is 'divided between Brahmanism and Muhammadanism.' His general proposition as to the influence of religion upon nationality seems, moreover, to lose sight of the historical fact that while community of religion strengthens and consolidates national sentiment, religious differences create distinct types within a nation and tend to perpetuate separate and antagonistic interests. This difficulty has not escaped the observation of Sir Henry Cotton, who rightly points out that 'it is impossible to be blind to the general character of the relations between Hindus and Muhammadans; to the jealousy which exists and manifests itself so frequently, even under British rule, in local outbursts of popular fanaticism; to the kine-killing riots and to the religious friction which occasionally accompanies the celebration of the Ram Lila or the Bakr Id or the Muharram.'* Mr. Theodore Morison† approaches the question from a different point of view. Writing of the educated Muhammadans, he says:—'The possibility of fusion with

Religion.

* *New India*, p. 228.

† *Quarterly Review*, April 1906.

the Hindus, and the creation by this fusion of an Indian nationality, does not commend itself to Muhammadan sentiment. The idea has been brought forward only to be flouted; the pride of Muhammadans revolts at such a sacrifice of their individuality.' But in the same article he seems to admit the possibility of the conception of territorial nationality, irrespective of race or creed, taking hold of the Indian Muhammadans and bringing them into the same political fold with the Hindus. In the case of the most advanced Muhammadans such a *rapprochement* is perhaps conceivable. But even with them it will take a long time to effect, and great changes of religious feeling and practice will have to take place before they can induce the main body of their co-religionists to follow their lead. The problem is a difficult one. As long as Muhammadans are accustomed to kill for food or sacrifice the animal deemed sacred by the Hindus, occasions for deadly strife are bound to arise when the passion of religious animosity will overpower the weaker sentiment of common nationality.

It will be observed that the right of free intermarriage, the *jus connubii* which played so large a part in the growth and progress of the Roman Empire, finds no place in Sidgwick's catalogue of the essential characteristics of nationality. No one writing in Europe would imagine that people who were capable of conceiving the idea of national unity had not long ago passed the stage at which restrictions on intermarriage could form part of their code of social custom. Yet this, which may be called the physiological aspect of the question, is one of the first points that strike an observer in India. It was referred to, as long ago as 1889, by Sir Comer Petheram, Chief Justice of Bengal, in an address delivered by him as Vice-Chancellor of the Calcutta University:—

Intermarriage.

'Above all,' he said, 'it should be borne in mind by those who aspire to lead the people of this country into the untried regions of political life, that all the recognized nations of the world have been produced by the freest possible intermingling and fusing of the different race stocks inhabiting a common territory. The horde, the tribe, the caste, the clan, all the smaller separate and often warring groups characteristic of the earlier stages of civilisation, must, it would seem, be welded together by a process of unrestricted crossing before a nation can be produced. Can we suppose that Germany would ever have arrived at her present greatness, or would indeed have come to be a nation at all, if the numerous tribes mentioned by Tacitus, or the three hundred petty princedoms of last century, had been stereotyped and their social fusion rendered impossible by a system forbidding intermarriage between the members of different tribes or the inhabitants of different jurisdictions? If the tribe in Germany had, as in India, developed into the caste, would German unity ever have been heard of? Everywhere in history we see the same contest going forward between the earlier, the more barbarous instinct of separation, and the modern civilising tendency towards unity, but we can point to no instance where the former principle, the principle of disunion and isolation, has succeeded in producing anything resembling a nation. History, it may be said, abounds in surprises, but I do not believe that what has happened nowhere else is likely to happen in India in the present generation.'

The view there stated is borne out by Rivier's* observation.

'On ne peut guère douter que ce ne soit en grande partie aux mélanges infinis qui, durant des siècles, ont pétri et trituré les Européens d'aujourd'hui, qu'est du la suprematie *mondiale* actuelle de notre continent.'

So long as a regime of caste persists, it is difficult to see how the sentiment of unity and solidarity can penetrate and inspire all classes of the community, from the highest to the lowest, in the manner that it has done in Japan where, if true caste ever existed, restrictions on intermarriage have long ago disappeared. It may be said on the other hand that the caste system itself, with its singularly perfect communal organization, is a machinery admirably fitted for the diffusion of new ideas; that castes may in course of time group themselves into classes representing the different strata of society; and that India may thus attain, by the agency of these indigenous corporations, the results which have been arrived at elsewhere through the fusion of individual types. The problem is a novel one, but so are the conditions which give rise to it, and the ferment of new ideas acting upon ancient institutions may bring about a solution the nature of which cannot now be foreseen.

The basis of Indian nationality.

We have seen that the factors which in other countries are regarded as essential to the growth of national sentiment either do not exist at all in India, or tend to produce separation rather than cohesion. We have also observed that the influence of caste seems at first sight to favour particularist rather than nationalist tendencies. Are we then to conclude that the conception of an Indian nationality rests upon no substantial or even intelligible basis, and may be brushed aside as a figment of the prolific oriental imagination stimulated by its recent contact with Western thought? Such a conclusion would, I think, be premature. Indian national sentiment is, indeed, at present in rather a fluid condition, but its existence within a certain section of the community can hardly be denied, and the causes which have led to its development are plainly discernible. They may be said to be two in number :—

* Rivier: *Principes du Droit des Gens.*

(1) The consciousness of a certain community of intellectual pursuits and aspirations, derived from the common study of the history and literature of England, and from the common use, for certain special purposes, of the English language in addition to a provincial vernacular.

(2) The consciousness of being united and drawn together by living under a single government, by taking part in the administration of a common system of laws, and by sharing in the material benefits of a common civilisation.

Here one naturally looks for some instance in history of a genuine nationality arising from the partial adoption of a foreign language and the partial assimilation of a few foreign institutions. Within the modern period the search for such a parallel would be fruitless. The modern theory of nationality figured prominently among the original doctrines of the French Revolution, but in the hands of Napoleon it speedily became an instrument of territorial aggrandisement, and it can hardly be said to have attained general recognition in Europe before about 1830. Long before that time all the peoples affected by it had formed their own languages, had made their own history, and had developed characteristic institutions to which they were passionately attached. Even the oppressed nationalities, whom other powers were trying to absorb, cherished these feelings in unabated strength. Going back some centuries earlier it may perhaps be thought that the common use of Latin by the learned classes of Europe as a medium of communication on political and literary subjects offers a resemblance to the common use of English by the educated class in India. But the survival of Latin as the language of diplomacy, science and scholarship down to the middle of the 18th century did no more towards developing any consciousness of common nationality among Europeans as such than the remotely analogous fact that under the rule of the Moghuls in India Hindu officials were in the habit of addressing their conquerors and of transacting public business in Persian. In neither case did the practice of the learned give rise to any community of political sentiment either among them or among the people at large.

Has it any parallel in history?

If we travel still further back in the history of Europe an approach to a precedent of the kind we are in search of seems at first sight to be furnished by the intellectual and social development of Gaul under Roman rule. In

The example of Gaul.

B. C. 38 when Julius Cæsar. yielding to the entreaties of the Gauls for aid against the Helvetii, entered upon the shortest of Roman wars,* he found the country between the Rhine and the Pyrenees in the possession of about eighty independent political communities (*Civitates*). These were united by no federal tie; they recognised no superior authority; they had not risen to the idea of a common country or a national life; and their local patriotism was bounded by their own little territories, and inspired by hatred of their immediate neighbours. Most of them were in form aristocratic republics governed by Senates in which the educated classes had a decided preponderance. But they were torn by internal factions ever ready to call in a foreign ally, and were in constant danger of being overthrown by any ambitious chief who was rich enough to gather round himself a small army of rudely equipped retainers. Independent Gaul was a chaos of disorderly local jealousies aggravated by perpetual war. When the Romans appeared on the scene, some of the States hastened to make terms; others offered a fitful and ineffectual resistance under leaders whose real object was to set up tyrannies of their own. With an army consisting mainly of Gallic levies, drilled and disciplined on the Roman system and stiffened by a few Italian legions, Cæsar subdued the country in five campaigns, and substituted a single Roman supremacy for a confused medley of local supremacies. On the establishment of the *pax Romana* an era of civilization commenced which resulted in the development of political and religious unity.

The influence of language was the chief factor in the change. From the first century onwards all the inscriptions that have been discovered, whether dedications to the gods, family epitaphs, or municipal decrees are without exception in Latin. Among the common people the ancient Celtic dialect seems to have survived down to the middle of the third century and then to have died out so completely that in the fifth century, when Gaul was converted to Christianity by Latin speaking missionaries, no trace of the original language remained.† As Coulanges observes, when two peoples are in contact, it is not always the less numerous that gives up its language; it is rather the one that has the most need of the other.

---

* Si cuncta bella recenseas nullum breviore spatio quam adversus Gallos confectum. Tac. Ann XI. 24.

† Here I follow Coulanges, *La Gaule Romaine*. *Mommsen* in *The Provinces of the Roman Empire* takes a different view of the scanty evidence available.

Here the need was all on the side of the Gauls. Their own language was poor and was unable to express the new ideas that came in with advancing civilization. They had no literature and no art of their own. They borrowed both from Roman sources and they founded schools all over Gaul to teach poetry, rhetoric, mathematics, the entire harmony of studies which the Latins called humanity. Religion, law, social usage followed in the same path, and in all departments of life Gallic culture perished and Latin culture took its place. Yet the result of this process of assimilation was not to produce an independent Gallic nationality, but to merge the people of Gaul in the Roman nation. The Gauls ceased to be Gauls in any but a geographical sense and became Romans with a Gallic tinge. The process is a remarkable one, and many of its incidents seem almost to have repeated themselves in the history of India. But it throws no direct light on the problems connected with the idea of an Indian nationality.

The example of Japan.

It is in no way surprising that the imagination of the Indian nationalists should have been deeply touched by the rise of Japan, or even that some of the more ardent spirits among them should have formed the opinion that if forty years of contact with European thought could make a nation of the Japanese, more than a century of similar experience ought to have done the same for the people of India. Here there seems to be some misconception of the facts. Japan has many lessons for the Indians of today, but when they begin to study her history they will assuredly not learn from it that Japanese nationalism was the work of two generations, or that it owed anything at all to foreign culture or influence. Centuries before Commodore Perry landed in Yokohama the various race elements out of which the Japanese people have been formed, had been crushed together and consolidated by the sternest discipline that any nation has ever undergone. In all the stages of this process religion was the dominant influence. *Shinto* or 'The way of the gods,' a form of Animism coloured and idealised by the belief that the dead are ever present with the living and take an unseen but active share in the fortunes of their descendants, lent itself to a social regime of extraordinary stringency. Under the rule of the dead no man could call his soul his own. His actions, his words, his demeanour, his thoughts, his emotions were perpetually watched by a ghostly company of ancestors, who were grieved at any wrong conduct and visited it on the family at large. Thus the rights of the dead came to be enforced by the living, and formed the basis of a domestic despotism of the most searching kind. Even the quality of a smile was defined by inviolable convention, and to smile at a superior so broadly as to show the back teeth was reckoned as a mortal offence.

The minute regulations promulgated in 681 A. D. by the Emperor Temmu, and expanded, a thousand years later, by the great Shogun Iyéyasu, afford many illustrations of the coercion employed. 'Every member of a Kumi',* says one of these, 'must carefully watch the conduct of his fellow members. If any one violates these regulations without due excuse, he is to be punished; and his *Kumi* will also be held responsible.' Behind the Kumi was the clan, then came the community, then the tribe—a hierarchy of groups, ruled by the 'Heavenly Sovereign,' the divinely incarnate Mikado, and all working together to suppress independent personality and to produce a uniform type of character for the service of the nation. The ordinances cover every incident of life from marriage to the material or cut of a dress, or the value of a birthday present to a child. They lay infinite stress on obedience to parents and superiors, respect for elders, faithful service to masters, and friendly feelings towards all members of the community. Intrigue, party spirit, the formation of cliques, competition for leadership, appeals to the passions of the ignorant—in short, all forms of political selfishness are condemned in scathing terms. The patriot must put aside personal vanity and may not play for his own hand. Breaches of the rules were punished by social ostracism, by flogging, by torture, and in the last resort by banishment for life or for a term of years. In old Japan the banished man was dead to human society. Even the outcast classes would not receive him; without permission he could not become a Buddhist monk; and the last resource of selling himself as a slave was withdrawn from him by the later Shoguns. The religion of loyalty could make no terms with the rebel or the renegade. It demanded absolute submission as the first condition of national unity.

The centuries of coercion which the Japanese passed through produced in them a superb heredity, moulded by discipline and instinct with loyalty. When the new era opened and the Mikado resumed his temporal power, he found ready to his hand a nation

* A *Kumi* was a group of five or more households under a Kumi-gashira or group-chief who was responsible for the conduct of the *Kumi* and of each of its members.

that moved like one man, and was inspired through all its ranks with the single sentiment of devotion to the country and to the ever present ancestors of the race. The world is still wondering at the achievements of the last forty years. But these were rendered possible by the training of the ages that had gone before. Japanese nationalism did not originate in the theoretical sentiment of a literate class which may or may not work down to the lower strata of society. It is rooted in the popular religion and bound up with the life of the race. To my mind the most striking among the many evidences of the diffusion of the spirit of unity in Japan is to be found in the extraordinary secrecy maintained during the war with Russia. The correspondents of foreign papers, ready to pay any price for news, saw one Division after another vanish into space, but no foreigner could find out where the troops embarked, where they would land, or what was their ultimate destination. At a time when the issue of the contest hung upon the command of the sea two great battleships were lost by misadventure, and the disaster was concealed until its disclosure could no longer imperil the national existence. These things were known to thousands but the secret was safe, because all classes were inspired by the passionate enthusiasm and self-devotion which the Shinto religion has developed into an instinct, so that the low-born coolie is as fine a patriot as the *Samurai* of ancient descent. When India can rise to these heights of discipline and self-control, India may rival Japan. But those who cherish that lofty ideal must bear in mind that in the region of evolution there is no such thing as a short cut.

The future of Indian Nationalism.

Having brought the enquiry to this point and having attempted to show what factors have and what have not contributed to the growth of national sentiment in India, one is left with the uncomfortable feeling that one has by no means got to the root of the matter. Analysis has its limits and a people, like an individual, is something more than a bundle of tendencies. The mysterious thing called personality, the equally mysterious thing called national character, has in either case to be reckoned with. Beneath the manifold diversity of physical and social type, language, custom and religion which strikes the observer in India, there can still be discerned, as Mr. Yusuf Ali has pointed out, a certain 'underlying uniformity of life from the Himalayas to Cape Comorin.' There is in fact an Indian character, a general Indian personality, which we cannot resolve into its component elements.

How is this character to be inspired and transfused by that consciousness of common interests and ideals which is the predominant feature of the sentiment of nationality? The question admits of being answered either on idealist or on evolutionary lines—in the light of Indian theory or of European or Japanese experience. It may be said on the one hand that the idea of nationality is in itself nothing more than an impalpable mental attitude, a subjective conviction which may subsist independently of any objective reality, a fine flower of sentiment, springing from an unknown germ and nourished on Maya or illusion. But once planted on Indian soil it may spread far and wide as its seeds are blown hither and thither by the breath of popular imagination. We have seen how the legend of the four original castes, evolved in the active brain of some systematising pandit, has filtered downwards, has taken hold of the mind of the people, and has become almost an article of faith with the general body of Hindus. No one cares to enquire whether it rests on any basis of fact, yet it holds its ground, it gains constantly wider currency, and it undoubtedly does in a way influence practice in matters of social usage. It is conceivable that the idea of nationality may run a similar course, that it may possess the mind of the upper classes and may be diffused thence through wider circles until it reaches the rank and file of the Indian people. The process will take time, and even when it is completed, the result will be wanting in substance and vitality. If on the other hand we look to the history of Europe, and more especially to the history of Japan, we shall see that wherever genuine nationalities have arisen, they have been the product of character and circumstances—common character and common experience acting and reacting on each other through a long period of time. There is no doubt that the common character exists in India, if only in the rather shadowy and undeveloped form in which Mr. Yusuf Ali depicts it. It has still to undergo the common experience necessary to mould it into national character. This apprenticeship, if it is to be of any real effect, must be based upon facts, not upon fancies, and must extend to the masses of the people. A mere top-dressing of idealism will not make a nationality. How then are the people to be reached? Japan supplies the answer—by the development of indigenous beliefs and institutions. The vast majority of the people of India are as yet untouched by the idea of nationality. This cannot be impressed upon them through their own vernaculars, the influence of which would make for separatism rather than for unity. Nor can they be reached through English, at least not for many generations. But they might be drawn together by the common interests which would be created by a genuine form of popular self-government. This should be built up from the bottom on the basis of two indigenous institutions—the village community and the village council—the common property of the Aryan people both in Europe and in India. Reconstruction on these lines offers the best prospect of realizing the national ideal, and of controlling the separatist tendencies of caste. It may be that in the first instance the process will produce not an Indian nationality but a number of provincial nationalities. But history shows this to be the natural course of evolution. Everywhere particularism has come first, just as crystallisation takes place by centres, and nationalities have been formed by the agglomeration of the particularist units into a larger whole.

Let us now try to draw together the threads of this discussion. The standard elements of nationality either do not exist in India or make for diversity rather than uniformity. Caste in particular, an institution peculiar to India, seems at first sight to be absolutely incompatible with the idea of nationality, but the history of the Marāthas suggests that a caste or a group of castes might harden into a nation, and that the caste organization itself might be employed with effect to bring about such a consummation. The factors of nationality in India are two—the common use of the English language for certain purposes and the common employment of Indians in English administration. At present these factors affect only a limited group of persons, among whom the Muhammadans have hitherto stood rather aloof. The masses have not been affected at all. They cannot be reached through language, but they might be reached through the agency of self-governing institutions. The orderly development of the indigenous germs of such institutions ought to be the immediate object of the Indian nationalists. In this direction and, I believe, in this direction alone, is it possible to advance towards real political representation. Progress will in any case be slow, but nothing will retard it more certainly than the 'impatient idealism' which insists upon beginning at the wrong end.

NOTES

Introduction

1. Some of the arguments draw upon my previous work on colonial discourse (Nayar 2008, 2012).

Imperial Business

1. It could be argued that the Charter's dismissal of the non-Christian prince and his possessions, discussed later in the chapter, was be a version of the *terra nullius*.
2. The 1793 Charter Act ended the Company's monopoly.
3. Sen writes of this insecure nature of the Company's transactions:

   There was much fear that, with the weakening of Mughal authority, local rulers would plunder one another's territories and impede the trade of the Company "at every turn by vexatious exactions. Such apprehensions were consistent with the established belief that Indian rulers, particularly the Moorish princes, were by nature despotic and always capable of despoiling rightful trade. (63)
4. As Anna Kurian argues when speaking of the Charter in her MA (English) class: 'they're [the Company and its "servants"] subject as per the Charter. But due to the distance, that subjection is very far away and minimal. It made it possible to be a Warren Hastings … the "man on the spot", emboldened and empowered by a Charter that gives them nearly infinite powers' (personal communication). Regarding the "man on the spot", see Kathryn Tridrick, *Empire and English Character* (1990).
5. Stern argues that the British Empire's structure and process was built on such associations:

   Accordingly, the governance of the "English" empire at home and abroad was a layered and hybrid affair, resting on multiple constitutional foundations and constantly negotiated among a variety of royal agencies, local governors, councils, assemblies, courts, and corporate and legal communities. With some notable exceptions, like Jamaica and Tangier, this was an empire founded and often administered by corporations, companies, and proprietors, each built on a variety of contrasting ideological, religious, political, and legal foundations. Though theoretically dependent upon the Crown, in both principle and practice, these corporate colonies exercised a great deal of autonomy; some were even literally self-constituting… (10)

Imperial Prospecting

1. Benjamin Schmidt writes of Early Modern geography and exoticism:

   Europe gains its identity *through* the exotic world; in both, global exotica and their pleasures coalesce around a freshly constituted idea of – Europe. (2015: 5, emphasis in original)

2. The 'Inquiries' resonate Early modern descriptive geography, with its emphasis on enumerative modes such as surveys, detailed description, chorography—as modes of writing and as a mode of self-definition (Cormack 1997).

Imperial Vulnerability

1. Chatterjee notes:

   There is one more account—the fourteenth—by John Cooke, who was in the fort at the time of its fall, but who narrated his version of the Black Hole story before a select committee of the House of Commons in 1772, sixteen years after the incident. Gupta shows with impeccable reasoning that Holwell was directly involved in the production of every single one of these narratives—that is, they are not independent pieces of evidence but rather all the result of consultations with Holwell or a reading of his various descriptions of the event. (19)

   Brijen K. Gupta lists the accounts of the incident in his essay, 'The Black Hole Incident' (1959) and concludes that the 'other French and Dutch accounts, and other references in Holwell's correspondence, … are based on the accounts mentioned above' (54).

2. Some of the arguments here draw upon my work in *English Siege and Prison Writings: From the 'Black Hole' to the 'Mutiny'* (2017).
3. In *Cartographies of Desire* (1999), Rebecca Blevins Faery makes a similar argument about the figure of the *white* woman captive as site for the making of an American culture.

Imperial Cartography

1. As Mark Harrison has persuasively argued, the differences in the climate between England and India were often treated as embodying

and emblematic of the *essential* differences between races (Harrison 1999).

2. Raj also comments on the cartouche to the first edition of the *Memoir*:

   > in the emblematic cartouche in the lower right hand side of the first edition of the map of the peninsula, one sees an open acknowledgement of co-operation between South Asian and British elites, a Brahman giving sacred manuscripts ('*Shasters*') to Britannia while other Brahmans, carrying other manuscripts in envelopes, patiently await their turn. (77; also see Edney, 13–15)

Imperial Eyewitnessing

1. The term sati itself has a number of meanings. As John Stratton Hawley puts it:

   > The term *sati* has a wide semantic range, with marked differences of emphasis depending on what language is being spoken. *Sati* can refer to the action or event whereby a woman is immolated on her husband's pyre, to the woman who is at the center of this spectacle, or to Sati as a goddess. In English, the first meaning is dominant: sati as an action or ritual. English usage sometimes makes sati the object of the verb "to perform," but the more common habit is to associate it with the verb "to commit," which tends to characterize sati as something in the nature of a crime or a form of suicide. In English, one commits suicide; one commits a crime. But whether one performs sati or commits it, the noun itself describes not a person but a thing—often, implicitly, something that ought to be halted. (1994, 11–12)

2. The reference is to William Guthrie's *Geographical Grammar* of 1770, a bestselling work which, according to Robert Mayhew, was a major Scottish intervention in the British geography debates and perspectives (Mayhew 2008).
3. Later Indian/Hindu nationalist representations of the 'true' Hindu womanhood were central to the construction of a certain Indianness. Ania Loomba writes:

   > The colonial disenfranchisement of Indian men led to a situation whereby women became the grounds and signs for the colonial struggle. Indian nationalisms of different shades produced their own versions of the good Hindu wife, each of which became emblematic of Indian-ness and tradition, a sign of rebellion against colonial authority and a symbol of the vision of the future. (211)

   Whether the Wilson kind of representation of the sati as agential and virtuous Hindu woman who followed her husband beyond the bounds of life fed into the nationalist discourse around the true Hindu wife is a moot point.

4. Paul Courtright writes of the conclusion and climax of this process:

   > Consensus emerged among colonial authorities and some Hindu reformists that sati was not an integral part of Hinduism but a medieval perversion of its core values. The principal beneficiaries of these religiously glossed murders of women were Brahman priests who collected fees for performing the rituals and family members who stood to benefit from inheritances that otherwise might have come to the surviving widow. Consequently the British authorities and their client Hindu states banned the practice. (185)

5. The ban on sati was itself not conclusive.

   > The British encounter with sati in early nineteenth-century Bengal left a lasting legacy, both judicially and ideologically, emphasising the question of the widow's volition, while at the same time undermining her agency and casting her as a passive victim of a barbaric oriental practice. (Major 2011, 5)

6. The British were less keen on intervening in the princely states because, Major writes:

   > The ineffectual interference in the matter would damage the dignity both of the princely house in question and of the paramount power that sponsored the reform, while authoritative intervention might provoke a hostile and destabilising response. (49)

Imperial Education

1. K. Narayana Chandran writes on the social, economic and political advantages to having an English degree in India:

   > I heard it said in India, not without some truth to the claim, that with good English you don't just make a living, you can make a killing. (2006, 151)

2. The question of the moral training of the colonial subject would become a serious concern and point of debate especially after the 1857 'Mutiny'. English educators, commentators and statesmen would recommend a manual of moral instruction in many regions of the subcontinent. For example, John Murdoch writes in *Hints on Government Education in India, With Special Reference to School Books* (1873):

   > The defrauding of masters by servants under the name of 'custom' should be exposed. Honesty towards government as well as individuals should be taught.... Purity in speech and behaviour should be enforced.... Respect for authority ought to be instilled. (61)

The Report of the Indian Education Commission stated:

> In all colleges, and under all courses of instruction, the most effective moral training consists in inculcating habits of order, diligence, truthfulness, and due self-respect combined with submission to authority, all of which lessons a good teacher finds useful opportunities of imparting. The formation of such habits is promoted by the study of the lives and actions of great men, such as the student finds in the course of his English reading; and, it may also be hoped, by the silent influence upon his character of constant intercourse with teachers whom he is able to regard with respect and affection. (1882, 307)

On the English debate, textbooks and curriculum for the moral training of the colonial subject in India, see Topdar 2015, Nayar 2020, 'Moral Readership').

3. Braj Kachru wrote in *The Alchemy of English*:

   > [K]nowing English is like possessing the fabled Aladdin's lamp, which permits one to open, as it were, the linguistic gates to international business, technology, science and travel. (Cited in Chandran 2009, 310)

Imperial Control

1. Kim Wagner writes:

   > It would be implausible to deny that the accounts do refer – in one way or the other – to a social reality. In other words it is not plausible that these individuals should have invented so similar stories at different times and places, when interrogated by different British officials, without reflecting related patterns of practices. When thuggee was first encountered in the South and Northern India there was no formal exchange of information on the subject between the authorities and yet the information collected about the phenomenon is virtually identical. Comparing the content of the depositions of, for instance, Ghulam Hussain given in 1810 at Mainpuri before the local Magistrate and that of Ameer Alee given in 1832 at Sagar before Sleeman also reveals that there were few temporal changes. What was different was the way the depositions were interpreted according to the changing discursive contexts of the colonial administration. (2007, 23)

2. Sagnik Bhattacharya writes:

   > What made the *thugs* such a dreadful obsession for the British administration that the latter was motivated to grant unchecked powers to the *Thug Department* (formed in the 1830s), I will argue is the elusive nature of the thugs. The very fact that British colonial

law was powerless in identifying and locating them, transformed it into a "metaphor" and a personification of the fear of the "other" and the unknown. As stated before, I am not concerned with the actual positive reality of the thugs per se, as much as I am with the image of the thug(s) and with *thuggee* as a phenomenon as it was known to the British. The reasons for avoiding direct engagement with the positive "actuality" of the *thugs* is not only motivated by the fact that the largest volume of sources about them are colonial products and as such suffer from the errors and misconceptions inherent in the nineteenth century colonial knowledge production apparatus, but also because what or who the thugs were in reality is not a matter of concern anymore when the thug as a metaphor has outlived the so called community that gave birth to the notion and has entered common parlance and popular imagination. (2020: 2)

3. The Thugi and Dacoity Department would eventually evolve into the Criminal Investigation Department, the CID.

BIBLIOGRAPHY

Primary Texts

1600. 'Charter Granted by Queen Elizabeth, To the Governor and Company of Merchants of London, Trading Into the East Indies, Dated the 31st December, in the 43rd Year of Her Reign, *Anno domini*, 1600'. In *Indian Constitutional Documents (1600–1618)*, edited by Panchanandas Mukherji, 2nd Edition, Volume 1, 1–20. Calcutta: Thacker, Spink & Co.

Anon. 1875. *The Gospel in Santhalisthan*. London: James Nisbet.

Bacon, Francis. 1860 [1625]. 'Of Travel'. Available at http://ebooks.adelaide.edu.au/b/bacon/francis/ b12e/essay18.html (accessed 26 May 2010).

Baden-Powell, R.S.S. 1920. *Memories of India*. Philadelphia: David McKay.

Buchanan, Claudius. 1813. *An Apology for Promoting Christianity in India*. London: T. Cadell and W. Davies.

Campbell, George. 1893. *Memoirs of My Indian Career*, edited by C.E. Bernard. London: Macmillan.

Campbell, Walter. 1853. *The Old Forest Ranger, or the Wild Sports of India*. 3rd edition. London: Arthur Hall, Virtue.

Clarkson, William. 1850. *Missionary Encouragements in India, or, the Christian Village in Gujarat*, 9th Edition. London: John Snow.

Colebrooke, H.T. 1795. *Remarks on the Present State of the Husbandry and Commerce of Bengal*. Calcutta.

D'Oyly, Charles. 1995. *The European in India*. New Delhi: Asian Educational Services.

Duff, Alexander. 1839. *India, and India Missions*. Edinburgh: J. Johnstone.

Duncan, Jonathan. 'Letter [to the Earl of Cornwallis]' Dated 1 January 1792. In *Colonial Education and India 1781–1945*, edited by Pramod K. Nayar (2020), Volume I, 12–13. Oxford: Routledge.

Elwood, Katherine A. 1830. *Narrative of a Journey Overland from England, by the Continent of Europe, Egypt, and the Red Sea To India* (two volumes). London: Henry Colburn & Richard Bentley.

Fergusson, James. 1866 (1977). *On the Study of Indian Architecture*. Varanasi: Indological Book House.

Forster, George. 1798. *A Journey from Bengal to England* (two volumes). London: R. Faulder.

Grant, Charles. 1792 (2020). 'Observations on the State of Society Among the Asiatic Subjects of Great Britain'. In *Colonial Education and India 1781–1945*, edited by Pramod K. Nayar, Volume 1, 16–30. Oxford: Routledge.

Herbert, Thomas. 1634. *A Relation of Some Years Travels, Began Anno 1626*. London: William Stansby & Jacob Bloome.

Hickey, William. 1925. *Memoirs* (four volumes), edited by A. Spencer. London: Hurst & Blackett.

Hodges, William. 1999. *Travels in India, During the Years 1780, 1781, 1782 and 1783*. New Delhi: Munshiram Manoharlal.

Holwell, J.Z. 1764. *A Genuine Narrative of the Deplorable Deaths of the English Gentlemen, and Others, Who Were Suffocated in the Black-Hole in Fort William, in Calcutta, in the Kingdom of Bengal; in the Night Succeeding the 20th Day of June, 1756*. In *India Tracts* by J.Z. Holwell. London: T. Becket and P.A. de Hondt.

Inglis, James. 1892. *Tent Life in Tigerland*. London: Sampson Low, Marston.

Johnson [Surgeon]. 1806. *An Account of a Voyage to India, China & C*. London: Richard Phillips.

Jones, William. 1901 (2021). *Shakuntala or the Fatal Ring: An Indian Drama*. New Delhi: Gyan Books.

______. 1772 (2009). 'On the Poetry of the Eastern Nations'. In Jones' *Poems, Consisting Chiefly of Translations from the Asiatick Tongues*, edited by Rudolf Beck. Augsburg: Universität Augsburg. Available at https://d-nb.info/1077698518/34 (accessed 8 December 2021).

______. 1824. 'On the Mystical Poetry of the Persians and Hindus'. In Jones' *Discourses Delivered Before the Asiatick Society: And Miscellaneous Papers on the Religion, Poetry, Literature, etc, of the Nations of India*, Volume 2, 131–150. London: Charles S. Arnold.

______. 1807. 'On the Literature of the Hindus, From the Sanscrit. Communicated by Govardhan Caul. Translated, With a Short Commentary by the President [William Jones]'. In *The Works of William Jones*, Volume 4, 92–113 London: John Stockdale.

______. 1824. 'On the Hindus [Discourse III, Delivered Before the Asiatick Society, February 2, 1786]'. In *Discourses Delivered Before the Asiatic Society: And Miscellaneous Papers, on the Religion, Poetry, Literature, Etc., of the Nations of India* by Jones, Volume 1, 20–37. London: Charles S. Arnold.

Kindersley, Jemima. 1777. *Letters From the Island of Teneriffe, Brazil, the Cape of Good Hope, and the East Indies*. London: J. Nourse.

Locke, J. Courtenay, ed. 1997. *The First Englishmen in India*. 1930. New Delhi: Munshiram Manoharlal.

Macaulay, T.B. 1833. 'Government of India'. Speech in the English Parliament, 10 July. Available at http://www.columbia.edu/itc/mealac/pritchett/00generallinks/macaulay/txt_commons_indiagovt_1833.html (accessed 14 July 2022).

______. 1835 (2020). 'Minute'. In *Colonial Education and India 1781–1945*, edited by Pramod K. Nayar, Volume 1, 55–64. Oxford: Routledge.

Mill, James. 1817. *The History of British India* (three volumes). London: Baldwin, Cradock, & Joy.

Mundy, Godfrey Charles. 1995. *Journal of a Tour in India in 1827–1830*. New Delhi: Asian Educational Publishers.

Murdoch, John. 1873. *Hints on Government Education in India, With Special Reference To School Books*. Madras: C. Foster.

'Narrative of an Hindoo Woman, Who Lately Burnt Herself on the Funeral Pyre of Her Husband'. 1804. *The Weekly Entertainer*, 25 June. Reprinted in *Women in Colonial India: Documents and Sources*, edited by Pramod K. Nayar (2013), Volume 3, 18–19. London and New York: Routledge.

Orme, Robert. 1782 (1974). *Historical Fragments of the Mogul Empire*, edited by J.P. Guha. New Delhi: Associated.

Ovington, John. 1696. *A Voyage to Surat, in the Year 1689*. London: Jacob Jonson.

Parliamentary Papers, Vol. 18, No. 749. 1821. Reprinted in *Women in Colonial India: Documents and Sources,* edited by Pramod K. Nayar (2013), Volume 3, 98–99. London and New York: Routledge.

Parliamentary Papers, No. 749. 1821. Reprinted in *Women in Colonial India: Documents and Sources* (2013), edited by Pramod K. Nayar, Vol. 3, 111–115. London and New York: Routledge.

Parliamentary Papers, No. 550. 1830. Reprinted in *Women in Colonial India: Documents and Sources,* edited by Pramod K. Nayar (2013), Volume 3, 415. London and New York: Routledge.

Purchas, Samuel. 1625 (1905). *Hakluytus Posthumus, or, Purchas His Pilgrimes,* (20 volumes). Glasgow: James MacLehose.

'A Regulation for Maintaining an Observance of the Restrictions Prescribed by the Shaster in the Burning of Hindoo Widows on the Funeral Piles of Their Husbands, or Otherwise'. 1821.

Rennell, James. 1788. *Memoir of a Map of Hindoostan, or the Mogul Empire.* London: M. Brown.

Report of the Indian Education Commission. 1882. Calcutta: Superintendent of Government Printing.

'Review of *Sacontalá*'. 1790. *Analytical Review* 7 (August): 361–373.

———. 1791. *Monthly Review*, February: 121–137.

———. *Blackwood's Edinburgh Magazine* 6 (Oct. 1819–Mar. 1820): 417–430.

———. 1851. *Calcutta Review* 15: 97–117.

Risley, Herbert. 1908 (1915 [2021]). *The People of India*. New Delhi: Gyan.

Roe, T. 1926 (1990). *The Embassy of Sir Thomas Roe to India, 1615–1619*, edited by William Foster. New Delhi: Munshiram Manoharlal.

Roy, Rammohan. 2020. 'Letter to Amherst, 11th December 1823'. In *Colonial Education and India 1781–1945*, edited by Pramod K. Nayar, Volume 4, 1–4. Oxford: Routledge.

Shakespear, Henry. 1862. *The Wild Sports of India*, London: Smith, Elder.

Sleeman, W.H. 1839. *Thugs or, Phansigars of India: Comprising a History of the Rise and Progress of That Extraordinary Fraternity of Assassins, and a Description of the System Which It Pursues and of the Measures Which Have Been Adopted by the Supreme Government of India for Its Suppression* (two volumes). Philadelphia: Carey & Hart.

Steel, Flora Annie and Grace Gardiner. 1888 (1898 [2010]). *The Complete Indian Housekeeper and Cook: Giving the Duties of Mistress and Servants, the General Management of the House and No Practical Recipes for Cooking in All Its Branches*, edited by Ralph Crane and Anna Johnstone. New York and Oxford: Oxford University Press.

Steel, Flora Annie. 1929. *The Garden of Fidelity: Being the Autobiography of Flora Annie Steel, 1847–1929*. London: Macmillan.

Terry, Edward. 1655. *A Voyage to East-India*. London: Martin & T. Allestrye.

Trevelyan, Charles. 1838. *On the Education of the People of India*. London: Longman, Orme, Brown, Green & Longmans.

Trevelyan, G.O. 1866 (1992). *The Competitionwallah*. New Delhi: HarperCollins.

Tucker, Sarah. 1842–1843. *South Indian Sketches* (two volumes). London: James Nisbet.

Tyndale-Biscoe, C.E. 1920. *Character Building in Kashmir*. Salisbury: Church Missionary Society.

Ward, William. 1822. *An Account of the Writings, Religion and Manners of the Hindoos* (three volumes). London: Kingsbury, Parbury and Allen.

Welsh, James. 1830. *Military Reminiscences From a Journal of Nearly Forty Years Active Service in the East Indies* (two volumes). London: Smith, Elder & Co.

Wilson, Joseph. 1788 (2013). 'The Custom of Women Burning Themselves With Their Husbands Still Practised in India'. In *Women in Colonial India:*

Historical Documents and Sources, edited by Pramod K. Nayar, Volume III, 15–17. London and New York: Routledge.

Secondary Texts

Ahmed, Siraj. 2009. 'Orientalism and the Permanent Fix of War'. In *The Postcolonial Enlightenment: Eighteenth-Century Colonialism and Postcolonial Theory*, edited by Daniel Carey and Lynn Festa, 167–206. Oxford: Oxford University Press.

Arnold, David. 1985. 'Crime in Madras'. In *Crime and Criminality*, edited by Anand A. Yang, 62–88. Tucson: University of Arizona Press.

Asad, Talal, ed. 1973. *Anthropology and the Colonial Encounter*. London: Humanities Press.

Banerjee, Rita. 2021. *India in Early Modern English Travel Writings: Protestantism, Enlightenment, and Toleration*. Leiden and Boston: Brill.

Bann, Stephen. 1999. *Under the Sign: John Bargrave as Collector, Traveler, and Witness*. Ann Arbor, Michigan: University of Michigan Press.

Bassnett, Susan. 2002. *Translation Studies* (third edition). London: Routledge.

Bayly, C.A. 1999. *Empire and Information: Intelligence Gathering and Social Communication in India, 1780–1870*. Cambridge: Cambridge University Press.

Bayon, H.P. 1944. 'John Zephaniah Holwell (1711–1798) and the Black Hole of Calcutta'. *Proceedings of the Royal Society of Medicine*, 38(1): 15–18.

Bhattacharya, Sagnik. 2020. 'Monsters in the Dark: The Discovery of Thuggee and Demographic Knowledge in Colonial India'. *Palgrave Communication*, 6. Available at https://www.nature.com/articles/s41599-020-0458-8 (accessed 4 July 2022).

Blunt, Alison. 1999. 'Imperial Geographies of Home: British Domesticity in India, 1886–1925'. *Transactions of the British Institute of Geographers, New Series*, 24(4): 221–440.

Brown, Mark. 2002. 'Crime, Governance and the Company Raj: *The Discovery of Thuggee*'. *British Journal of Criminology*, 42: 77–95.

———. 2003. 'Ethnology and Colonial Administration in Nineteenth-Century British India: The Question of Native Crime and Criminality'. *British Journal for the History of Science*, 36(2): 201–219.

Brunner, Claudia. 2021. 'Conceptualizing Epistemic Violence: An Interdisciplinary Assemblage for IR'. *International Politics Reviews*, 9: 193–212.

Buettner, Elizabeth. 2004. *Empire Families: Britons and Late Imperial India*. Oxford: Oxford University Press.

Burke, Peter. 2001. *Eyewitnessing: The Uses of Images as Historical Evidence*. London: Reaktion.

Campbell, Mary Baine. 1988. *The Witness and the Other World: Exotic European Travel Writing, 400–1600*. Ithaca, New York: Cornell University Press.

Cannon, Garland. 1990. *The Life and Mind of Oriental Jones: Sir William Jones, the Father of Modern Linguistics*. Cambridge: Cambridge University Press.

Castro-Gómez, S. 2002. 'The Social Sciences, Epistemic Violence, and the Problem of the "Invention of the Other"'. *Nepantla: Views from South*, 3(2): 269–285.

Chandran, K. Narayana. 2006. 'On English from India: Prepositions to Post-Positions'. *The Cambridge Quarterly*, 35(2): 151–168.

______. 2009. 'English for "Specific"/"Special" Purposes: An Essay Concerning Indian Understanding'. *Changing English*, 16(3): 301–312.

______. 2018. 'To the Manner Born: How English Tells Its Stories'. *Hermeneus*, 20: 87–104.

Chatterjee, Baijayanti. 2021. 'Founding Empire: James Rennell and the Eighteenth-Century Survey of British Bengal', *Revue de la Société D'études Anglo-Américaines des XVIIe et XVIIIe Siècles*, XVII–XVIII (78). Available at https://journals.openedition.org/1718/8375 (accessed 15 June 2022).

Chatterjee, Partha. 2012. *The Black Hole of Empire: History of a Global Practice of Power*. Princeton: Princeton University Press.

Chattopadhyay, Swati. 2000. 'Blurring Boundaries: The Limits of the "White Town" in Colonial Calcutta'. *Journal of the Society of Architectural Historians*, 59(2): 154–179.

Chaudhuri, K.N. 1978. T*he Trading World of Asia and the English East India Company, 1660–1760*. Cambridge: Cambridge University Press.

Chaudhuri, Nupur. 1992. 'Shawls, Jewelry, Curry, and Rice in Victorian Britain'. In *Western Women and Imperialism*, edited by Chaudhuri and Margaret Strobel. Bloomington: Indiana University Press.

Cohen, B.B. 2009. 'Networks of Sociability: Women's Clubs in Colonial and Postcolonial India'. *Frontiers*, 30(3): 168–195.

Colley, Linda. 2004. *Captives: Britain, Empire, and the World, 1600–1850*. New York: Anchor.

Colvin, Sarah. 2021. 'The Credibility of Elves: Narrative Exclusion and Prison Writing'. In *Prison Writing and the Literary World: Imprisonment, Institutionality and Questions of Literary Practice*, edited by Michelle Kelly and Claire Westall, 21–37. New York and London: Routledge.

______. 2002. 'Goods, Chattels and Sundry Items': Constructing Nineteenth-Century Anglo-Indian Domestic Life'. *Journal of Material Culture*, 7(3): 243–271.

Cosgrove, Denis E. 2001. *Apollo's Eye: A Cartographic Genealogy of the Earth in the Western Imagination*. Baltimore, Maryland: Johns Hopkins University Press.

Courtright, Paul B. 1994. 'The Iconographies of Sati'. In *Sati, the Blessing and the Curse: The Burning of Wives in India*, edited by John Stratton Hawley, 27–48. New York: Oxford University Press.

______. 1995. 'Sati, Sacrifice, and Marriage: The Modernity of Tradition'. In *From the Margins of Hindu Marriage: Essays on Gender, Religion, and Culture*, edited by Lindsay Harlan and Paul B. Courtright, 184–203. Oxford: Oxford University Press.

Crane, Ralph and Anna Johnstone. 2010. 'Introduction'. In *The Complete Indian Housekeeper and Cook* (by F.A. Steel and G. Gardiner), edited by Crane and Johnston. Oxford: Oxford University Press.

Cutts, Elmer H. 1953. 'The Background of Macaulay's Minute'. *American Historical Review*, 58(4): 824–853.

Dear, Peter. 2015. '*Totius in verba:* Rhetoric and Authority in the Early Royal Society'. In *Rhetoric and the Early Royal Society: A Sourcebook*, edited by Tina Skouen and Ryan J. Stark, 53–76. Leiden and Boston: Brill.

Dirks, Nicholas. 2001. *Castes of Mind: Colonialism and the Making of Modern India*. New Jersey: Princeton University Press.

Dodson, Michael S. 2007. *Orientalism, Empire, and National Culture: India, 1770–1880*. London: Palgrave Macmillan.

Dube, Saurubh. 2004. *Stitches on Time: Colonial Textures and Postcolonial Tangles*. Oxford: Oxford University Press.

Dussart, Fae Ceridwen. 2015. 'That "Unit of Civilisation" and "The Talent Peculiar to Women": British Employers and their Servants in the Nineteenth-Century Indian Empire'. *Identities*, 22(6): 706–721.

Eaton, Natasha. 2006. 'Nostalgia for the Exotic: Creating an Imperial Art in London, 1750–1793'. *Eighteenth-Century Studies*, 39: 227–250.

Edgerton, Franklin. 2002. 'Sir William Jones'. In *Portrait of Linguists: A Biographical Source Book for the History of Western Linguistics, 1746–1963. Vol. 1. Sir William Jones to Karl Brugmann*, edited by Thomas A. Sebeok, 1–57. Bristol: Thoemmes Press.

Edney, Matthew H. 1997. *Mapping an Empire: The Geographical Construction of British India, 1765–1843*. Chicago: University of Chicago Press.

Erikson, Emily. 2014. *Between Monopoly and Free Trade: The English East India Company, 1600–1757*. Princeton and Oxford: Princeton University Press.

Evans, Stephen. 2002. 'Macaulay's Minute Revisited: Colonial Language Policy in Nineteenth-Century India'. *Journal of Multilingual and Multicultural Development*, 23(4): 260–281.

Faery, Rebecca Blevins. 1999. *Cartographies of Desire: Captivity, Race, and Sex in the Shaping of an American Nation*. Norman: University of Oklahoma Press.

Figueira, Dorothy Matilda. 1991. *Translating the Orient: The Reception of* Sakuntala *in Nineteenth-Century Europe*. Albany: State University of New York Press.

Fhlathuin, Máire Ní. 2001. 'That solitary Englishman': W.H. Sleeman and the Biography of British India'. *Victorian Review*, 27(1): 69–85.

———. 2004. 'The Campaign Against Thugs in the Bengal Press of the 1830s'. *Victorian Periodicals Review*, 37(2): 124–140.

Franklin, Michael J. 2011. *Orientalist Jones: Sir William Jones, Poet, Lawyer, and Linguist, 1746–1794*. Oxford: Oxford University Press.

Freitag, Sandria. 1985. 'Collective Crime and Authority in North India'. In *Crime and Criminality in British India*, edited by Anand A. Yang, 140–164. Tucson: University of Arizona Press.

Fuller, C.J. 2016. 'Anthropologists and Viceroys: Colonial Knowledge and Policy Making in India, 1871–1911'. *Modern Asian Studies*, 50(1): 217–258.

———. 2017. 'Ethnographic Inquiry in Colonial India: Herbert Risley, William Crooke, and the Study of Tribes and Castes'. *Journal of the Royal Anthropological Institute*, 23(3): 603–621.

George, Rosemary Marangoly. 1993–1994. 'Homes in the Empire, Empires in the Home'. *Cultural Critique*, 26: 95–127.

Ghosh, Suresh Chandra. 1995. 'Bentinck, Macaulay and the introduction of English education in India'. *History of Education*, 24(1): 17–24.

Glover, W.J. 2004. '"A Feeling of Absence from Old England": The Colonial Bungalow'. *Home Cultures*, 1: 61–82.

Gordon, Stewart N. 1969. 'Scarf and Sword: Thugs, Marauders, and State-Formation in 18th Century Malwa'. *The Indian Economic & Social History Review*, 6(4): 403–429.

Gottschalk, Peter. 2013. *Religion, Science, and Empire: Classifying Hinduism and Islam in British India*. New York: Oxford University Press.

Grewal, Inderpal. 1996. *Home and Harem: Nation, Gender, Empire and Cultures of Travel*. London: Leicester University Press.

Hassan, Narin. 2016. 'Feeding Empire: Wet Nursing and Colonial Domesticity in India'. *Nineteenth-Century Contexts*, 38(5): 353–363.

Hatcher, Brian A. 2005. 'What's Become of the Pandit? Rethinking the History of Sanskrit Scholars in Colonial Bengal'. *Modern Asian Studies*, 39(3): 683–723.

Hawley, John Stratton. 1994. 'Introduction'. In *Sati, the Blessing and the Curse: The Burning of Wives in India,* edited by John Stratton Hawley, 3–25. New York: Oxford University Press.

Helsinger, Elizabeth K. 1997. 'Land and National Representation in Britain'. In *Prospects for the Nation: Recent Essays in British Landscape, 1750–1880,* edited by Michael Rosenthal, Christiana Payne and Scott Wilcox, 13–35. New Haven, CT: Yale University Press.

Home, R.W. 2002. 'The Royal Society and the Empire: The Colonial and Commonwealth Fellowship. Part 1. 1731–1847'. Notes and Records of the Royal Society of London, 56(3): 307–332.

Jay, Martin. 1998. 'Scopic Regimes of Modernity'. In *The Visual Culture Reader*, edited by Nicholas Mirzoeff, 66–69. London: Routledge.

Joseph, Betty. 2004. *Reading the East India Company, 1720–1840: Colonial Currencies of Gender*. Chicago: University of Chicago Press.

Keay, John. 1993. *The Honourable Company: A History of the English East India Company*. London: HarperCollins.

Lawrence, Jonathan. 2021. 'Building a Library: The Arabic and Persian Manuscript Collection of Sir William Jones'. *Journal of the Royal Asiatic Society*, 31(1): 1–70.

Leonard, Zak. 2016. 'Colonial Ethnography on India's North-West Frontier, 1850–1910'. *The Historical Journal*, 59(1): 175–196.

Leong-Salobir, Cecilia. 2014. 'Spreading the Word: Using Cookbooks and Colonial Memoirs to Examine the Foodways of British Colonials in Asia, 1850–1900'. In *The Routledge History of Food*, edited by Carol Helstosky, 131–155. London and New York: Routledge.

Lewis, Diane. 1973. 'Anthropology and Colonialism'. *Current Anthropology*, 14(5): 581–602.

Lloyd, Tom. 2006. 'Acting in the "Theatre of Anarchy": The "Anti-Thug Campaign" and Elaborations of Colonial Rule in Early Nineteenth-Century India'. *Edinburgh Papers in South Asian Studies,* 19: 1–50.

Loomba, A. 1993. 'Dead Women Tell No Tales: Issues of Female Subjectivity, Subaltern Agency and Tradition in Colonial and Post-Colonial Writings on Widow Immolation in India'. *History Workshop Journal*, 36.1: 209–227.

Major, Andrea. 2011. *Sovereignty and Social Reform in India: British Colonialism and the Campaign against Sati, 1830–60.* Oxford: Routledge.

Mani, Lata. 1998. *Contentious Traditions: The Debate on Sati in Colonial India*. Berkeley: University of California Press.

Mayhew, Robert J. 1999. 'William Guthrie's *Geographical Grammar*, the Scottish Enlightenment and the Politics of British Geography'. *Scottish Geographical Journal*, 115(1): 19–34.

———. 2000. *Enlightenment Geography: The Political Languages of British Geography, 1650–1850*. Basingstoke: Palgrave Macmillan.

McClintock, Anne. 1994. *Imperial Leather: Race, Gender and Sexuality in the Colonial Contest*. London: Routledge.

Meyns, Chris. 2020. '"Data" in the Royal Society's Philosophical Transactions, 1665–1886'. *Notes and Records*, 74: 507–528.

Midgley, Clare. 2000. 'Female Emancipation in an Imperial Frame: English Women and the Campaign Against Sati (Widow-Burning) in India, 1813–30'. *Women's History Review*, 9(1): 95–121.

Morris, Jan. 1982. *The Spectacle of Empire: Style, Effect and the Pax Britannica*. London: Faber & Faber.

Moseley, C.W.R.D. 2011. '"New Things to Speak of": Money, Memory, and Mandeville's Travels in Early Modern England'. *The Yearbook of English Studies*, 41(1): 5–20.

Mukherjee, Alok. 2009. *The Gift of English: English Education and the Formation of Alternative Hegemonies in India*. Orient BlackSwan.

Mukherjee, S.N. 1968. *Sir William Jones: A Study in Eighteenth-Century British Attitudes to India*. Cambridge: Cambridge University Press.

Murdoch, John. 1990. 'The Landscape of Labour: Transformations of the Georgic'. In *Romantic Revolutions: Criticism and Theory*, edited by Kenneth R. Johnston, Karen Hanson, Gilbert D. Chaitin and Herbert Marks, 176–193. Bloomington, Indiana: Indiana University Press.

Nair, Janaki. 1994. 'On the Question of Agency in Indian Feminist Historiography'. *Gender & History*, 6(1): 82–100.

Nayar, Pramod K. 2008. *English Writings on India, 1600–1920: Colonizing Aesthetics*. London and New York: Routledge.

———. 2012. 'The "Disorderly Memsahib": Political Domesticity in Alice Perrin's Empire Fiction'. *Brno Studies in English*, 38(1): 123–138.

———. 2012. *Colonial Voices: The Discourses of Empire*. Marlden, Massachusetts: Wiley-Blackwell.

———. 2016. 'Civil Modernity: The Management of Manners and Polite Imperial Relations in India, 1880–1930'. *South Asia: Journal of South Asian Studies*, 39(4): 740–757.

———, ed. 2017. *English Siege and Prison Writings: From the 'Black Hole' to the 'Mutiny'*. Oxford: Routledge.

Nayar, Pramod K. 2020. 'The Colonial Home: Managing Objects and Servants in British India'. *Anglo-Saxonica*, 17(1): 1–9.

______. 2020. 'Moral Readership and Political Apprenticeship: Commentaries on English Education in India, 1875-1930'. In *The Edinburgh History of Reading. Vol. IV. Subversive Readers*, edited by Jonathan Rose, 138–161. Edinburgh: Edinburgh University Press.

Niranjana, Tejaswini. 1992. *Siting Translation: History, Post-Structuralism and the Colonial Context*. Berkeley: University of California Press.

Ogborn, Miles. 2007. *Indian Ink: Script and Print in the Making of the English East India Company*. Chicago and London: Chicago University Press.

Pandian, A.S. 2001. 'Predatory Care: The Imperial Hunt in Mughal and British India'. *Journal of Historical Sociology*, 14(1): 79–107.

Poovey, Mary. 1998. *A History of the Modern Fact: Problems of Knowledge in the Sciences of Wealth and Society*. Chicago and London: University of Chicago Press.

Procida, Mary. 2003. 'Feeding the Imperial Appetite: Imperial Knowledge and Anglo-Indian Discourse'. *Journal of Women's History*, 15(2): 123–149.

Quadflieg, Helga. 2016. '"As Mannerly and Civill as Any of Europe": Early Modern Travel Writing and the Exploration of the English Self'. In *Perspectives on Travel Writing*, edited by Glenn Hooper and Tim Youngs, 27–40. Aldershot, UK: Ashgate.

Raj, Kapil. 2007. *Relocating Modern Science: Circulation and the Construction of Knowledge in South Asia and Europe, 1650–1900*. London: Palgrave Macmillan.

Ramaswamy, Sumathi. 2017. *Terrestrial Lessons: The Conquest of the World as Globe*. Hyderabad: Orient BlackSwan.

Rangarajan, Mahesh. 1996. *Fencing the Forest: Conservation and Ecological Change in India's Central Provinces 1860–1914*. Delhi: Oxford University Press.

Robins, Nick. 2006. *The Corporation That Changed the World: How the East India Company Shaped the Modern Multinational*. London: Pluto.

Rocher, Rosane. 1989. 'The Career of Rādhākānta Tarkavāgīśa, an Eighteenth-Century Pandit in British Employ'. *Journal of the American Oriental Society*, 109(4): 627–633.

______. 1993. 'British Orientalism in the Eighteenth Century: The Dialectics of Knowledge and Government'. In *Orientalism and the Postcolonial Predicament: Perspectives on South Asia*, edited by Carol A. Breckenridge and Peter van der Veer, 215–249. Philadelphia: University of Pennsylvania Press.

Rousseau, G.S. and Roy Porter, eds. 1990. *Exoticism in the Enlightenment*. Manchester: Manchester University Press.

Roy, Parama. 1998. Indian Traffic: *Identities in Question in Colonial and Postcolonial India*. Berkeley: University of California Press.

Rubiés, Joan-Pau. 2000. *Travel and Ethnology in the Renaissance: South India through European Eyes, 1250–1625*. Cambridge: Cambridge University Press.

Rubiés, Joan-Pau and Manel Ollé. 2016. 'The Comparative History of a Genre: The Production and Circulation of Books on Travel and Ethnographies in Early Modern Europe and China.' *Modern Asian Studies*, 50(1): 259–309.

Said, Edward W. 1985. *Orientalism*. Harmondsworth: Penguin.

Savory, Isabel. 1900. *A Sportswoman in India: Personal Adventures and Experiences of Travel in Known and Unknown India*. London: Hutchinson.

Schwab, Raymond. 1984. *The Oriental Renaissance: Europe's Rediscovery of India and the East, 1680–1880*. Trans. Gene Patterson-Black and Victor Reinking. New York: Columbia University Press.

Schwan, Anne. 2014. *Convict Voices: Women, Class, and Writing About Prison in Nineteenth-Century England*. Durham: New Hampshire Press.

Sen, Sudipta. 1998. *The Empire of Free Trade: The East India Company and the Making of the Colonial Marketplace*. Philadelphia: University of Pennsylvania Press.

Shapiro, Barbara. 1983. *A Culture Probability and Certainty in Seventeenth-Century England: A Study of the Relationships Between Natural Science, Religion, History, Law, and Literature*. Chicago and London: University of Chicago.

Sharma, Arvind with Ajit Ray, Alaka Hejib, Katharine K. Young. 1988. *Sati: Historical and Phenomenological Essays*. Delhi: Motilal Banarsidass.

Sharpe, Jenny. 1993. *Allegories of Empire: The Figure of Woman in the Colonial Text*. Minneapolis: Minnesota University Press.

Shiva, Vandana. 1990. 'Reductionist Science as Epistemological Violence. In *Science, Hegemony and Violence. A Requiem for Modernity*, edited by Ashis Nandy, 232–256. Oxford: Oxford University Press.

Singha, Radhika. 2000. *A Despotism of Law: Crime and Justice in Early Colonial India*. New Delhi: Oxford University Press.

Sinha, Mrinalini. 1995. *Colonial Masculinity: The 'Manly Englishman' and the 'Effeminate Bengali' in the Nineteenth Century*. Manchester: Manchester University Press.

Sinha, Mrinalini. 2001. 'Britishness, Clubbability and the Colonial Public Sphere: The Genealogy of an Imperial Institution in Colonial India'. *Journal of British Studies*, 40: 489–521.

Sleeman. 1839. *Ramaseeana, Or A Vocabulary of the Peculiar Language Used by the Thugs*. Calcutta: G.H. Huttman, the Military Orphan Press.

______. 1844. *Rambles and Recollections of an Indian Official* (2 volumes). Piccadilly: J. Hatchard.

Spivak, Gayatri Chakravarty. 1988. 'Can the Subaltern Speak?' In *Marxism and the Interpretation of Culture*, edited by Cary Nelson and Lawrence Grossberg, 271–313. Urbana-Champaign, IL: University of Illinois Press.

Stern, Philip J. 2011. *The Company-State: Corporate Sovereignty and the Early Modern Foundations of the British Empire in India*. Oxford: Oxford University Press.

Teltscher, Kate. 1993. *India Inscribed: European and British Writing on India 1600–1800*. Delhi: Oxford University Press.

______. 1996. '"The Fearful Name of the Black Hole": Fashioning an Imperial Myth'. In *Writing India, 1757–1990*, edited by Bart Moore-Gilbert, 30–51. Manchester: Manchester University Press.

Thapar, Romila. 2010. *Sakuntala: Texts, Readings, Histories*. New York: Columbia University Press.

Tidrick, Kathryn. 1990. *Empire and the English Character*. London: I.B. Tauris.

Tinnemeyer, Andrea. 2006. *Identity Politics of the Captivity Narrative After 1848*. Lincoln: University of Nebraska Press.

Topdar, Sudipa. 2015. 'Duties of a "Good Citizen": Colonial Secondary School Textbook Policies in Late Nineteenth-Century India'. *South Asian History and Culture*, 6(3): 417–439.

Trivedi, Harish. 1995. *Colonial Transactions: English Literature and India*. Manchester: Manchester University Press.

Trollope, Joanna. 1983. *Britannia's Daughters: Women of the British Empire*. London: Hutchinson.

Tschurenev, Jana. 2004. 'Between Non-Interference in Matters of Religion and the Civilizing Mission: The Prohibition of Suttee in 1829'. In *Colonialism as Civilizing Mission: Cultural Ideology in British India*, edited by Harald Fischer-Tine and Michael Mann, 68–91. Ashgate: London.

Vishwanathan, Gauri. 2015. *Masks of Conquest: Literary Study and British Rule in India*. New York: Columbia University Press.

Wagner, Kim A. 2007. *Thuggee: Banditry and the British in Early Nineteenth-Century India*. London: Palgrave Macmillan.

Wagner, Kim A. 2009. 'Introduction'. In *Stranglers and Bandits: A Historical Anthology*, edited by Wagner, 1–48. Oxford: Oxford University Press.

Winterbottom, Anna. 2016. *Hybrid Knowledge in the Early East India Company World*. London: Palgrave Macmillan.

Yang, Anand A. 1985. 'Dangerous Castes and Tribes: The Criminal Tribes Act and the Magahiya Doms of Northeast India'. In *Crime and Criminality in British India*, edited by Yang, 108–127. Tucson: University of Arizona Press.

Zastoupil, Lynn and Martin Moir. 1999. 'Preface'. In *The Great Indian Education Debate: Documents Relating to the Orientalist-Anglicist Controversy, 1781–1843*, edited by Zastoupil and Moir, ix–xii. London: Curzon.

Zlotnick, Susan. 1996. 'Domesticating Imperialism: Curry and Cookbooks in Victorian England'. *Frontiers: A Journal of Women Studies*, 16(2–3): 51–68.

ABOUT THE AUTHOR

Pramod K. Nayar, FEA, FRHistS, teaches at the Department of English, University of Hyderabad, India. His most recent books include *Alzheimer's Disease Memoirs* (2021), *The Human Rights Graphic Novel* (2021), *Ecoprecarity: Vulnerable Lives in Literature and Culture* (2019), *Brand Postcolonial: 'Third World' Texts and the Global* (2018), *Bhopal's Ecological Gothic: Disaster, Precarity and the Biopolitical Uncanny* (2017), *Human Rights and Literature: Writing Right* (2016) and the edited collection *Indian Travel Writing 1830–1947* (2016). His essays have appeared in *Modern Fiction Studies, South Asian Review, South Asia, Narrative, Celebrity Studies, Asiatic, Journal of Postcolonial Writing, Prose Studies, a/b: Auto/Biography Studies, Biography, Image and Text* and *Postcolonial Text*, among others.

Nayar also holds the UNESCO Chair in Vulnerability Studies at the University of Hyderabad.